Love Hina

Vol. 10

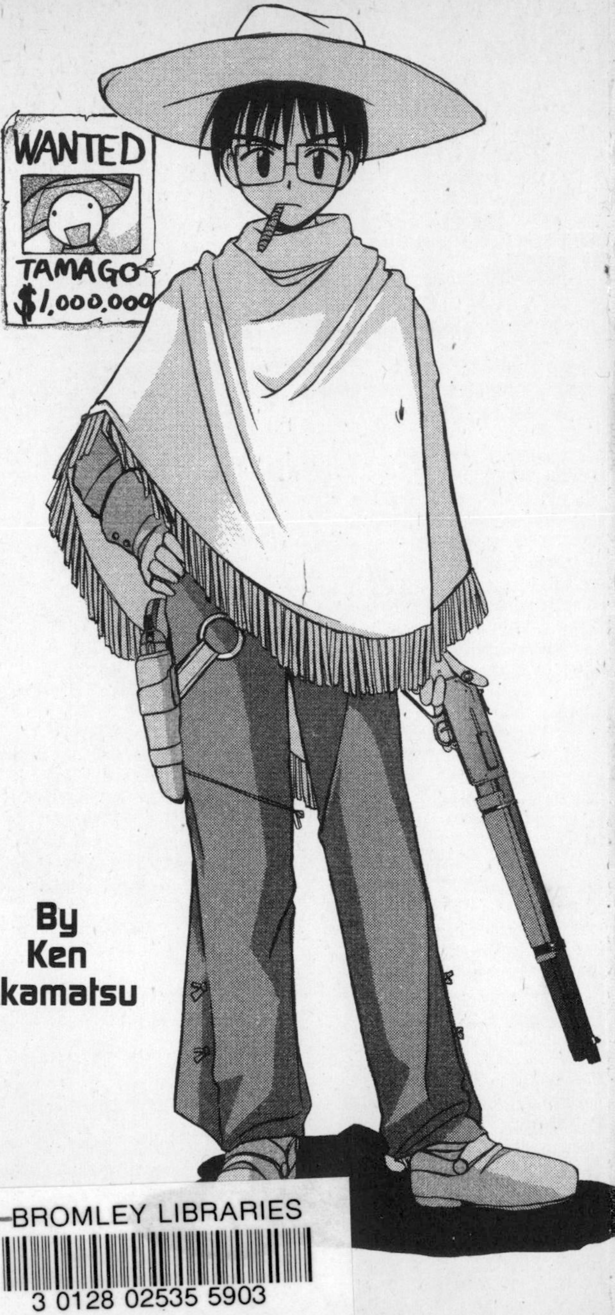
WANTED
TAMAGO
$1,000,000

By
Ken
Akamatsu

ALSO AVAILABLE FROM ☻TOKYOPOP®

MANGA

ANGELIC LAYER*
BABY BIRTH* (September 2003)
BATTLE ROYALE*
BRAIN POWERD* (June 2003)
BRIGADOON* (August 2003)
CARDCAPTOR SAKURA
CARDCAPTOR SAKURA: MASTER OF THE CLOW*
CLAMP SCHOOL DETECTIVES*
CHOBITS*
CHRONICLES OF THE CURSED SWORD (July 2003)
CLOVER
CONFIDENTIAL CONFESSIONS* (July 2003)
CORRECTOR YUI
COWBOY BEBOP*
COWBOY BEBOP: SHOOTING STAR* (June 2003)
DEMON DIARY (May 2003)
DIGIMON
DRAGON HUNTER (June 2003)
DRAGON KNIGHTS*
DUKLYON: CLAMP SCHOOL DEFENDERS* (September 2003)
ERICA SAKURAZAWA* (May 2003)
ESCAFLOWNE* (July 2003)
FAKE*(May 2003)
FLCL* (September 2003)
FORBIDDEN DANCE* (August 2003)
GATE KEEPERS*
G-GUNDAM* (June 2003)
GRAVITATION* (June 2003)
GTO*
GUNDAM WING
GUNDAM WING: ENDLESS WALTZ*
GUNDAM: THE LAST OUTPOST*
HAPPY MANIA*
HARLEM BEAT
INITIAL D*
I.N.V.U.
ISLAND
JING: KING OF BANDITS* (June 2003)
JULINE
KARE KANO*
KINDAICHI CASE FILES* (June 2003)
KING OF HELL (June 2003)

KODOCHA*
LOVE HINA*
LUPIN III*
MAGIC KNIGHT RAYEARTH* (August 2003)
MAN OF MANY FACES* (May 2003)
MARMALADE BOY*
MARS*
MIRACLE GIRLS
MIYUKI-CHAN IN WONDERLAND* (October 2003)
MONSTERS, INC.
NIEA_7* (August 2003)
PARADISE KISS*
PARASYTE
PEACH GIRL
PEACH GIRL: CHANGE OF HEART*
PET SHOP OF HORRORS* (June 2003)
PLANET LADDER
PLANETS* (October 2003)
PRIEST
RAGNAROK
RAVE MASTER*
REAL BOUT HIGH SCHOOL*
REALITY CHECK
REBIRTH
REBOUND*
SABER MARIONETTE J* (July 2003)
SAILOR MOON
SAINT TAIL
SAMURAI DEEPER KYO* (June 2003)
SCRYED*
SHAOLIN SISTERS*
SHIRAHIME-SYO* (December 2003)
THE SKULL MAN*
SORCERER HUNTERS
TOKYO MEW MEW*
UNDER THE GLASS MOON (June 2003)
VAMPIRE GAME* (June 2003)
WILD ACT* (July 2003)
WISH*
X-DAY* (August 2003)
ZODIAC P.I.* (July 2003)

CINE-MANGA™

AKIRA*
CARDCAPTORS
JIMMY NEUTRON (COMING SOON)
KIM POSSIBLE
LIZZIE McGUIRE
SPONGEBOB SQUAREPANTS (COMING SOON)
SPY KIDS 2

NOVELS

SAILOR MOON
KARMA CLUB (COMING SOON)

TOKYOPOP KIDS

STRAY SHEEP (September 2003)

ART BOOKS

CARDCAPTOR SAKURA*
MAGIC KNIGHT RAYEARTH*

ANIME GUIDES

GUNDAM TECHNICAL MANUALS
COWBOY BEBOP
SAILOR MOON SCOUT GUIDES

Love Hina

By
Ken Akamatsu

Volume 10

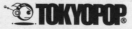

Los Angeles • Tokyo • London • Hamburg

Translator - Nan Rymer
English Adaptation - Adam Arnold
Associate Editor - Bryce P. Coleman
Retouch and Lettering - Steve Avooski, Bryce P. Coleman & Paul Morissey
Cover Layout - Anna Kernbaum

Digital Imaging Manager - Chris Buford
Pre-Press Manager - Antonio DePietro
Production Managers - Jennifer Miller, Mutsumi Miyazaki
Art Director - Matt Alford
Managing Editor - Jill Freshney
VP of Production - Ron Klamert
President & C.O.O. - John Parker
Publisher & C.E.O. - Stuart Levy

E-mail: info@TOKYOPOP.com
Come visit us online at www.TOKYOPOP.com

A 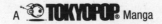 Manga

TOKYOPOP Inc.
5900 Wilshire Blvd. Suite 2000
Los Angeles, CA 90036

Love Hina Vol. 10

©1999 Ken Akamatsu. First published in 1999 by Kodansha Ltd., Tokyo.
English publication rights arranged through Kodansha Ltd., Tokyo.

English text copyright ©2004 TOKYOPOP Inc.

ISBN: 1-59182-116-9

First TOKYOPOP® printing: May 2003

10 9 8
Printed in U.S.A.

Love Hina

The Story Thus Far...

Fifteen years ago, Keitaro Urashima made a promise to a girl that the two of them would go to Tokyo University together. For fifteen long years, Keitaro has slaved away at the books, stumbling through academia until the day he could take the university's entrance exam. Having failed three times already, having readied himself so thoroughly as to fail again, and having discovered that the girl to whom he made that fateful promise is the girl that has recently studied with him, helping beat his fear of tests, at last the saga has ended, the impossible has become reality. Keitaro Urashima has finally managed to pass the entrance exam. This is one boy that won't live another year as a ronin. He is finally going to Tokyo U. or so he thought. For all the good twists of fate Keitaro had been given, sooner or later his bad luck would regain control. In a shocking turn of events, Keitaro breaks his leg just minutes before the opening ceremonies are about to commence. Hospitalized with no way of attending college, Keitaro goes for broke and confesses his love for Naru. But perhaps we are getting ahead of ourselves.

This chapter in Keitaro Urashima's life began over a year ago when he inherited from his globe-trotting grandmother the Hinata House, an all-girls dormitory whose clientele is none too pleased that their new, live-in landlord is a man... or as close to a man as poor Keitaro can be. The lanky loser incessantly (and accidentally) crashes their sessions in the hot springs, walks in on them changing, and pokes his nose pretty much everywhere that it can get broken, if not by the hot-headed Naru—the mystery girl from fifteen years ago—then by one of the other Hinata inmates: Kitsune, a late-teen alcoholic with a diesel libido; Motoko, a swordsman who struggles with a feminine identity; Shinobu, a pre teen princess with a colossal crush on Keitaro; Su, a foreign girl with a big appetite; Sarah, an orphaned ward resentful of being left there by her archeologist guardian; Mutsumi, an accident-prone lily also studying for her exams; and Haruka, Keitaro's aunt and de facto matriarch of Hinata House.

Now, back to full health, Keitaro and Naru's relationship is finally beginning to crawl out of the starting gate. But Mutsumi might have other plans for the lovebird's budding romance. And yet, something is digging at Keitaro's subconscious that is nudging him towards a colossal decision that could very well affect the lives of everyone at Hinata House.

CONTENTS

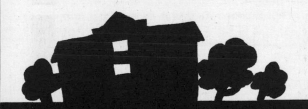

LOVE♡HINA

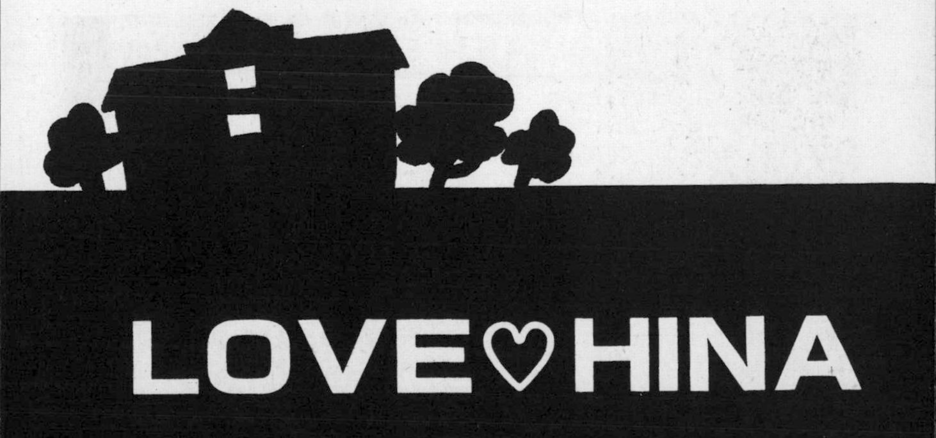

Love Hina 「ラブひな」

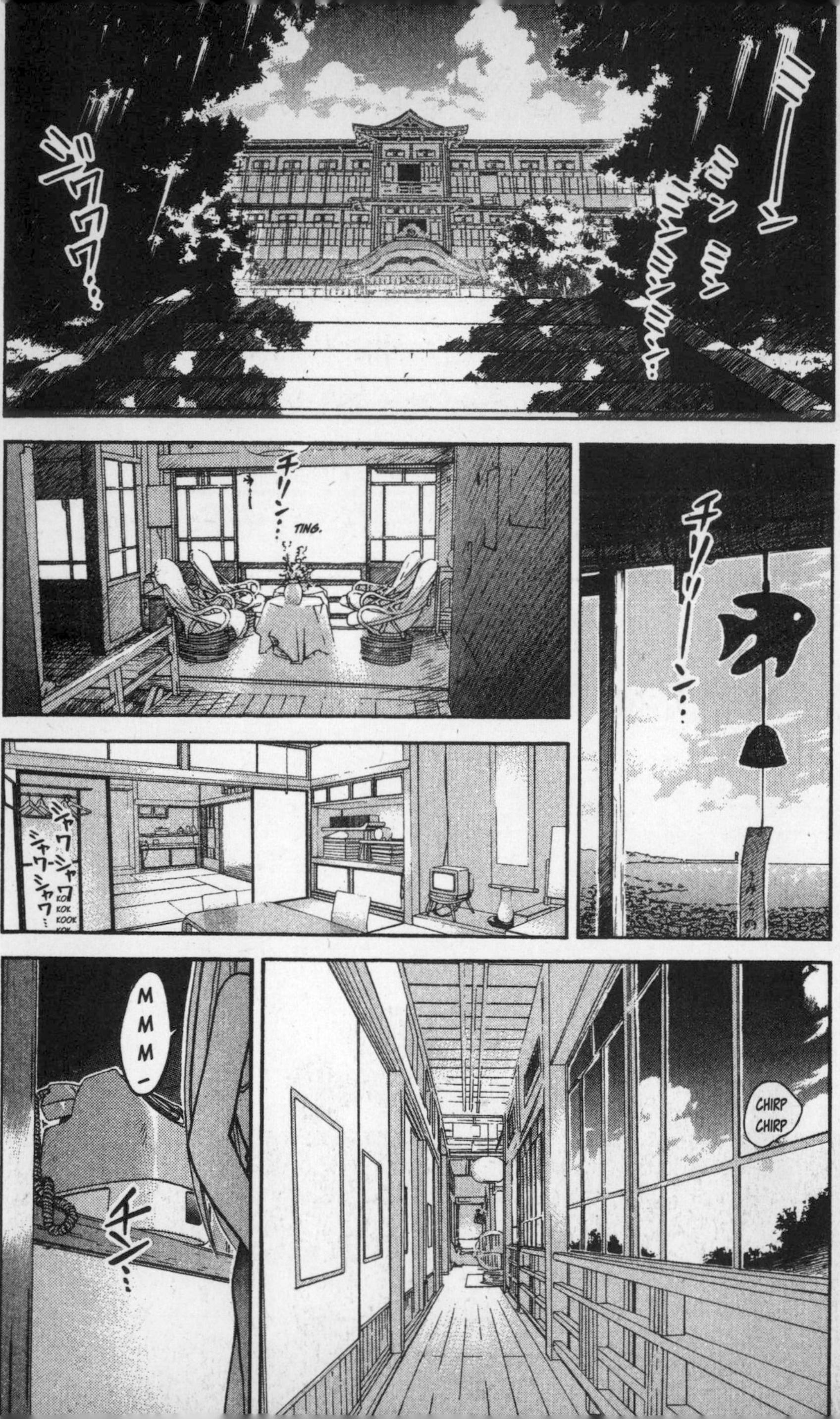
ミーン ミン ミン ミンミンミン…
ジワワワ…
チリリリーン…
チリン…
TING.
シャワシャワ シャワシャワ…
KOK KOK KOOK
CHIRP CHIRP
MMM–
チン…

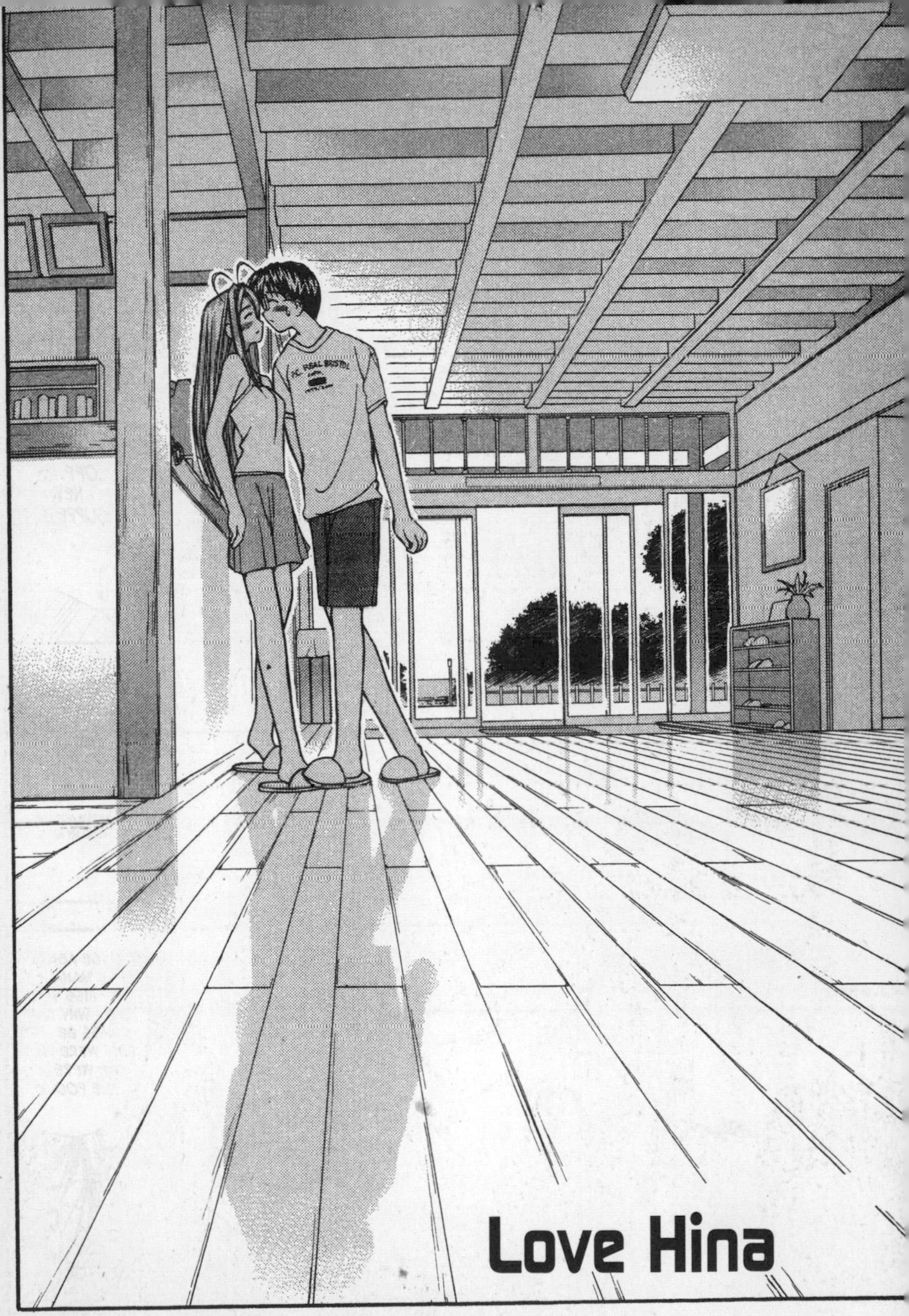
Love Hina

HINATA.79 Kiss, Kiss, Kiss!

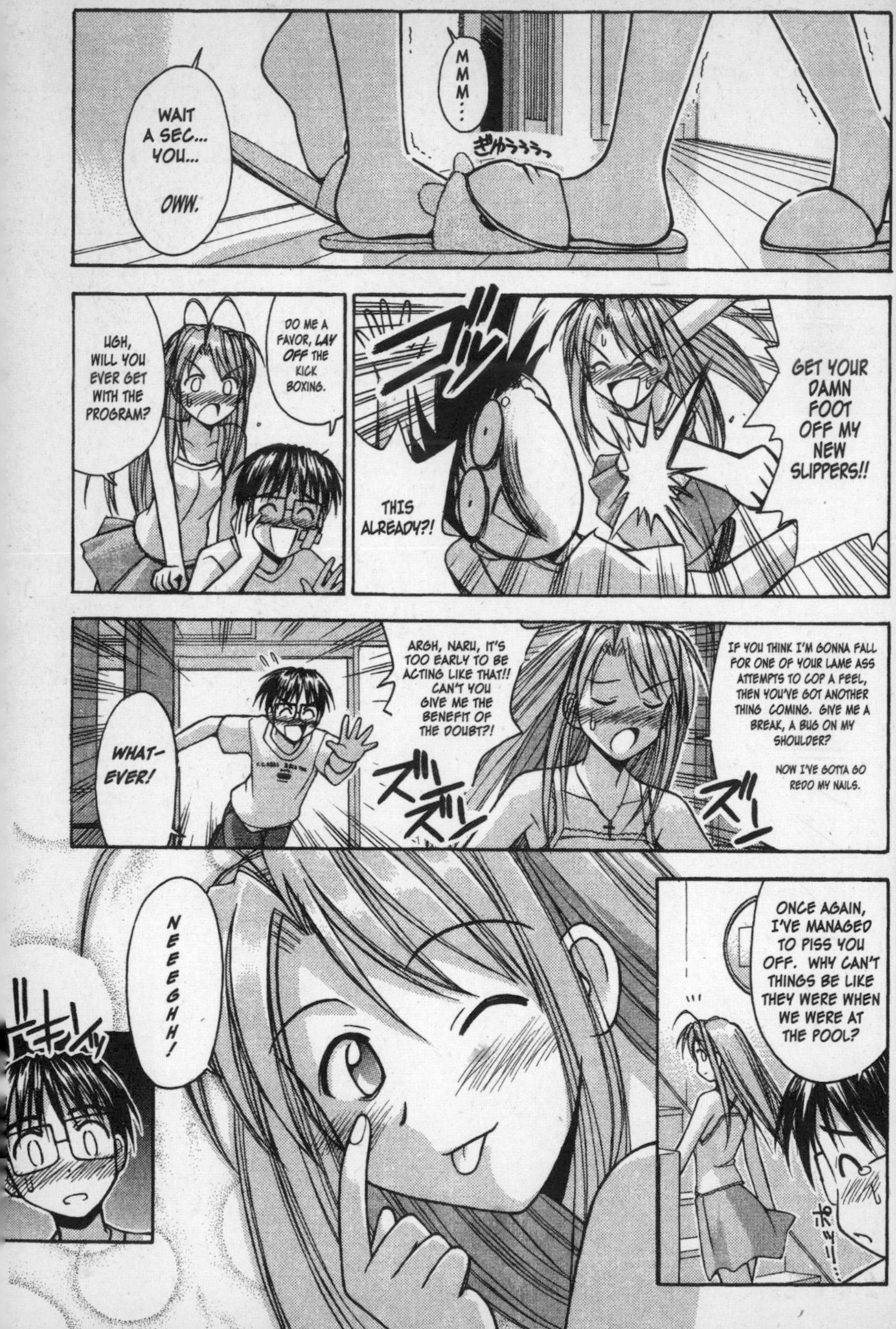
MMM...
WAIT A SEC... YOU... OWW.
GET YOUR DAMN FOOT OFF MY NEW SLIPPERS!!
THIS ALREADY?!
DO ME A FAVOR, LAY OFF THE KICK BOXING.
UGH, WILL YOU EVER GET WITH THE PROGRAM?
IF YOU THINK I'M GONNA FALL FOR ONE OF YOUR LAME ASS ATTEMPTS TO COP A FEEL, THEN YOU'VE GOT ANOTHER THING COMING. GIVE ME A BREAK, A BUG ON MY SHOULDER?
NOW I'VE GOTTA GO REDO MY NAILS.
ARGH, NARU, IT'S TOO EARLY TO BE ACTING LIKE THAT!! CAN'T YOU GIVE ME THE BENEFIT OF THE DOUBT?!
WHAT-EVER!
ONCE AGAIN, I'VE MANAGED TO PISS YOU OFF. WHY CAN'T THINGS BE LIKE THEY WERE WHEN WE WERE AT THE POOL?
NEEEGHH!

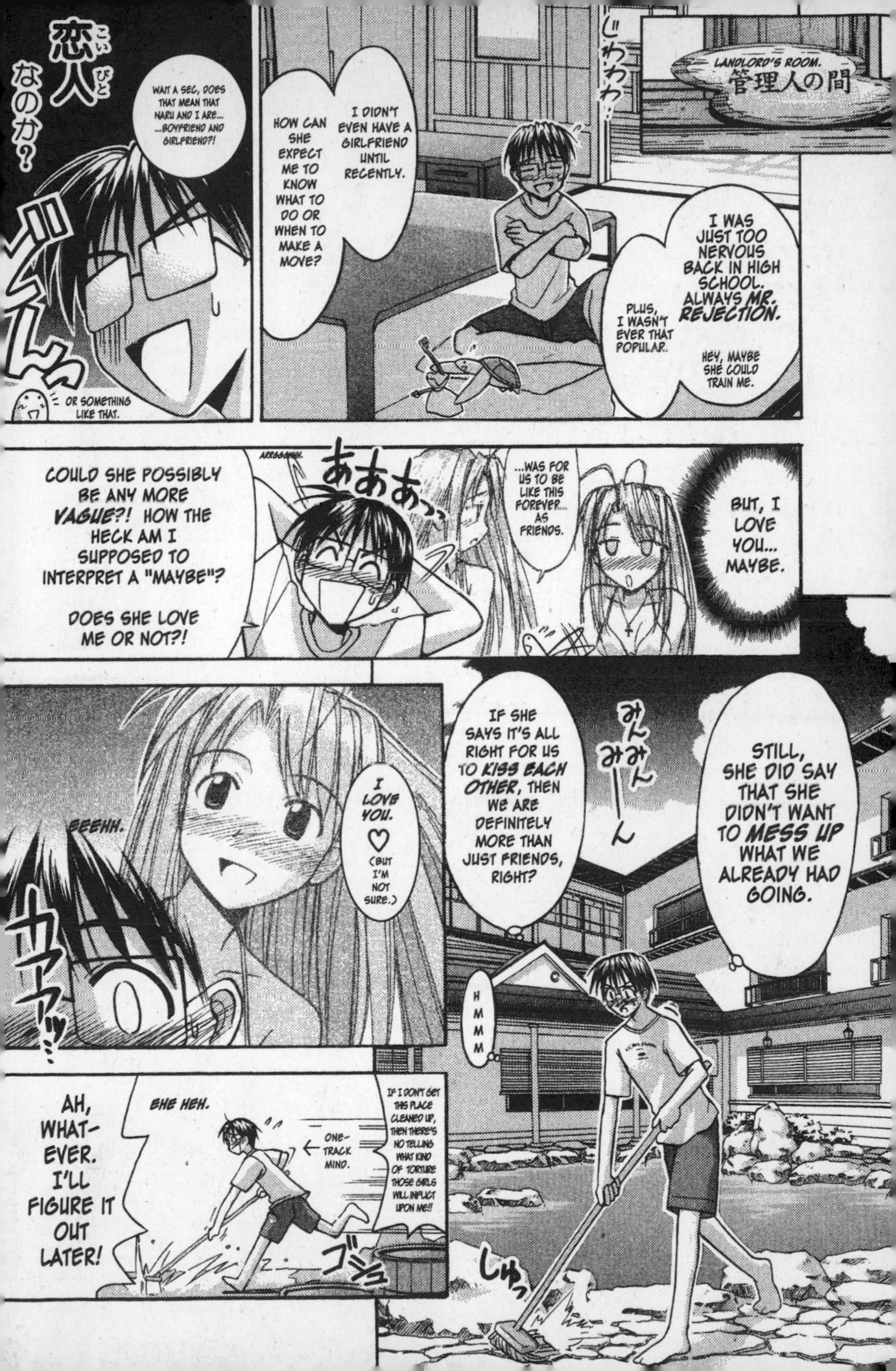
LANDLORD'S ROOM.
管理人の間
じわわわ…
I WAS JUST TOO NERVOUS BACK IN HIGH SCHOOL. ALWAYS MR. REJECTION.
PLUS, I WASN'T EVER THAT POPULAR.
HEY, MAYBE SHE COULD TRAIN ME.
I DIDN'T EVEN HAVE A GIRLFRIEND UNTIL RECENTLY.
HOW CAN SHE EXPECT ME TO KNOW WHAT TO DO OR WHEN TO MAKE A MOVE?
恋人なのか?
WAIT A SEC, DOES THAT MEAN THAT NARU AND I ARE... ...BOYFRIEND AND GIRLFRIEND?!
OR SOMETHING LIKE THAT.
BUT, I LOVE YOU... MAYBE.
...WAS FOR US TO BE LIKE THIS FOREVER... AS FRIENDS.
あああああっ
COULD SHE POSSIBLY BE ANY MORE VAGUE?! HOW THE HECK AM I SUPPOSED TO INTERPRET A "MAYBE"?
DOES SHE LOVE ME OR NOT?!
STILL, SHE DID SAY THAT SHE DIDN'T WANT TO MESS UP WHAT WE ALREADY HAD GOING.
みんみんみーん
IF SHE SAYS IT'S ALL RIGHT FOR US TO KISS EACH OTHER, THEN WE ARE DEFINITELY MORE THAN JUST FRIENDS, RIGHT?
HMMM
I LOVE YOU. ♡ (BUT I'M NOT SURE.)
EEEHH.
しゅっ
IF I DON'T GET THIS PLACE CLEANED UP, THEN THERE'S NO TELLING WHAT KIND OF TORTURE THOSE GIRLS WILL INFLICT UPON ME!!
ONE-TRACK MIND.
EHE HEH.
ゴシュ
AH, WHATEVER. I'LL FIGURE IT OUT LATER!

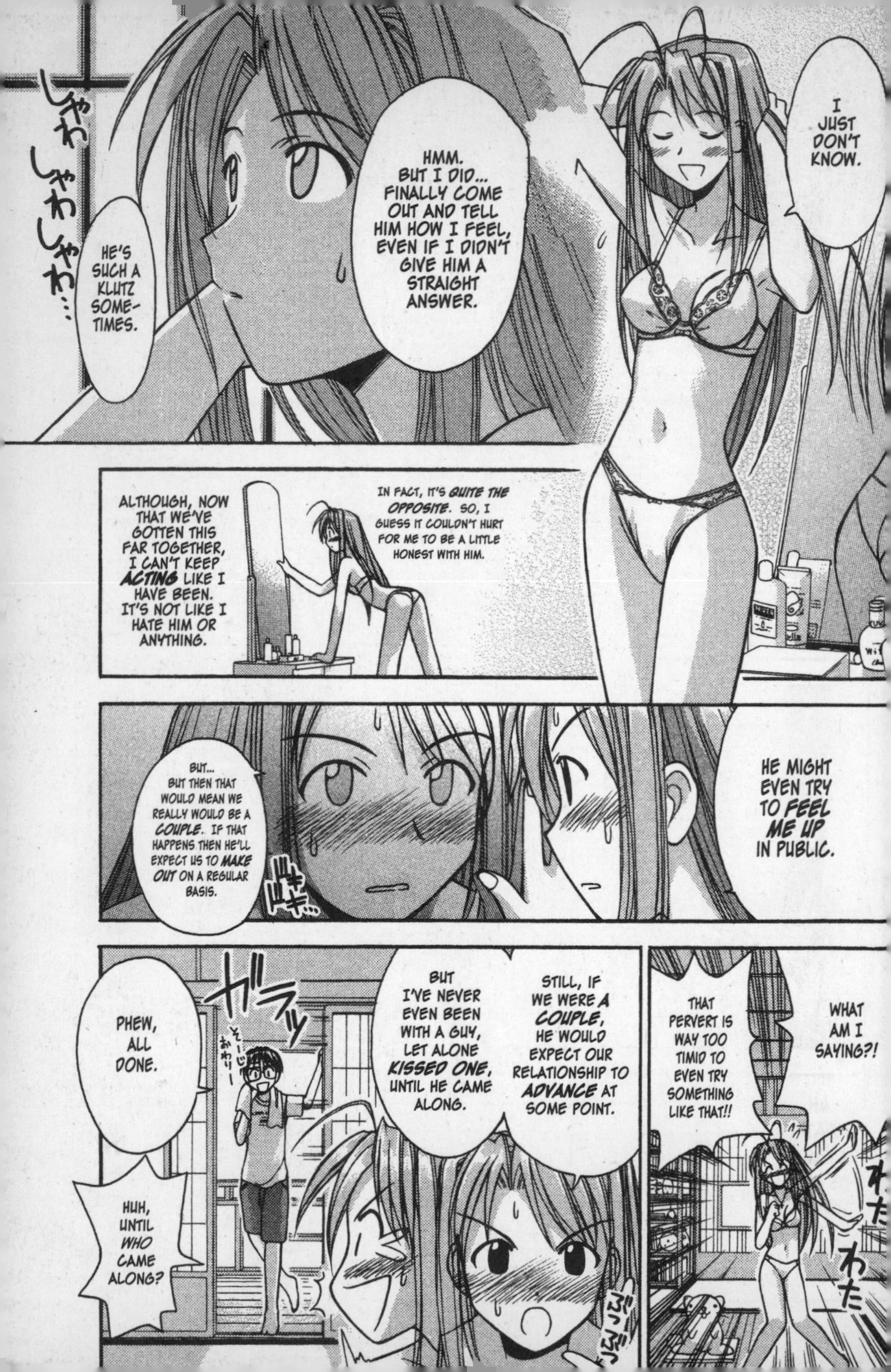
I JUST DON'T KNOW.
HMM. BUT I DID... FINALLY COME OUT AND TELL HIM HOW I FEEL, EVEN IF I DIDN'T GIVE HIM A STRAIGHT ANSWER.
HE'S SUCH A KLUTZ SOMETIMES.
しゃわしゃわしゃわ…
ALTHOUGH, NOW THAT WE'VE GOTTEN THIS FAR TOGETHER, I CAN'T KEEP ACTING LIKE I HAVE BEEN. IT'S NOT LIKE I HATE HIM OR ANYTHING.
IN FACT, IT'S QUITE THE OPPOSITE. SO, I GUESS IT COULDN'T HURT FOR ME TO BE A LITTLE HONEST WITH HIM.
BUT... BUT THEN THAT WOULD MEAN WE REALLY WOULD BE A COUPLE. IF THAT HAPPENS THEN HE'LL EXPECT US TO MAKE OUT ON A REGULAR BASIS.
HE MIGHT EVEN TRY TO FEEL ME UP IN PUBLIC.
ドキ…
WHAT AM I SAYING?!
THAT PERVERT IS WAY TOO TIMID TO EVEN TRY SOMETHING LIKE THAT!!
わたわた
STILL, IF WE WERE A COUPLE, HE WOULD EXPECT OUR RELATIONSHIP TO ADVANCE AT SOME POINT.
BUT I'VE NEVER EVEN BEEN WITH A GUY, LET ALONE KISSED ONE, UNTIL HE CAME ALONG.
ガラッ
そーじおわりー
PHEW, ALL DONE.
HUH, UNTIL WHO CAME ALONG?

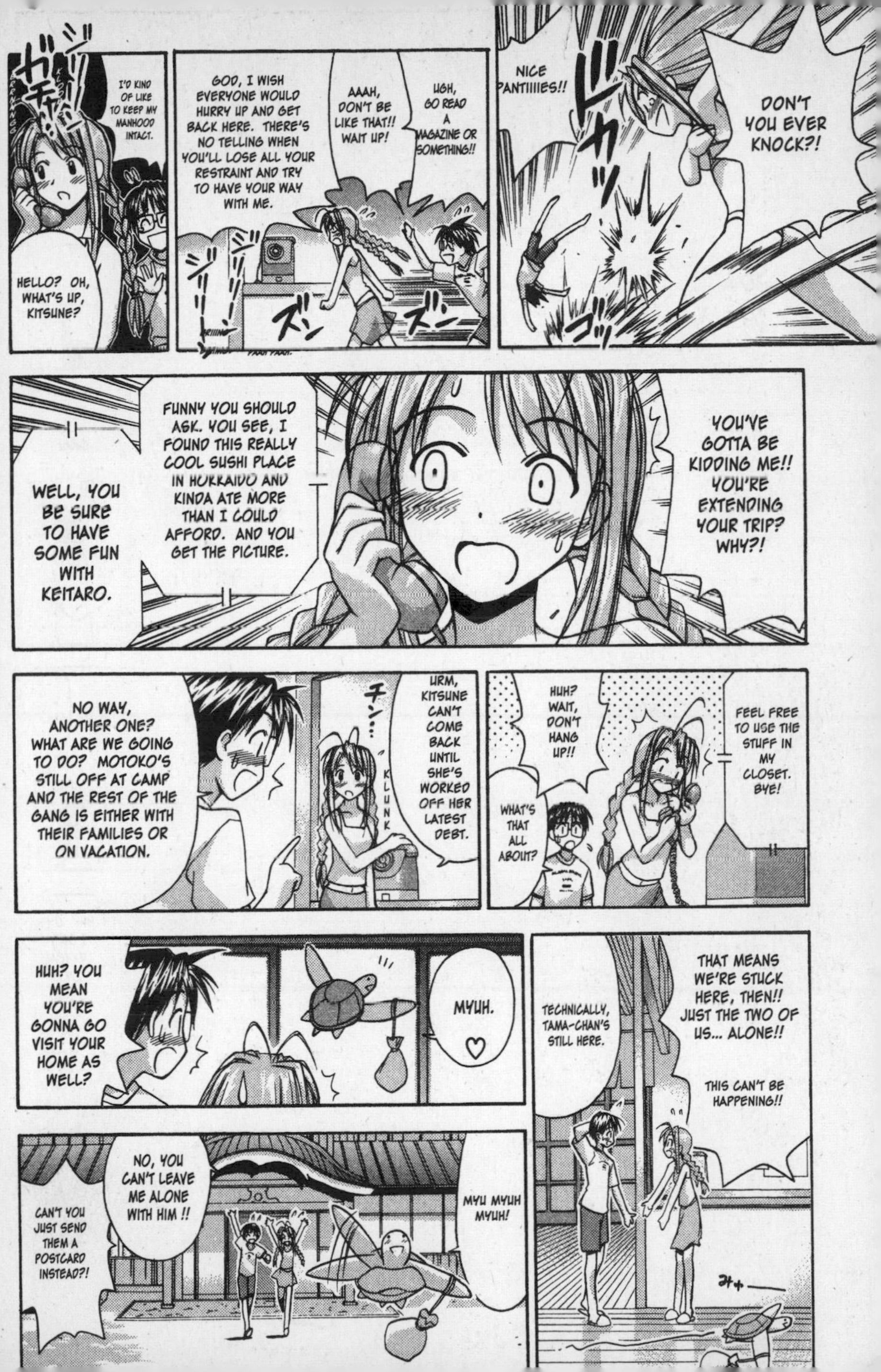
DON'T YOU EVER KNOCK?!
NICE PANTIIIIIES!!
UGH, GO READ A MAGAZINE OR SOMETHING!!
AAAH, DON'T BE LIKE THAT!! WAIT UP!
GOD, I WISH EVERYONE WOULD HURRY UP AND GET BACK HERE. THERE'S NO TELLING WHEN YOU'LL LOSE ALL YOUR RESTRAINT AND TRY TO HAVE YOUR WAY WITH ME.
I'D KIND OF LIKE TO KEEP MY MANHOOD INTACT.
HELLO? OH, WHAT'S UP, KITSUNE?
YOU'VE GOTTA BE KIDDING ME!! YOU'RE EXTENDING YOUR TRIP? WHY?!
FUNNY YOU SHOULD ASK. YOU SEE, I FOUND THIS REALLY COOL SUSHI PLACE IN HOKKAIDO AND KINDA ATE MORE THAN I COULD AFFORD. AND YOU GET THE PICTURE.
WELL, YOU BE SURE TO HAVE SOME FUN WITH KEITARO.
FEEL FREE TO USE THE STUFF IN MY CLOSET. BYE!
HUH? WAIT, DON'T HANG UP!!
WHAT'S THAT ALL ABOUT?
URM, KITSUNE CAN'T COME BACK UNTIL SHE'S WORKED OFF HER LATEST DEBT.
KLUNK
NO WAY, ANOTHER ONE? WHAT ARE WE GOING TO DO? MOTOKO'S STILL OFF AT CAMP AND THE REST OF THE GANG IS EITHER WITH THEIR FAMILIES OR ON VACATION.
THAT MEANS WE'RE STUCK HERE, THEN!! JUST THE TWO OF US... ALONE!!
TECHNICALLY, TAMA-CHAN'S STILL HERE.
THIS CAN'T BE HAPPENING!!
MYUH. ♥
HUH? YOU MEAN YOU'RE GONNA GO VISIT YOUR HOME AS WELL?
MYU MYUH MYUH!
NO, YOU CAN'T LEAVE ME ALONE WITH HIM !!
CAN'T YOU JUST SEND THEM A POSTCARD INSTEAD?!

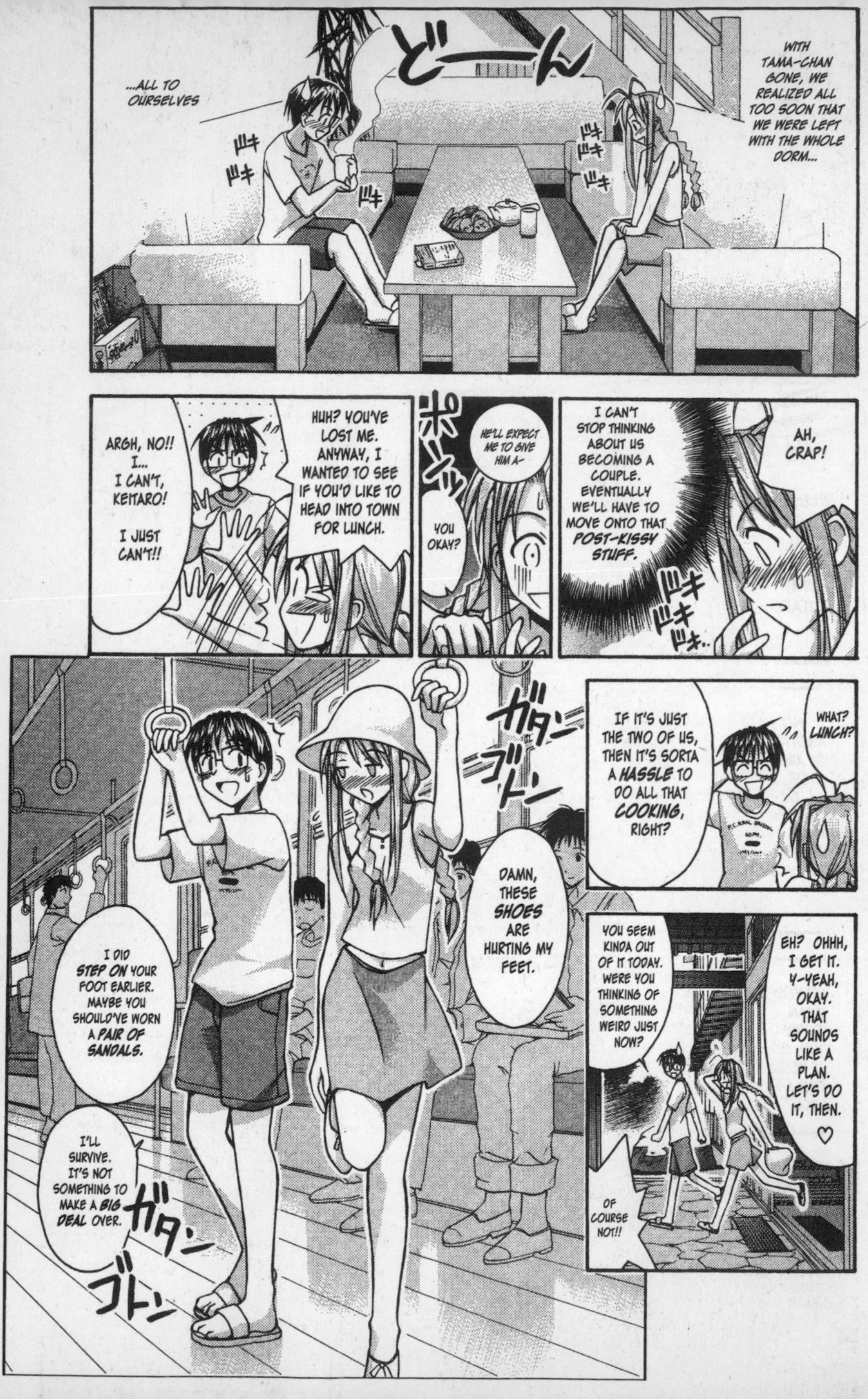
WITH TAMA-CHAN GONE, WE REALIZED ALL TOO SOON THAT WE WERE LEFT WITH THE WHOLE DORM...
どーん
...ALL TO OURSELVES
ドキ ドキ ドキ
ドキ ドキ ドキ
AH, CRAP!
I CAN'T STOP THINKING ABOUT US BECOMING A COUPLE. EVENTUALLY WE'LL HAVE TO MOVE ONTO THAT POST-KISSY STUFF.
ドキ ドキ ドキ..
ポーッ
HE'LL EXPECT ME TO GIVE HIM A-
YOU OKAY?
HUH? YOU'VE LOST ME. ANYWAY, I WANTED TO SEE IF YOU'D LIKE TO HEAD INTO TOWN FOR LUNCH.
ARGH, NO!! I... I CAN'T, KEITARO! I JUST CAN'T!!
WHAT? LUNCH?
IF IT'S JUST THE TWO OF US, THEN IT'S SORTA A HASSLE TO DO ALL THAT COOKING, RIGHT?
EH? OHHH, I GET IT. Y-YEAH, OKAY. THAT SOUNDS LIKE A PLAN. LET'S DO IT, THEN. ♡
YOU SEEM KINDA OUT OF IT TODAY. WERE YOU THINKING OF SOMETHING WEIRD JUST NOW?
OF COURSE NOT!!
ガタン ゴトン
DAMN, THESE SHOES ARE HURTING MY FEET.
I DID STEP ON YOUR FOOT EARLIER. MAYBE YOU SHOULD'VE WORN A PAIR OF SANDALS.
I'LL SURVIVE. IT'S NOT SOMETHING TO MAKE A BIG DEAL OVER.
ガタン ゴトン

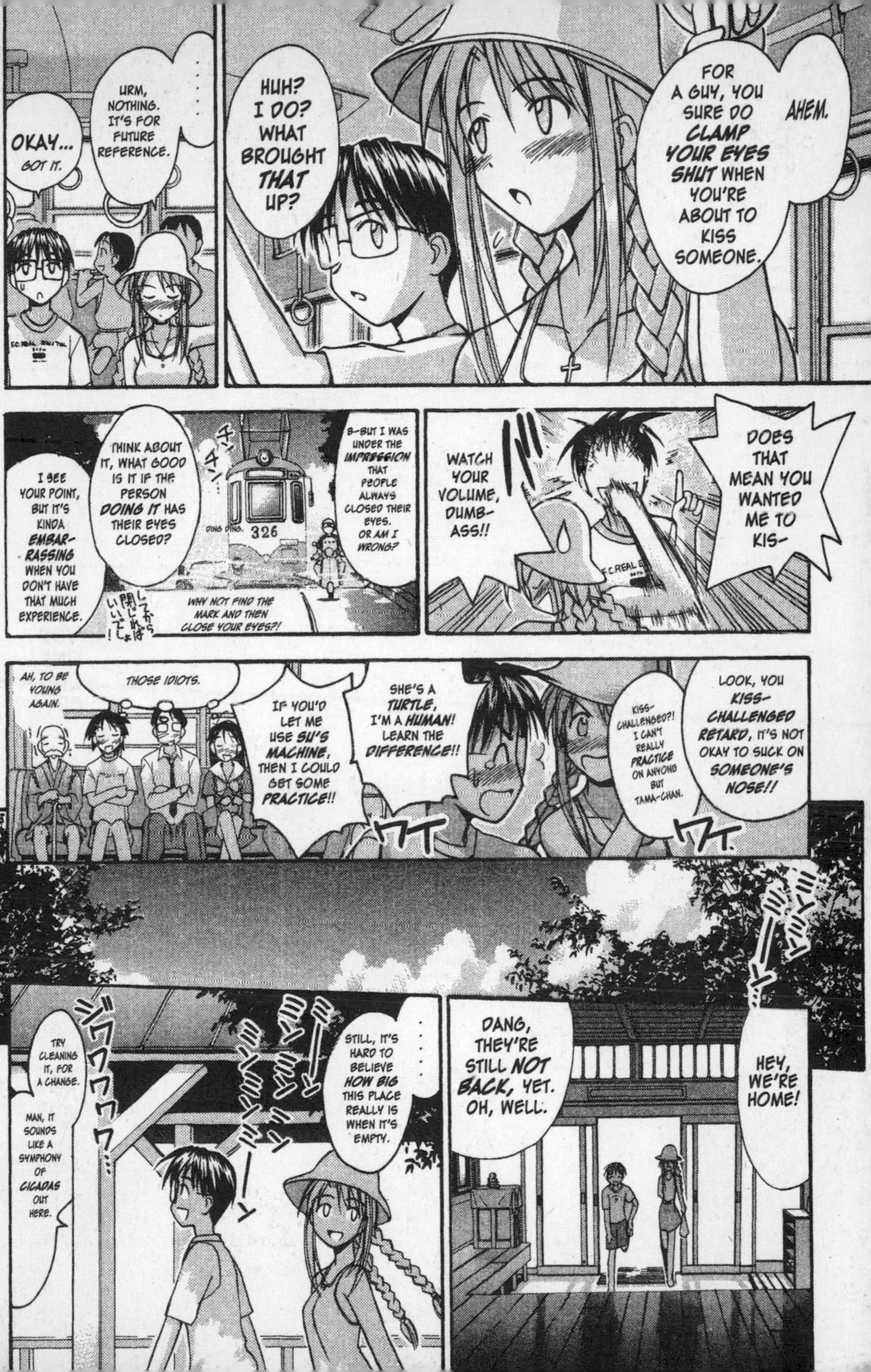
AHEM.
FOR A GUY, YOU SURE DO CLAMP YOUR EYES SHUT WHEN YOU'RE ABOUT TO KISS SOMEONE.
HUH? I DO? WHAT BROUGHT THAT UP?
URM, NOTHING. IT'S FOR FUTURE REFERENCE.
OKAY... GOT IT.
DOES THAT MEAN YOU WANTED ME TO KIS-
WATCH YOUR VOLUME, DUMB-ASS!!
B-BUT I WAS UNDER THE IMPRESSION THAT PEOPLE ALWAYS CLOSED THEIR EYES. OR AM I WRONG?
チン チン…
DING DING.
326
THINK ABOUT IT, WHAT GOOD IS IT IF THE PERSON DOING IT HAS THEIR EYES CLOSED?
I SEE YOUR POINT, BUT IT'S KINDA EMBARRASSING WHEN YOU DON'T HAVE THAT MUCH EXPERIENCE.
してから閉じればいいでしょ!
WHY NOT FIND THE MARK AND THEN CLOSE YOUR EYES?!
LOOK, YOU KISS-CHALLENGED RETARD, IT'S NOT OKAY TO SUCK ON SOMEONE'S NOSE!!
KISS-CHALLENGED?! I CAN'T REALLY PRACTICE ON ANYONE BUT TAMA-CHAN.
ワイ
SHE'S A TURTLE, I'M A HUMAN! LEARN THE DIFFERENCE!!
IF YOU'D LET ME USE SU'S MACHINE, THEN I COULD GET SOME PRACTICE!!
ワイ
THOSE IDIOTS.
AH, TO BE YOUNG AGAIN.
ミーン…
HEY, WE'RE HOME!
DANG, THEY'RE STILL NOT BACK, YET. OH, WELL.
STILL, IT'S HARD TO BELIEVE HOW BIG THIS PLACE REALLY IS WHEN IT'S EMPTY.
ミーンミンミーン
ジワワワワ…
MAN, IT SOUNDS LIKE A SYMPHONY OF CICADAS OUT HERE.
TRY CLEANING IT, FOR A CHANGE.

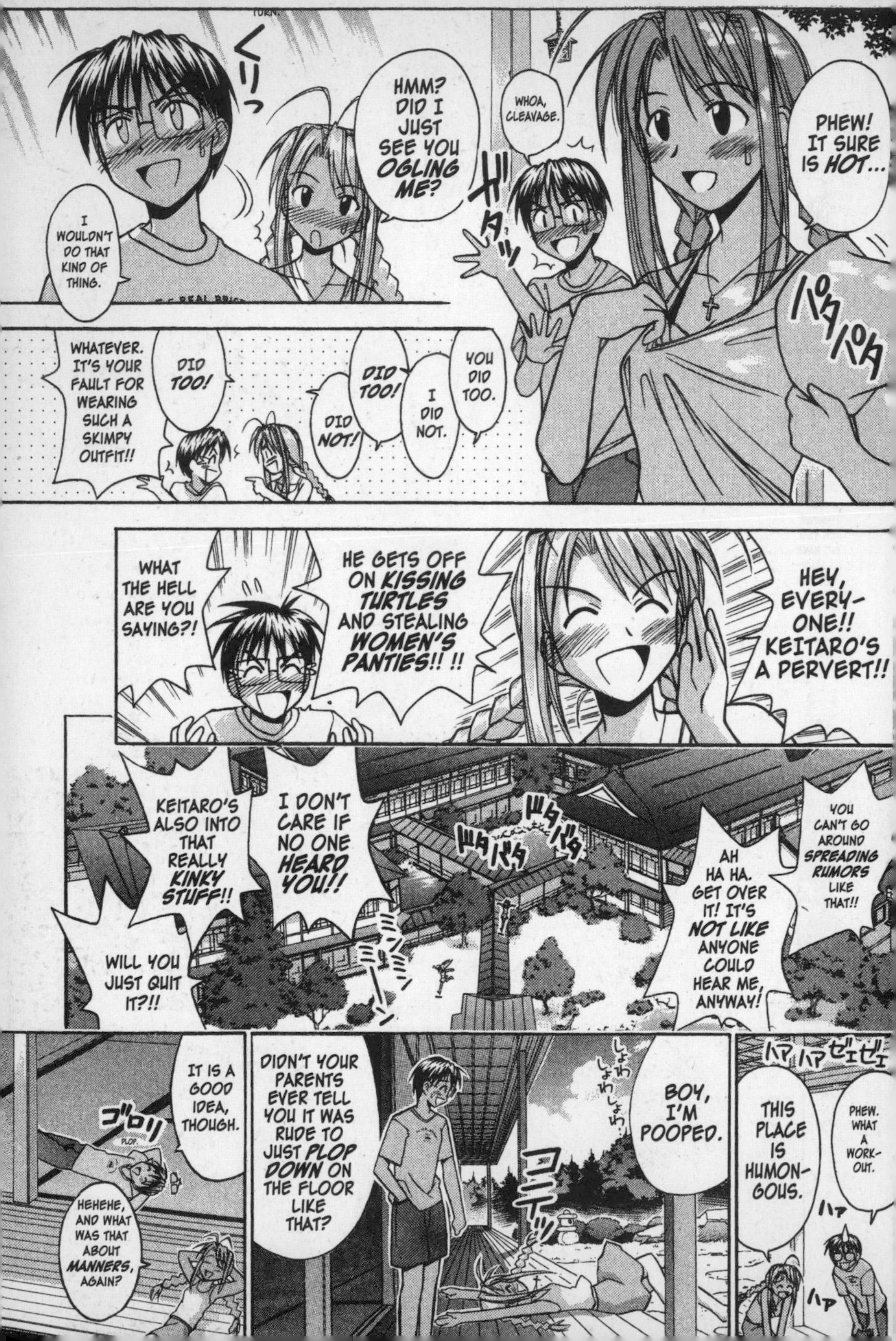
PHEW! IT SURE IS HOT...
WHOA, CLEAVAGE.
TURN
HMM? DID I JUST SEE YOU OGLING ME?
I WOULDN'T DO THAT KIND OF THING.
YOU DID TOO.
I DID NOT.
DID TOO!
DID NOT!
DID TOO!
WHATEVER. IT'S YOUR FAULT FOR WEARING SUCH A SKIMPY OUTFIT!!
HEY, EVERYONE!! KEITARO'S A PERVERT!!
HE GETS OFF ON KISSING TURTLES AND STEALING WOMEN'S PANTIES!! !!
WHAT THE HELL ARE YOU SAYING?!
YOU CAN'T GO AROUND SPREADING RUMORS LIKE THAT!!
AH HA HA. GET OVER IT! IT'S NOT LIKE ANYONE COULD HEAR ME, ANYWAY!
I DON'T CARE IF NO ONE HEARD YOU!!
KEITARO'S ALSO INTO THAT REALLY KINKY STUFF!!
WILL YOU JUST QUIT IT?!!
PHEW. WHAT A WORK-OUT.
THIS PLACE IS HUMON-GOUS.
BOY, I'M POOPED.
DIDN'T YOUR PARENTS EVER TELL YOU IT WAS RUDE TO JUST PLOP DOWN ON THE FLOOR LIKE THAT?
IT IS A GOOD IDEA, THOUGH.
PLOP.
HEHEHE, AND WHAT WAS THAT ABOUT MANNERS, AGAIN?

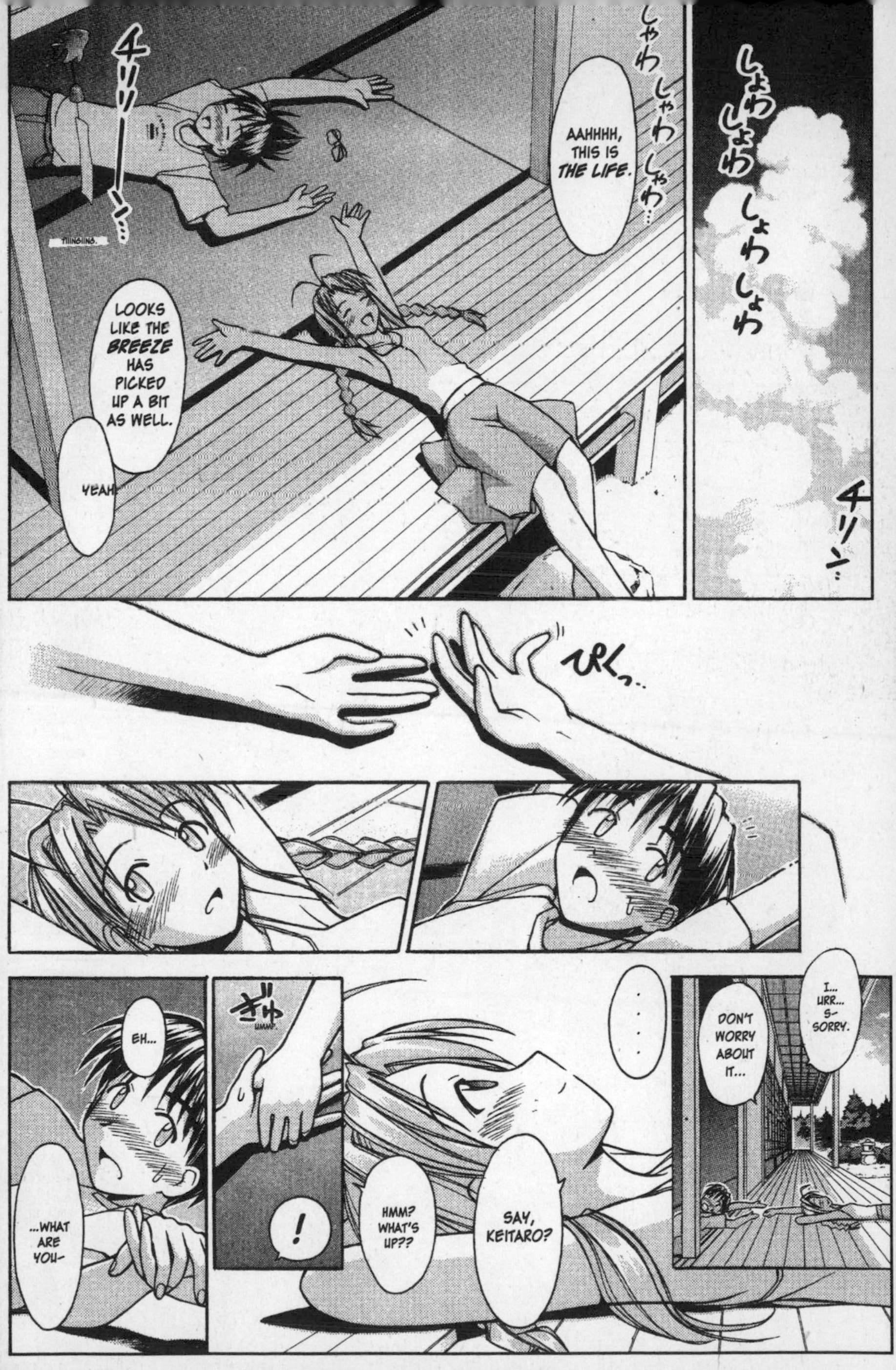
しょわしょわ しょわしょわ
チリン
しゃわしゃわしゃわしゃわ…
AAHHHH, THIS IS THE LIFE.
チリリーーン…
TIIINGIING.
LOOKS LIKE THE BREEZE HAS PICKED UP A BIT AS WELL.
YEAH
ぴくっ…
I... URR... S-SORRY.
DON'T WORRY ABOUT IT...
. . . .
SAY, KEITARO?
HMM? WHAT'S UP??
ぎゅ
UMMP.
!
EH...
...WHAT ARE YOU-

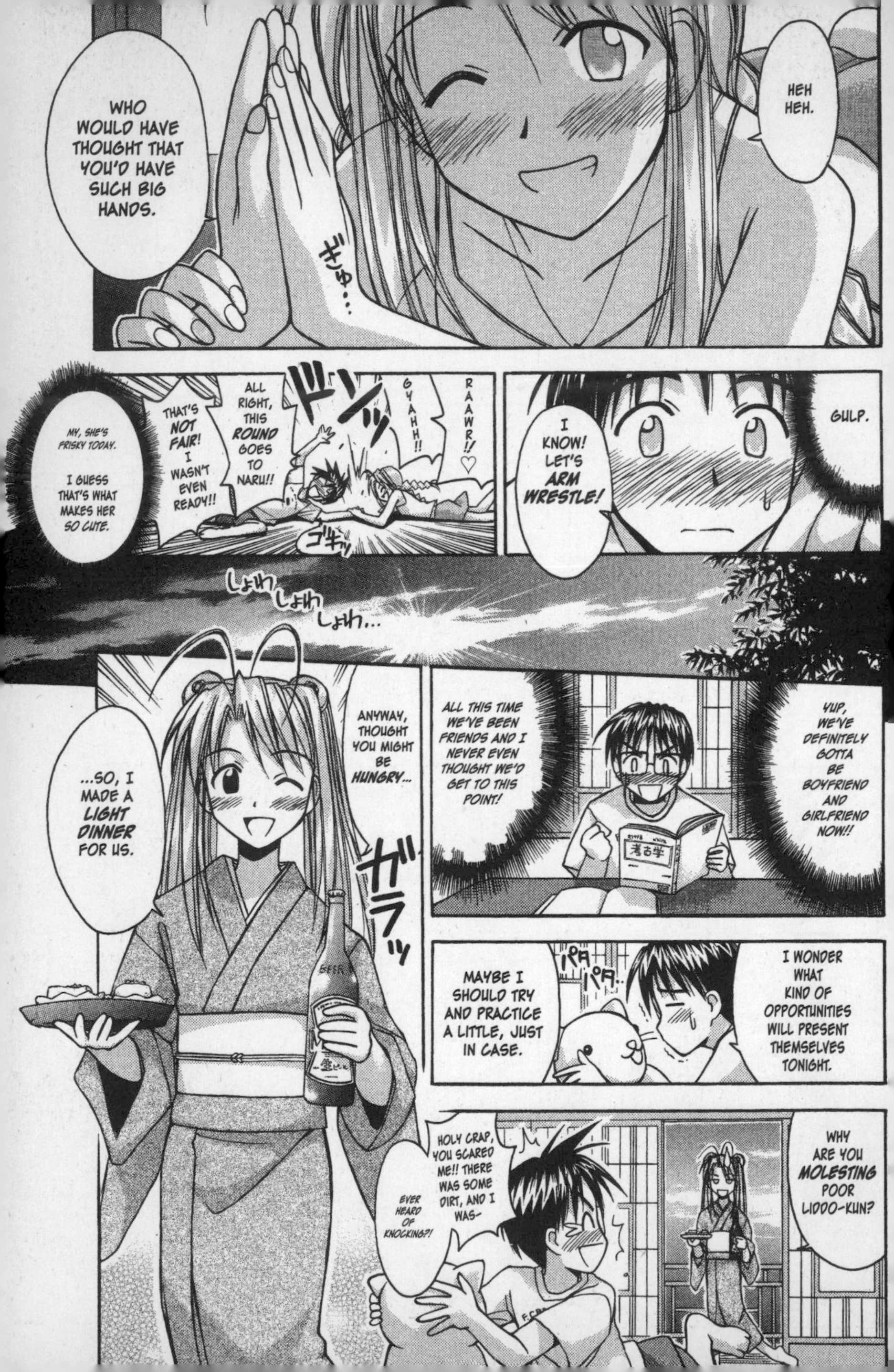
HEH HEH.
WHO WOULD HAVE THOUGHT THAT YOU'D HAVE SUCH BIG HANDS.
ぎゅ...
GULP.
I KNOW! LET'S ARM WRESTLE!
RAAWR!!♡
GYAHH!!
ドンッ
ALL RIGHT, THIS ROUND GOES TO NARU!!
THAT'S NOT FAIR! I WASN'T EVEN READY!!
ゴキッ
MY, SHE'S FRISKY TODAY.
I GUESS THAT'S WHAT MAKES HER SO CUTE.
しょわ しょわ しょわ...
YUP, WE'VE DEFINITELY GOTTA BE BOYFRIEND AND GIRLFRIEND NOW!!
ALL THIS TIME WE'VE BEEN FRIENDS AND I NEVER EVEN THOUGHT WE'D GET TO THIS POINT!
I WONDER WHAT KIND OF OPPORTUNITIES WILL PRESENT THEMSELVES TONIGHT.
MAYBE I SHOULD TRY AND PRACTICE A LITTLE, JUST IN CASE.
パタ パタ..
WHY ARE YOU MOLESTING POOR LIDDO-KUN?
HOLY CRAP, YOU SCARED ME!! THERE WAS SOME DIRT, AND I WAS-
EVER HEARD OF KNOCKING?!
ガラッ
ANYWAY, THOUGHT YOU MIGHT BE HUNGRY...
...SO, I MADE A LIGHT DINNER FOR US.

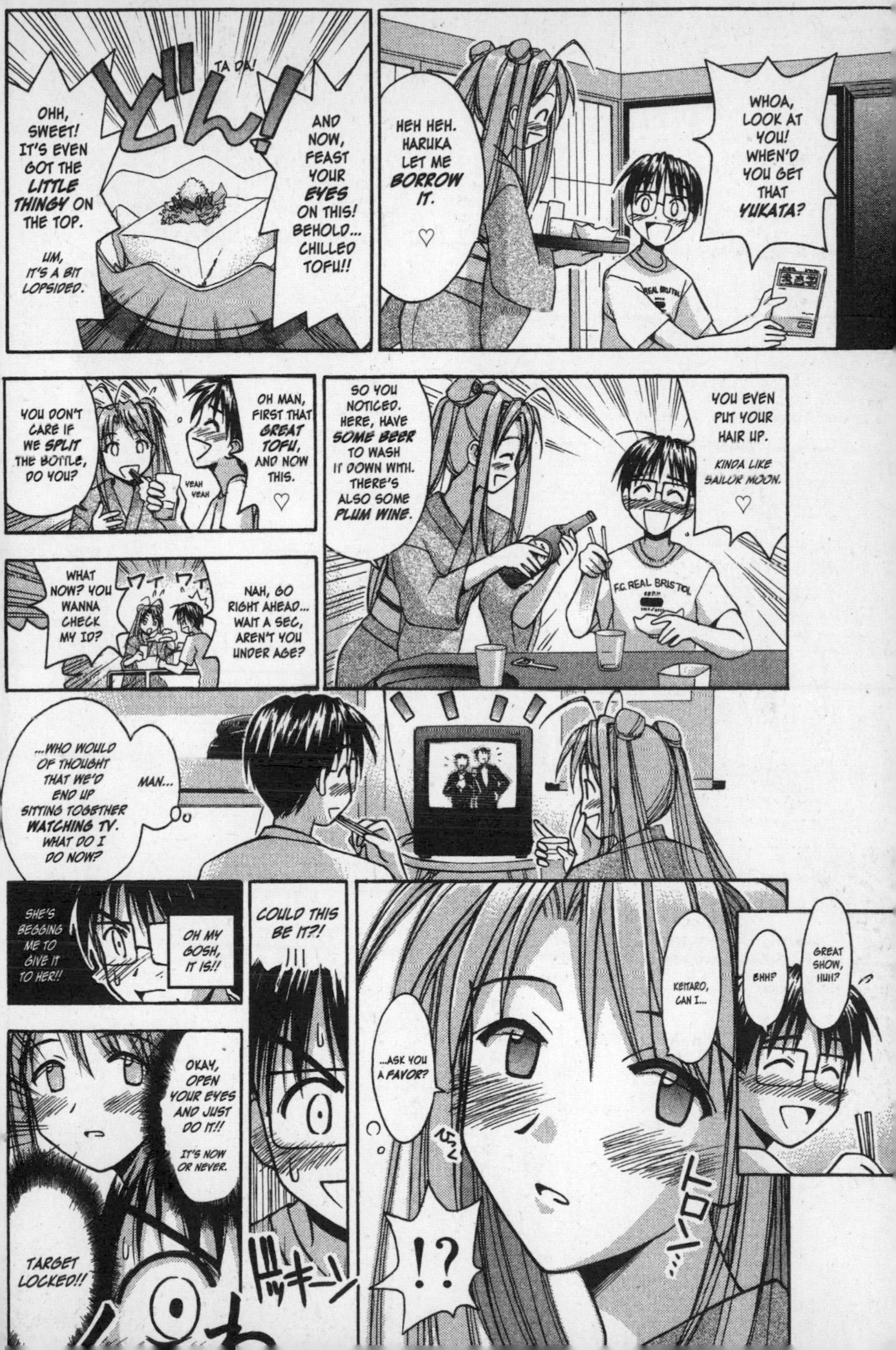
WHOA, LOOK AT YOU! WHEN'D YOU GET THAT YUKATA?
HEH HEH. HARUKA LET ME BORROW IT. ♡
TA DA!
AND NOW, FEAST YOUR EYES ON THIS! BEHOLD... CHILLED TOFU!!
OHH, SWEET! IT'S EVEN GOT THE LITTLE THINGY ON THE TOP.
UM, IT'S A BIT LOPSIDED.
YOU EVEN PUT YOUR HAIR UP.
KINDA LIKE SAILOR MOON. ♡
SO YOU NOTICED. HERE, HAVE SOME BEER TO WASH IT DOWN WITH. THERE'S ALSO SOME PLUM WINE.
OH MAN, FIRST THAT GREAT TOFU, AND NOW THIS. ♡
YOU DON'T CARE IF WE SPLIT THE BOTTLE, DO YOU?
YEAH YEAH
NAH, GO RIGHT AHEAD... WAIT A SEC, AREN'T YOU UNDER AGE?
WHAT NOW? YOU WANNA CHECK MY ID?
MAN...
...WHO WOULD OF THOUGHT THAT WE'D END UP SITTING TOGETHER WATCHING TV. WHAT DO I DO NOW?
GREAT SHOW, HUH?
EHH?
KEITARO, CAN I...
...ASK YOU A FAVOR?
!?
COULD THIS BE IT?!
OH MY GOSH, IT IS!!
SHE'S BEGGING ME TO GIVE IT TO HER!!
OKAY, OPEN YOUR EYES AND JUST DO IT!!
IT'S NOW OR NEVER.
TARGET LOCKED!!

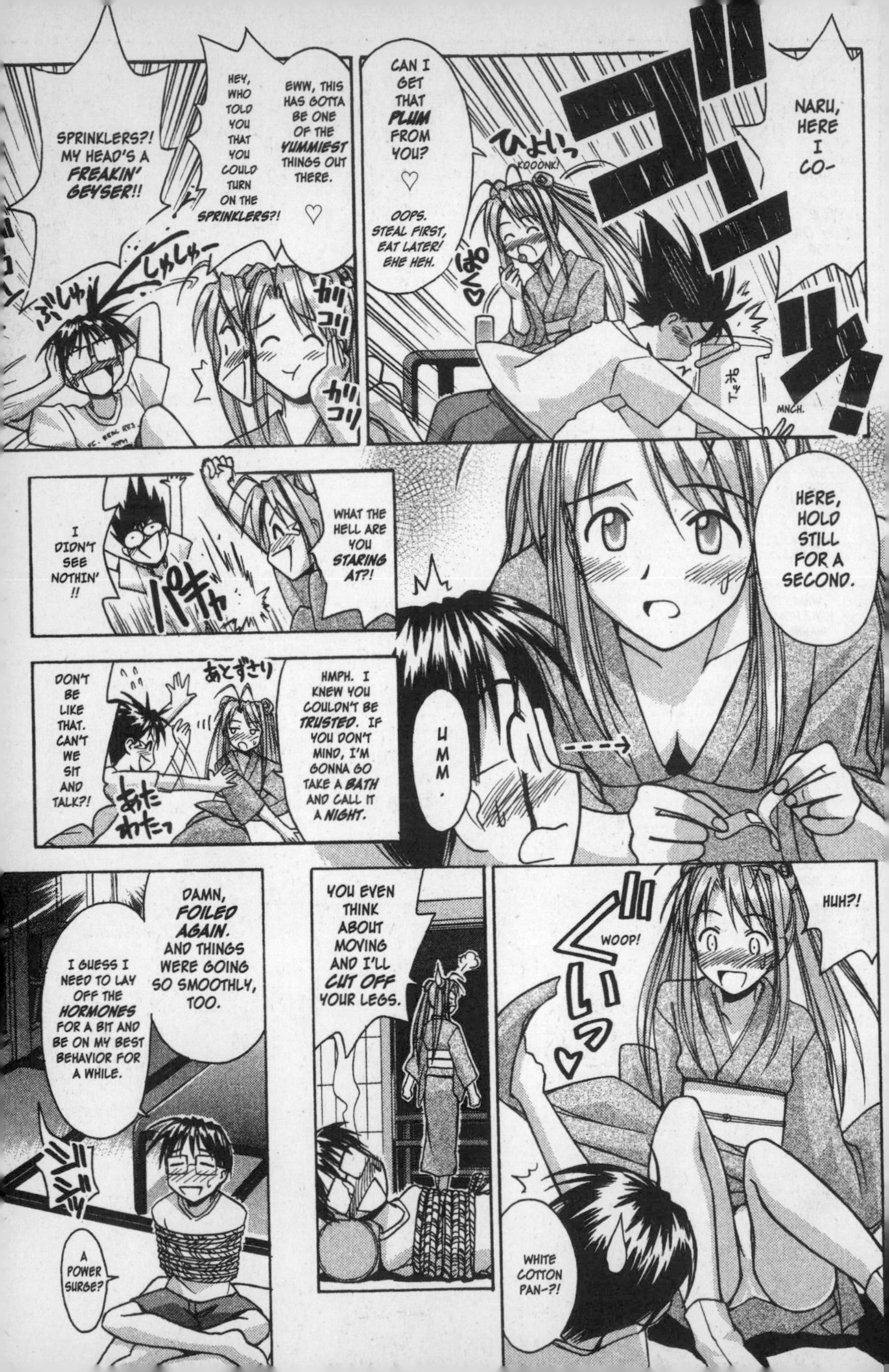
NARU, HERE I CO-
ひょいっ
KOOONK!
CAN I GET THAT PLUM FROM YOU? ♡
OOPS. STEAL FIRST, EAT LATER! EHE HEH.
ぱく♡
MNCH.
EWW, THIS HAS GOTTA BE ONE OF THE YUMMIEST THINGS OUT THERE. ♡
HEY, WHO TOLD YOU THAT YOU COULD TURN ON THE SPRINKLERS?!
SPRINKLERS?! MY HEAD'S A FREAKIN' GEYSER!!
しゅしゅー
ぶしゅ
HERE, HOLD STILL FOR A SECOND.
UMM.
WHAT THE HELL ARE YOU STARING AT?!
I DIDN'T SEE NOTHIN'!!
あとずさり
HMPH. I KNEW YOU COULDN'T BE TRUSTED. IF YOU DON'T MIND, I'M GONNA GO TAKE A BATH AND CALL IT A NIGHT.
DON'T BE LIKE THAT. CAN'T WE SIT AND TALK?!
HUH?!
WOOP!
WHITE COTTON PAN-?!
YOU EVEN THINK ABOUT MOVING AND I'LL CUT OFF YOUR LEGS.
DAMN, FOILED AGAIN. AND THINGS WERE GOING SO SMOOTHLY, TOO.
I GUESS I NEED TO LAY OFF THE HORMONES FOR A BIT AND BE ON MY BEST BEHAVIOR FOR A WHILE.
A POWER SURGE?

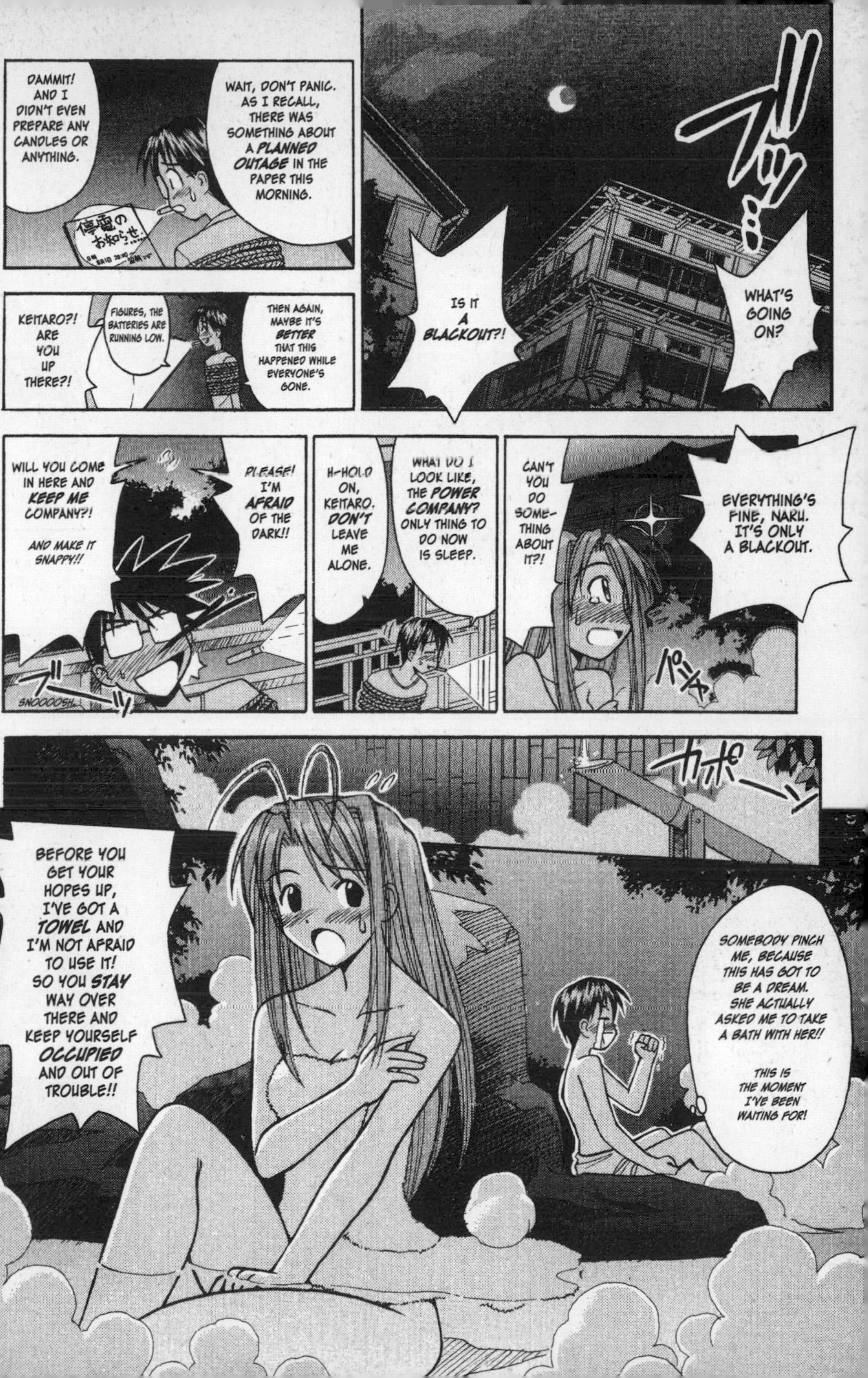

ブツッ
WHAT'S GOING ON?
IS IT A BLACKOUT?!
WAIT, DON'T PANIC. AS I RECALL, THERE WAS SOMETHING ABOUT A PLANNED OUTAGE IN THE PAPER THIS MORNING.
DAMMIT! AND I DIDN'T EVEN PREPARE ANY CANDLES OR ANYTHING.
停電のお知らせ
THEN AGAIN, MAYBE IT'S BETTER THAT THIS HAPPENED WHILE EVERYONE'S GONE.
FIGURES, THE BATTERIES ARE RUNNING LOW.
KEITARO?! ARE YOU UP THERE?!
EVERYTHING'S FINE, NARU. IT'S ONLY A BLACKOUT.
CAN'T YOU DO SOMETHING ABOUT IT?!
パシャ
WHAT DO I LOOK LIKE, THE POWER COMPANY? ONLY THING TO DO NOW IS SLEEP.
H-HOLD ON, KEITARO. DON'T LEAVE ME ALONE.
PLEASE! I'M AFRAID OF THE DARK!!
WILL YOU COME IN HERE AND KEEP ME COMPANY?!
AND MAKE IT SNAPPY!!
SNOOOOSH
カポーン
SOMEBODY PINCH ME, BECAUSE THIS HAS GOT TO BE A DREAM. SHE ACTUALLY ASKED ME TO TAKE A BATH WITH HER!!
THIS IS THE MOMENT I'VE BEEN WAITING FOR!
BEFORE YOU GET YOUR HOPES UP, I'VE GOT A TOWEL AND I'M NOT AFRAID TO USE IT! SO YOU STAY WAY OVER THERE AND KEEP YOURSELF OCCUPIED AND OUT OF TROUBLE!!

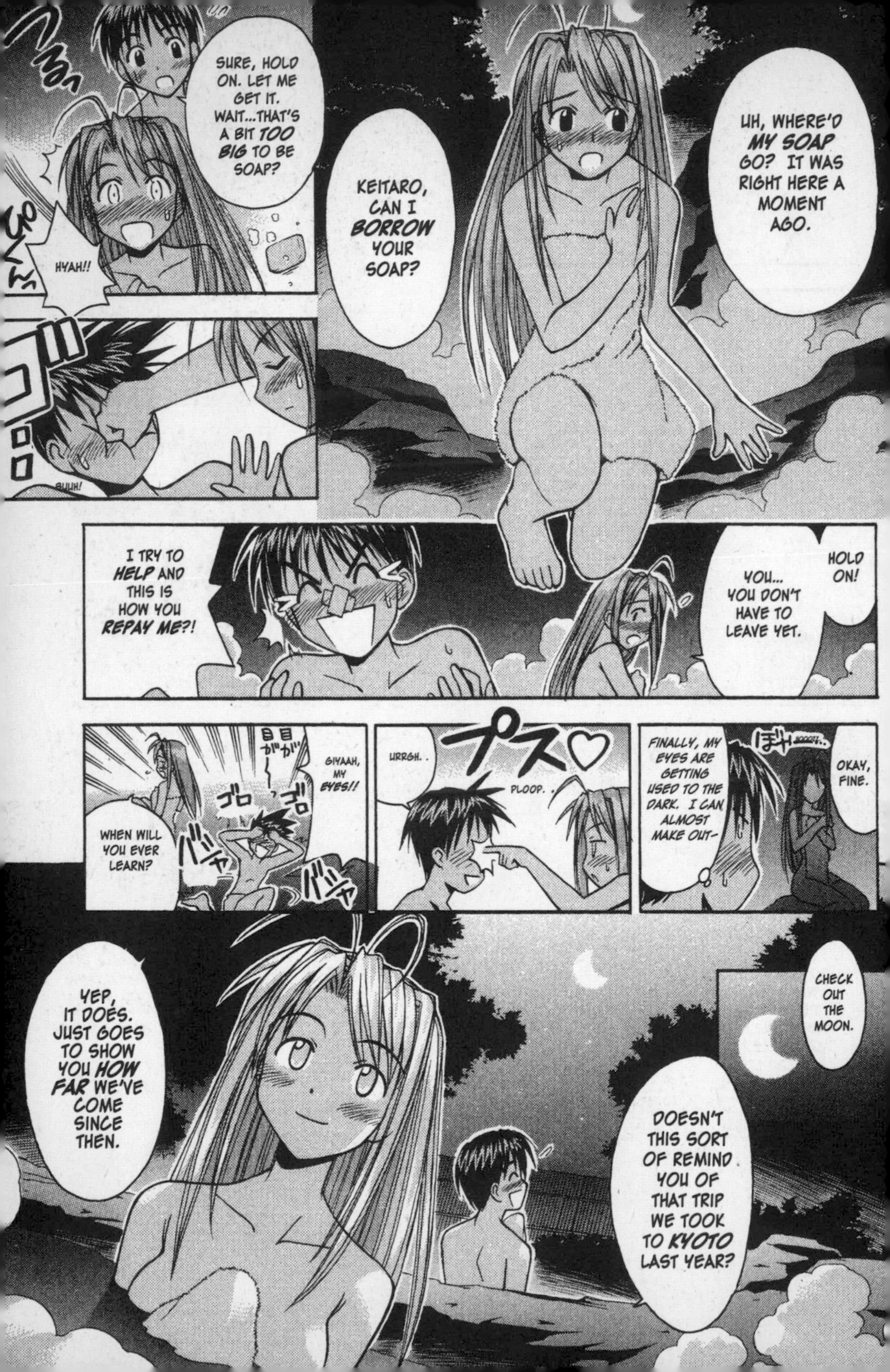
UH, WHERE'D MY SOAP GO? IT WAS RIGHT HERE A MOMENT AGO.
KEITARO, CAN I BORROW YOUR SOAP?
SURE, HOLD ON. LET ME GET IT. WAIT...THAT'S A BIT TOO BIG TO BE SOAP?
HYAH!!
BUUH!
HOLD ON!
YOU... YOU DON'T HAVE TO LEAVE YET.
I TRY TO HELP AND THIS IS HOW YOU REPAY ME?!
ぽや
OKAY, FINE.
FINALLY, MY EYES ARE GETTING USED TO THE DARK. I CAN ALMOST MAKE OUT-
URRGH. .
プス♡
PLOOP. .
目が目が～
GIYAAH, MY EYES!!
ゴロ ゴロ
バシャ バシャ
WHEN WILL YOU EVER LEARN?
CHECK OUT THE MOON.
DOESN'T THIS SORT OF REMIND YOU OF THAT TRIP WE TOOK TO KYOTO LAST YEAR?
YEP, IT DOES. JUST GOES TO SHOW YOU HOW FAR WE'VE COME SINCE THEN.

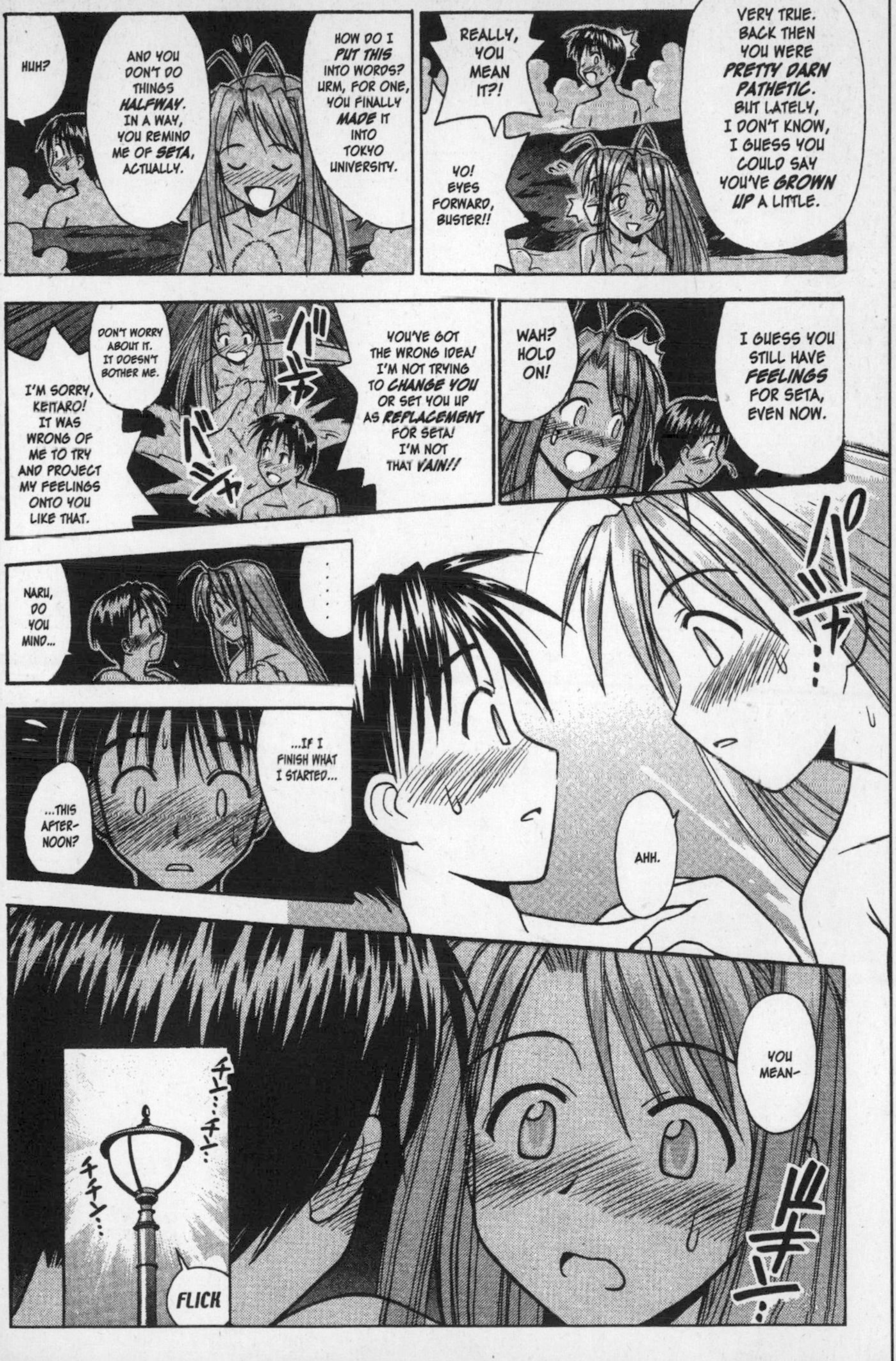
VERY TRUE. BACK THEN YOU WERE PRETTY DARN PATHETIC. BUT LATELY, I DON'T KNOW, I GUESS YOU COULD SAY YOU'VE GROWN UP A LITTLE.
REALLY, YOU MEAN IT?!
YO! EYES FORWARD, BUSTER!!
HOW DO I PUT THIS INTO WORDS? URM, FOR ONE, YOU FINALLY MADE IT INTO TOKYO UNIVERSITY.
AND YOU DON'T DO THINGS HALFWAY. IN A WAY, YOU REMIND ME OF SETA, ACTUALLY.
HUH?
I GUESS YOU STILL HAVE FEELINGS FOR SETA, EVEN NOW.
WAH? HOLD ON!
YOU'VE GOT THE WRONG IDEA! I'M NOT TRYING TO CHANGE YOU OR SET YOU UP AS REPLACEMENT FOR SETA! I'M NOT THAT VAIN!!
DON'T WORRY ABOUT IT. IT DOESN'T BOTHER ME.
I'M SORRY, KEITARO! IT WAS WRONG OF ME TO TRY AND PROJECT MY FEELINGS ONTO YOU LIKE THAT.
.....
NARU, DO YOU MIND...
...IF I FINISH WHAT I STARTED...
...THIS AFTER-NOON?
AHH.
YOU MEAN-
FLICK

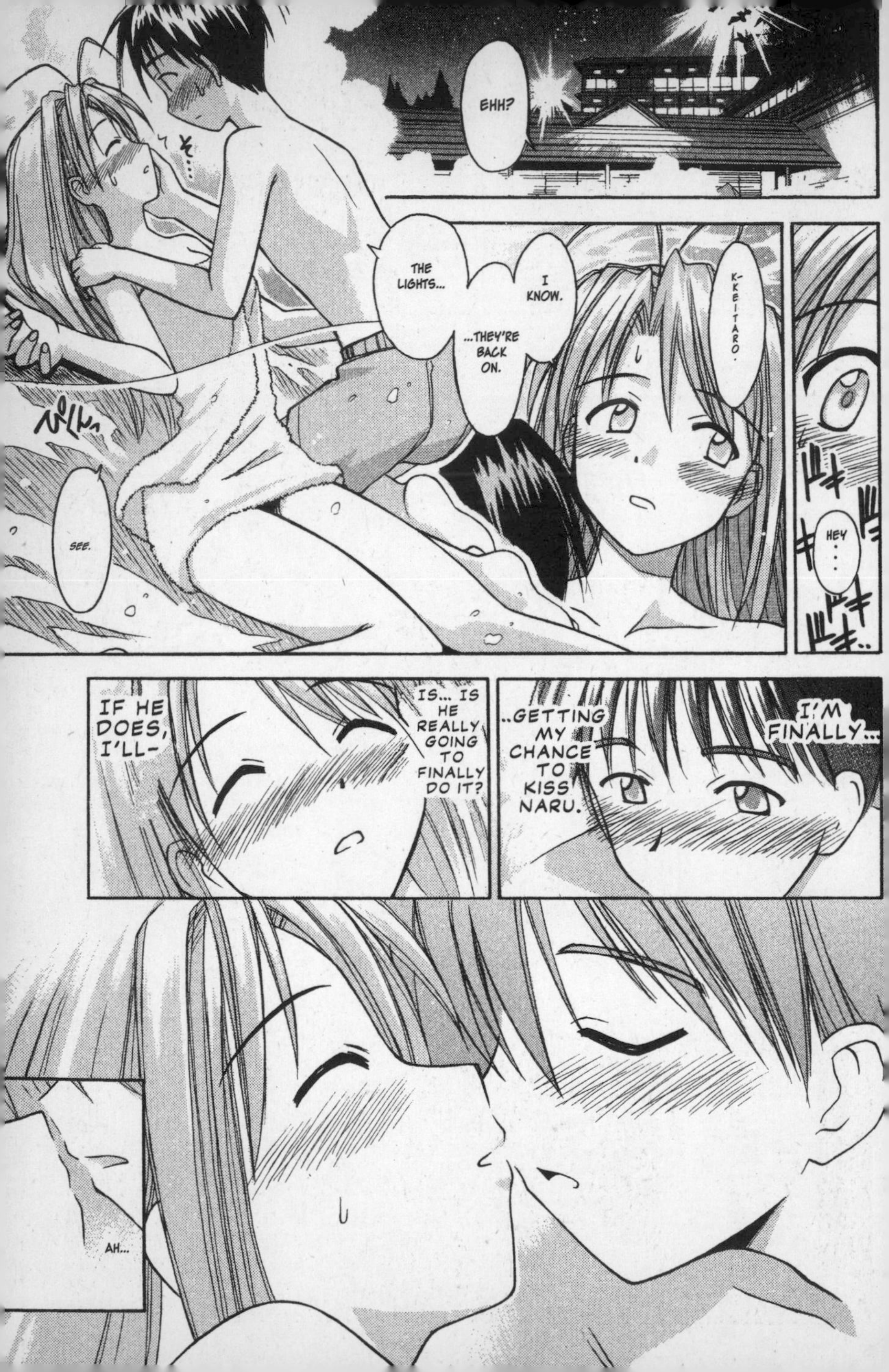
EHH?
HEY...
K-KEITARO.
THE LIGHTS...
I KNOW.
...THEY'RE BACK ON.
SEE.
I'M FINALLY...
..GETTING MY CHANCE TO KISS NARU.
IS... IS HE REALLY GOING TO FINALLY DO IT?
IF HE DOES, I'LL-
AH...

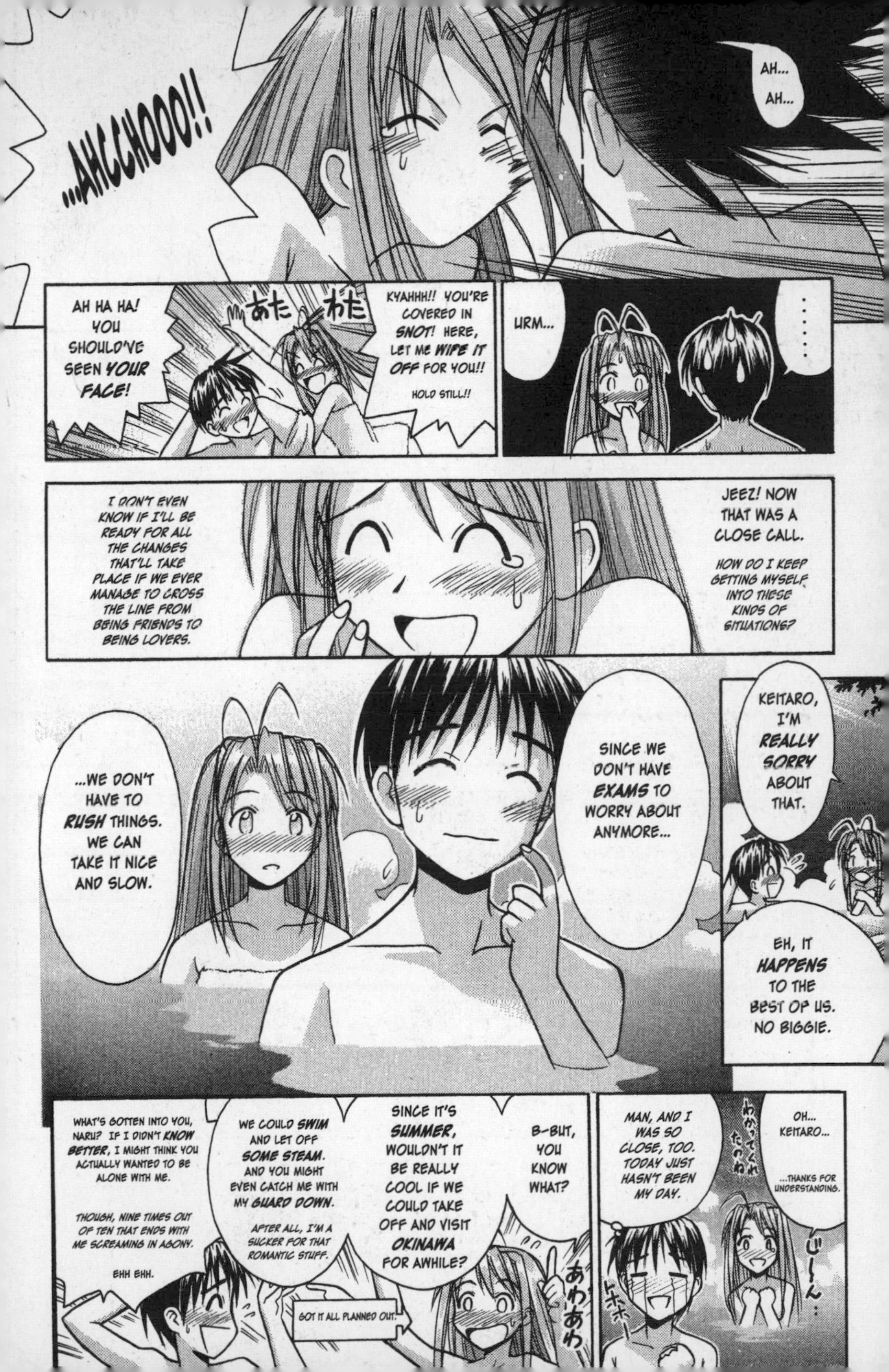
AH... AH...
...AHCCHOOO!!
......
URM...
KYAHHH!! YOU'RE COVERED IN SNOT! HERE, LET ME WIPE IT OFF FOR YOU!!
HOLD STILL!!
あた わた
AH HA HA! YOU SHOULD'VE SEEN YOUR FACE!
JEEZ! NOW THAT WAS A CLOSE CALL.
HOW DO I KEEP GETTING MYSELF INTO THESE KINDS OF SITUATIONS?
I DON'T EVEN KNOW IF I'LL BE READY FOR ALL THE CHANGES THAT'LL TAKE PLACE IF WE EVER MANAGE TO CROSS THE LINE FROM BEING FRIENDS TO BEING LOVERS.
KEITARO, I'M REALLY SORRY ABOUT THAT.
EH, IT HAPPENS TO THE BEST OF US. NO BIGGIE.
SINCE WE DON'T HAVE EXAMS TO WORRY ABOUT ANYMORE...
...WE DON'T HAVE TO RUSH THINGS. WE CAN TAKE IT NICE AND SLOW.
OH... KEITARO...
...THANKS FOR UNDERSTANDING.
わかってくれたのね
じ～ん...
MAN, AND I WAS SO CLOSE, TOO. TODAY JUST HASN'T BEEN MY DAY.
トホホ
B-BUT, YOU KNOW WHAT?
SINCE IT'S SUMMER, WOULDN'T IT BE REALLY COOL IF WE COULD TAKE OFF AND VISIT OKINAWA FOR AWHILE?
あわあわ
GOT IT ALL PLANNED OUT.
WE COULD SWIM AND LET OFF SOME STEAM. AND YOU MIGHT EVEN CATCH ME WITH MY GUARD DOWN.
AFTER ALL, I'M A SUCKER FOR THAT ROMANTIC STUFF.
WHAT'S GOTTEN INTO YOU, NARU? IF I DIDN'T KNOW BETTER, I MIGHT THINK YOU ACTUALLY WANTED TO BE ALONE WITH ME.
THOUGH, NINE TIMES OUT OF TEN THAT ENDS WITH ME SCREAMING IN AGONY.
EHH EHH.

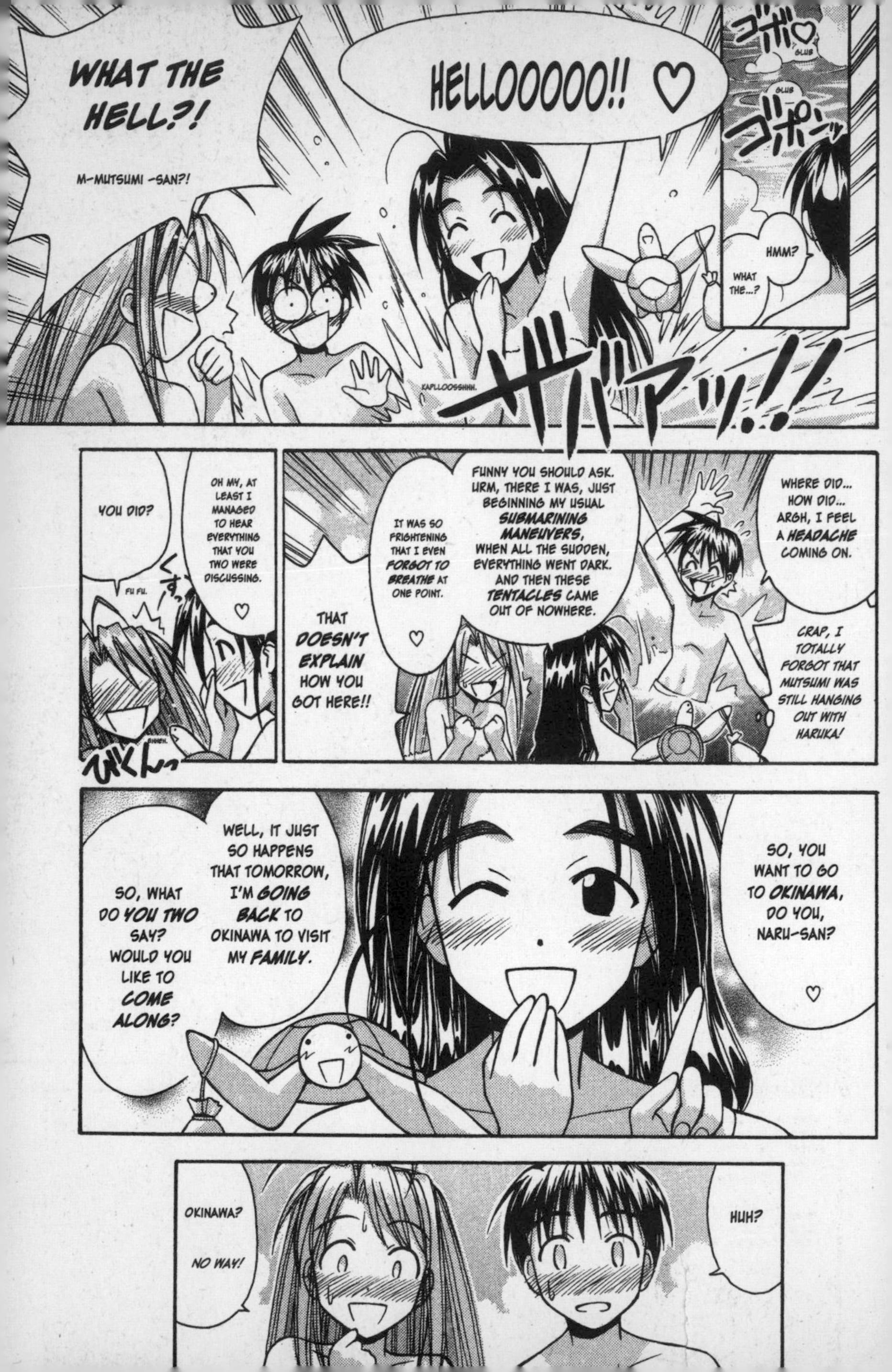
ゴポ♡
GLUB
GLUB
ゴポーッ
HMM?
WHAT THE...?
HELLOOOOO!! ♡
WHAT THE HELL?!
M-MUTSUMI -SAN?!
KAPLLOOSSHHH.
ザバアッ!!
WHERE DID... HOW DID... ARGH, I FEEL A HEADACHE COMING ON.
CRAP, I TOTALLY FORGOT THAT MUTSUMI WAS STILL HANGING OUT WITH HARUKA!
FUNNY YOU SHOULD ASK. URM, THERE I WAS, JUST BEGINNING MY USUAL SUBMARINING MANEUVERS, WHEN ALL THE SUDDEN, EVERYTHING WENT DARK. AND THEN THESE TENTACLES CAME OUT OF NOWHERE.
IT WAS SO FRIGHTENING THAT I EVEN FORGOT TO BREATHE AT ONE POINT. ♡
THAT DOESN'T EXPLAIN HOW YOU GOT HERE!!
OH MY, AT LEAST I MANAGED TO HEAR EVERYTHING THAT YOU TWO WERE DISCUSSING. ♡
YOU DID?
FU FU.
くすっ
びくんっ
SO, YOU WANT TO GO TO OKINAWA, DO YOU, NARU-SAN? ♡
WELL, IT JUST SO HAPPENS THAT TOMORROW, I'M GOING BACK TO OKINAWA TO VISIT MY FAMILY.
SO, WHAT DO YOU TWO SAY? WOULD YOU LIKE TO COME ALONG?
HUH?
OKINAWA?
NO WAY!

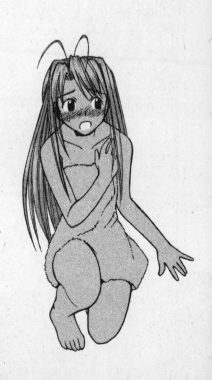

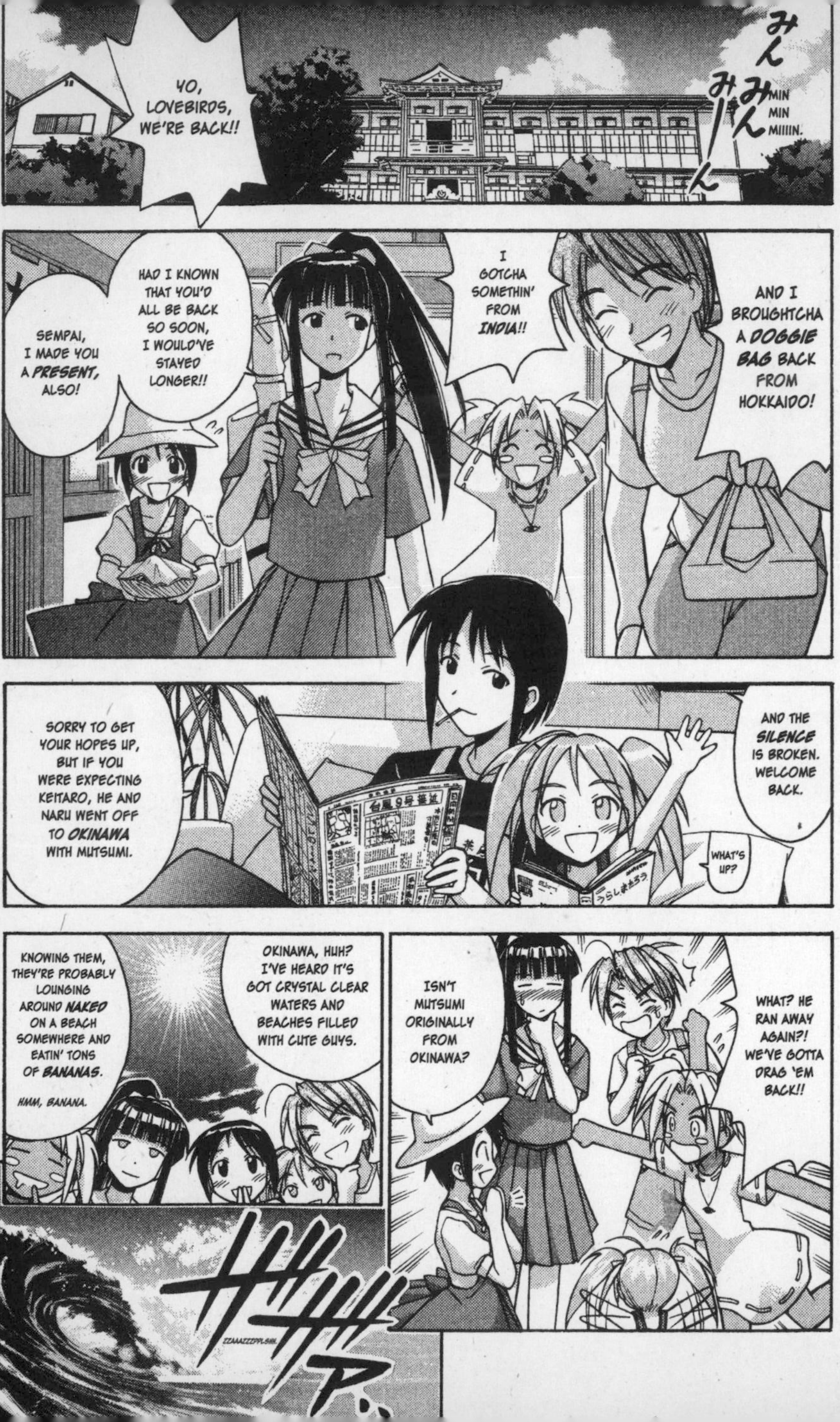
みんみんみーん
MIN MIN MIIIN.
YO, LOVEBIRDS, WE'RE BACK!!
AND I BROUGHTCHA A DOGGIE BAG BACK FROM HOKKAIDO!
I GOTCHA SOMETHIN' FROM INDIA!!
HAD I KNOWN THAT YOU'D ALL BE BACK SO SOON, I WOULD'VE STAYED LONGER!!
SEMPAI, I MADE YOU A PRESENT, ALSO!
AND THE SILENCE IS BROKEN. WELCOME BACK.
WHAT'S UP?
SORRY TO GET YOUR HOPES UP, BUT IF YOU WERE EXPECTING KEITARO, HE AND NARU WENT OFF TO OKINAWA WITH MUTSUMI.
WHAT? HE RAN AWAY AGAIN?! WE'VE GOTTA DRAG 'EM BACK!!
ISN'T MUTSUMI ORIGINALLY FROM OKINAWA?
OKINAWA, HUH? I'VE HEARD IT'S GOT CRYSTAL CLEAR WATERS AND BEACHES FILLED WITH CUTE GUYS.
KNOWING THEM, THEY'RE PROBABLY LOUNGING AROUND NAKED ON A BEACH SOMEWHERE AND EATIN' TONS OF BANANAS.
HMM, BANANA.
ザザァ

「ラブひな」

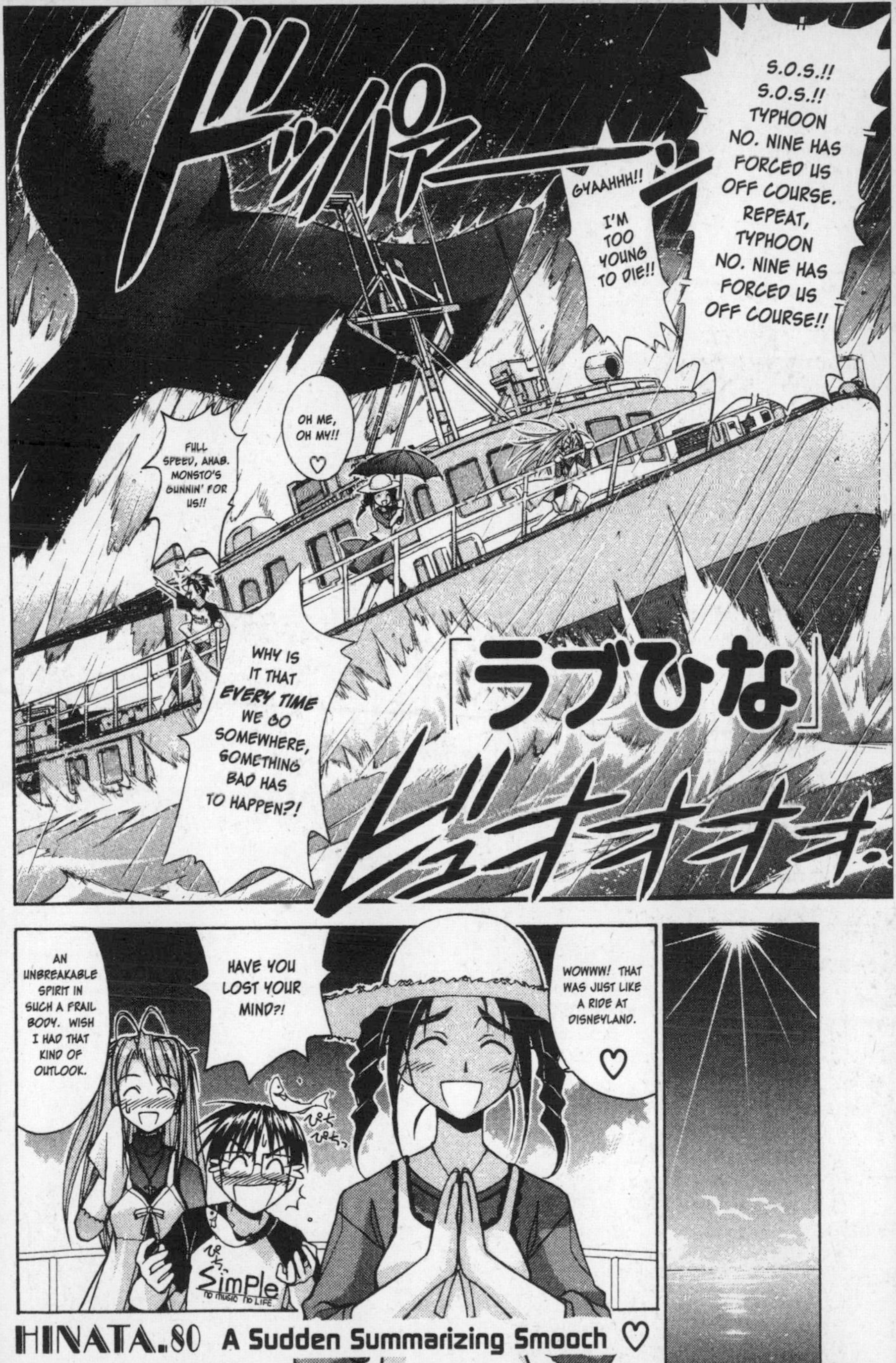
S.O.S.!! S.O.S.!! TYPHOON NO. NINE HAS FORCED US OFF COURSE. REPEAT, TYPHOON NO. NINE HAS FORCED US OFF COURSE!!
GYAAHHH!!
I'M TOO YOUNG TO DIE!!
ドッパァーン
OH ME, OH MY!! ♡
FULL SPEED, AHAB. MONSTO'S GUNNIN' FOR US!!
WHY IS IT THAT EVERY TIME WE GO SOMEWHERE, SOMETHING BAD HAS TO HAPPEN?!
「ラブひな」
ビュオオオオ
WOWWW! THAT WAS JUST LIKE A RIDE AT DISNEYLAND. ♡
HAVE YOU LOST YOUR MIND?!
AN UNBREAKABLE SPIRIT IN SUCH A FRAIL BODY. WISH I HAD THAT KIND OF OUTLOOK.
Simple
NO MUSIC NO LIFE

HINATA.80 A Sudden Summarizing Smooch ♡

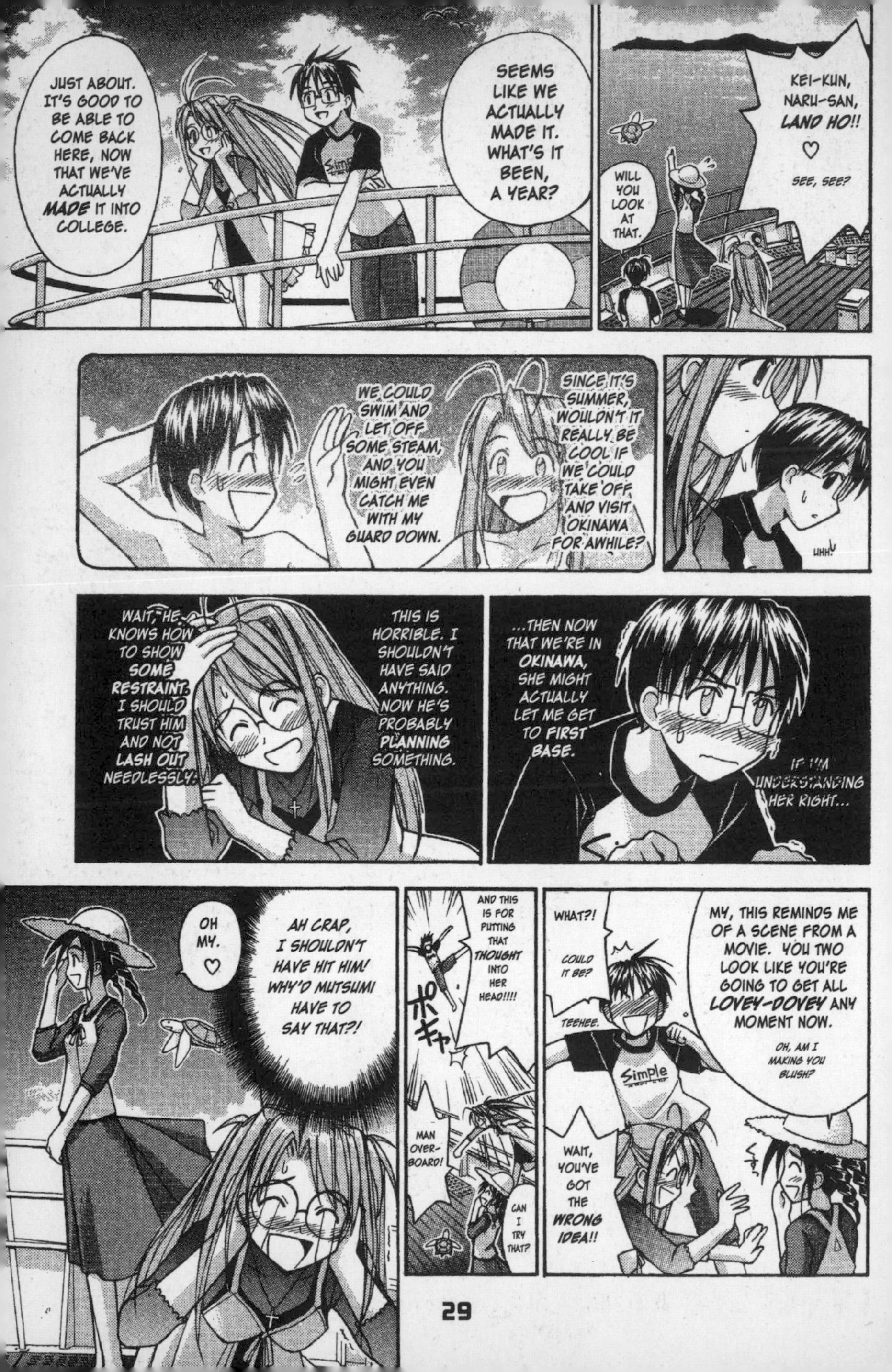
KEI-KUN, NARU-SAN, LAND HO!! ♡
SEE, SEE?
WILL YOU LOOK AT THAT.
SEEMS LIKE WE ACTUALLY MADE IT. WHAT'S IT BEEN, A YEAR?
JUST ABOUT. IT'S GOOD TO BE ABLE TO COME BACK HERE, NOW THAT WE'VE ACTUALLY MADE IT INTO COLLEGE.
UHH.
SINCE IT'S SUMMER, WOULDN'T IT REALLY BE COOL IF WE COULD TAKE OFF AND VISIT OKINAWA FOR AWHILE?
WE COULD SWIM AND LET OFF SOME STEAM, AND YOU MIGHT EVEN CATCH ME WITH MY GUARD DOWN.
IF I'M UNDERSTANDING HER RIGHT...
...THEN NOW THAT WE'RE IN OKINAWA, SHE MIGHT ACTUALLY LET ME GET TO FIRST BASE.
THIS IS HORRIBLE. I SHOULDN'T HAVE SAID ANYTHING. NOW HE'S PROBABLY PLANNING SOMETHING.
WAIT, HE KNOWS HOW TO SHOW SOME RESTRAINT. I SHOULD TRUST HIM AND NOT LASH OUT NEEDLESSLY.
MY, THIS REMINDS ME OF A SCENE FROM A MOVIE. YOU TWO LOOK LIKE YOU'RE GOING TO GET ALL LOVEY-DOVEY ANY MOMENT NOW.
OH, AM I MAKING YOU BLUSH?
WHAT?!
COULD IT BE?
TEEHEE.
WAIT, YOU'VE GOT THE WRONG IDEA!!
AND THIS IS FOR PUTTING THAT THOUGHT INTO HER HEAD!!!!
ポキャ
MAN OVERBOARD!
CAN I TRY THAT?
AH CRAP, I SHOULDN'T HAVE HIT HIM! WHY'D MUTSUMI HAVE TO SAY THAT?!
OH MY. ♡

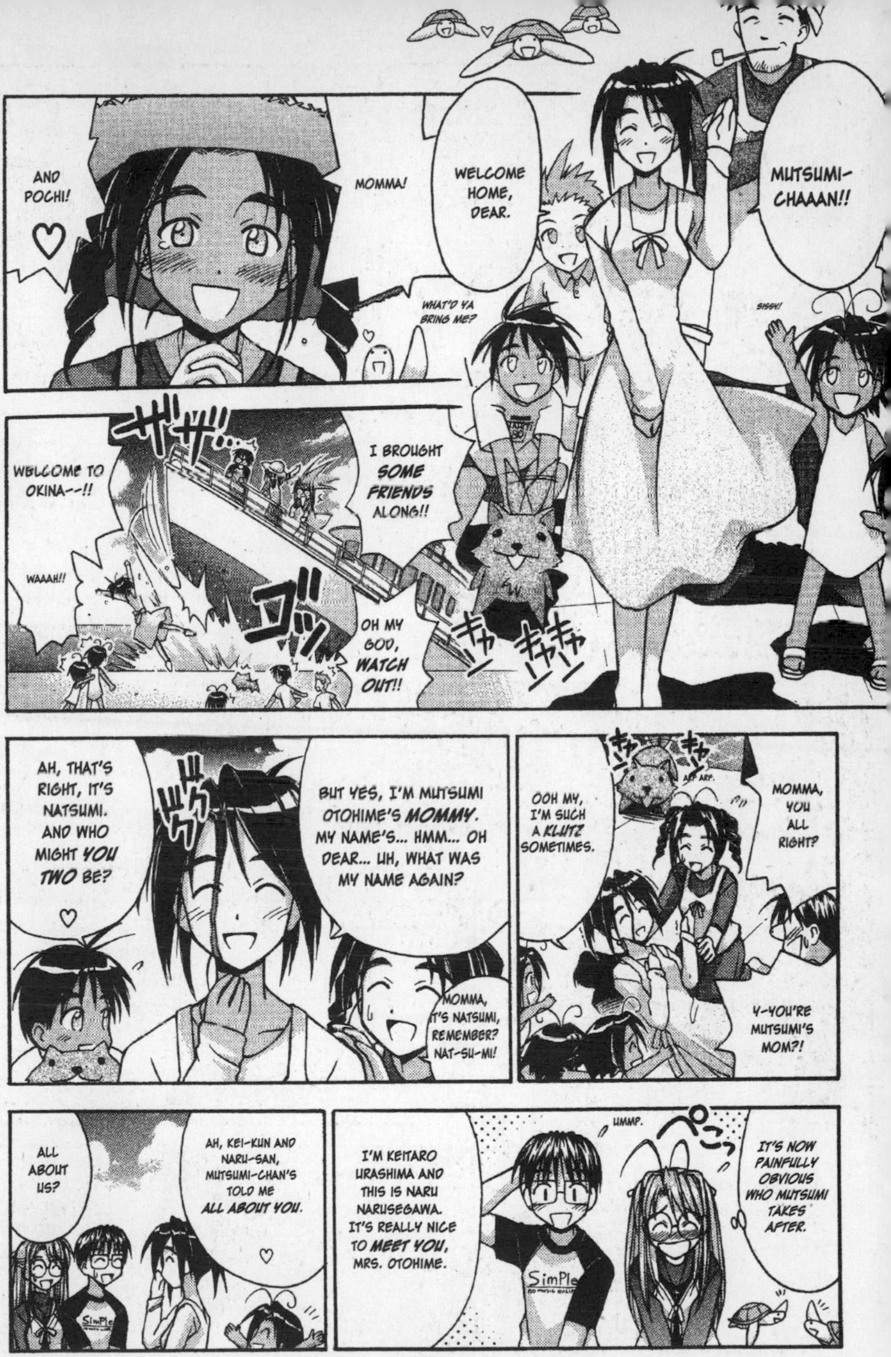

MUTSUMI-CHAAAN!!
SISSY!
WELCOME HOME, DEAR.
WHAT'D YA BRING ME?
MOMMA!
AND POCHI! ♡
I BROUGHT SOME FRIENDS ALONG!!
キャ キャキャ
OH MY GOD, WATCH OUT!!
ゴッ
ザザ…
WELCOME TO OKINA--!!
WAAAH!!
キャ キャ
MOMMA, YOU ALL RIGHT?
ARF ARF.
OOH MY, I'M SUCH A KLUTZ SOMETIMES.
Y-YOU'RE MUTSUMI'S MOM?!
BUT YES, I'M MUTSUMI OTOHIME'S MOMMY. MY NAME'S... HMM... OH DEAR... UH, WHAT WAS MY NAME AGAIN?
MOMMA, IT'S NATSUMI, REMEMBER? NAT-SU-MI!
ドクン
AH, THAT'S RIGHT, IT'S NATSUMI. AND WHO MIGHT YOU TWO BE? ♡
IT'S NOW PAINFULLY OBVIOUS WHO MUTSUMI TAKES AFTER.
ぺこっ
UMMP.
I'M KEITARO URASHIMA AND THIS IS NARU NARUSEGAWA. IT'S REALLY NICE TO MEET YOU, MRS. OTOHIME.
AH, KEI-KUN AND NARU-SAN, MUTSUMI-CHAN'S TOLD ME ALL ABOUT YOU. ♡
ALL ABOUT US?

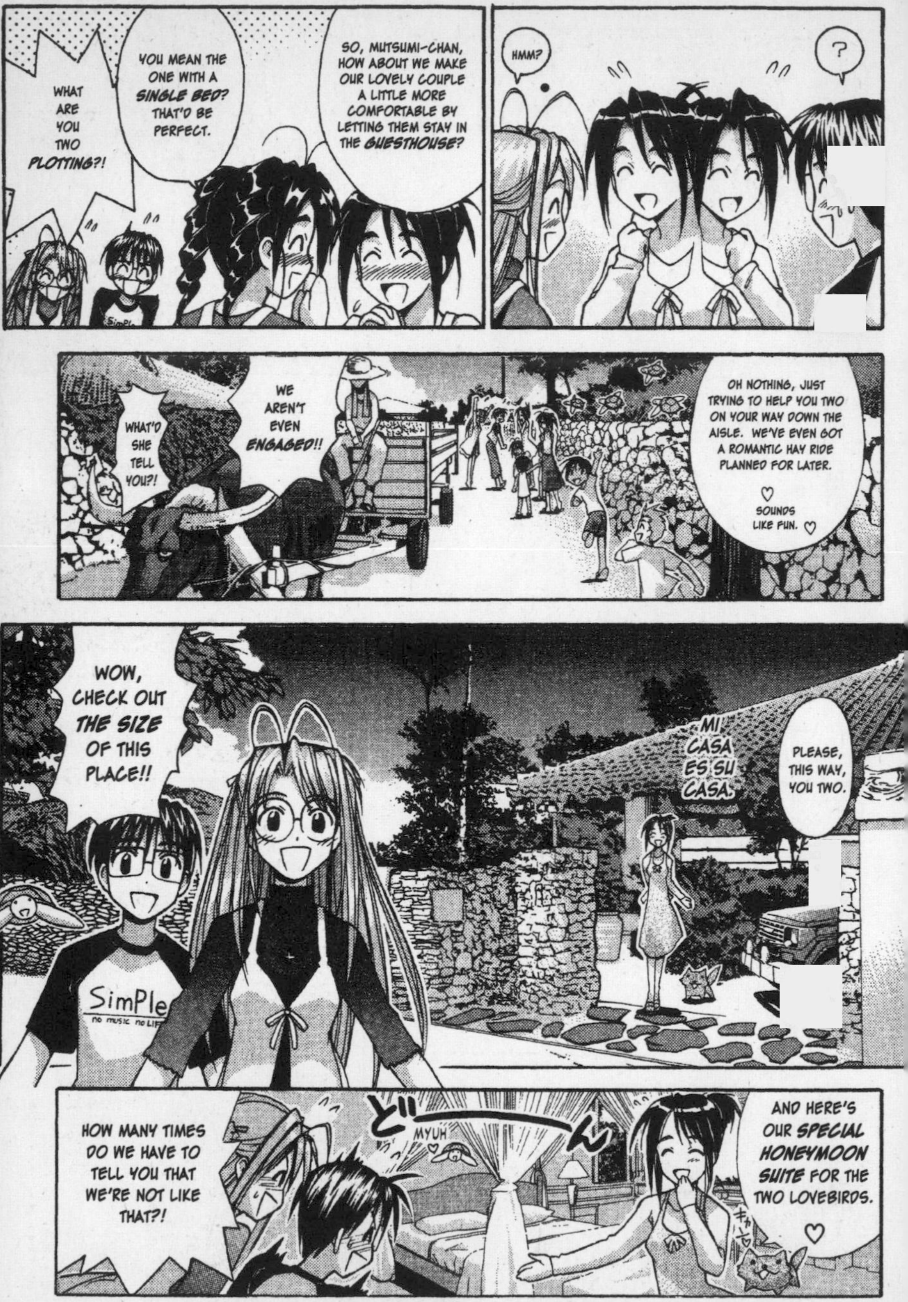
HMM?
?
SO, MUTSUMI-CHAN, HOW ABOUT WE MAKE OUR LOVELY COUPLE A LITTLE MORE COMFORTABLE BY LETTING THEM STAY IN THE GUESTHOUSE?
YOU MEAN THE ONE WITH A SINGLE BED? THAT'D BE PERFECT.
WHAT ARE YOU TWO PLOTTING?!
OH NOTHING, JUST TRYING TO HELP YOU TWO ON YOUR WAY DOWN THE AISLE. WE'VE EVEN GOT A ROMANTIC HAY RIDE PLANNED FOR LATER.
SOUNDS LIKE FUN.
WE AREN'T EVEN ENGAGED!!
WHAT'D SHE TELL YOU?!
PLEASE, THIS WAY, YOU TWO.
MI CASA ES SU CASA.
WOW, CHECK OUT THE SIZE OF THIS PLACE!!
SimPle no music no LIFE
AND HERE'S OUR SPECIAL HONEYMOON SUITE FOR THE TWO LOVEBIRDS.
どーーん
MYUH
HOW MANY TIMES DO WE HAVE TO TELL YOU THAT WE'RE NOT LIKE THAT?!

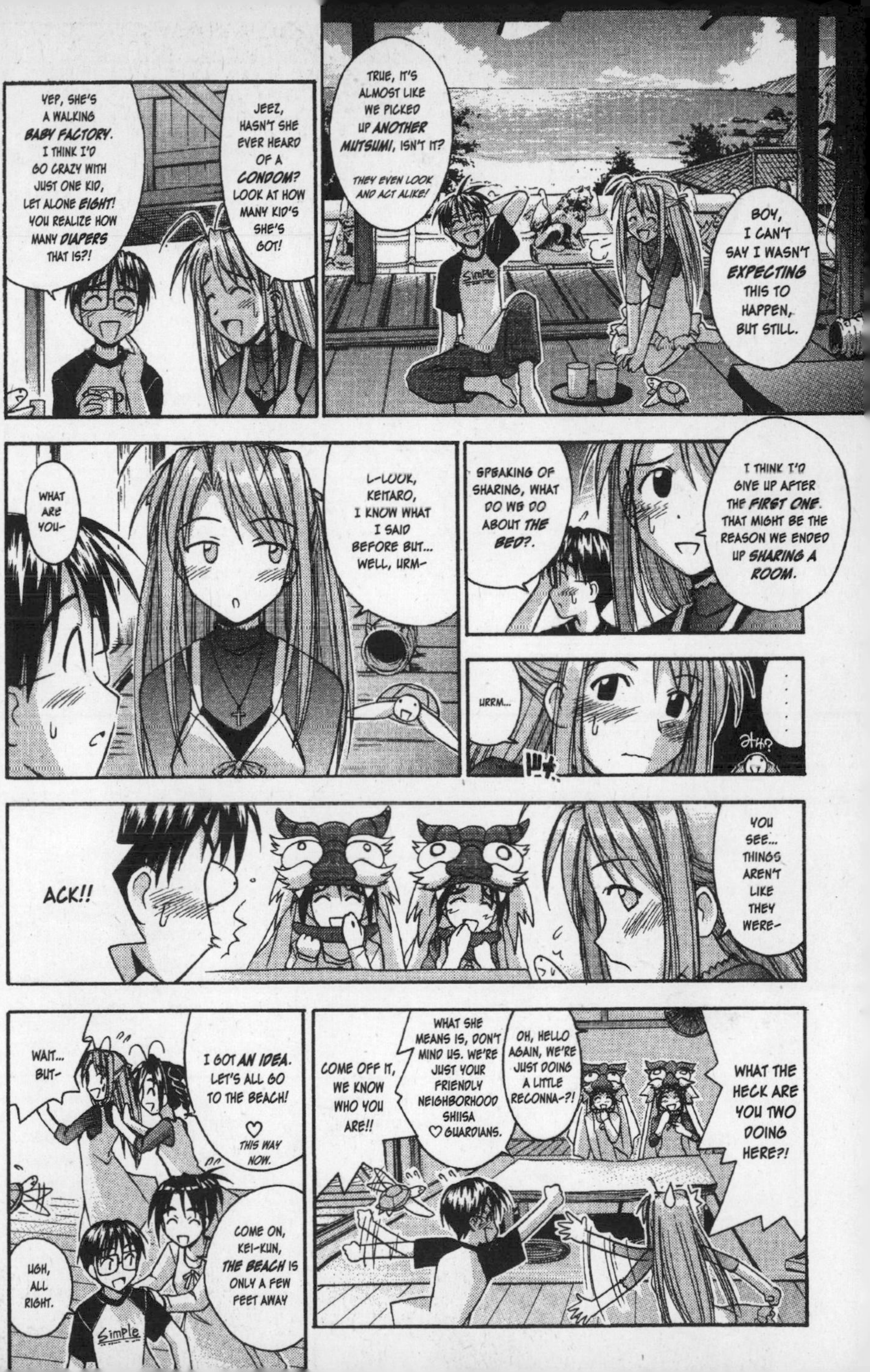
BOY, I CAN'T SAY I WASN'T EXPECTING THIS TO HAPPEN, BUT STILL.
TRUE, IT'S ALMOST LIKE WE PICKED UP ANOTHER MUTSUMI, ISN'T IT?
THEY EVEN LOOK AND ACT ALIKE!
JEEZ, HASN'T SHE EVER HEARD OF A CONDOM? LOOK AT HOW MANY KID'S SHE'S GOT!
YEP, SHE'S A WALKING BABY FACTORY. I THINK I'D GO CRAZY WITH JUST ONE KID, LET ALONE EIGHT! YOU REALIZE HOW MANY DIAPERS THAT IS?!
I THINK I'D GIVE UP AFTER THE FIRST ONE. THAT MIGHT BE THE REASON WE ENDED UP SHARING A ROOM.
SPEAKING OF SHARING, WHAT DO WE DO ABOUT THE BED?.
. . . . .
URRM...
みゅ?
L-LOOK, KEITARO, I KNOW WHAT I SAID BEFORE BUT... WELL, URM-
WHAT ARE YOU-
YOU SEE... THINGS AREN'T LIKE THEY WERE-
ACK!!
WHAT THE HECK ARE YOU TWO DOING HERE?!
OH, HELLO AGAIN, WE'RE JUST DOING A LITTLE RECONNA-?!
WHAT SHE MEANS IS, DON'T MIND US. WE'RE JUST YOUR FRIENDLY NEIGHBORHOOD SHIISA ♡ GUARDIANS.
COME OFF IT, WE KNOW WHO YOU ARE!!
I GOT AN IDEA. LET'S ALL GO TO THE BEACH! ♡
THIS WAY NOW.
WAIT... BUT-
COME ON, KEI-KUN, THE BEACH IS ONLY A FEW FEET AWAY
UGH, ALL RIGHT.

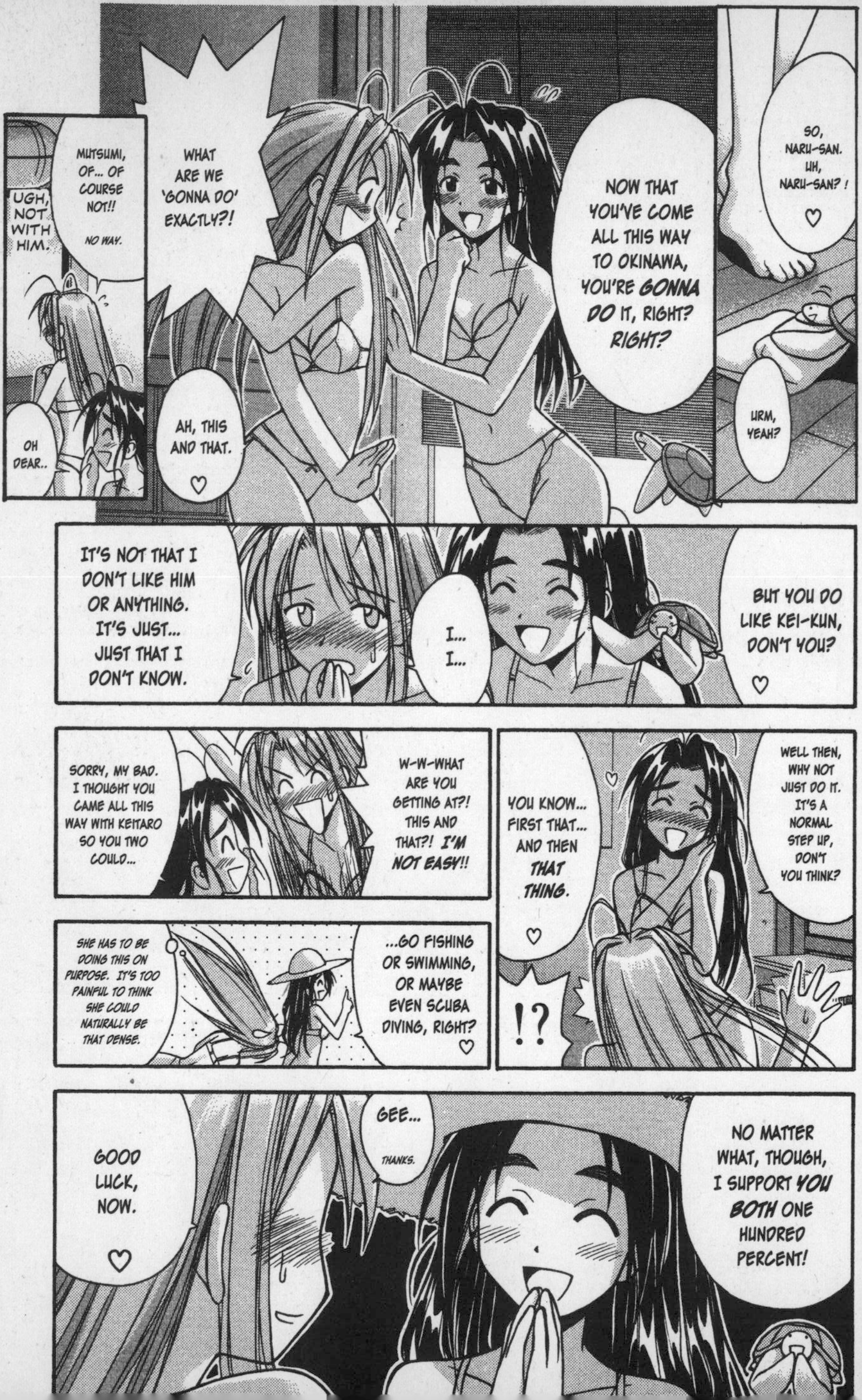
SO, NARU-SAN. UH, NARU-SAN? ! ♡
URM, YEAH?
NOW THAT YOU'VE COME ALL THIS WAY TO OKINAWA, YOU'RE *GONNA DO* IT, RIGHT? *RIGHT?*
WHAT ARE WE 'GONNA DO' EXACTLY?!
AH, THIS AND THAT. ♡
MUTSUMI, OF... OF COURSE NOT!!
NO WAY.
UGH, NOT WITH HIM.
OH DEAR..
BUT YOU DO LIKE KEI-KUN, DON'T YOU? ♡
I... I...
IT'S NOT THAT I DON'T LIKE HIM OR ANYTHING. IT'S JUST... JUST THAT I DON'T KNOW.
WELL THEN, WHY NOT JUST DO IT. IT'S A NORMAL STEP UP, DON'T YOU THINK?
YOU KNOW... FIRST THAT... AND THEN *THAT THING.* ♡
!?
W-W-WHAT ARE YOU GETTING AT?! THIS AND THAT?! *I'M NOT EASY!!*
SORRY, MY BAD. I THOUGHT YOU CAME ALL THIS WAY WITH KEITARO SO YOU TWO COULD...
...GO FISHING OR SWIMMING, OR MAYBE EVEN SCUBA DIVING, RIGHT? ♡
SHE HAS TO BE DOING THIS ON PURPOSE. IT'S TOO PAINFUL TO THINK SHE COULD NATURALLY BE THAT DENSE.
NO MATTER WHAT, THOUGH, I SUPPORT *YOU BOTH* ONE HUNDRED PERCENT!
GEE...
THANKS.
GOOD LUCK, NOW. ♡

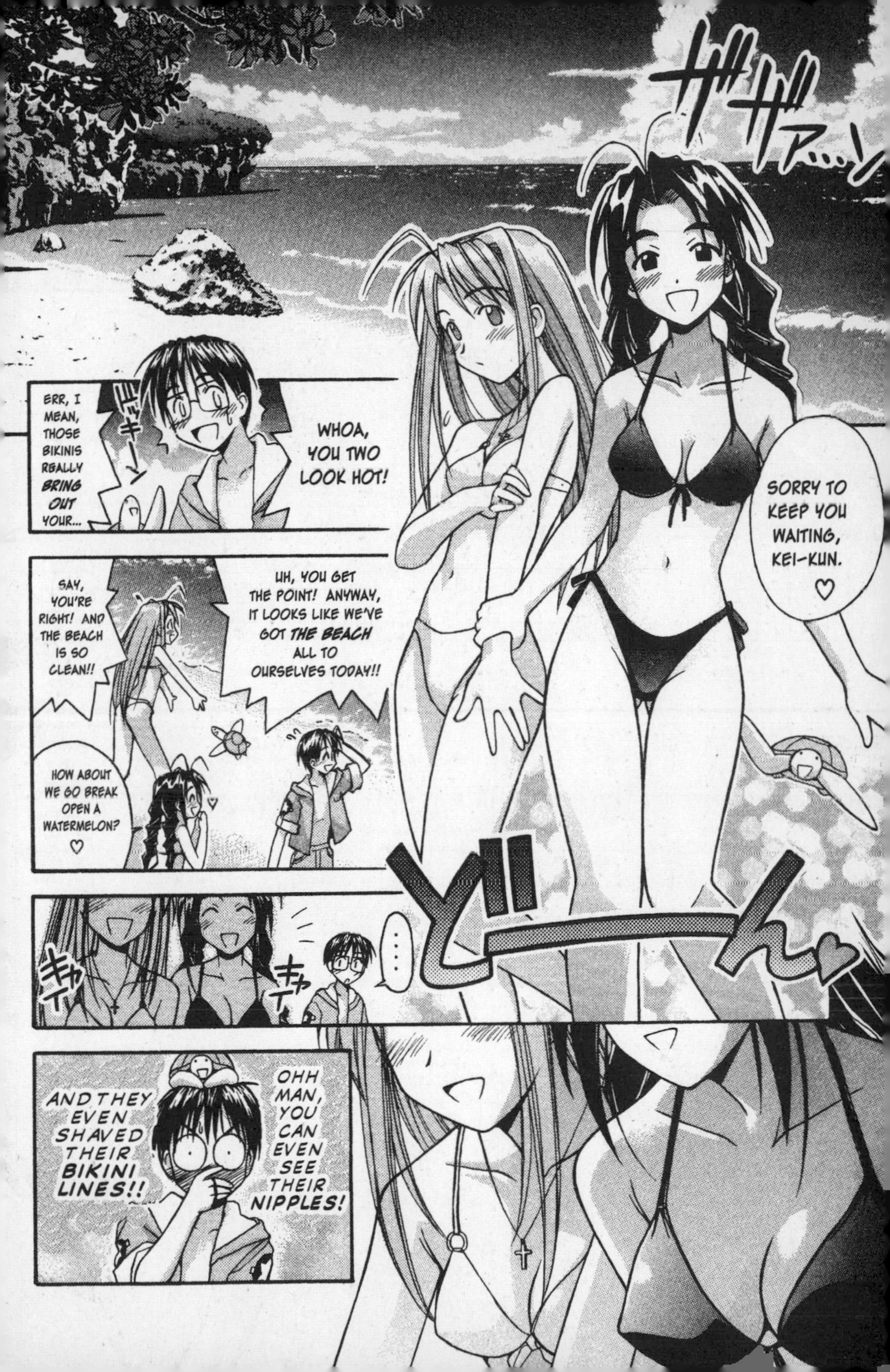

ザザァ…ッ
SORRY TO KEEP YOU WAITING, KEI-KUN. ♡
WHOA, YOU TWO LOOK HOT!
ドッキーン
ERR, I MEAN, THOSE BIKINIS REALLY BRING OUT YOUR...
UH, YOU GET THE POINT! ANYWAY, IT LOOKS LIKE WE'VE GOT THE BEACH ALL TO OURSELVES TODAY!!
SAY, YOU'RE RIGHT! AND THE BEACH IS SO CLEAN!!
HOW ABOUT WE GO BREAK OPEN A WATERMELON? ♡
どーん♡
....
キャ
キャ
OHH MAN, YOU CAN EVEN SEE THEIR NIPPLES!
AND THEY EVEN SHAVED THEIR BIKINI LINES!!

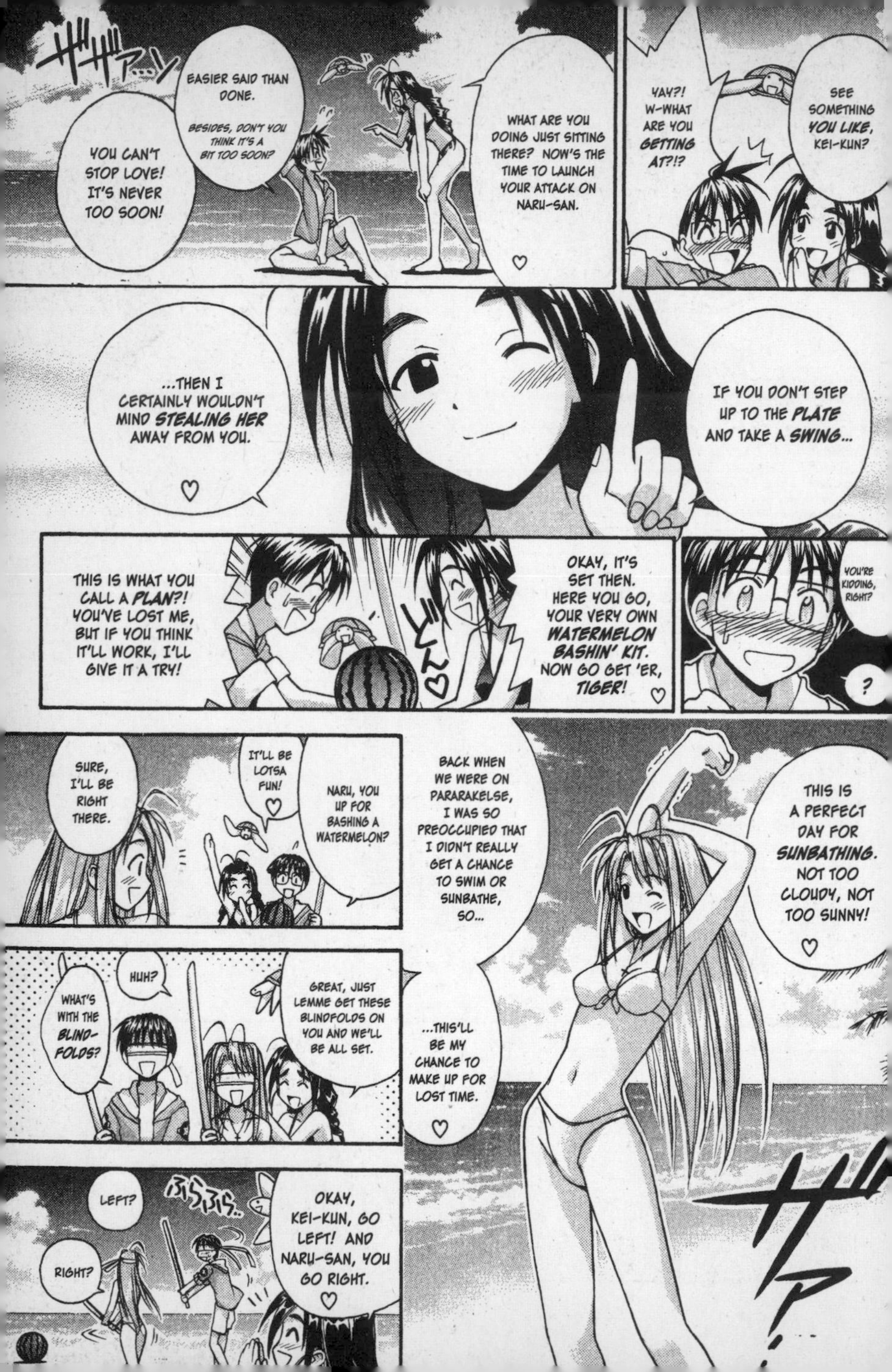
SEE SOMETHING YOU LIKE, KEI-KUN?
YAY?! W-WHAT ARE YOU GETTING AT?!?
WHAT ARE YOU DOING JUST SITTING THERE? NOW'S THE TIME TO LAUNCH YOUR ATTACK ON NARU-SAN. ♡
EASIER SAID THAN DONE.
BESIDES, DON'T YOU THINK IT'S A BIT TOO SOON?
YOU CAN'T STOP LOVE! IT'S NEVER TOO SOON!
IF YOU DON'T STEP UP TO THE PLATE AND TAKE A SWING...
...THEN I CERTAINLY WOULDN'T MIND STEALING HER AWAY FROM YOU. ♡
YOU'RE KIDDING, RIGHT?
?
OKAY, IT'S SET THEN. HERE YOU GO, YOUR VERY OWN WATERMELON BASHIN' KIT. NOW GO GET 'ER, TIGER! ♡
THIS IS WHAT YOU CALL A PLAN?! YOU'VE LOST ME, BUT IF YOU THINK IT'LL WORK, I'LL GIVE IT A TRY!
THIS IS A PERFECT DAY FOR SUNBATHING. NOT TOO CLOUDY, NOT TOO SUNNY! ♡
BACK WHEN WE WERE ON PARARAKELSE, I WAS SO PREOCCUPIED THAT I DIDN'T REALLY GET A CHANCE TO SWIM OR SUNBATHE, SO...
...THIS'LL BE MY CHANCE TO MAKE UP FOR LOST TIME. ♡
NARU, YOU UP FOR BASHING A WATERMELON?
IT'LL BE LOTSA FUN! ♡
SURE, I'LL BE RIGHT THERE.
GREAT, JUST LEMME GET THESE BLINDFOLDS ON YOU AND WE'LL BE ALL SET.
HUH?
WHAT'S WITH THE BLIND-FOLDS?
OKAY, KEI-KUN, GO LEFT! AND NARU-SAN, YOU GO RIGHT. ♡
ふらふら..
LEFT?
RIGHT?

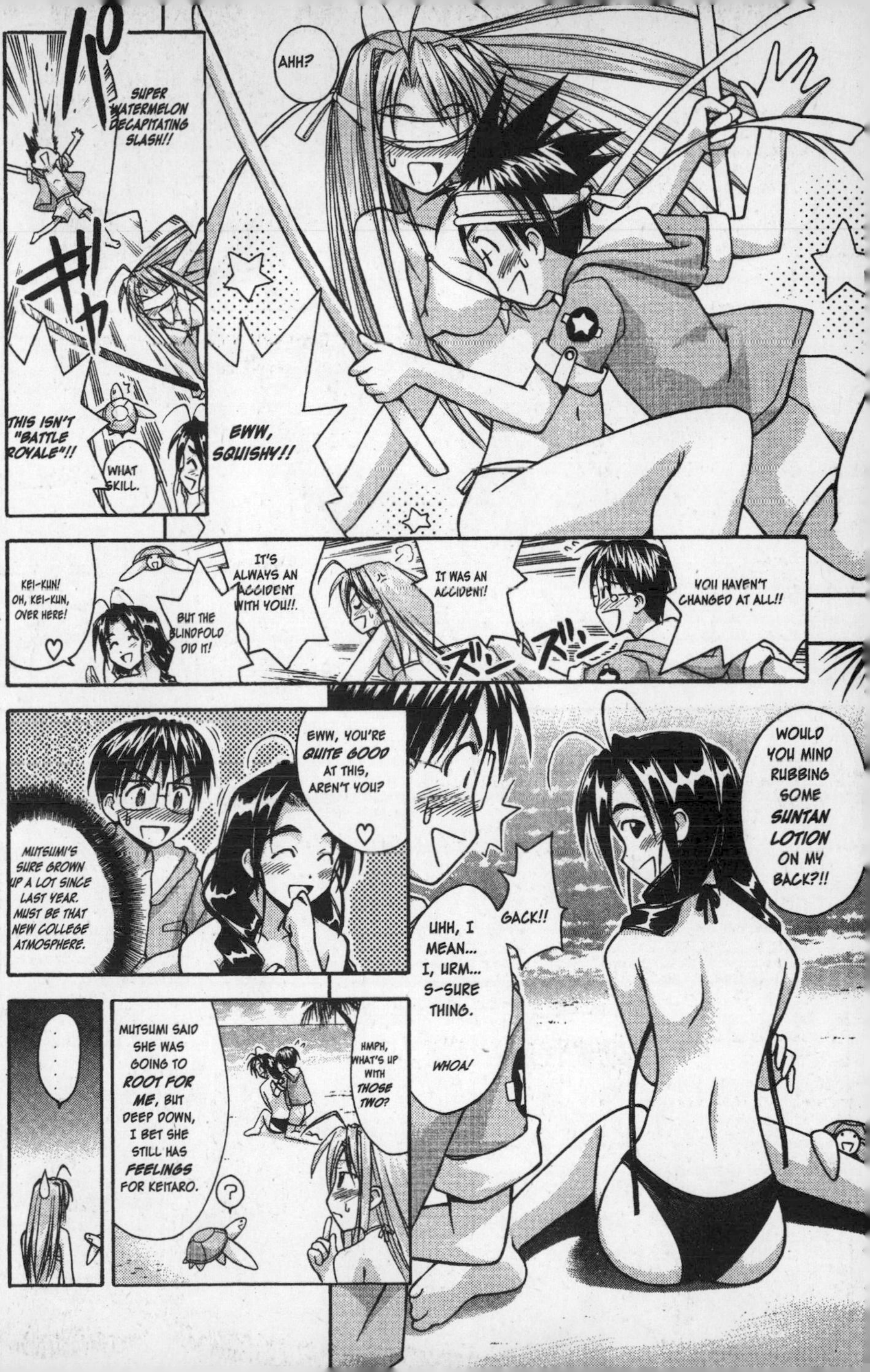
AHH?
EWW, SQUISHY!!
SUPER WATERMELON DECAPITATING SLASH!!
THIS ISN'T "BATTLE ROYALE"!!
WHAT SKILL.
YOU HAVEN'T CHANGED AT ALL!!
IT WAS AN ACCIDENT!
IT'S ALWAYS AN ACCIDENT WITH YOU!!
BUT THE BLINDFOLD DID IT!
KEI-KUN! OH, KEI-KUN, OVER HERE!
WOULD YOU MIND RUBBING SOME SUNTAN LOTION ON MY BACK?!!
GACK!!
UHH, I MEAN... I, URM... S-SURE THING.
WHOA!
EWW, YOU'RE QUITE GOOD AT THIS, AREN'T YOU?
MITSUMI'S SURE GROWN UP A LOT SINCE LAST YEAR. MUST BE THAT NEW COLLEGE ATMOSPHERE.
HMPH, WHAT'S UP WITH THOSE TWO?
MUTSUMI SAID SHE WAS GOING TO ROOT FOR ME, BUT DEEP DOWN, I BET SHE STILL HAS FEELINGS FOR KEITARO.
?
. . . . .

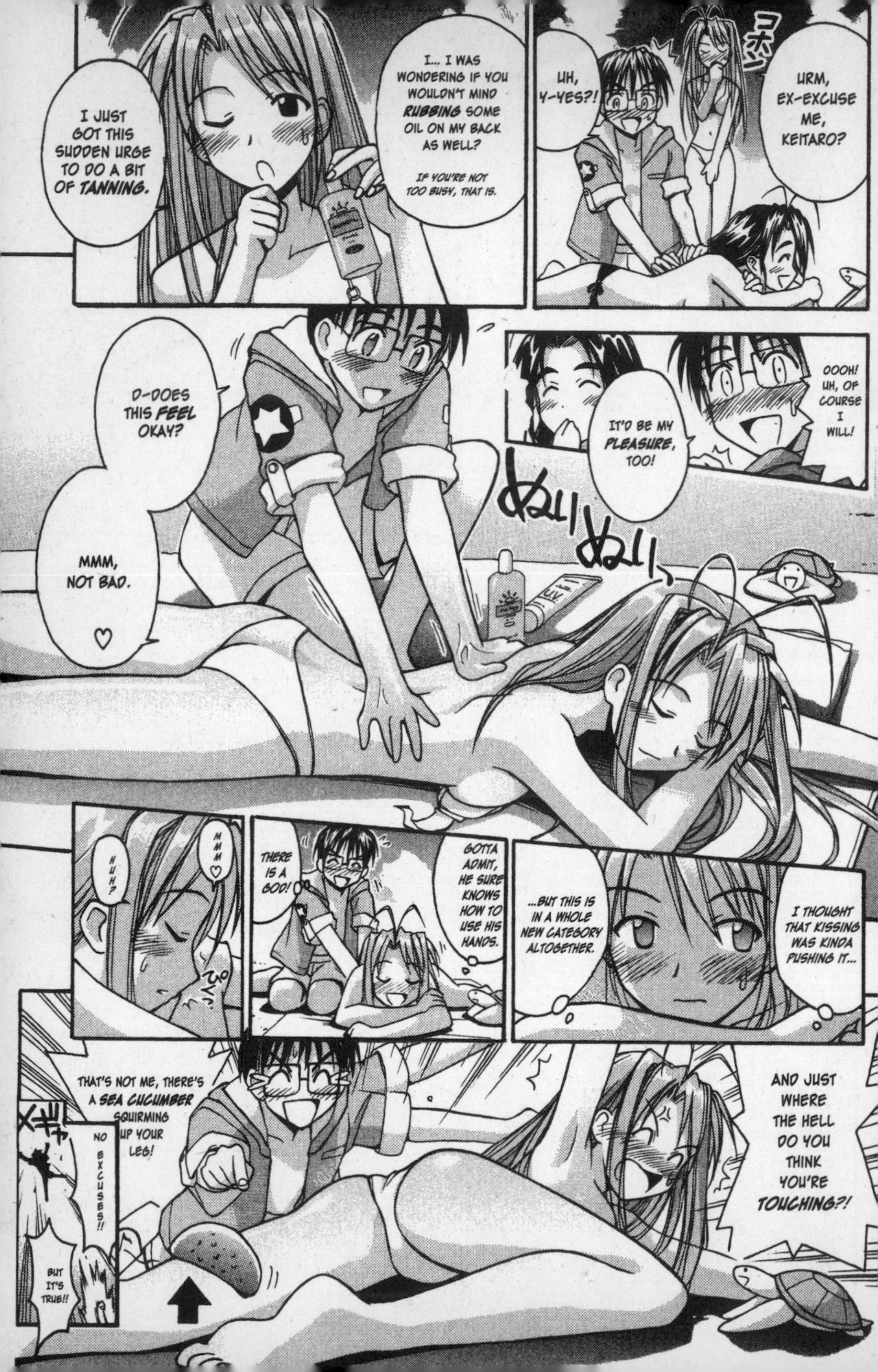
URM, EX-EXCUSE ME, KEITARO?
UH, Y-YES?!
I... I WAS WONDERING IF YOU WOULDN'T MIND RUBBING SOME OIL ON MY BACK AS WELL?
IF YOU'RE NOT TOO BUSY, THAT IS.
I JUST GOT THIS SUDDEN URGE TO DO A BIT OF TANNING.
OOOH! UH, OF COURSE I WILL!
IT'D BE MY PLEASURE, TOO!
D-DOES THIS FEEL OKAY?
MMM, NOT BAD. ♡
I THOUGHT THAT KISSING WAS KINDA PUSHING IT...
...BUT THIS IS IN A WHOLE NEW CATEGORY ALTOGETHER.
GOTTA ADMIT, HE SURE KNOWS HOW TO USE HIS HANDS.
THERE IS A GOD!
MMM ♡
HUH?
AND JUST WHERE THE HELL DO YOU THINK YOU'RE TOUCHING?!
THAT'S NOT ME, THERE'S A SEA CUCUMBER SQUIRMING UP YOUR LEG!
NO EXCUSES!!
BUT IT'S TRUE!!

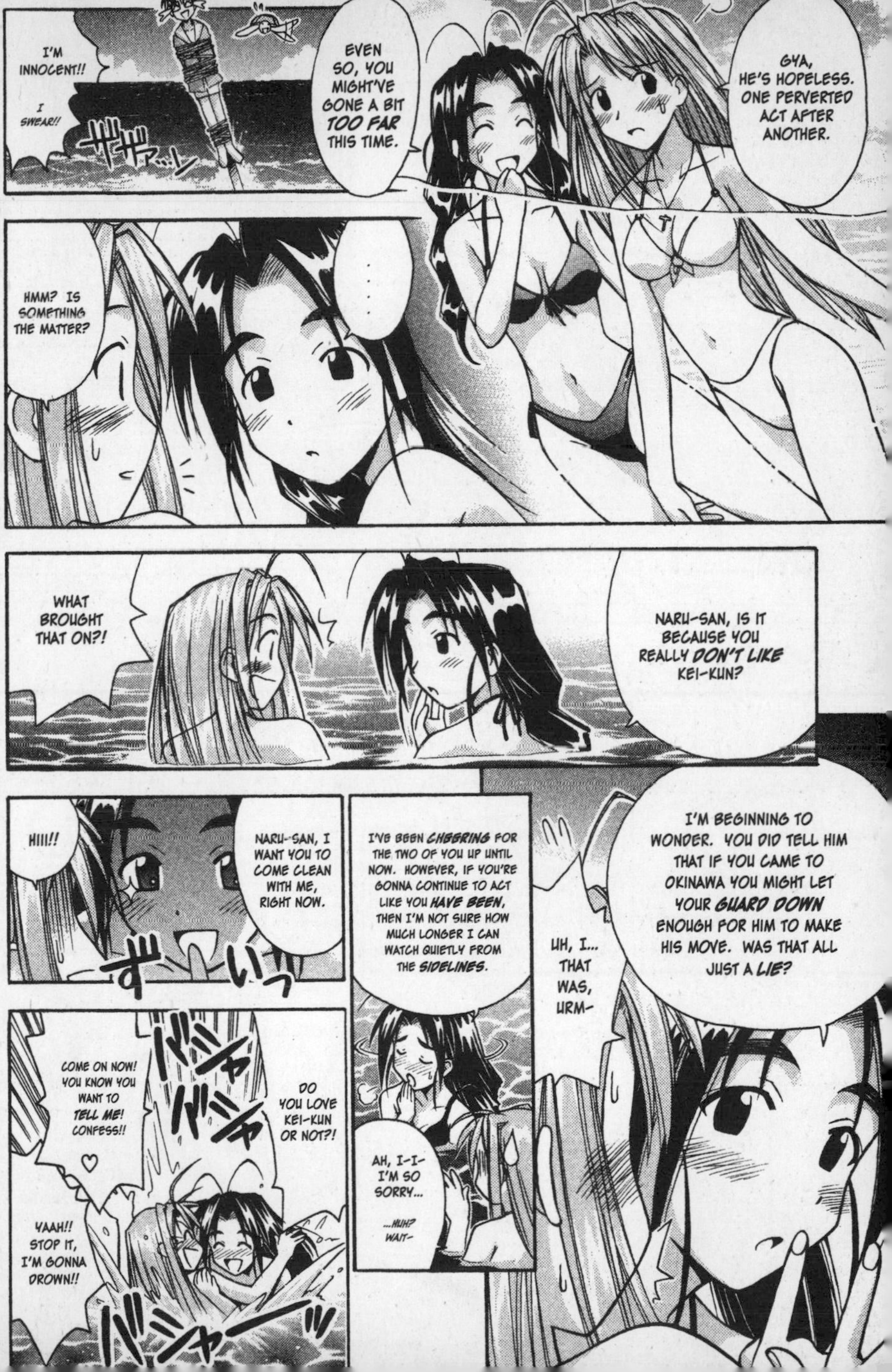
GYA, HE'S HOPELESS. ONE PERVERTED ACT AFTER ANOTHER.
EVEN SO, YOU MIGHT'VE GONE A BIT TOO FAR THIS TIME.
I'M INNOCENT!!
I SWEAR!!
...
HMM? IS SOMETHING THE MATTER?
NARU-SAN, IS IT BECAUSE YOU REALLY DON'T LIKE KEI-KUN?
WHAT BROUGHT THAT ON?!
I'M BEGINNING TO WONDER. YOU DID TELL HIM THAT IF YOU CAME TO OKINAWA YOU MIGHT LET YOUR GUARD DOWN ENOUGH FOR HIM TO MAKE HIS MOVE. WAS THAT ALL JUST A LIE?
UH, I... THAT WAS, URM-
I'VE BEEN CHEERING FOR THE TWO OF YOU UP UNTIL NOW. HOWEVER, IF YOU'RE GONNA CONTINUE TO ACT LIKE YOU HAVE BEEN, THEN I'M NOT SURE HOW MUCH LONGER I CAN WATCH QUIETLY FROM THE SIDELINES.
AH, I-I- I'M SO SORRY...
...HUH? WAIT-
NARU-SAN, I WANT YOU TO COME CLEAN WITH ME, RIGHT NOW.
HIII!!
ずいっ
DO YOU LOVE KEI-KUN OR NOT?!
COME ON NOW! YOU KNOW YOU WANT TO TELL ME! CONFESS!!
YAAH!! STOP IT, I'M GONNA DROWN!!

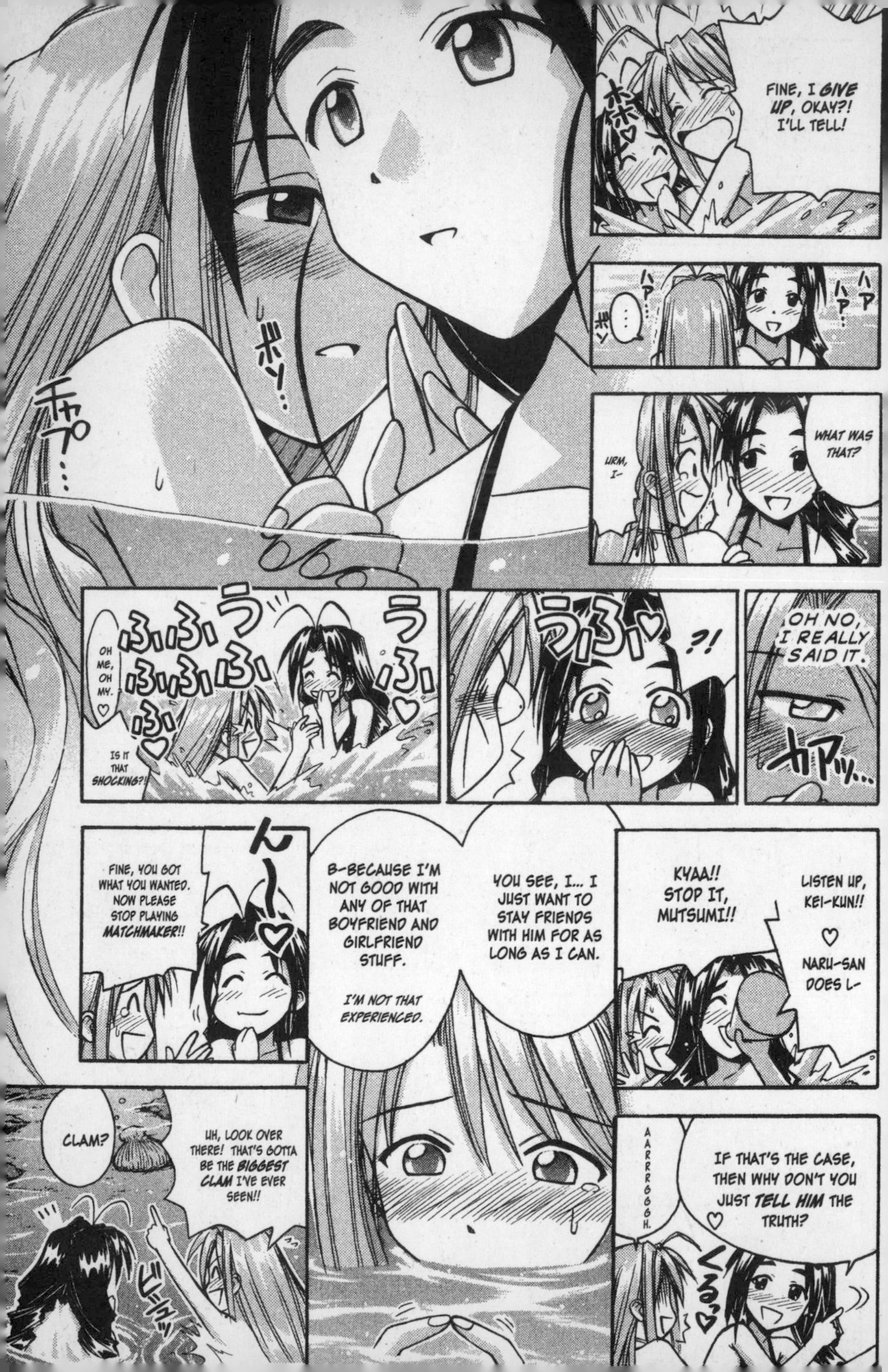
FINE, I GIVE UP, OKAY?! I'LL TELL!
ハァ ハァ…
…
ボソ
ハァ ハァ…
WHAT WAS THAT?
URM, I-
ボソ…
チャプ…
OH NO, I REALLY SAID IT.
カァッ…
うふふ♡
?!
うふふ ふふふ ふ♡
OH ME, OH MY. ♡
IS IT THAT SHOCKING?!
LISTEN UP, KEI-KUN!! ♡ NARU-SAN DOES L-
KYAA!! STOP IT, MUTSUMI!!
YOU SEE, I... I JUST WANT TO STAY FRIENDS WITH HIM FOR AS LONG AS I CAN.
B-BECAUSE I'M NOT GOOD WITH ANY OF THAT BOYFRIEND AND GIRLFRIEND STUFF.
I'M NOT THAT EXPERIENCED.
ん～♡
FINE, YOU GOT WHAT YOU WANTED. NOW PLEASE STOP PLAYING MATCHMAKER!!
IF THAT'S THE CASE, THEN WHY DON'T YOU JUST TELL HIM THE TRUTH? ♡
くるっ
AARRRGGGH.
UH, LOOK OVER THERE! THAT'S GOTTA BE THE BIGGEST CLAM I'VE EVER SEEN!!
CLAM?
ビシッ

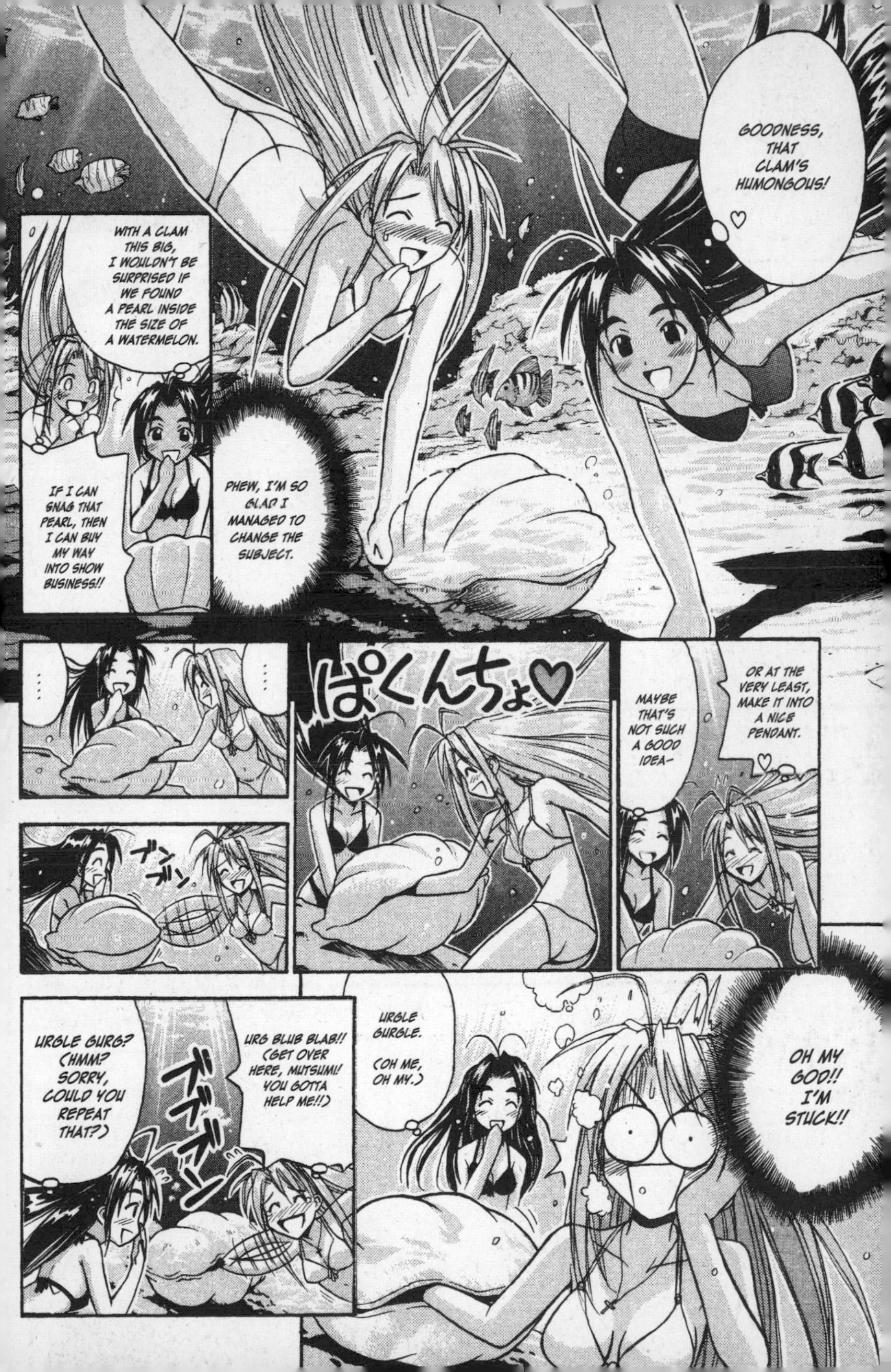

GOODNESS, THAT CLAM'S HUMONGOUS!
WITH A CLAM THIS BIG, I WOULDN'T BE SURPRISED IF WE FOUND A PEARL INSIDE THE SIZE OF A WATERMELON.
IF I CAN SNAG THAT PEARL, THEN I CAN BUY MY WAY INTO SHOW BUSINESS!!
PHEW, I'M SO GLAD I MANAGED TO CHANGE THE SUBJECT.
OR AT THE VERY LEAST, MAKE IT INTO A NICE PENDANT.
MAYBE THAT'S NOT SUCH A GOOD IDEA–
ぱくんちょ♥
....
....
ブンブン
OH MY GOD!! I'M STUCK!!
URGLE GURGLE. (OH ME, OH MY.)
URG BLUB BLAB!! (GET OVER HERE, MUTSUMI! YOU GOTTA HELP ME!!)
URGLE GURG? (HMM? SORRY, COULD YOU REPEAT THAT?)

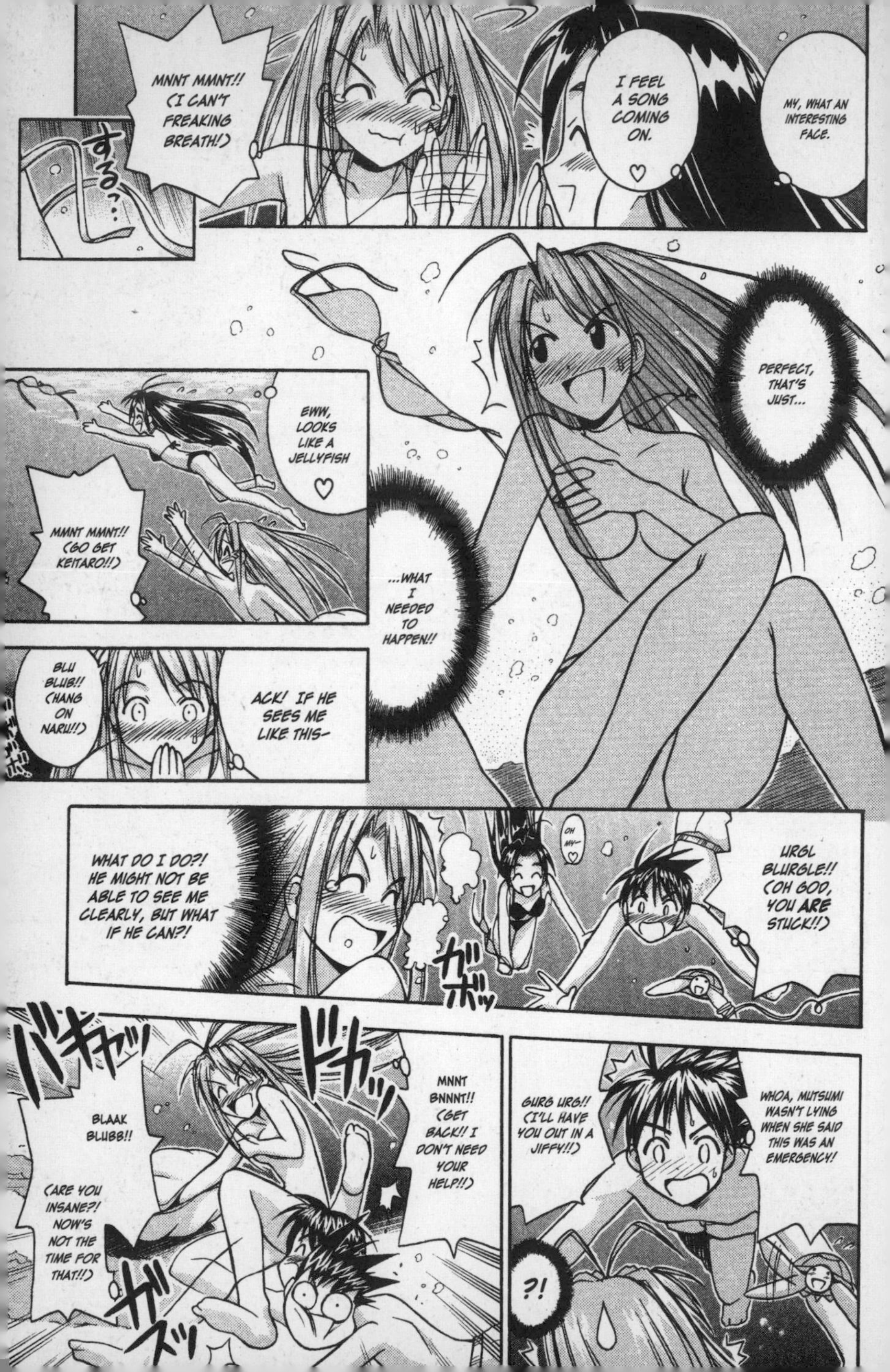
MY, WHAT AN INTERESTING FACE.
I FEEL A SONG COMING ON. ♥
MNNT MMNT!! (I CAN'T FREAKING BREATH!)
するっ…
PERFECT, THAT'S JUST...
...WHAT I NEEDED TO HAPPEN!!
EWW, LOOKS LIKE A JELLYFISH ♥
MMNT MMNT!! (GO GET KEITARO!!)
ACK! IF HE SEES ME LIKE THIS-
BLU BLUB!! (HANG ON NARU!!)
URGL BLURGLE!! (OH GOD, YOU ARE STUCK!!)
OH MY— ♡
WHAT DO I DO?! HE MIGHT NOT BE ABLE TO SEE ME CLEARLY, BUT WHAT IF HE CAN?!
ガボッ
WHOA, MUTSUMI WASN'T LYING WHEN SHE SAID THIS WAS AN EMERGENCY!
GURG URG!! (I'LL HAVE YOU OUT IN A JIFFY!!)
?!
ドカッ
MNNT BNNNT!! (GET BACK!! I DON'T NEED YOUR HELP!!)
バキャッ
BLAAK BLUBB!!
(ARE YOU INSANE?! NOW'S NOT THE TIME FOR THAT!!)
ガズッ

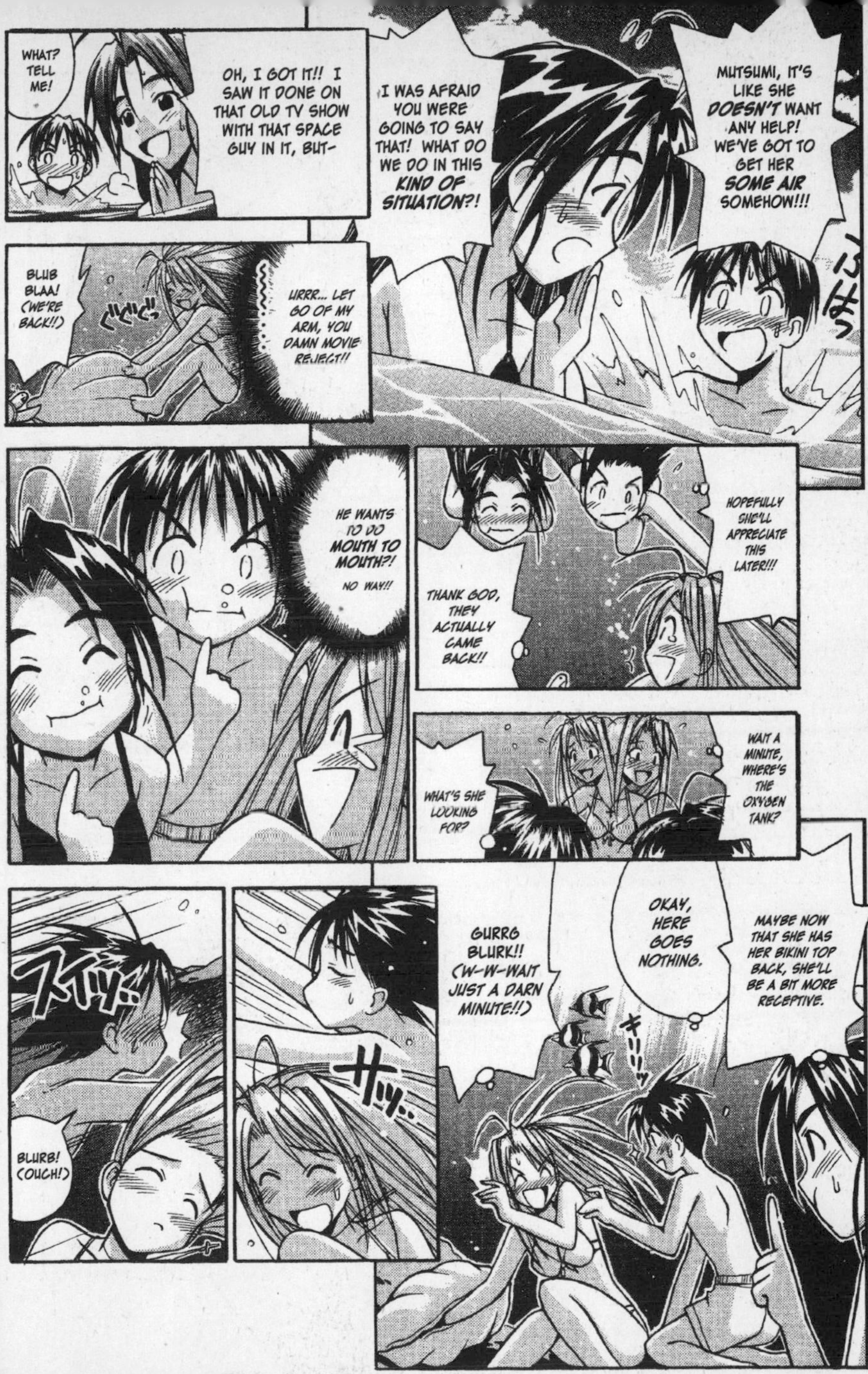
MUTSUMI, IT'S LIKE SHE **DOESN'T** WANT ANY HELP! WE'VE GOT TO GET HER **SOME AIR** SOMEHOW!!!
I WAS AFRAID YOU WERE GOING TO SAY THAT! WHAT DO WE DO IN THIS **KIND OF SITUATION?!**
ふはっ
OH, I GOT IT!! I SAW IT DONE ON THAT OLD TV SHOW WITH THAT SPACE GUY IN IT, BUT-
WHAT? TELL ME!
URRR... LET GO OF MY ARM, YOU DAMN MOVIE REJECT!!
ぐぐぐっ
BLUB BLAA! (WE'RE BACK!!)
HOPEFULLY SHE'LL APPRECIATE THIS LATER!!!
THANK GOD, THEY ACTUALLY CAME BACK!!
WAIT A MINUTE, WHERE'S THE OXYGEN TANK?
WHAT'S SHE LOOKING FOR?
HE WANTS TO DO **MOUTH TO MOUTH?!**
NO WAY!!
MAYBE NOW THAT SHE HAS HER BIKINI TOP BACK, SHE'LL BE A BIT MORE RECEPTIVE.
OKAY, HERE GOES NOTHING.
GURRG BLURK!! (W-W-WAIT JUST A DARN MINUTE!!)
キーッ
ハッ..
スイーッ
BLURB! (OUCH!)

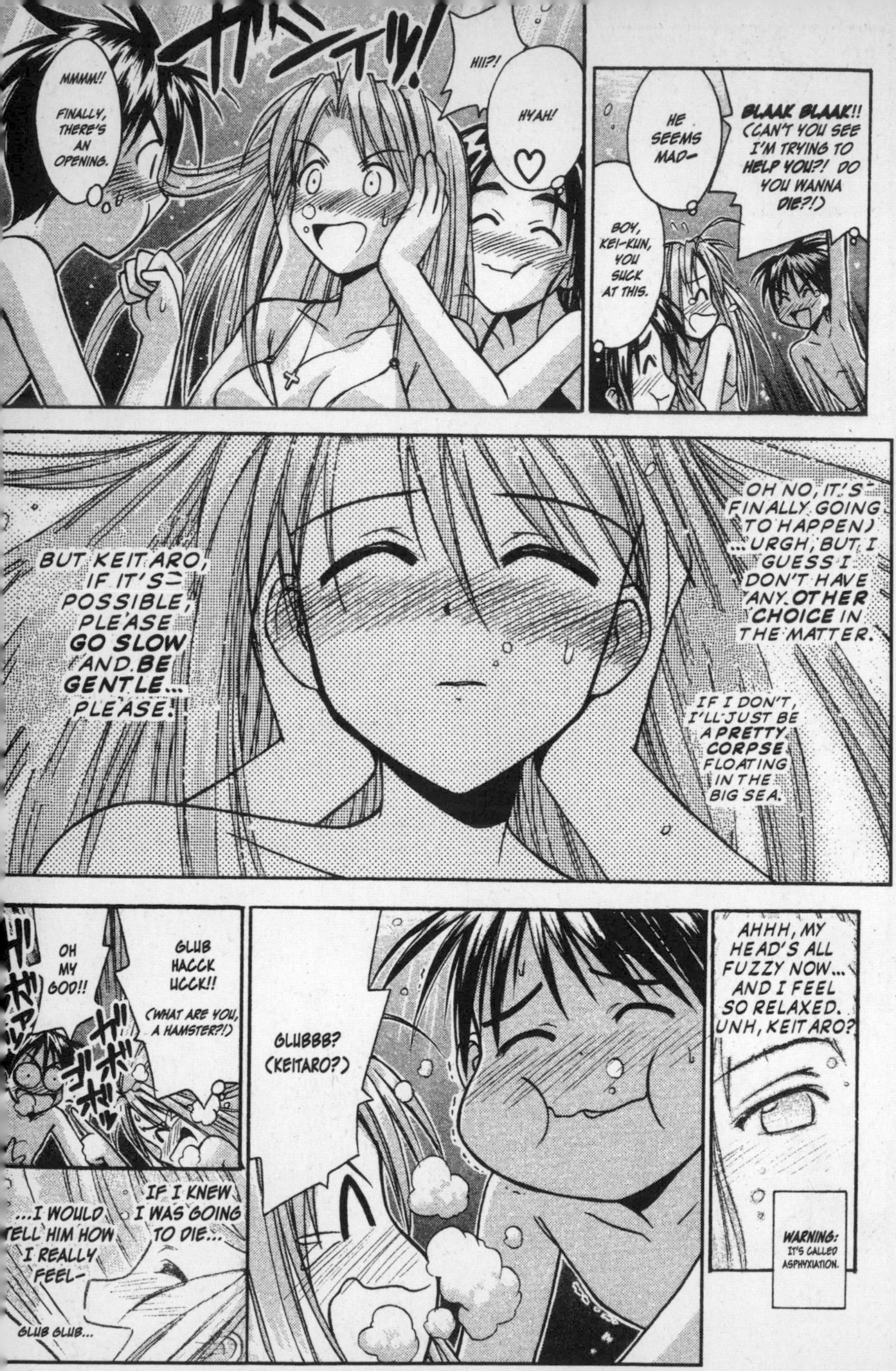
BLAAK BLAAK!! (CAN'T YOU SEE I'M TRYING TO HELP YOU?! DO YOU WANNA DIE?!)
HE SEEMS MAD-
BOY, KEI-KUN, YOU SUCK AT THIS.
HII?!
HYAH!
♥
MMMM!! FINALLY, THERE'S AN OPENING.
OH NO, IT'S FINALLY GOING TO HAPPEN) ...URGH, BUT I GUESS I DON'T HAVE ANY OTHER CHOICE IN THE MATTER.
IF I DON'T, I'LL JUST BE A PRETTY CORPSE FLOATING IN THE BIG SEA.
BUT KEITARO, IF IT'S POSSIBLE, PLEASE GO SLOW AND BE GENTLE... PLEASE.
AHHH, MY HEAD'S ALL FUZZY NOW... AND I FEEL SO RELAXED. UNH, KEITARO?
WARNING: IT'S CALLED ASPHYXIATION.
GLUBBB? (KEITARO?)
GLUB HACCK UCCK!!
(WHAT ARE YOU, A HAMSTER?!)
OH MY GOD!!
IF I KNEW I WAS GOING TO DIE...
...I WOULD TELL HIM HOW I REALLY FEEL-
GLUB GLUB...

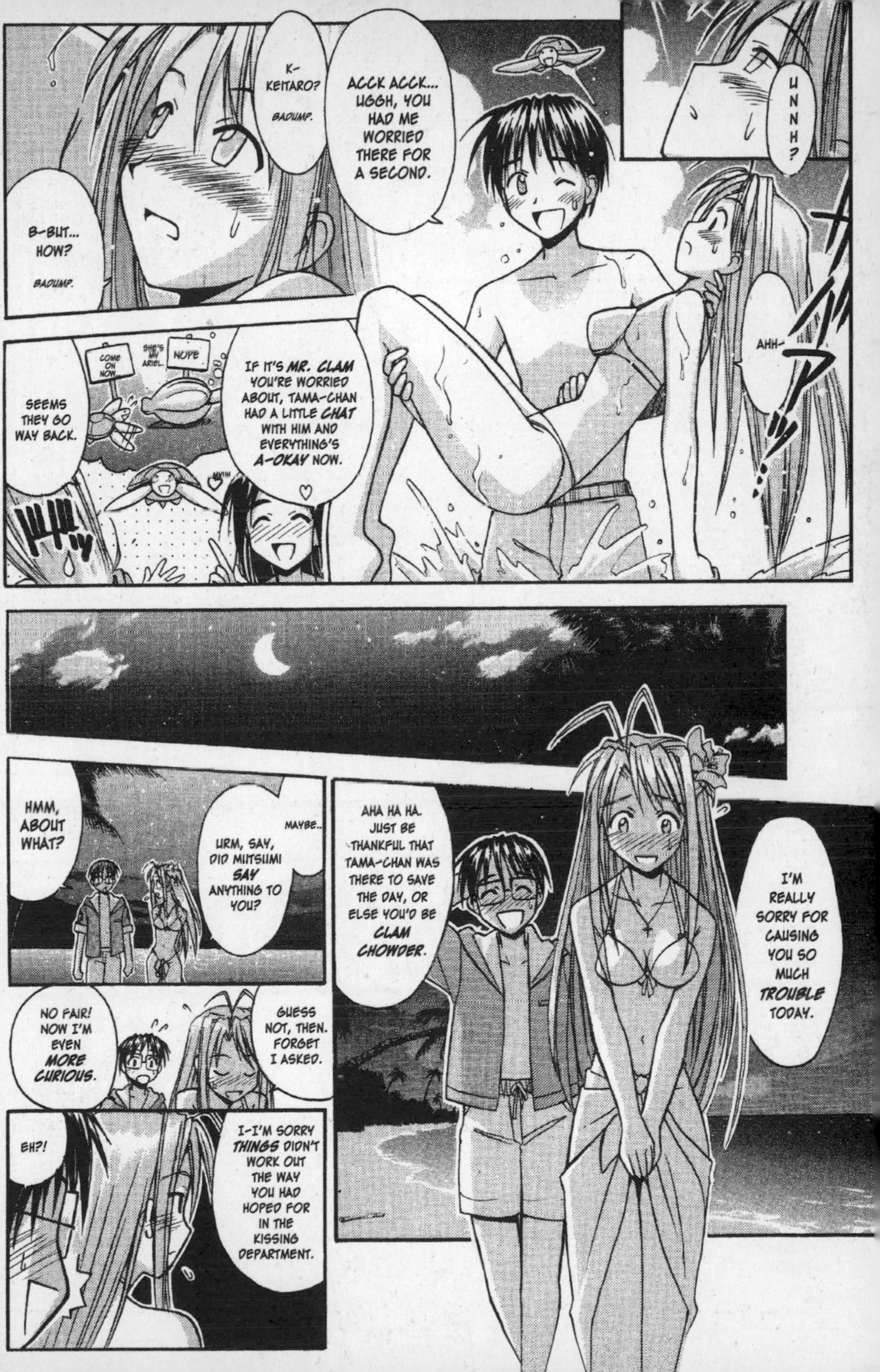
UNNH?
ACCK ACCK... UGGH, YOU HAD ME WORRIED THERE FOR A SECOND.
K-KEITARO?
BADUMP.
B-BUT... HOW?
BADUMP.
AHH-
IF IT'S MR. CLAM YOU'RE WORRIED ABOUT, TAMA-CHAN HAD A LITTLE CHAT WITH HIM AND EVERYTHING'S A-OKAY NOW.
NOPE
SHE'S MY ARIEL.
COME ON NOW...
SEEMS THEY GO WAY BACK.
I'M REALLY SORRY FOR CAUSING YOU SO MUCH TROUBLE TODAY.
AHA HA HA. JUST BE THANKFUL THAT TAMA-CHAN WAS THERE TO SAVE THE DAY, OR ELSE YOU'D BE CLAM CHOWDER.
MAYBE..
URM, SAY, DID MITSUMI SAY ANYTHING TO YOU?
HMM, ABOUT WHAT?
GUESS NOT, THEN. FORGET I ASKED.
NO FAIR! NOW I'M EVEN MORE CURIOUS.
I-I'M SORRY THINGS DIDN'T WORK OUT THE WAY YOU HAD HOPED FOR IN THE KISSING DEPARTMENT.
EH?!

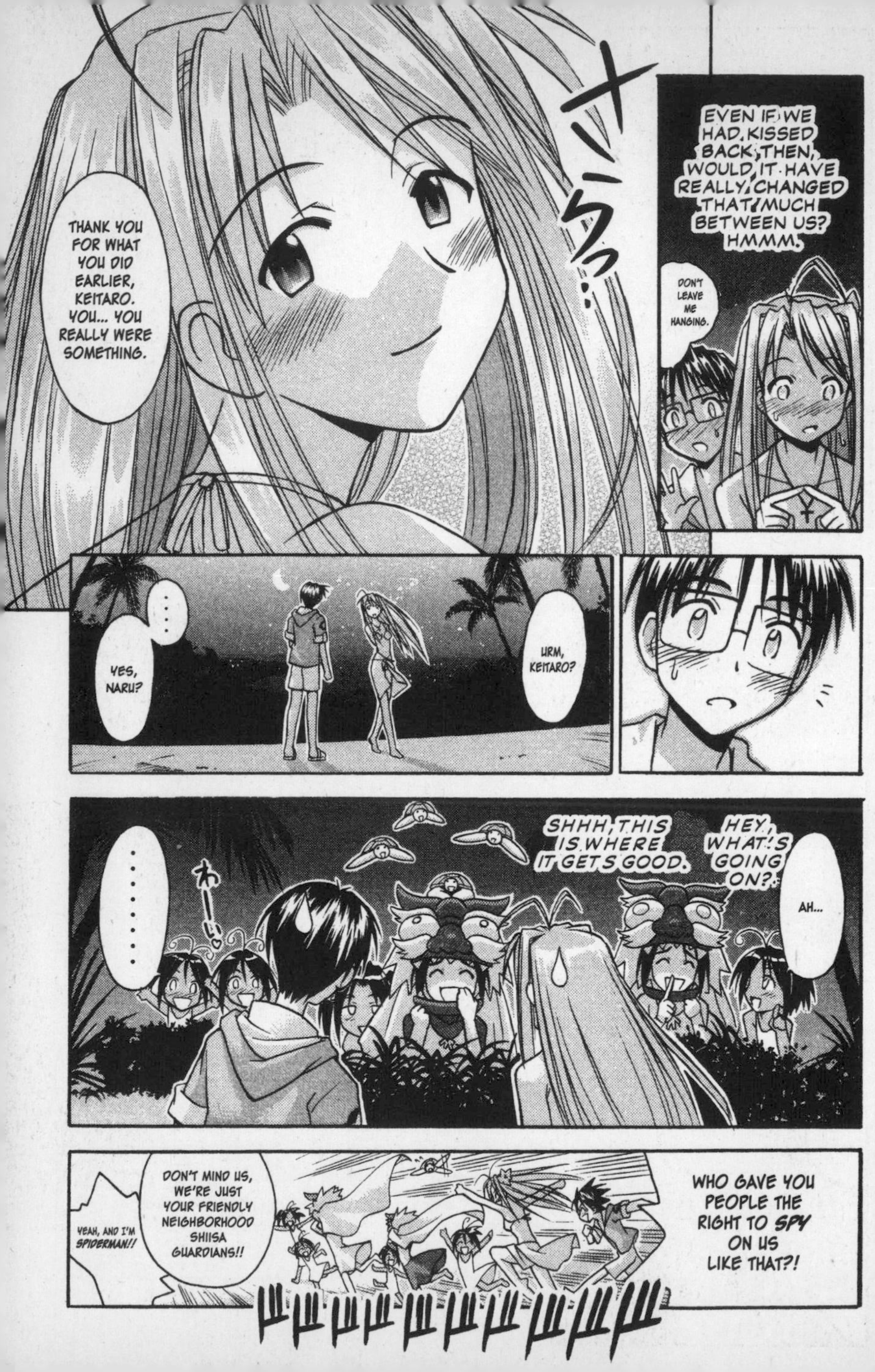
EVEN IF WE HAD KISSED BACK THEN, WOULD IT HAVE REALLY CHANGED THAT MUCH BETWEEN US? HMMM.
DON'T LEAVE ME HANGING.
さらっ
THANK YOU FOR WHAT YOU DID EARLIER, KEITARO. YOU... YOU REALLY WERE SOMETHING.
URM, KEITARO?
...
YES, NARU?
HEY, WHAT'S GOING ON?
SHHH, THIS IS WHERE IT GETS GOOD.
AH...
わーい♡
....
WHO GAVE YOU PEOPLE THE RIGHT TO *SPY* ON US LIKE THAT?!
DON'T MIND US, WE'RE JUST YOUR FRIENDLY NEIGHBORHOOD SHIISA GUARDIANS!!
YEAH, AND I'M *SPIDERMAN*!!

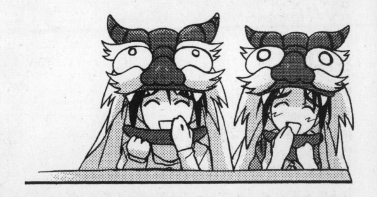

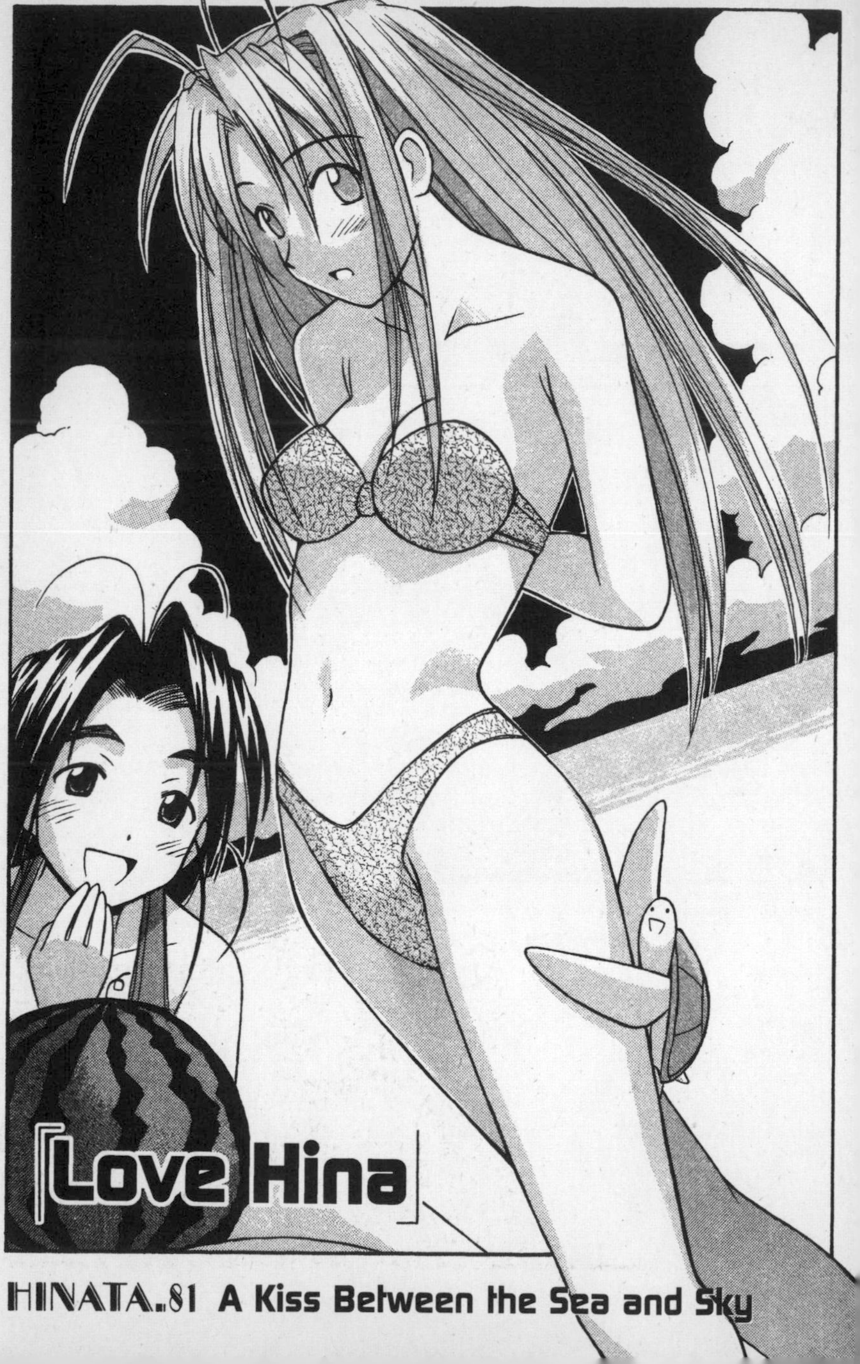
「Love Hina」

HINATA.81 A Kiss Between the Sea and Sky

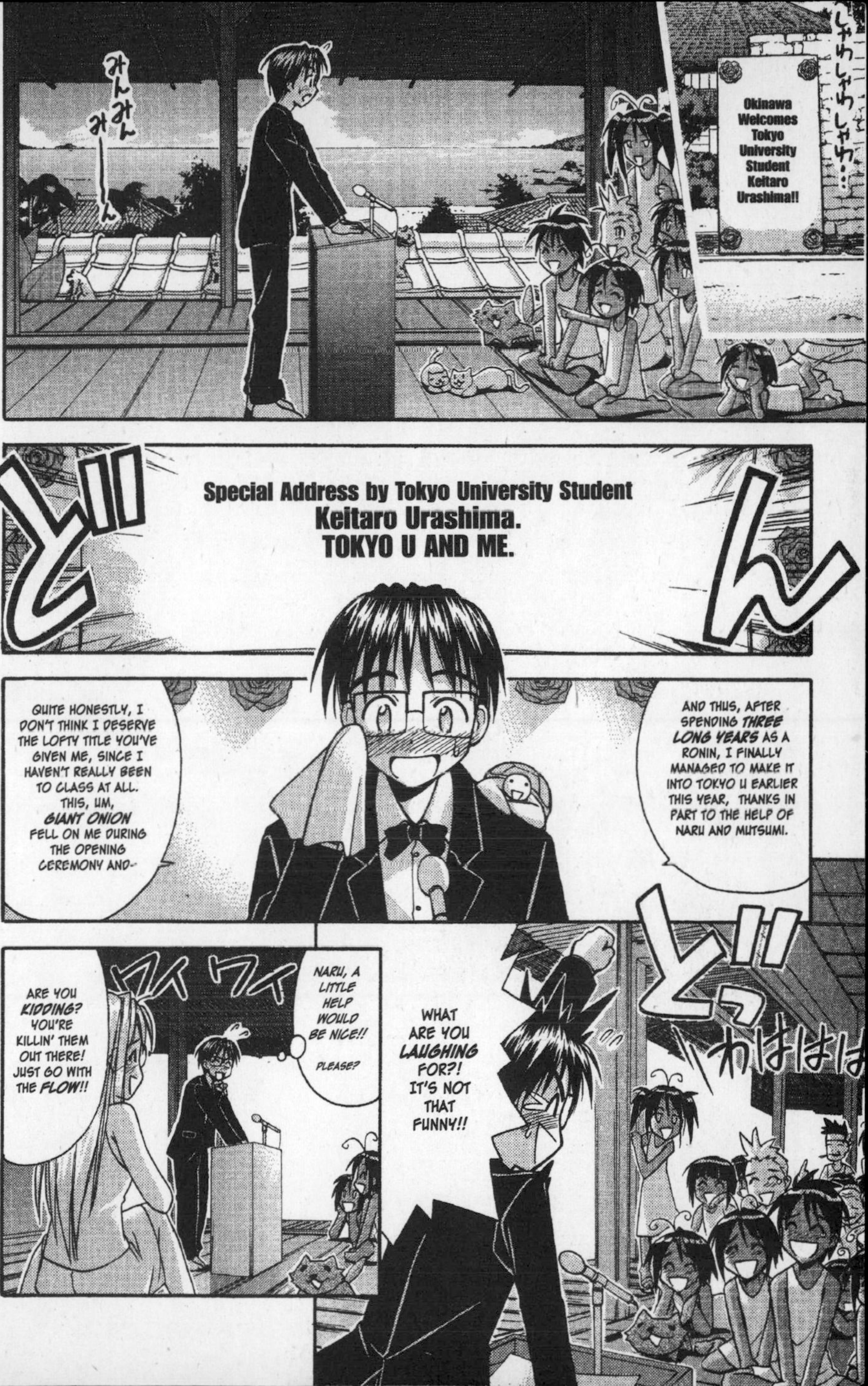
しゃわしゃわしゃわ・・
Okinawa Welcomes Tokyo University Student Keitaro Urashima!!
みんみんみーーん
どどん
Special Address by Tokyo University Student
Keitaro Urashima.
TOKYO U AND ME.
AND THUS, AFTER SPENDING THREE LONG YEARS AS A RONIN, I FINALLY MANAGED TO MAKE IT INTO TOKYO U EARLIER THIS YEAR, THANKS IN PART TO THE HELP OF NARU AND MUTSUMI.
QUITE HONESTLY, I DON'T THINK I DESERVE THE LOFTY TITLE YOU'VE GIVEN ME, SINCE I HAVEN'T REALLY BEEN TO CLASS AT ALL. THIS, UM, GIANT ONION FELL ON ME DURING THE OPENING CEREMONY AND--
どっ
わははは
WHAT ARE YOU LAUGHING FOR?! IT'S NOT THAT FUNNY!!
NARU, A LITTLE HELP WOULD BE NICE!!
PLEASE?
ワイワイ
ARE YOU KIDDING? YOU'RE KILLIN' THEM OUT THERE! JUST GO WITH THE FLOW!!

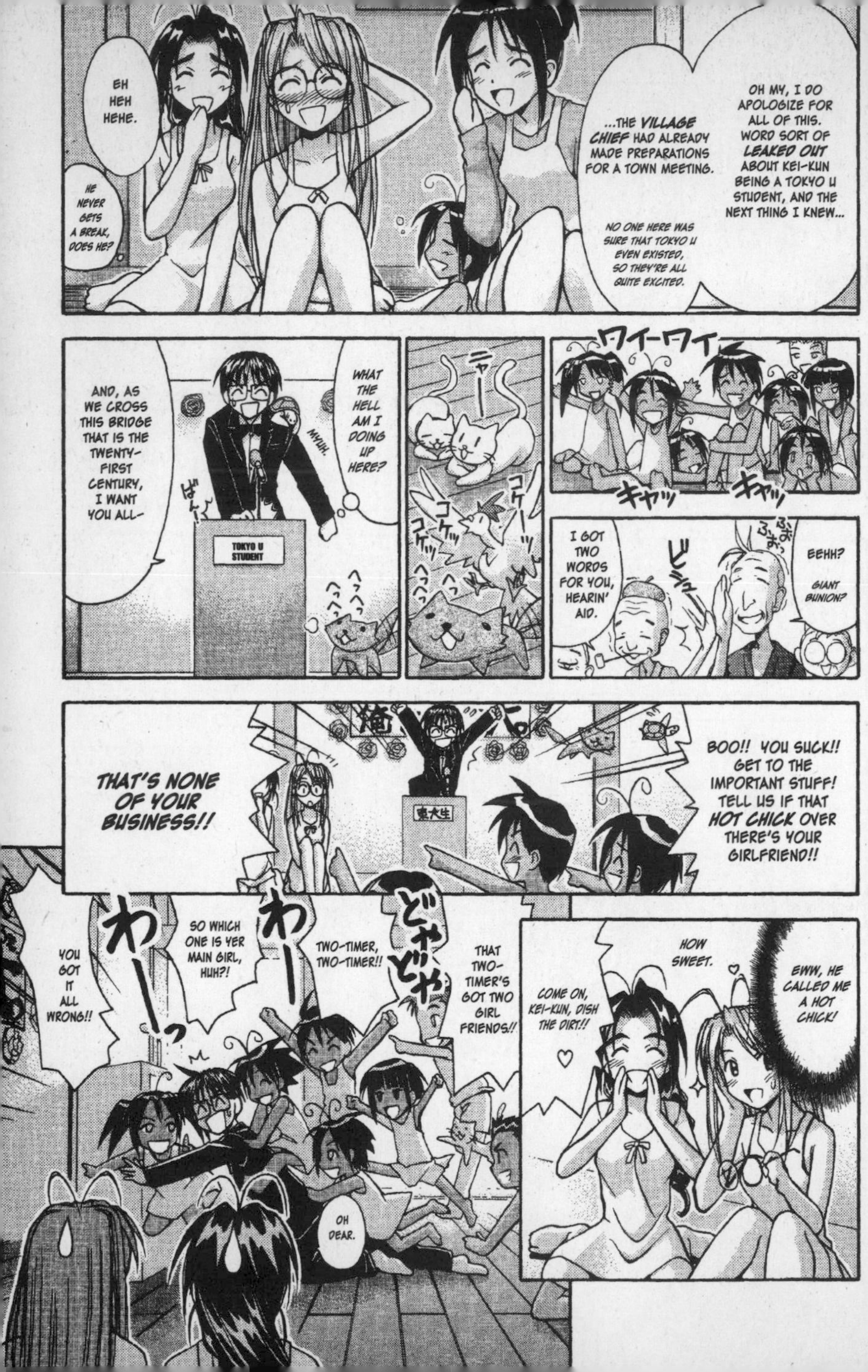

OH MY, I DO APOLOGIZE FOR ALL OF THIS. WORD SORT OF LEAKED OUT ABOUT KEI-KUN BEING A TOKYO U STUDENT, AND THE NEXT THING I KNEW...
...THE VILLAGE CHIEF HAD ALREADY MADE PREPARATIONS FOR A TOWN MEETING.
NO ONE HERE WAS SURE THAT TOKYO U EVEN EXISTED, SO THEY'RE ALL QUITE EXCITED.
EH HEH HEHE.
HE NEVER GETS A BREAK, DOES HE?
ワイーワイ
キャッ
キャッ
ふぉふぉ
EEHH?
GIANT BUNION?
I GOT TWO WORDS FOR YOU, HEARIN' AID.
ニャー
コケーッ
コケッ
コケッ
WHAT THE HELL AM I DOING UP HERE?
MYUH.
AND, AS WE CROSS THIS BRIDGE THAT IS THE TWENTY-FIRST CENTURY, I WANT YOU ALL-
ばん!
TOKYO U STUDENT
BOO!! YOU SUCK!! GET TO THE IMPORTANT STUFF! TELL US IF THAT HOT CHICK OVER THERE'S YOUR GIRLFRIEND!!
俺
東大生
THAT'S NONE OF YOUR BUSINESS!!
EWW, HE CALLED ME A HOT CHICK!
HOW SWEET.
COME ON, KEI-KUN, DISH THE DIRT!!
THAT TWO-TIMER'S GOT TWO GIRL FRIENDS!!
どやどや
TWO-TIMER, TWO-TIMER!!
わー
SO WHICH ONE IS YER MAIN GIRL, HUH?!
わーっ
YOU GOT IT ALL WRONG!!
OH DEAR.

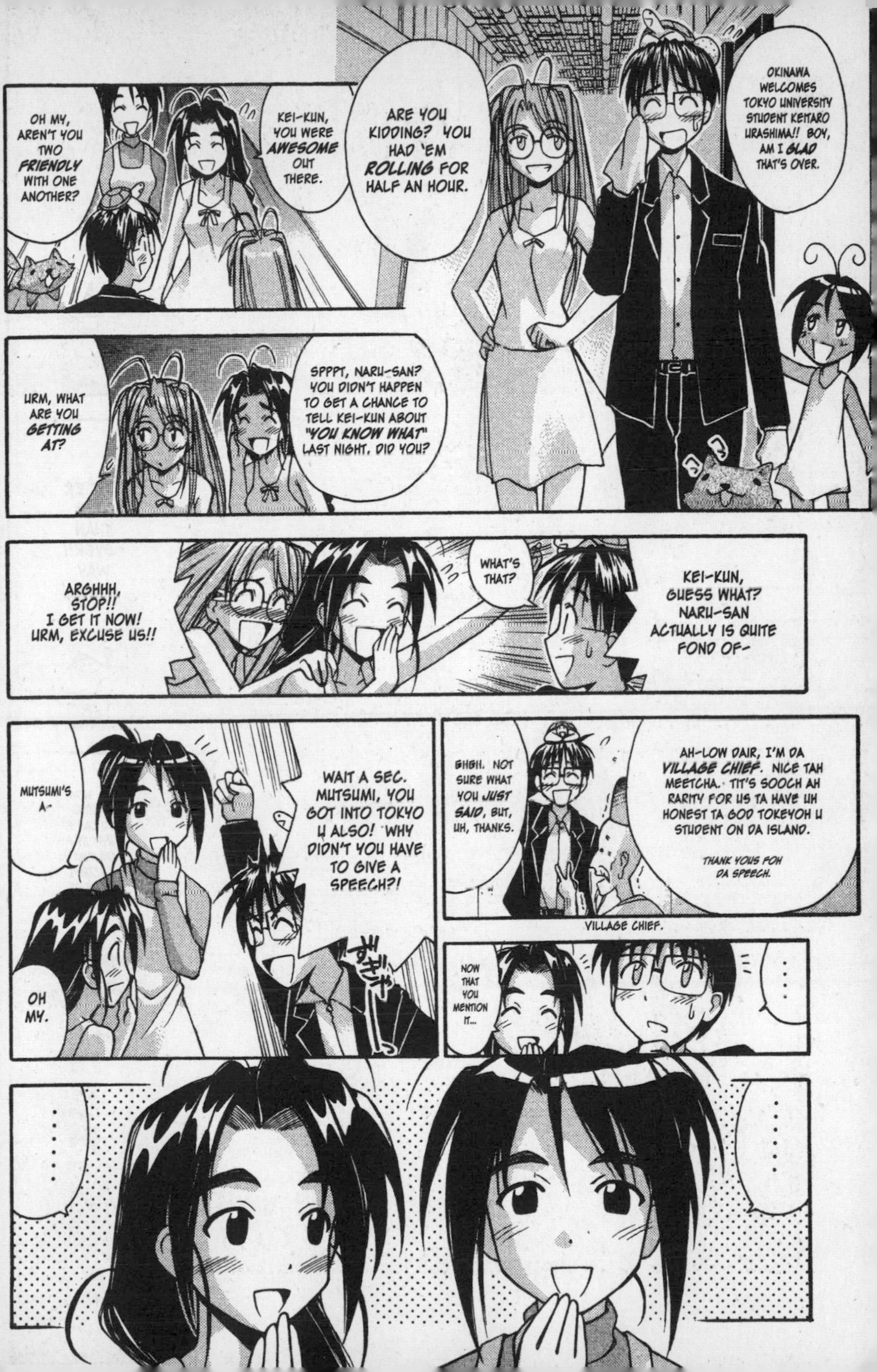
OKINAWA WELCOMES TOKYO UNIVERSITY STUDENT KEITARO URASHIMA!! BOY, AM I GLAD THAT'S OVER.
ARE YOU KIDDING? YOU HAD 'EM ROLLING FOR HALF AN HOUR.
KEI-KUN, YOU WERE AWESOME OUT THERE.
OH MY, AREN'T YOU TWO FRIENDLY WITH ONE ANOTHER?
SPPPT, NARU-SAN? YOU DIDN'T HAPPEN TO GET A CHANCE TO TELL KEI-KUN ABOUT "YOU KNOW WHAT" LAST NIGHT, DID YOU?
URM, WHAT ARE YOU GETTING AT?
KEI-KUN, GUESS WHAT? NARU-SAN ACTUALLY IS QUITE FOND OF-
WHAT'S THAT?
ARGHHH, STOP!! I GET IT NOW! URM, EXCUSE US!!
AH-LOW DAIR, I'M DA VILLAGE CHIEF. NICE TAH MEETCHA. TIT'S SOOCH AH RARITY FOR US TA HAVE UH HONEST TA GOD TOKEYOH U STUDENT ON DA ISLAND.
THANK YOUS FOH DA SPEECH.
EHEH. NOT SURE WHAT YOU JUST SAID, BUT, UH, THANKS.
VILLAGE CHIEF.
....
NOW THAT YOU MENTION IT...
WAIT A SEC. MUTSUMI, YOU GOT INTO TOKYO U ALSO! WHY DIDN'T YOU HAVE TO GIVE A SPEECH?!
MUTSUMI'S A-
OH MY.
....
....

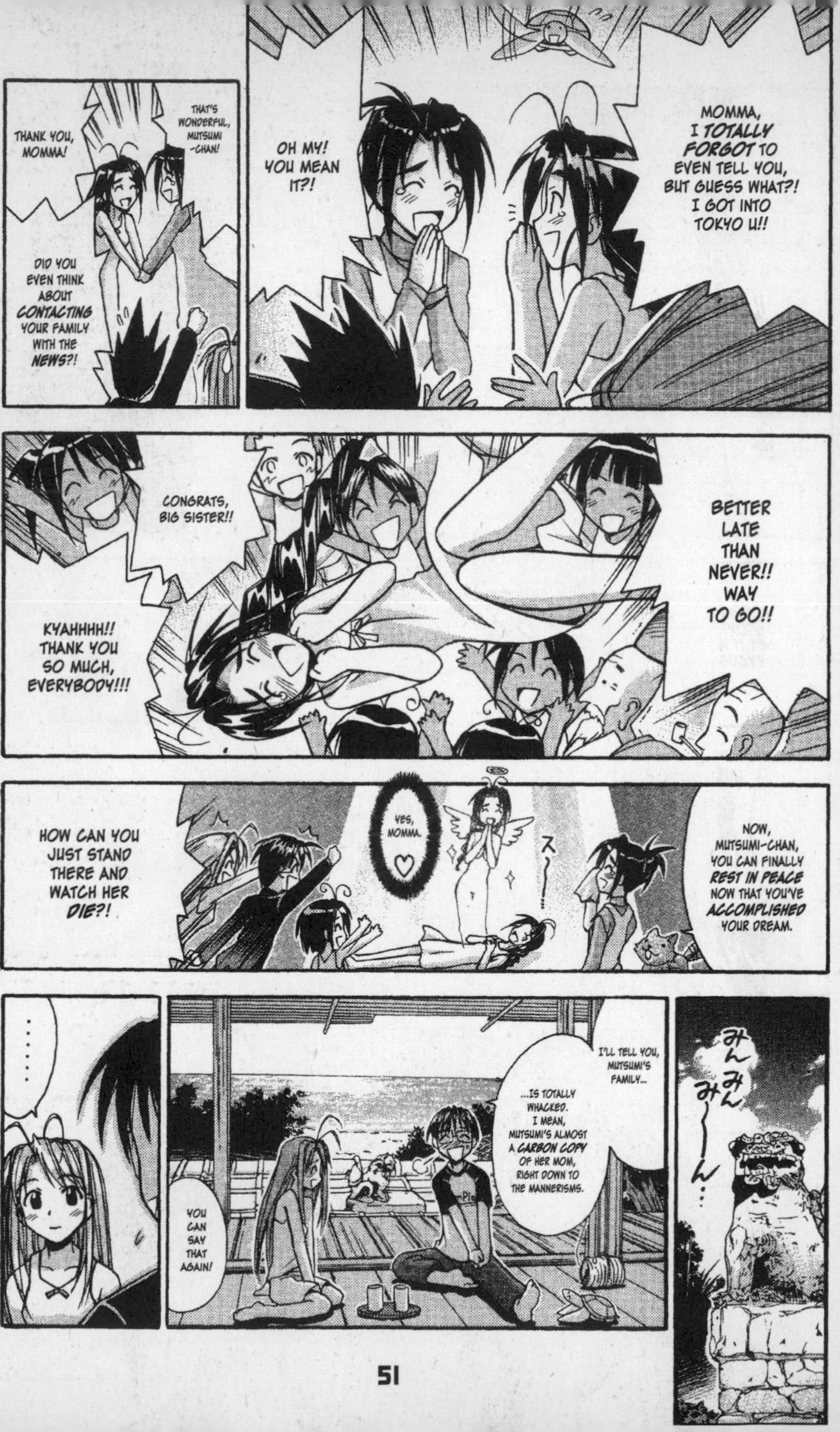
MOMMA, I *TOTALLY FORGOT* TO EVEN TELL YOU, BUT GUESS WHAT?! I GOT INTO TOKYO U!!
OH MY! YOU MEAN IT?!
THAT'S WONDERFUL, MUTSUMI-CHAN!
THANK YOU, MOMMA!
DID YOU EVEN THINK ABOUT *CONTACTING* YOUR FAMILY WITH THE *NEWS*?!
BETTER LATE THAN NEVER!! WAY TO GO!!
CONGRATS, BIG SISTER!!
KYAHHHH!! THANK YOU SO MUCH, EVERYBODY!!!
NOW, MUTSUMI-CHAN, YOU CAN FINALLY *REST IN PEACE* NOW THAT YOU'VE *ACCOMPLISHED* YOUR DREAM.
YES, MOMMA. ♥
ス～
HOW CAN YOU JUST STAND THERE AND WATCH HER *DIE*?!
みんみんみ～ん…
I'LL TELL YOU, MUTSUMI'S FAMILY...
...IS TOTALLY WHACKED. I MEAN, MUTSUMI'S ALMOST A *CARBON COPY* OF HER MOM, RIGHT DOWN TO THE MANNERISMS.
YOU CAN SAY THAT AGAIN!
......

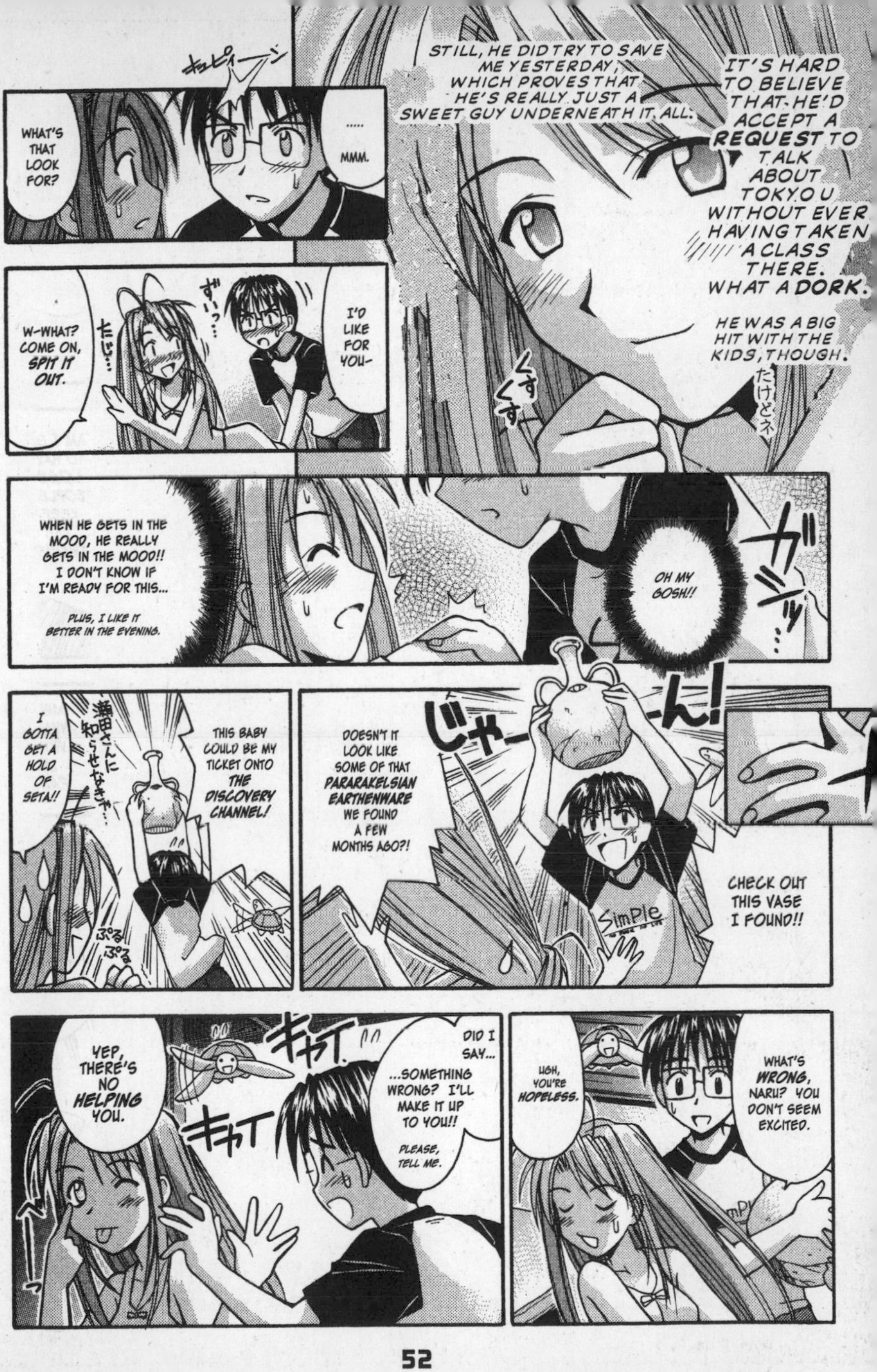
IT'S HARD TO BELIEVE THAT HE'D ACCEPT A REQUEST TO TALK ABOUT TOKYO U WITHOUT EVER HAVING TAKEN A CLASS THERE. WHAT A DORK.
STILL, HE DID TRY TO SAVE ME YESTERDAY, WHICH PROVES THAT HE'S REALLY JUST A SWEET GUY UNDERNEATH IT ALL.
HE WAS A BIG HIT WITH THE KIDS, THOUGH.
たけどネ
くすくす
キュピィーン
.....
MMM.
WHAT'S THAT LOOK FOR?
I'D LIKE FOR YOU-
ずいっ…
たじ…
W-WHAT? COME ON, SPIT IT OUT.
ガシッ…
OH MY GOSH!!
WHEN HE GETS IN THE MOOD, HE REALLY GETS IN THE MOOD!! I DON'T KNOW IF I'M READY FOR THIS...
PLUS, I LIKE IT BETTER IN THE EVENING.
じゃーん!
CHECK OUT THIS VASE I FOUND!!
DOESN'T IT LOOK LIKE SOME OF THAT PARARAKELSIAN EARTHENWARE WE FOUND A FEW MONTHS AGO?!
THIS BABY COULD BE MY TICKET ONTO THE DISCOVERY CHANNEL!
瀬田さんに知らせなきゃ…
I GOTTA GET A HOLD OF SETA!!
ぷるぷる
WHAT'S WRONG, NARU? YOU DON'T SEEM EXCITED.
UGH, YOU'RE HOPELESS.
DID I SAY...
...SOMETHING WRONG? I'LL MAKE IT UP TO YOU!!
PLEASE, TELL ME.
キャア
キャア
YEP, THERE'S NO HELPING YOU.

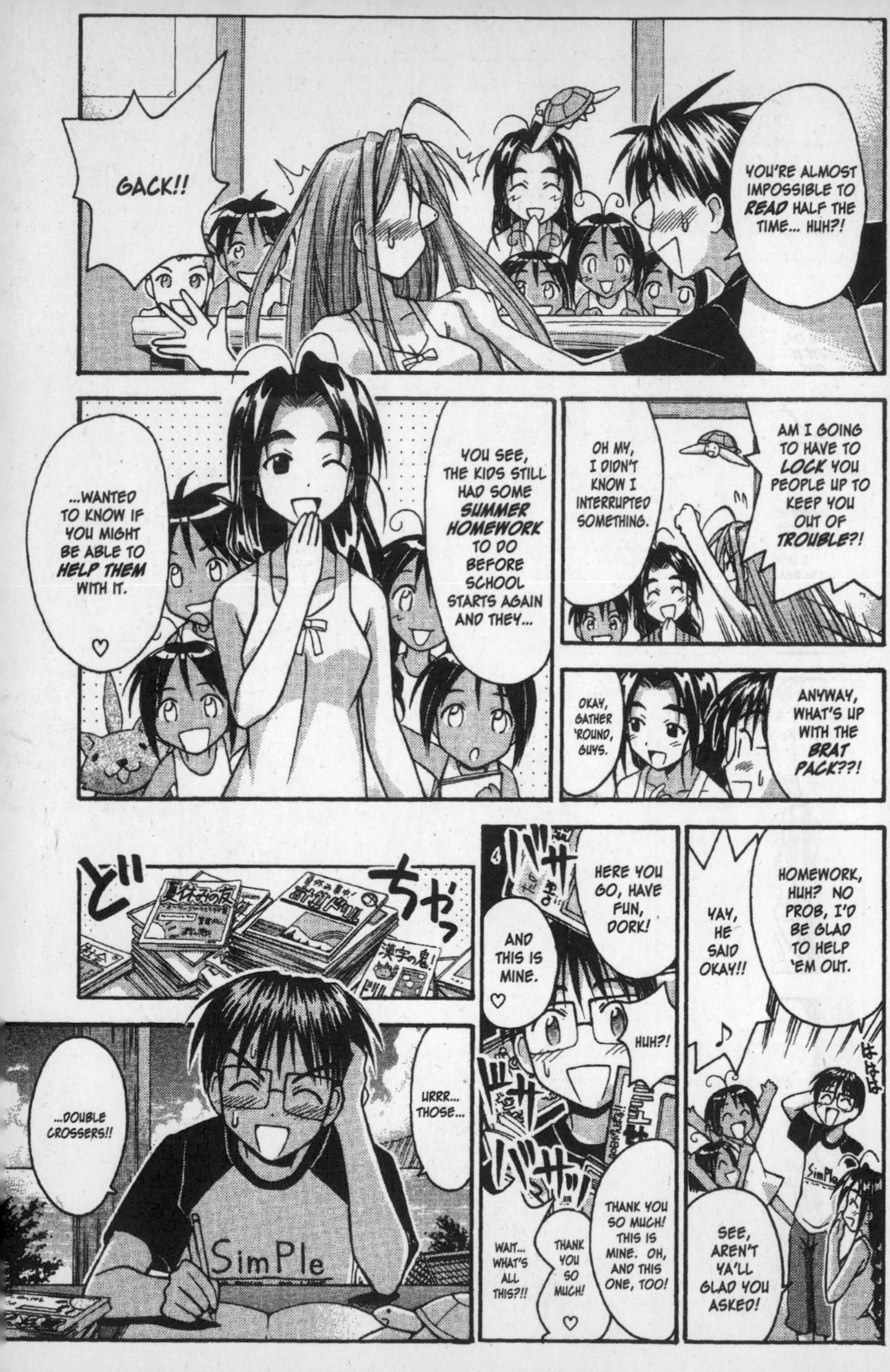
YOU'RE ALMOST IMPOSSIBLE TO READ HALF THE TIME... HUH?!
GACK!!
AM I GOING TO HAVE TO LOCK YOU PEOPLE UP TO KEEP YOU OUT OF TROUBLE?!
OH MY, I DIDN'T KNOW I INTERRUPTED SOMETHING.
ANYWAY, WHAT'S UP WITH THE BRAT PACK??!
OKAY, GATHER 'ROUND, GUYS.
YOU SEE, THE KIDS STILL HAD SOME SUMMER HOMEWORK TO DO BEFORE SCHOOL STARTS AGAIN AND THEY...
...WANTED TO KNOW IF YOU MIGHT BE ABLE TO HELP THEM WITH IT. ♡
HOMEWORK, HUH? NO PROB, I'D BE GLAD TO HELP 'EM OUT.
YAY, HE SAID OKAY!!
SEE, AREN'T YA'LL GLAD YOU ASKED!
HERE YOU GO, HAVE FUN, DORK!
AND THIS IS MINE. ♡
HUH?!
THANK YOU SO MUCH! THIS IS MINE. OH, AND THIS ONE, TOO!
THANK YOU SO MUCH! ♡
WAIT... WHAT'S ALL THIS?!!
URRR... THOSE...
...DOUBLE CROSSERS!!
SimPle

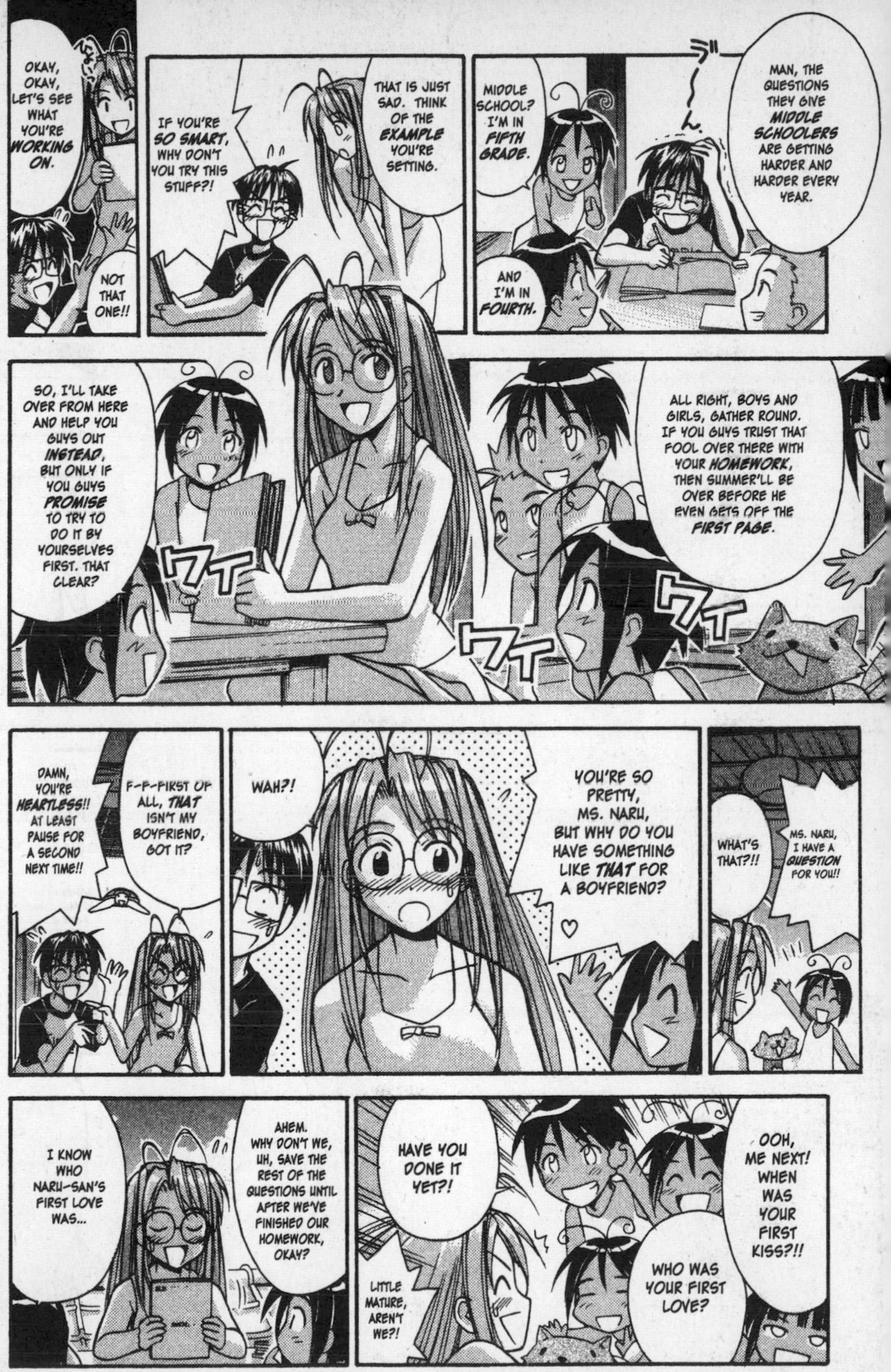
MAN, THE QUESTIONS THEY GIVE MIDDLE SCHOOLERS ARE GETTING HARDER AND HARDER EVERY YEAR.
MIDDLE SCHOOL? I'M IN FIFTH GRADE.
AND I'M IN FOURTH.
THAT IS JUST SAD. THINK OF THE EXAMPLE YOU'RE SETTING.
IF YOU'RE SO SMART, WHY DON'T YOU TRY THIS STUFF?!
OKAY, OKAY, LET'S SEE WHAT YOU'RE WORKING ON.
NOT THAT ONE!!
ALL RIGHT, BOYS AND GIRLS, GATHER ROUND. IF YOU GUYS TRUST THAT FOOL OVER THERE WITH YOUR HOMEWORK, THEN SUMMER'LL BE OVER BEFORE HE EVEN GETS OFF THE FIRST PAGE.
SO, I'LL TAKE OVER FROM HERE AND HELP YOU GUYS OUT INSTEAD, BUT ONLY IF YOU GUYS PROMISE TO TRY TO DO IT BY YOURSELVES FIRST. THAT CLEAR?
ワイ
ワイ
ワイ
MS. NARU, I HAVE A QUESTION FOR YOU!!
WHAT'S THAT?!!
YOU'RE SO PRETTY, MS. NARU, BUT WHY DO YOU HAVE SOMETHING LIKE THAT FOR A BOYFRIEND?
WAH?!
F-F-FIRST OF ALL, THAT ISN'T MY BOYFRIEND, GOT IT?
DAMN, YOU'RE HEARTLESS!! AT LEAST PAUSE FOR A SECOND NEXT TIME!!
OOH, ME NEXT! WHEN WAS YOUR FIRST KISS?!!
HAVE YOU DONE IT YET?!
WHO WAS YOUR FIRST LOVE?
LITTLE MATURE, AREN'T WE?!
AHEM. WHY DON'T WE, UH, SAVE THE REST OF THE QUESTIONS UNTIL AFTER WE'VE FINISHED OUR HOMEWORK, OKAY?
I KNOW WHO NARU-SAN'S FIRST LOVE WAS...

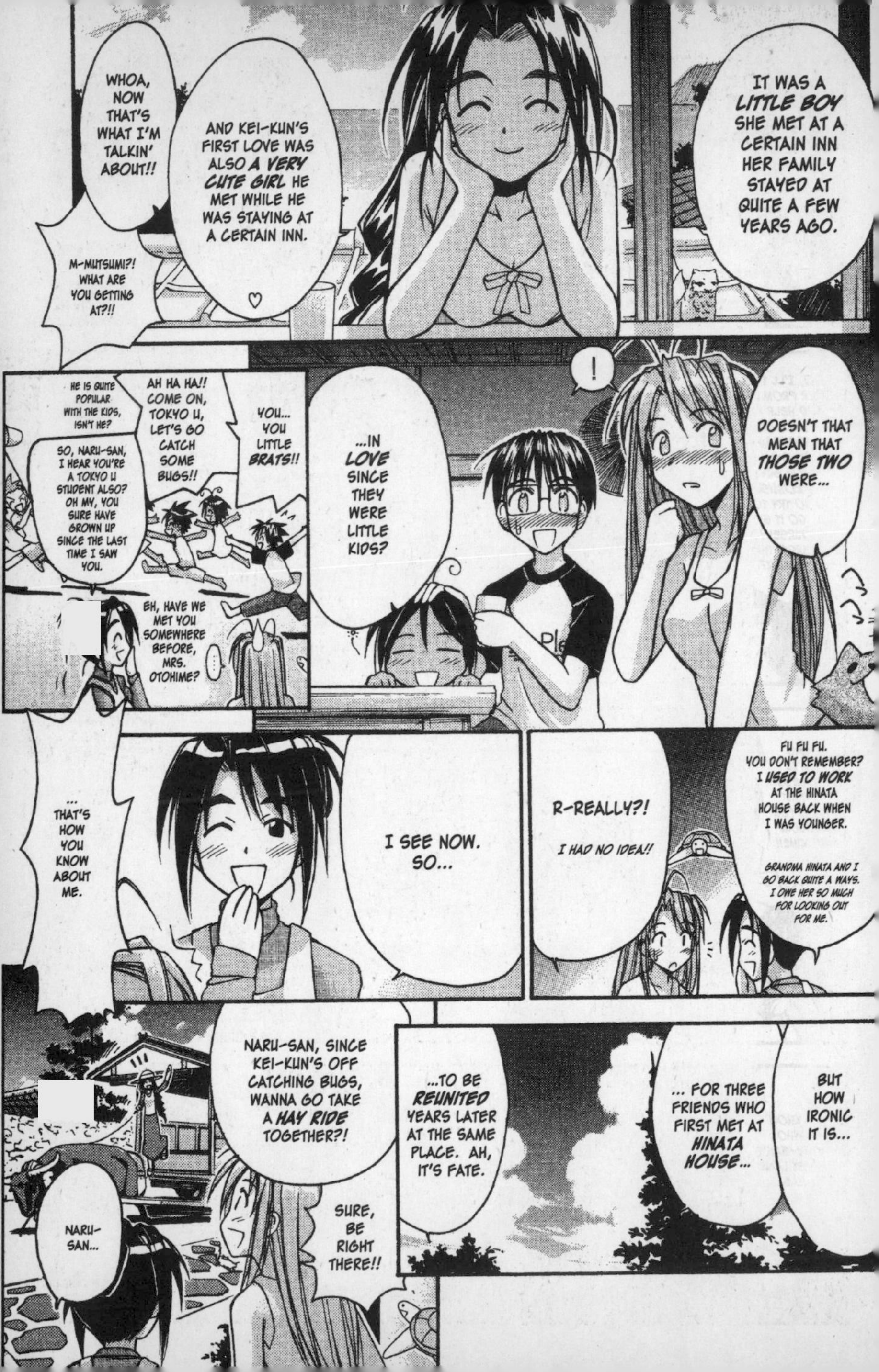
IT WAS A LITTLE BOY SHE MET AT A CERTAIN INN HER FAMILY STAYED AT QUITE A FEW YEARS AGO.
AND KEI-KUN'S FIRST LOVE WAS ALSO A VERY CUTE GIRL HE MET WHILE HE WAS STAYING AT A CERTAIN INN. ♡
WHOA, NOW THAT'S WHAT I'M TALKIN' ABOUT!!
M-MUTSUMI?! WHAT ARE YOU GETTING AT?!!
!
DOESN'T THAT MEAN THAT THOSE TWO WERE...
...IN LOVE SINCE THEY WERE LITTLE KIDS?
YOU... YOU LITTLE BRATS!!
AH HA HA!! COME ON, TOKYO U, LET'S GO CATCH SOME BUGS!!
HE IS QUITE POPULAR WITH THE KIDS, ISN'T HE?
SO, NARU-SAN, I HEAR YOU'RE A TOKYO U STUDENT ALSO? OH MY, YOU SURE HAVE GROWN UP SINCE THE LAST TIME I SAW YOU.
EH, HAVE WE MET YOU SOMEWHERE BEFORE, MRS. OTOHIME?
...
FU FU FU. YOU DON'T REMEMBER? I USED TO WORK AT THE HINATA HOUSE BACK WHEN I WAS YOUNGER.
GRANDMA HINATA AND I GO BACK QUITE A WAYS. I OWE HER SO MUCH FOR LOOKING OUT FOR ME.
R-REALLY?!
I HAD NO IDEA!!
I SEE NOW. SO...
... THAT'S HOW YOU KNOW ABOUT ME.
BUT HOW IRONIC IT IS...
... FOR THREE FRIENDS WHO FIRST MET AT HINATA HOUSE...
...TO BE REUNITED YEARS LATER AT THE SAME PLACE. AH, IT'S FATE.
NARU-SAN, SINCE KEI-KUN'S OFF CATCHING BUGS, WANNA GO TAKE A HAY RIDE TOGETHER?!
SURE, BE RIGHT THERE!!
NARU-SAN...

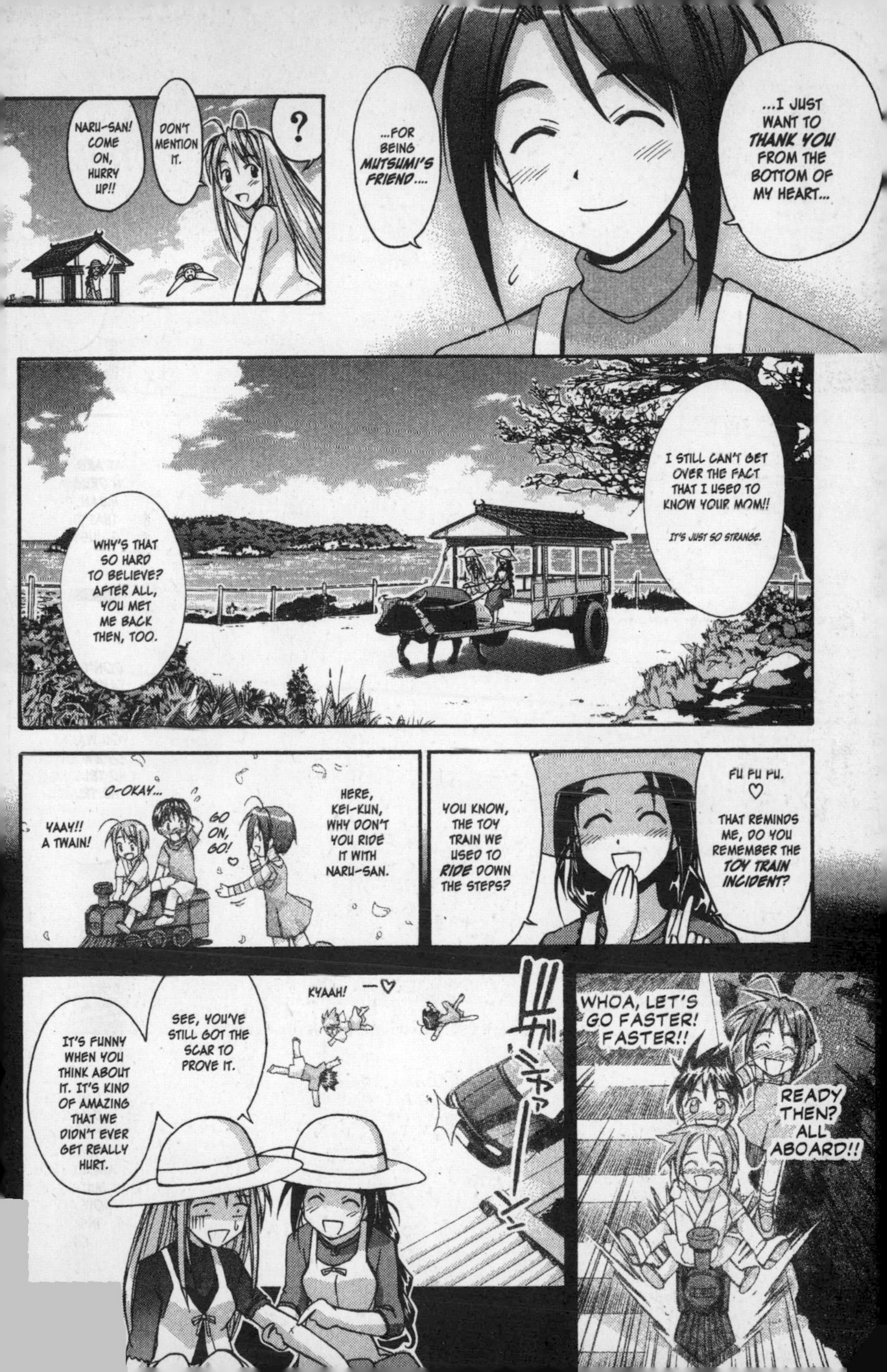
...I JUST WANT TO THANK YOU FROM THE BOTTOM OF MY HEART...
...FOR BEING MUTSUMI'S FRIEND....
?
DON'T MENTION IT.
NARU-SAN! COME ON, HURRY UP!!
I STILL CAN'T GET OVER THE FACT THAT I USED TO KNOW YOUR MOM!!
IT'S JUST SO STRANGE.
WHY'S THAT SO HARD TO BELIEVE? AFTER ALL, YOU MET ME BACK THEN, TOO.
FU FU FU. ♡
THAT REMINDS ME, DO YOU REMEMBER THE TOY TRAIN INCIDENT?
YOU KNOW, THE TOY TRAIN WE USED TO RIDE DOWN THE STEPS?
HERE, KEI-KUN, WHY DON'T YOU RIDE IT WITH NARU-SAN.
GO ON, GO!
O-OKAY...
YAAY!! A TWAIN!
READY THEN? ALL ABOARD!!
WHOA, LET'S GO FASTER! FASTER!!
KYAAH! —♡
SEE, YOU'VE STILL GOT THE SCAR TO PROVE IT.
IT'S FUNNY WHEN YOU THINK ABOUT IT. IT'S KIND OF AMAZING THAT WE DIDN'T EVER GET REALLY HURT.

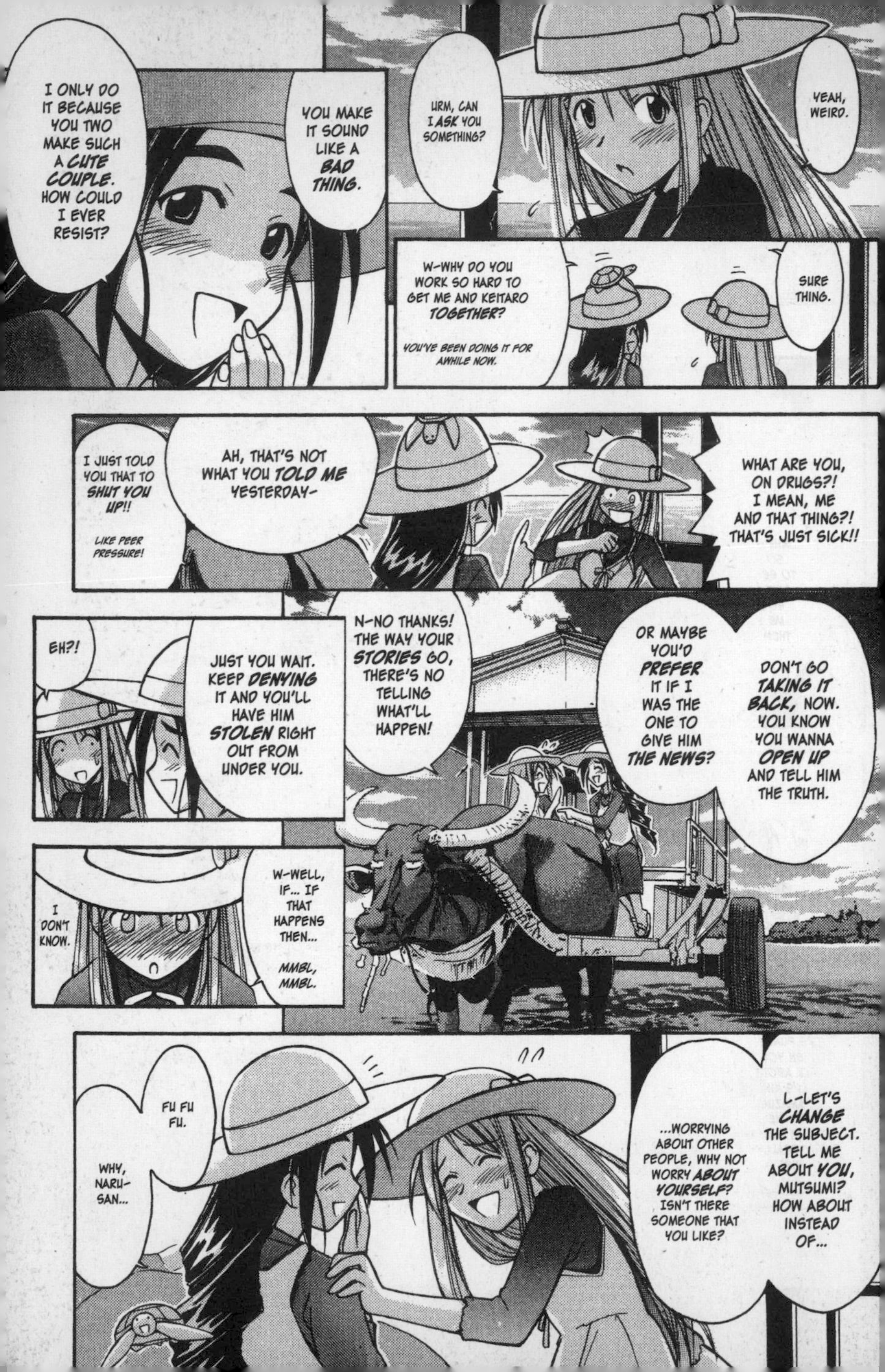
YEAH, WEIRD.
URM, CAN I ASK YOU SOMETHING?
SURE THING.
W-WHY DO YOU WORK SO HARD TO GET ME AND KEITARO TOGETHER?
YOU'VE BEEN DOING IT FOR AWHILE NOW.
YOU MAKE IT SOUND LIKE A BAD THING.
I ONLY DO IT BECAUSE YOU TWO MAKE SUCH A CUTE COUPLE. HOW COULD I EVER RESIST?
WHAT ARE YOU, ON DRUGS?! I MEAN, ME AND THAT THING?! THAT'S JUST SICK!!
AH, THAT'S NOT WHAT YOU TOLD ME YESTERDAY-
I JUST TOLD YOU THAT TO SHUT YOU UP!!
LIKE PEER PRESSURE!
DON'T GO TAKING IT BACK, NOW. YOU KNOW YOU WANNA OPEN UP AND TELL HIM THE TRUTH.
OR MAYBE YOU'D PREFER IT IF I WAS THE ONE TO GIVE HIM THE NEWS?
N-NO THANKS! THE WAY YOUR STORIES GO, THERE'S NO TELLING WHAT'LL HAPPEN!
JUST YOU WAIT. KEEP DENYING IT AND YOU'LL HAVE HIM STOLEN RIGHT OUT FROM UNDER YOU.
EH?!
W-WELL, IF... IF THAT HAPPENS THEN...
MMBL, MMBL.
I DON'T KNOW.
L-LET'S CHANGE THE SUBJECT. TELL ME ABOUT YOU, MUTSUMI? HOW ABOUT INSTEAD OF...
...WORRYING ABOUT OTHER PEOPLE, WHY NOT WORRY ABOUT YOURSELF? ISN'T THERE SOMEONE THAT YOU LIKE?
FU FU FU.
WHY, NARU-SAN...

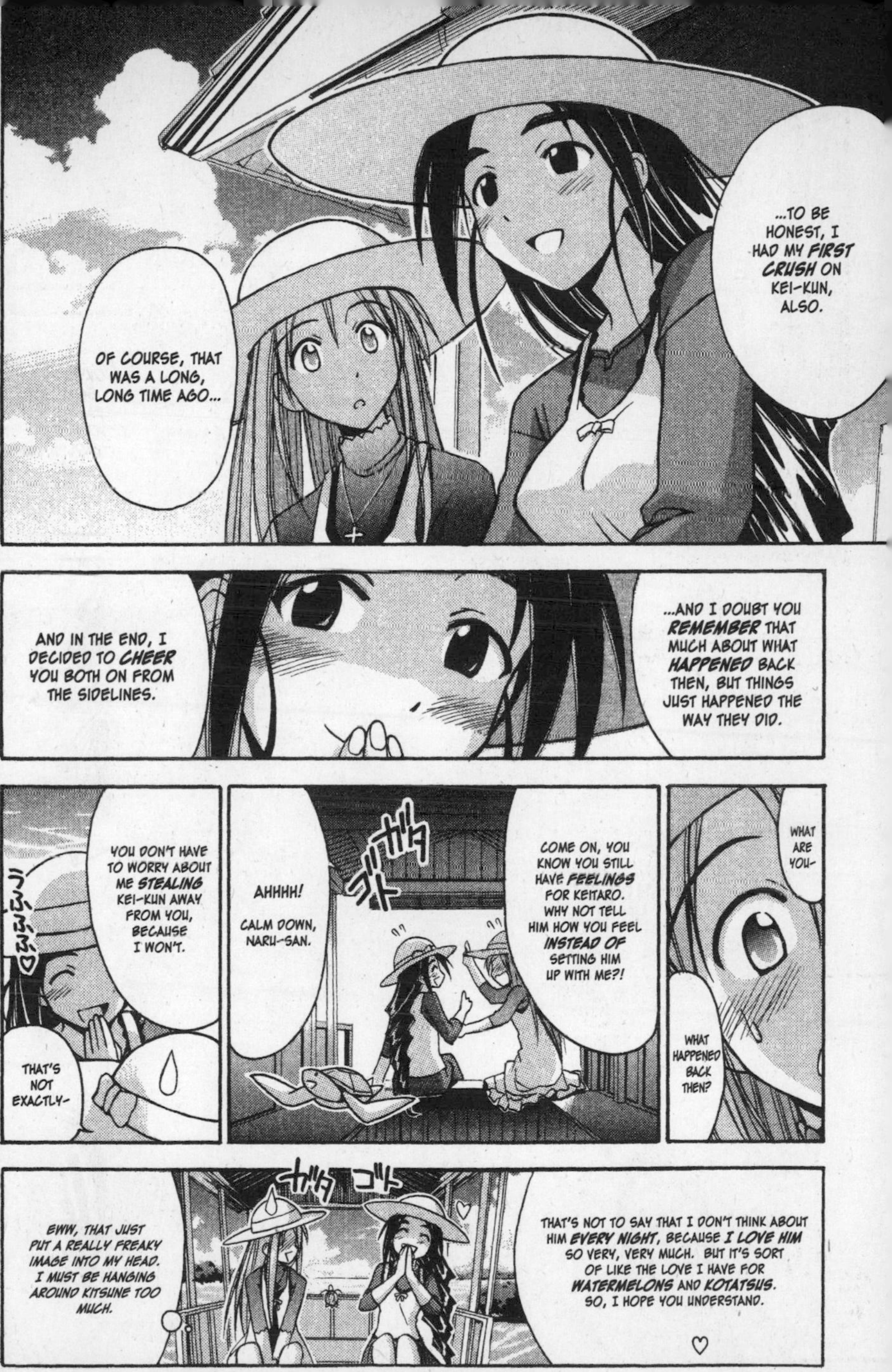
...TO BE HONEST, I HAD MY FIRST CRUSH ON KEI-KUN, ALSO.
OF COURSE, THAT WAS A LONG, LONG TIME AGO...
...AND I DOUBT YOU REMEMBER THAT MUCH ABOUT WHAT HAPPENED BACK THEN, BUT THINGS JUST HAPPENED THE WAY THEY DID.
AND IN THE END, I DECIDED TO CHEER YOU BOTH ON FROM THE SIDELINES.
WHAT ARE YOU-
WHAT HAPPENED BACK THEN?
COME ON, YOU KNOW YOU STILL HAVE FEELINGS FOR KEITARO. WHY NOT TELL HIM HOW YOU FEEL INSTEAD OF SETTING HIM UP WITH ME?!
AHHHH!
CALM DOWN, NARU-SAN.
YOU DON'T HAVE TO WORRY ABOUT ME STEALING KEI-KUN AWAY FROM YOU, BECAUSE I WON'T.
ふふふ♡
THAT'S NOT EXACTLY-
ガタ ゴト
THAT'S NOT TO SAY THAT I DON'T THINK ABOUT HIM EVERY NIGHT, BECAUSE I LOVE HIM SO VERY, VERY MUCH. BUT IT'S SORT OF LIKE THE LOVE I HAVE FOR WATERMELONS AND KOTATSUS. SO, I HOPE YOU UNDERSTAND.
EWW, THAT JUST PUT A REALLY FREAKY IMAGE INTO MY HEAD. I MUST BE HANGING AROUND KITSUNE TOO MUCH.

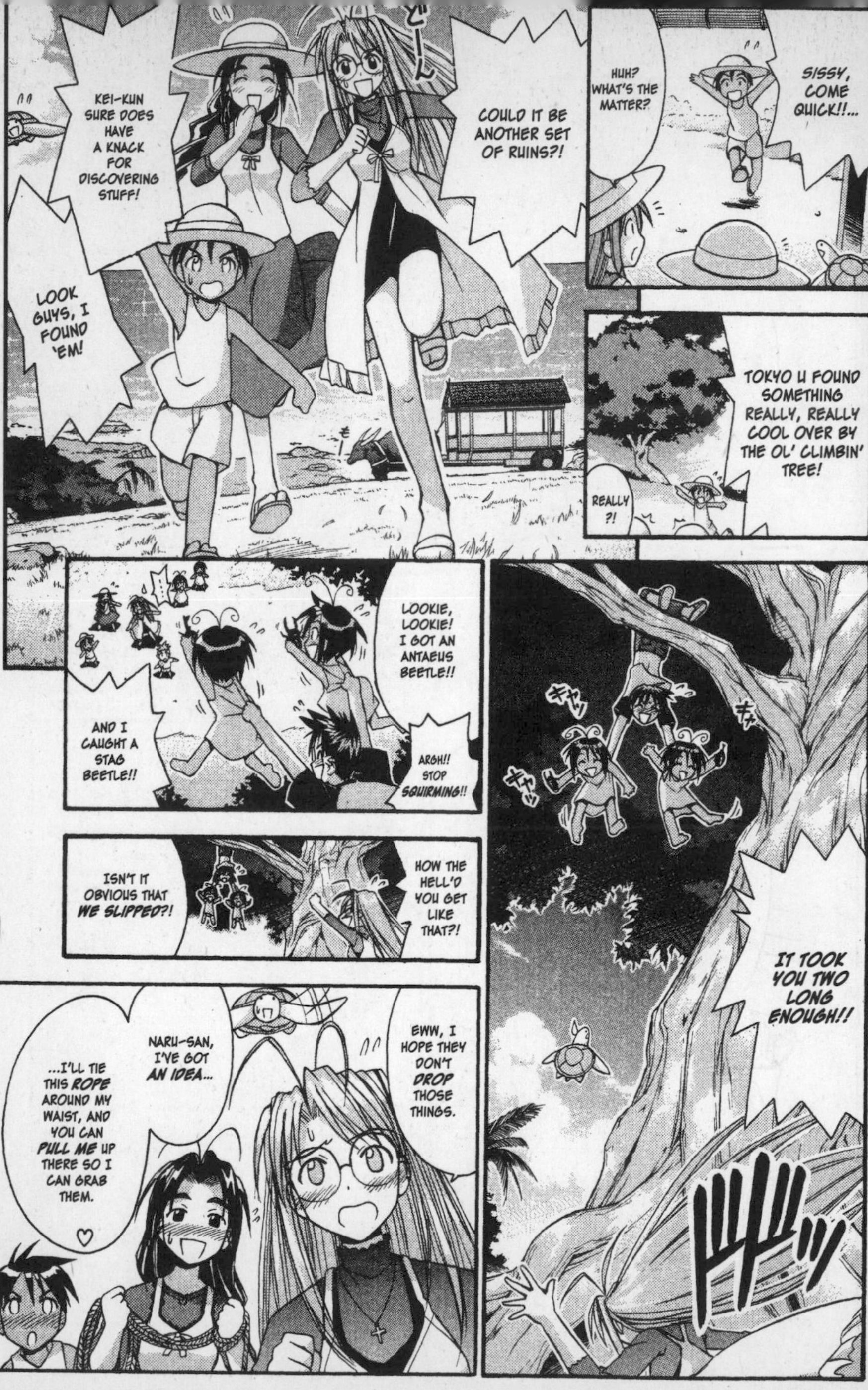
SISSY, COME QUICK!!...
HUH? WHAT'S THE MATTER?
TOKYO U FOUND SOMETHING REALLY, REALLY COOL OVER BY THE OL' CLIMBIN' TREE!
REALLY?!
COULD IT BE ANOTHER SET OF RUINS?!
KEI-KUN SURE DOES HAVE A KNACK FOR DISCOVERING STUFF!
LOOK GUYS, I FOUND 'EM!
IT TOOK YOU TWO LONG ENOUGH!!
LOOKIE, LOOKIE! I GOT AN ANTAEUS BEETLE!!
AND I CAUGHT A STAG BEETLE!!
ARGH!! STOP SQUIRMING!!
HOW THE HELL'D YOU GET LIKE THAT?!
ISN'T IT OBVIOUS THAT WE SLIPPED?!
EWW, I HOPE THEY DON'T DROP THOSE THINGS.
NARU-SAN, I'VE GOT AN IDEA...
...I'LL TIE THIS ROPE AROUND MY WAIST, AND YOU CAN PULL ME UP THERE SO I CAN GRAB THEM.

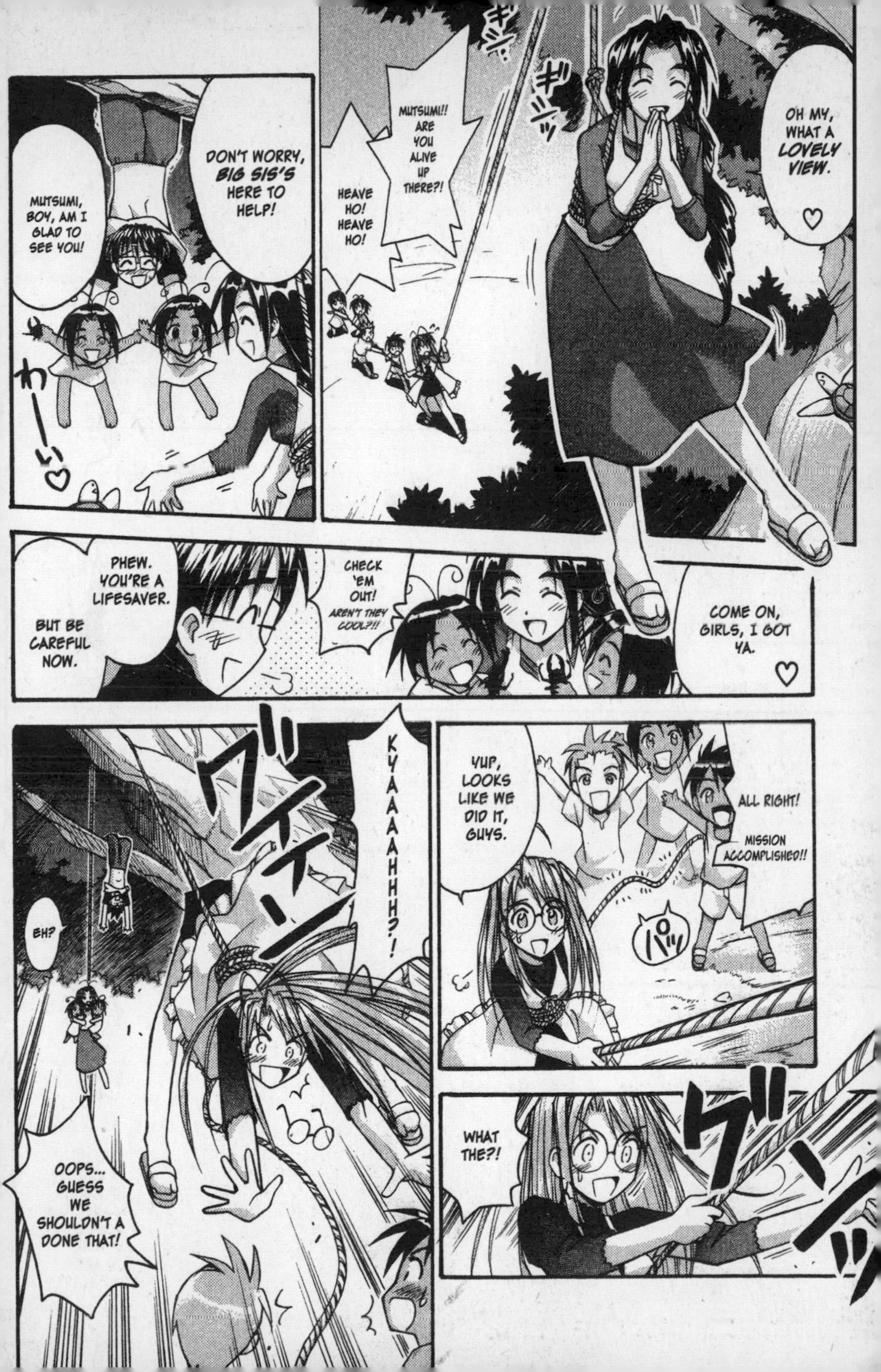
OH MY, WHAT A LOVELY VIEW. ♡
MUTSUMI!! ARE YOU ALIVE UP THERE?!
HEAVE HO! HEAVE HO!
DON'T WORRY, BIG SIS'S HERE TO HELP!
MUTSUMI, BOY, AM I GLAD TO SEE YOU!
わーい ♡
COME ON, GIRLS, I GOT YA. ♡
CHECK 'EM OUT! AREN'T THEY COOL?!!
PHEW. YOU'RE A LIFESAVER.
BUT BE CAREFUL NOW.
YUP, LOOKS LIKE WE DID IT, GUYS.
ALL RIGHT!
MISSION ACCOMPLISHED!!
パッ
WHAT THE?!
KYAAAAAAHHH?!
EH?
OOPS... GUESS WE SHOULDN'T A DONE THAT!

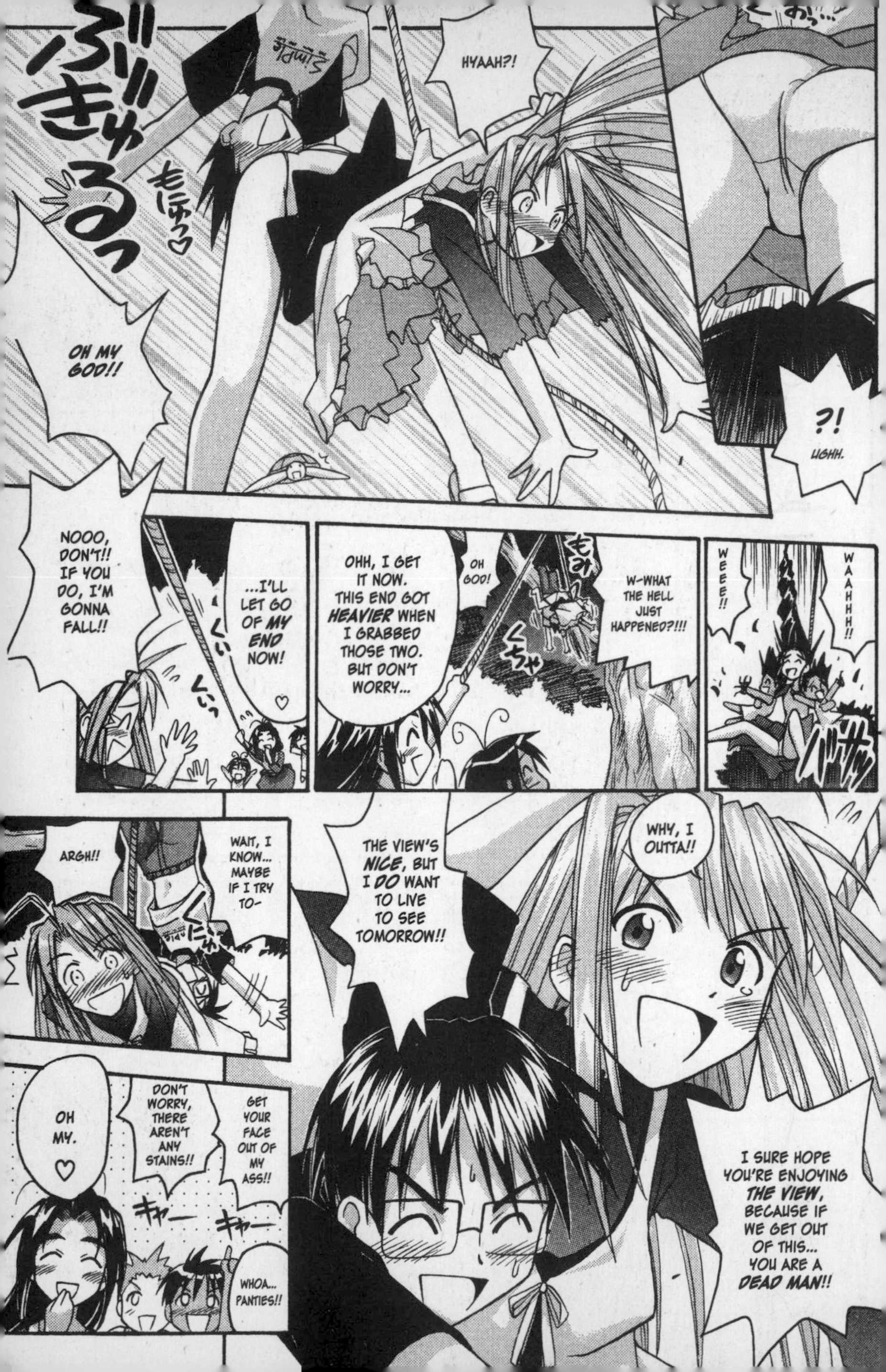

おっ…
?!
UGHH.
HYAAH?!
ぶりきゅるっ
もにゅっ♡
OH MY GOD!!
WAAHHH!!
WEEE!!
バサッ
W-WHAT THE HELL JUST HAPPENED?!!!
もみ
くちゃ
OH GOD!
OHH, I GET IT NOW. THIS END GOT HEAVIER WHEN I GRABBED THOSE TWO. BUT DON'T WORRY...
...I'LL LET GO OF MY END NOW! ♡
くい くいっ
NOOO, DON'T!! IF YOU DO, I'M GONNA FALL!!
I SURE HOPE YOU'RE ENJOYING THE VIEW, BECAUSE IF WE GET OUT OF THIS... YOU ARE A DEAD MAN!!
THE VIEW'S NICE, BUT I DO WANT TO LIVE TO SEE TOMORROW!!
WHY, I OUTTA!!
WAIT, I KNOW... MAYBE IF I TRY TO-
ARGH!!
GET YOUR FACE OUT OF MY ASS!!
DON'T WORRY, THERE AREN'T ANY STAINS!!
OH MY. ♡
キャー キャー
WHOA... PANTIES!!

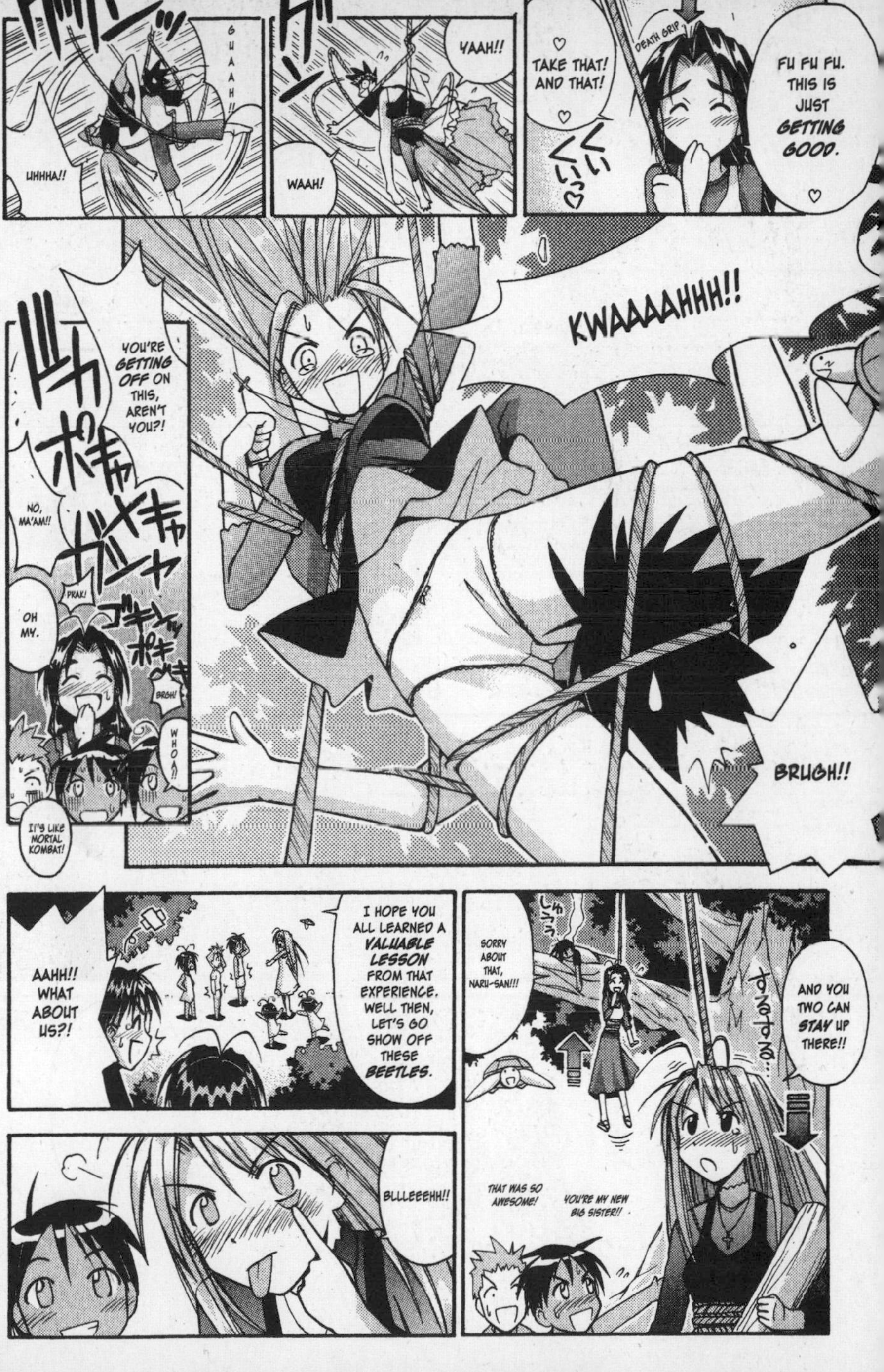
DEATH GRIP
FU FU FU. THIS IS JUST GETTING GOOD.
TAKE THAT! AND THAT!
くいくいくいっ
YAAH!!
WAAH!
GUAAAH!!
UHHHA!!
KWAAAAHHH!!
BRUGH!!
YOU'RE GETTING OFF ON THIS, AREN'T YOU?!
NO, MA'AM!!
PRAK!
OH MY.
BRGH!
WHOA!!
IT'S LIKE MORTAL KOMBAT!
SORRY ABOUT THAT, NARU-SAN!!!
AND YOU TWO CAN STAY UP THERE!!
THAT WAS SO AWESOME!
YOU'RE MY NEW BIG SISTER!!
I HOPE YOU ALL LEARNED A VALUABLE LESSON FROM THAT EXPERIENCE. WELL THEN, LET'S GO SHOW OFF THESE BEETLES.
AAHH!! WHAT ABOUT US?!
BLLLEEEHH!!

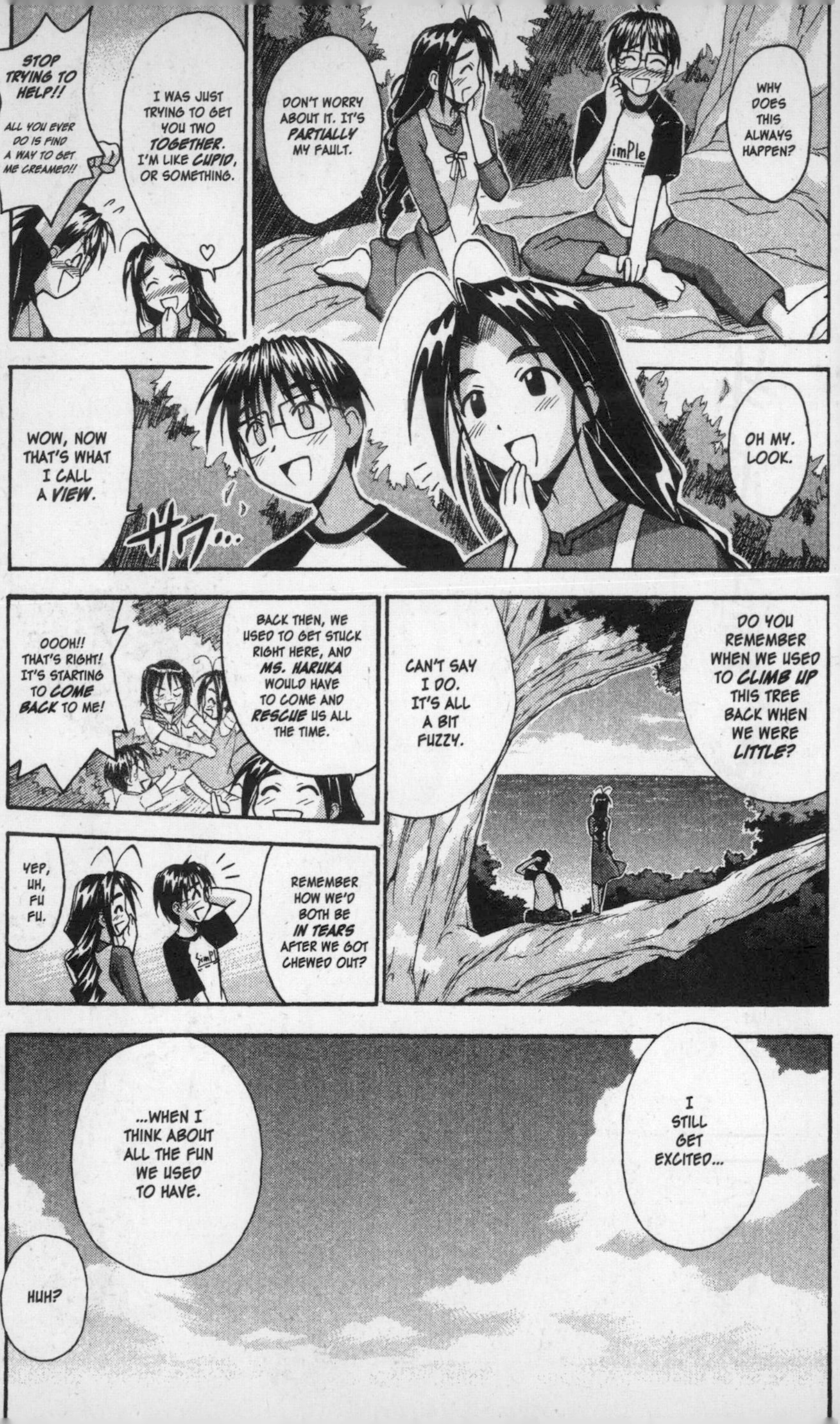
WHY DOES THIS ALWAYS HAPPEN?
DON'T WORRY ABOUT IT. IT'S PARTIALLY MY FAULT.
I WAS JUST TRYING TO GET YOU TWO TOGETHER. I'M LIKE CUPID, OR SOMETHING.
STOP TRYING TO HELP!!
ALL YOU EVER DO IS FIND A WAY TO GET ME CREAMED!!
OH MY. LOOK.
WOW, NOW THAT'S WHAT I CALL A VIEW.
サワ...
DO YOU REMEMBER WHEN WE USED TO CLIMB UP THIS TREE BACK WHEN WE WERE LITTLE?
CAN'T SAY I DO. IT'S ALL A BIT FUZZY.
BACK THEN, WE USED TO GET STUCK RIGHT HERE, AND MS. HARUKA WOULD HAVE TO COME AND RESCUE US ALL THE TIME.
OOOH!! THAT'S RIGHT! IT'S STARTING TO COME BACK TO ME!
REMEMBER HOW WE'D BOTH BE IN TEARS AFTER WE GOT CHEWED OUT?
YEP, UH, FU FU.
I STILL GET EXCITED...
...WHEN I THINK ABOUT ALL THE FUN WE USED TO HAVE.
HUH?

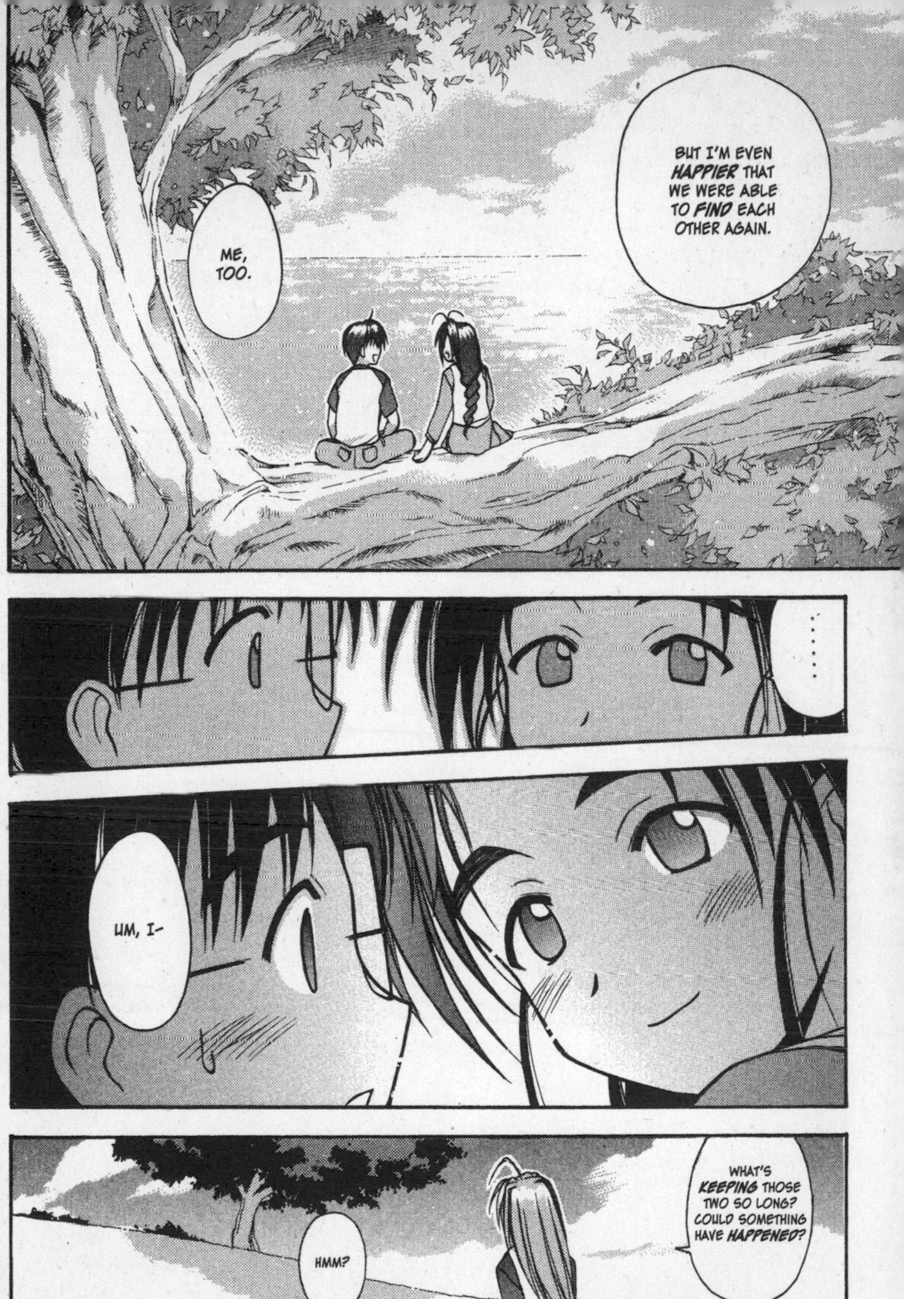
BUT I'M EVEN HAPPIER THAT WE WERE ABLE TO FIND EACH OTHER AGAIN.
ME, TOO.
......
UM, I-
WHAT'S KEEPING THOSE TWO SO LONG? COULD SOMETHING HAVE HAPPENED?
HMM?

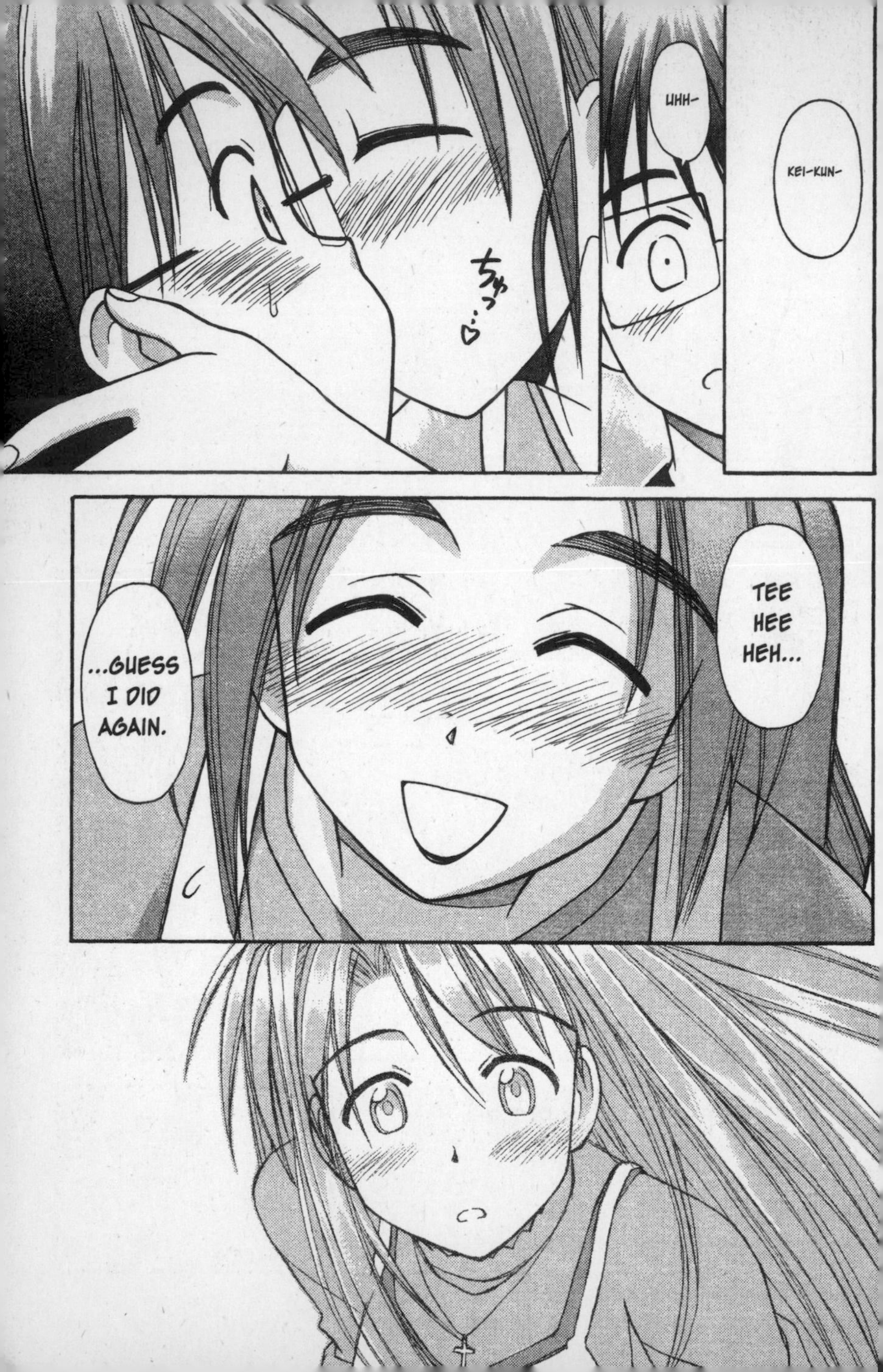
KEI-KUN-
UHH-
ちゅっ…♡
TEE HEE HEH...
...GUESS I DID AGAIN.

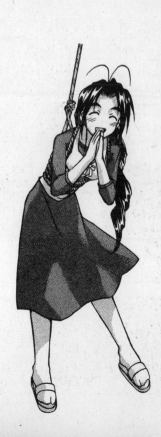

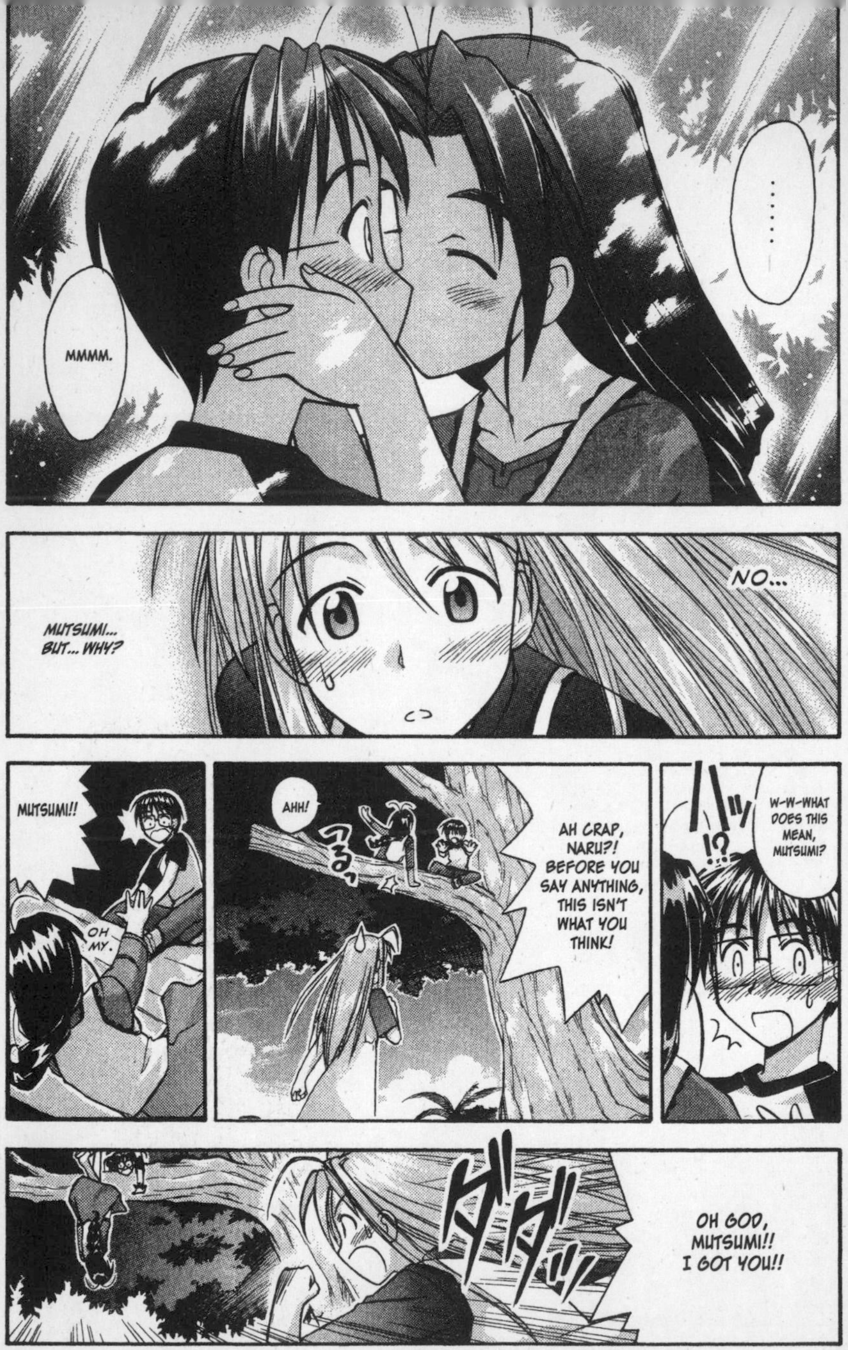
......
MMMM.
NO...
MUTSUMI... BUT... WHY?
W-W-WHAT DOES THIS MEAN, MUTSUMI?
!?
AH CRAP, NARU?! BEFORE YOU SAY ANYTHING, THIS ISN'T WHAT YOU THINK!
AHH!
MUTSUMI!!
OH MY.
OH GOD, MUTSUMI!! I GOT YOU!!

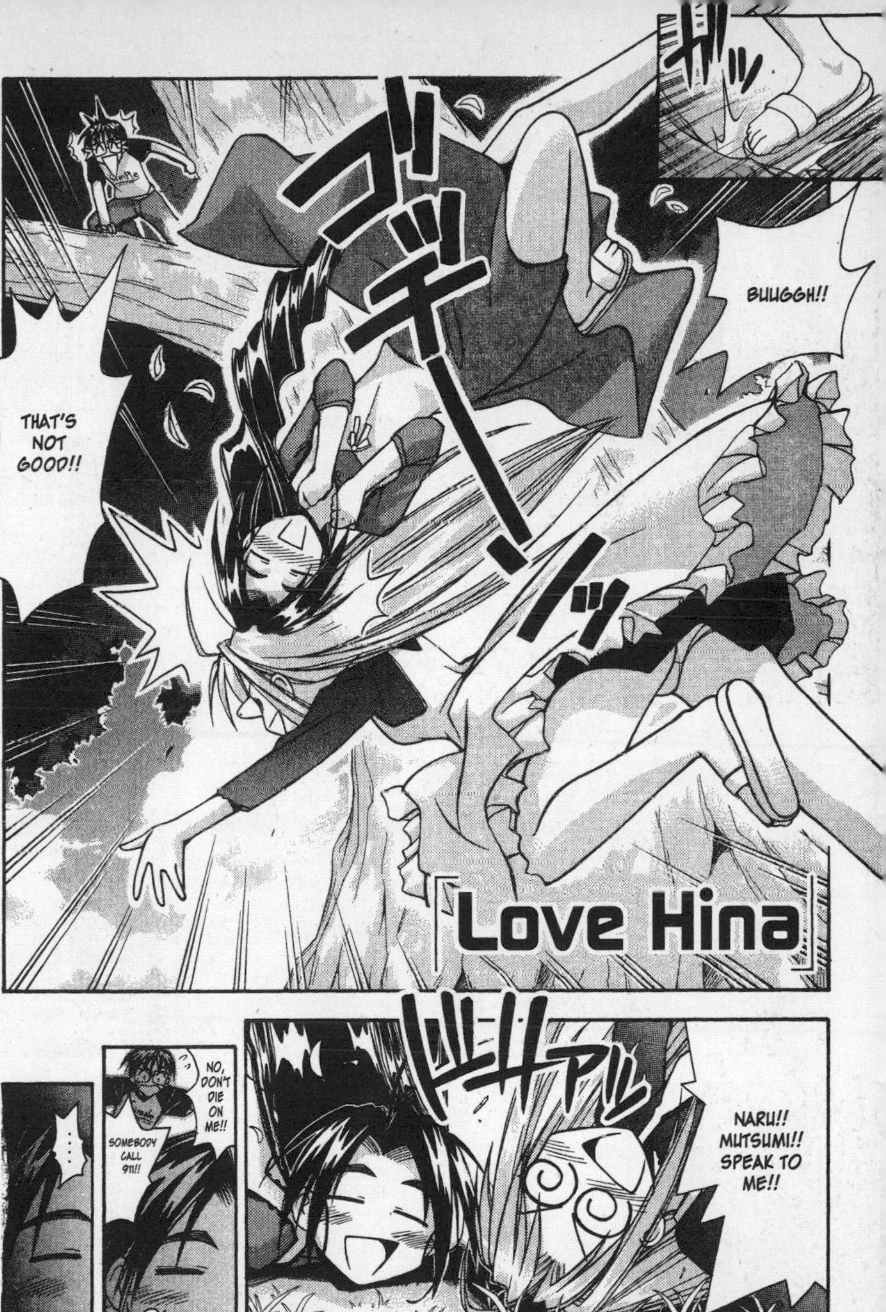
BUUGGH!!
THAT'S NOT GOOD!!
Love Hina
NARU!! MUTSUMI!! SPEAK TO ME!!
NO, DON'T DIE ON ME!!
SOMEBODY CALL 911!!
GUUGG
....

HINATA.82 Memories a Blur?!

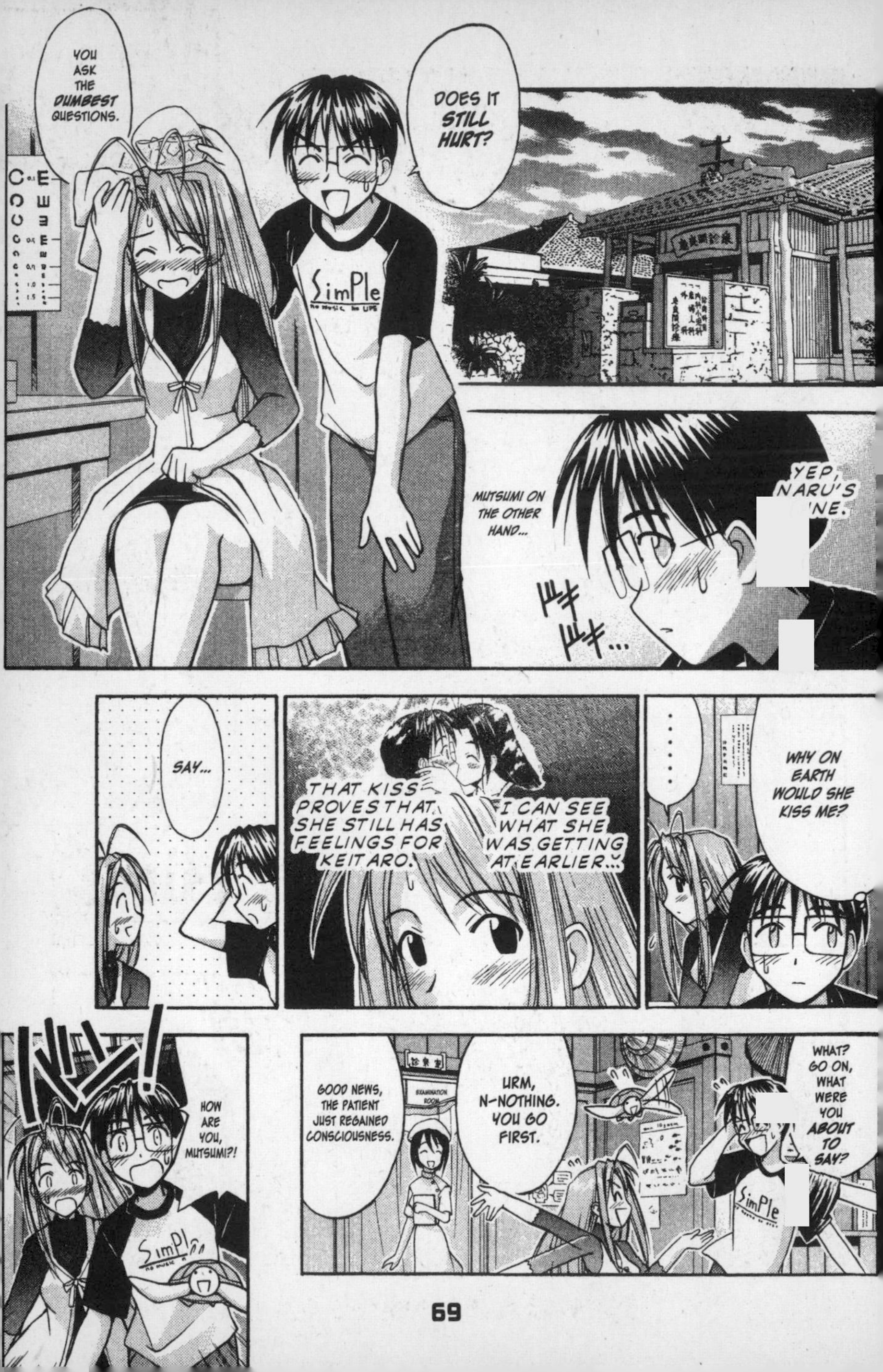
YEP, NARU'S
MUTSUMI ON THE OTHER HAND...
DOES IT STILL HURT?
YOU ASK THE DUMBEST QUESTIONS.
WHY ON EARTH WOULD SHE KISS ME?
......
I CAN SEE WHAT SHE WAS GETTING AT EARLIER...
THAT KISS PROVES THAT SHE STILL HAS FEELINGS FOR KEITARO.
SAY...
WHAT? GO ON, WHAT WERE YOU ABOUT TO SAY?
URM, N-NOTHING. YOU GO FIRST.
EXAMINATION ROOM
GOOD NEWS, THE PATIENT JUST REGAINED CONSCIOUSNESS.
HOW ARE YOU, MUTSUMI?!

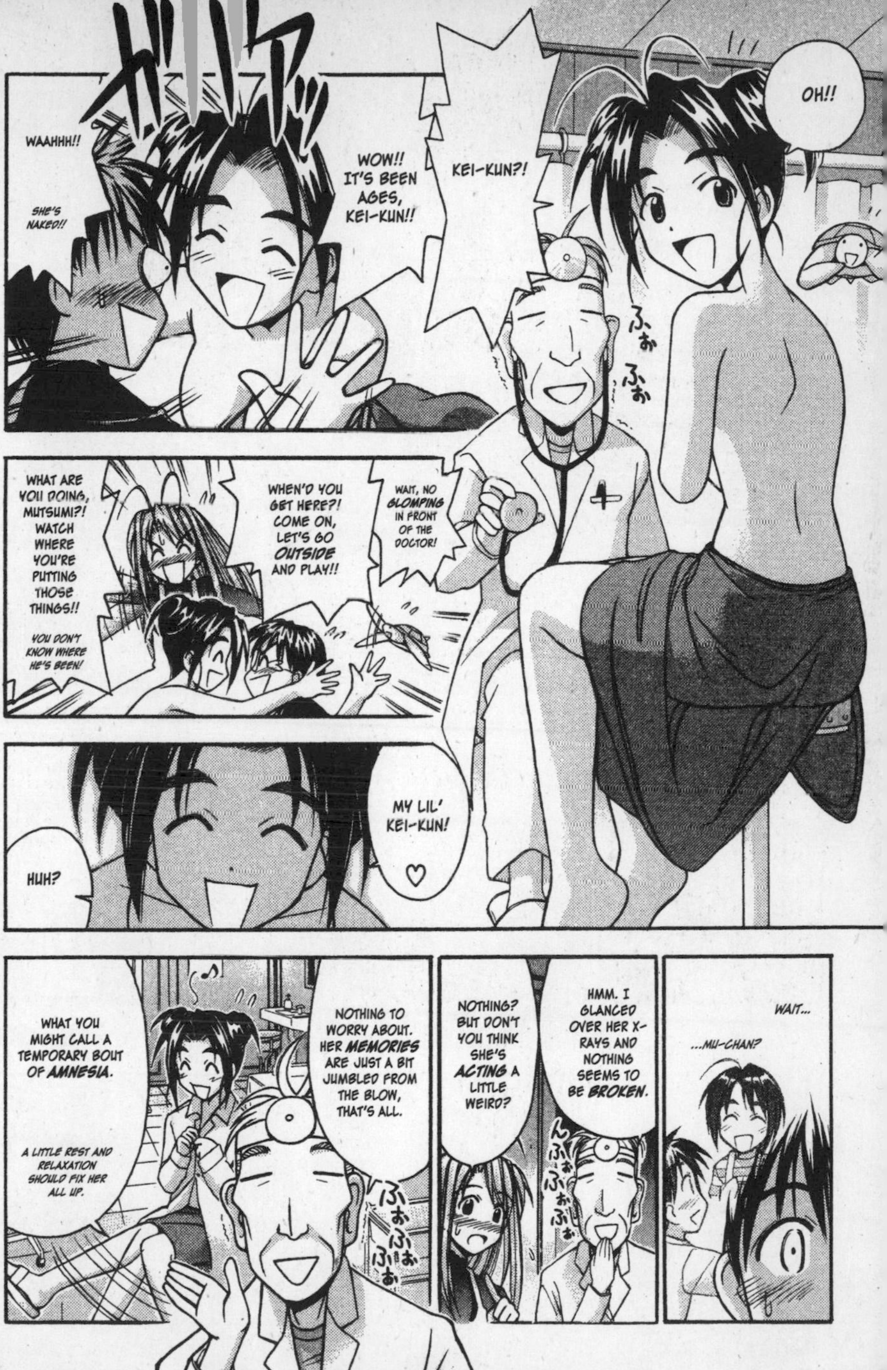

OH!!
KEI-KUN?!
ふぉ ふぉ
WOW!! IT'S BEEN AGES, KEI-KUN!!
WAAHHH!!
SHE'S NAKED!!
WAIT, NO GLOMPING IN FRONT OF THE DOCTOR!
WHEN'D YOU GET HERE?! COME ON, LET'S GO OUTSIDE AND PLAY!!
WHAT ARE YOU DOING, MUTSUMI?! WATCH WHERE YOU'RE PUTTING THOSE THINGS!!
YOU DON'T KNOW WHERE HE'S BEEN!
MY LIL' KEI-KUN! ♥
HUH?
WAIT...
...MU-CHAN?
HMM. I GLANCED OVER HER X-RAYS AND NOTHING SEEMS TO BE BROKEN.
NOTHING? BUT DON'T YOU THINK SHE'S ACTING A LITTLE WEIRD?
んふぉふぉふぉ
NOTHING TO WORRY ABOUT. HER MEMORIES ARE JUST A BIT JUMBLED FROM THE BLOW, THAT'S ALL.
ふぉふぉふぉ
WHAT YOU MIGHT CALL A TEMPORARY BOUT OF AMNESIA.
A LITTLE REST AND RELAXATION SHOULD FIX HER ALL UP.

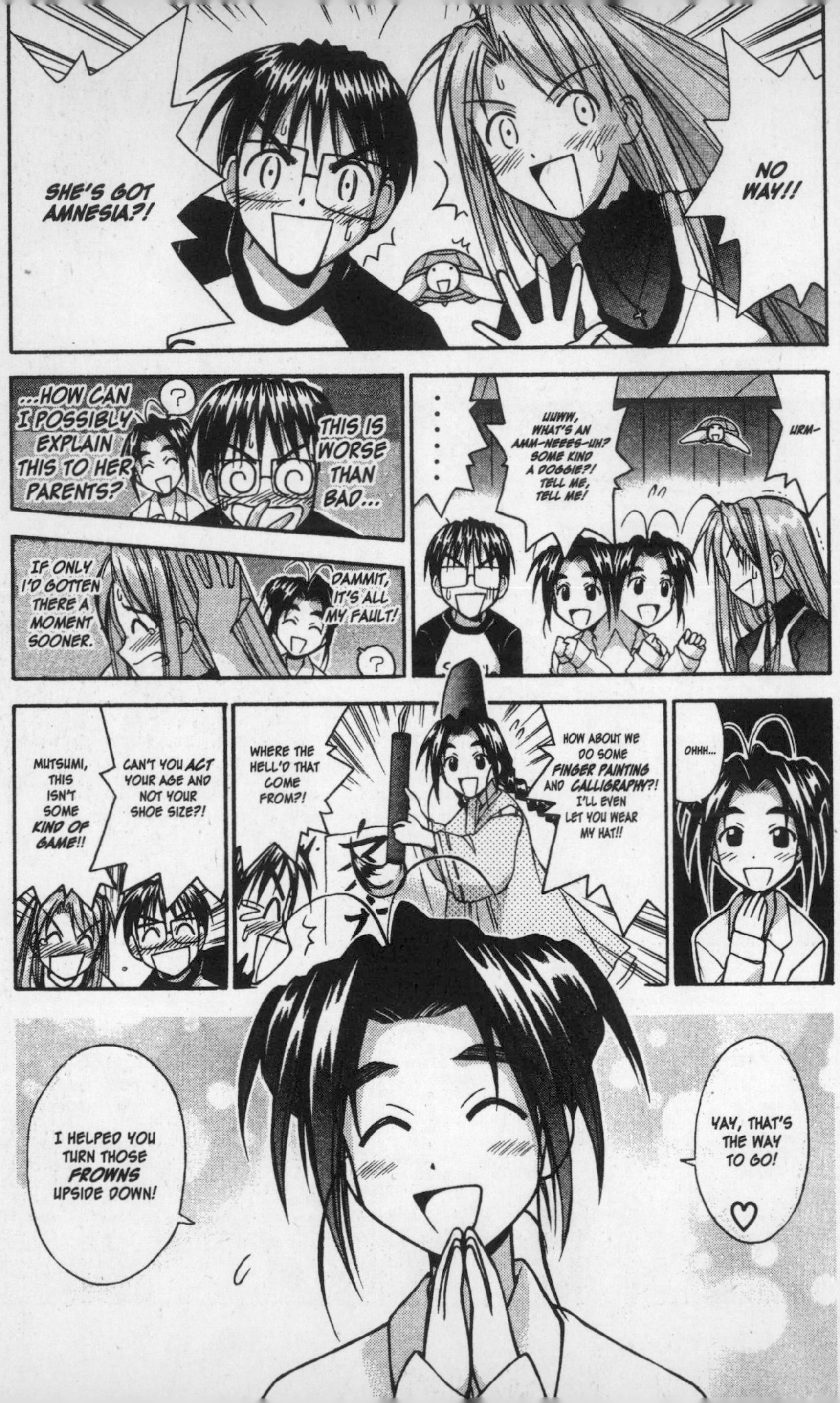
NO WAY!!
SHE'S GOT AMNESIA?!
URM-
UUWW, WHAT'S AN AMM-NEEES-UH? SOME KIND A DOGGIE?! TELL ME, TELL ME!
...
THIS IS WORSE THAN BAD...
...HOW CAN I POSSIBLY EXPLAIN THIS TO HER PARENTS?
?
DAMMIT, IT'S ALL MY FAULT!
IF ONLY I'D GOTTEN THERE A MOMENT SOONER.
?
OHHH...
HOW ABOUT WE DO SOME FINGER PAINTING AND CALLIGRAPHY?! I'LL EVEN LET YOU WEAR MY HAT!!
WHERE THE HELL'D THAT COME FROM?!
CAN'T YOU ACT YOUR AGE AND NOT YOUR SHOE SIZE?!
MUTSUMI, THIS ISN'T SOME KIND OF GAME!!
YAY, THAT'S THE WAY TO GO! ♥
I HELPED YOU TURN THOSE FROWNS UPSIDE DOWN!

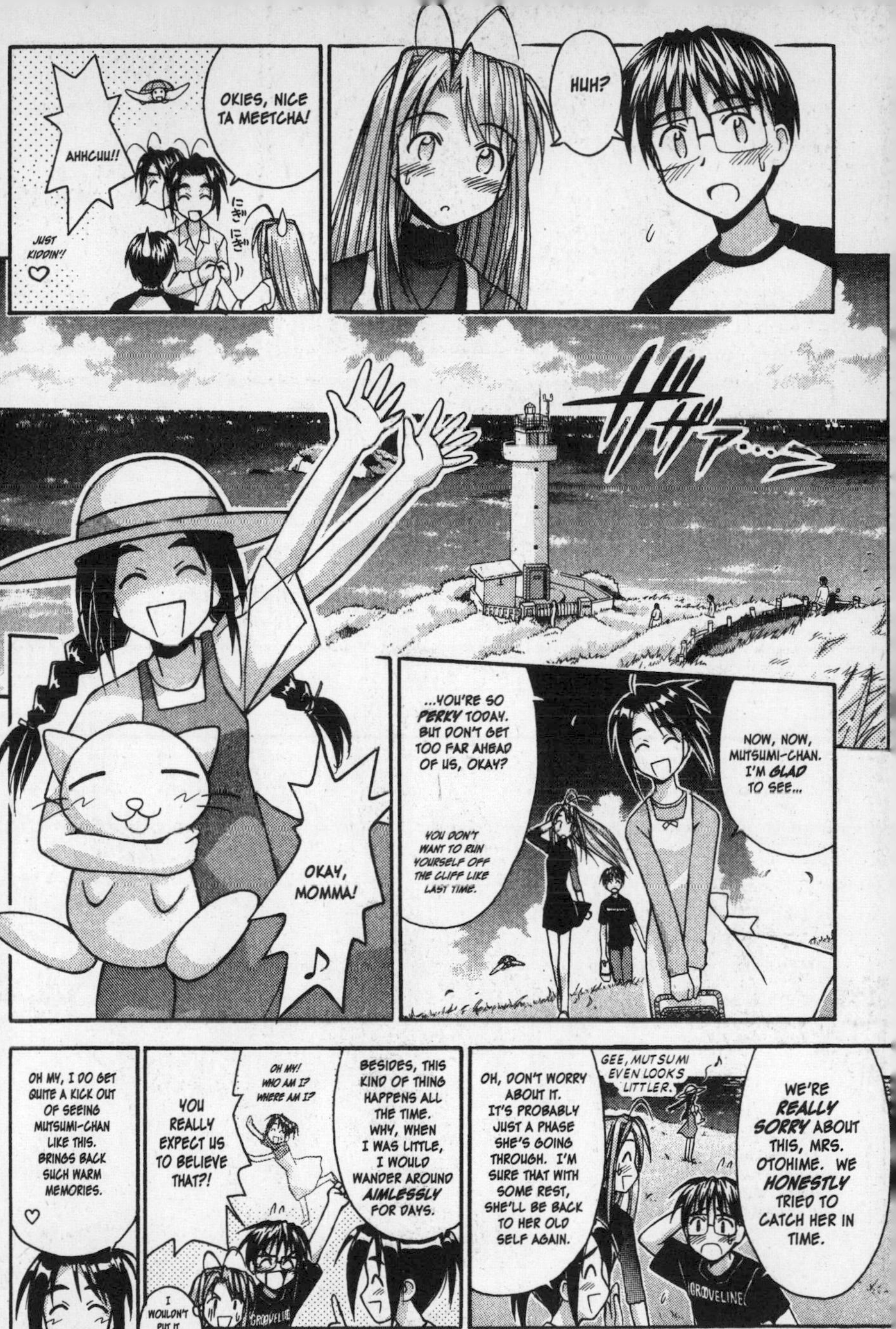
HUH?
OKIES, NICE TA MEETCHA!
AHHCUU!!
にぎにぎ
JUST KIDDIN'!!
ザザァ…
NOW, NOW, MUTSUMI-CHAN. I'M GLAD TO SEE...
...YOU'RE SO PERKY TODAY. BUT DON'T GET TOO FAR AHEAD OF US, OKAY?
YOU DON'T WANT TO RUN YOURSELF OFF THE CLIFF LIKE LAST TIME.
OKAY, MOMMA!
WE'RE REALLY SORRY ABOUT THIS, MRS. OTOHIME. WE HONESTLY TRIED TO CATCH HER IN TIME.
GEE, MUTSUMI EVEN LOOKS LITTLER.
OH, DON'T WORRY ABOUT IT. IT'S PROBABLY JUST A PHASE SHE'S GOING THROUGH. I'M SURE THAT WITH SOME REST, SHE'LL BE BACK TO HER OLD SELF AGAIN.
BESIDES, THIS KIND OF THING HAPPENS ALL THE TIME. WHY, WHEN I WAS LITTLE, I WOULD WANDER AROUND AIMLESSLY FOR DAYS.
OH MY! WHO AM I? WHERE AM I?
YOU REALLY EXPECT US TO BELIEVE THAT?!
I WOULDN'T PUT IT PAST HER, THOUGH.
OH MY, I DO GET QUITE A KICK OUT OF SEEING MUTSUMI-CHAN LIKE THIS. BRINGS BACK SUCH WARM MEMORIES.

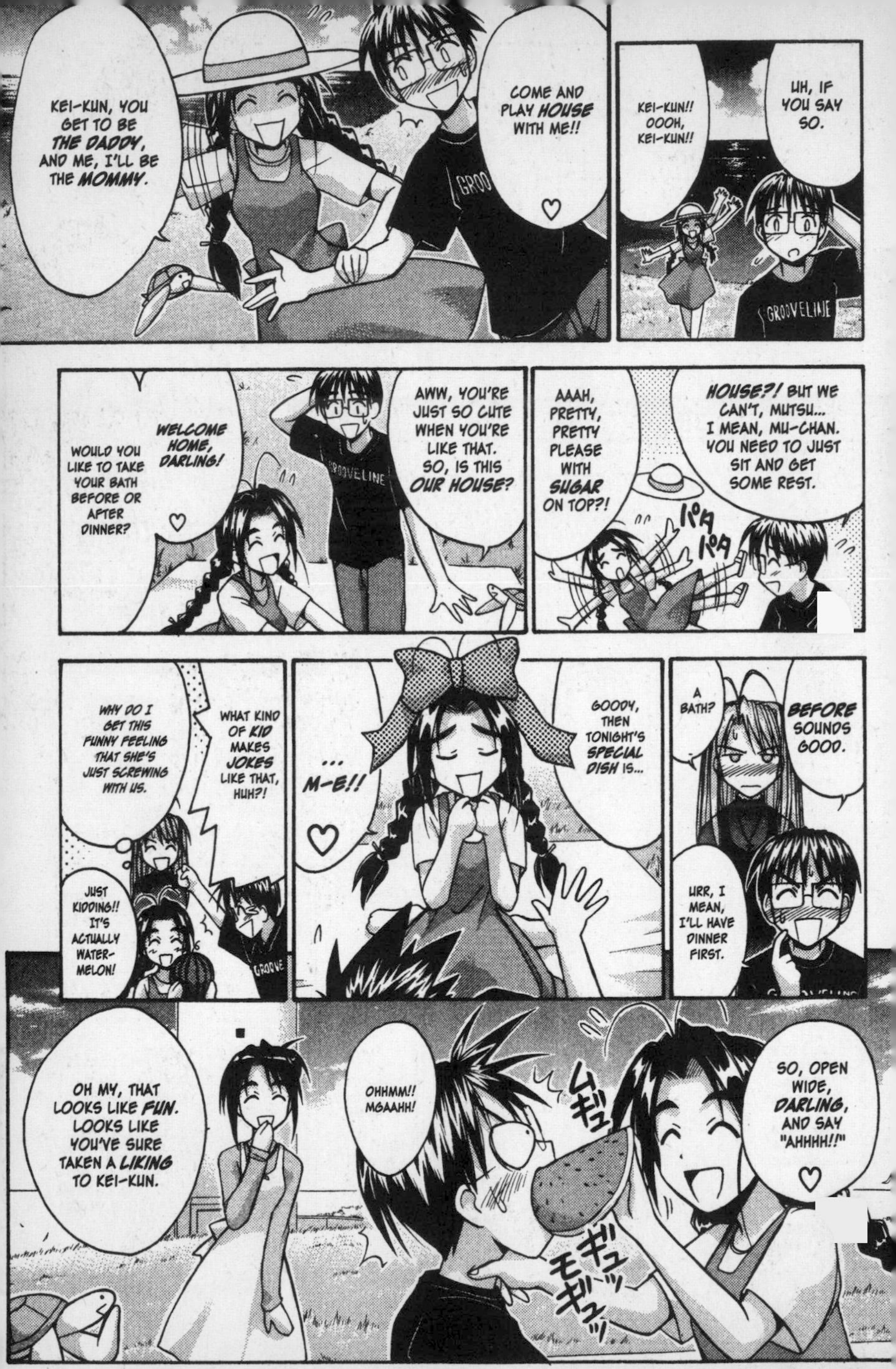
UH, IF YOU SAY SO.
KEI-KUN!! OOOH, KEI-KUN!!
COME AND PLAY HOUSE WITH ME!! ♥
KEI-KUN, YOU GET TO BE THE DADDY, AND ME, I'LL BE THE MOMMY.
GROOVELINE
HOUSE?! BUT WE CAN'T, MUTSU... I MEAN, MU-CHAN. YOU NEED TO JUST SIT AND GET SOME REST.
パタパタ
AAAH, PRETTY, PRETTY PLEASE WITH SUGAR ON TOP?!
AWW, YOU'RE JUST SO CUTE WHEN YOU'RE LIKE THAT. SO, IS THIS OUR HOUSE?
WELCOME HOME, DARLING!
WOULD YOU LIKE TO TAKE YOUR BATH BEFORE OR AFTER DINNER? ♥
BEFORE SOUNDS GOOD.
A BATH?
URR, I MEAN, I'LL HAVE DINNER FIRST.
GOODY, THEN TONIGHT'S SPECIAL DISH IS...
... M-E!! ♥
WHAT KIND OF KID MAKES JOKES LIKE THAT, HUH?!
WHY DO I GET THIS FUNNY FEELING THAT SHE'S JUST SCREWING WITH US.
JUST KIDDING!! IT'S ACTUALLY WATER-MELON!
SO, OPEN WIDE, DARLING, AND SAY "AHHHH!!" ♥
ムギュ
ギュッ
モギュッ
OHHMM!! MGAAHH!
OH MY, THAT LOOKS LIKE FUN. LOOKS LIKE YOU'VE SURE TAKEN A LIKING TO KEI-KUN.

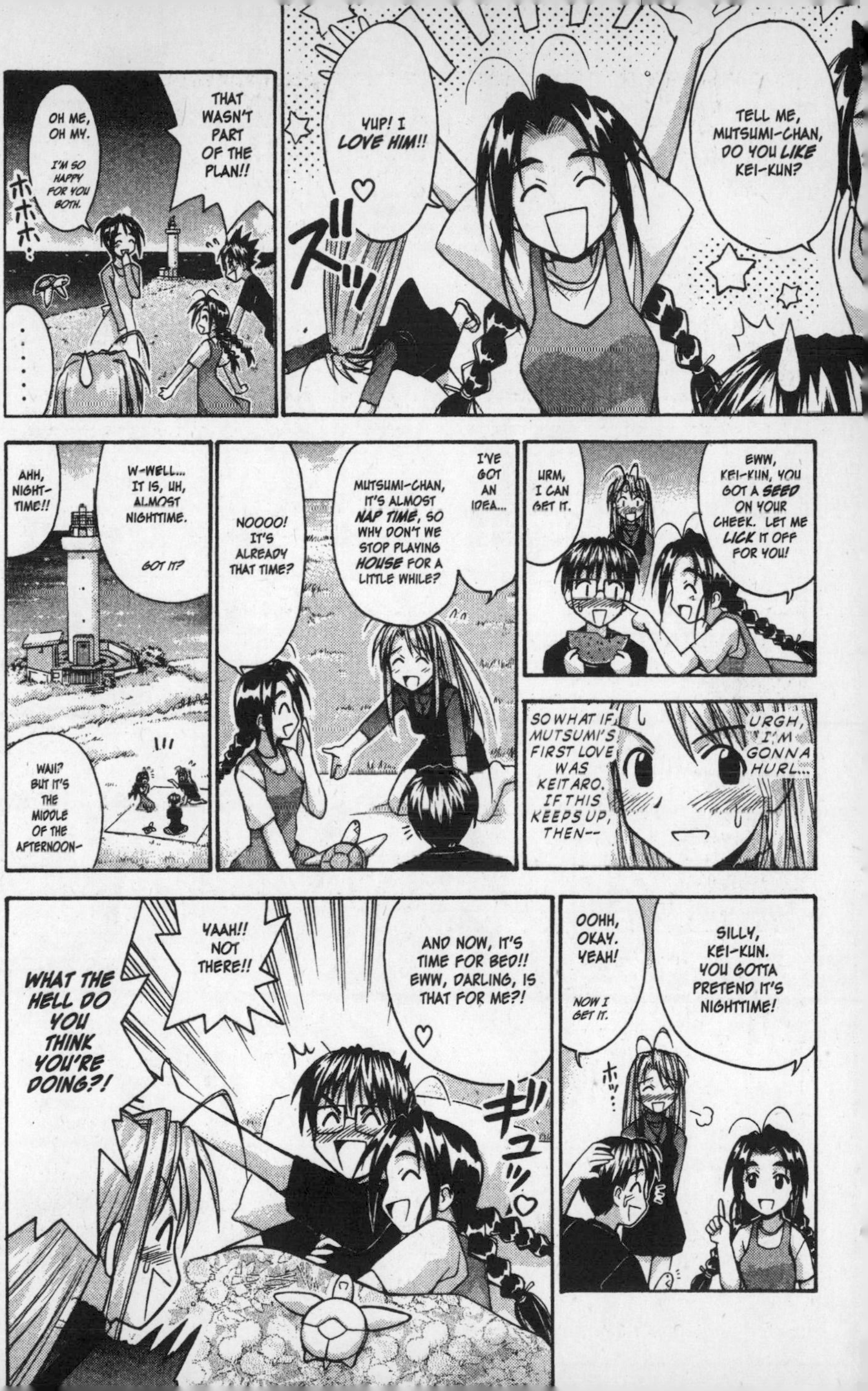
TELL ME, MUTSUMI-CHAN, DO YOU LIKE KEI-KUN?
YUP! I LOVE HIM!!
ズッ
THAT WASN'T PART OF THE PLAN!!
OH ME, OH MY.
I'M SO HAPPY FOR YOU BOTH.
ホホホ…
......
EWW, KEI-KUN, YOU GOT A SEED ON YOUR CHEEK. LET ME LICK IT OFF FOR YOU!
URM, I CAN GET IT.
URGH, I'M GONNA HURL...
SO WHAT IF MUTSUMI'S FIRST LOVE WAS KEITARO. IF THIS KEEPS UP, THEN--
I'VE GOT AN IDEA...
MUTSUMI-CHAN, IT'S ALMOST NAP TIME, SO WHY DON'T WE STOP PLAYING HOUSE FOR A LITTLE WHILE?
NOOOO! IT'S ALREADY THAT TIME?
W-WELL... IT IS, UH, ALMOST NIGHTTIME.
GOT IT?
AHH, NIGHT-TIME!!
WAIT? BUT IT'S THE MIDDLE OF THE AFTERNOON-
SILLY, KEI-KUN. YOU GOTTA PRETEND IT'S NIGHTTIME!
OOHH, OKAY. YEAH!
NOW I GET IT.
ホッ…
AND NOW, IT'S TIME FOR BED!! EWW, DARLING, IS THAT FOR ME?!
YAAH!! NOT THERE!!
WHAT THE HELL DO YOU THINK YOU'RE DOING?!
ギュッ

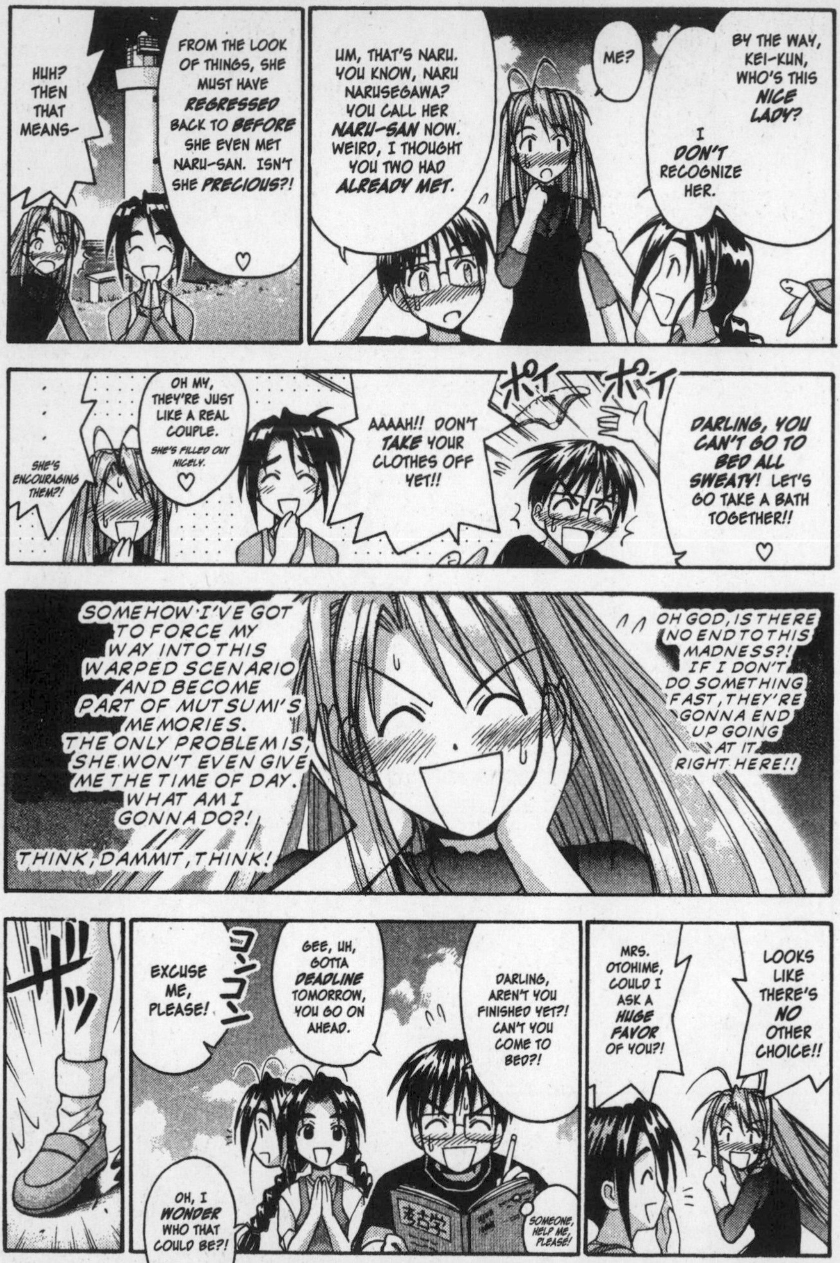

BY THE WAY, KEI-KUN, WHO'S THIS NICE LADY?
I DON'T RECOGNIZE HER.
ME?
UM, THAT'S NARU. YOU KNOW, NARU NARUSEGAWA? YOU CALL HER NARU-SAN NOW. WEIRD, I THOUGHT YOU TWO HAD ALREADY MET.
FROM THE LOOK OF THINGS, SHE MUST HAVE REGRESSED BACK TO BEFORE SHE EVEN MET NARU-SAN. ISN'T SHE PRECIOUS?!
HUH? THEN THAT MEANS-
DARLING, YOU CAN'T GO TO BED ALL SWEATY! LET'S GO TAKE A BATH TOGETHER!!
ポイ
ポイ
AAAAH!! DON'T TAKE YOUR CLOTHES OFF YET!!
OH MY, THEY'RE JUST LIKE A REAL COUPLE.
SHE'S FILLED OUT NICELY.
SHE'S ENCOURAGING THEM?!
OH GOD, IS THERE NO END TO THIS MADNESS?! IF I DON'T DO SOMETHING FAST, THEY'RE GONNA END UP GOING AT IT RIGHT HERE!!
SOMEHOW I'VE GOT TO FORCE MY WAY INTO THIS WARPED SCENARIO AND BECOME PART OF MUTSUMI'S MEMORIES. THE ONLY PROBLEM IS, SHE WON'T EVEN GIVE ME THE TIME OF DAY. WHAT AM I GONNA DO?!
THINK, DAMMIT, THINK!
LOOKS LIKE THERE'S NO OTHER CHOICE!!
MRS. OTOHIME, COULD I ASK A HUGE FAVOR OF YOU?!
DARLING, AREN'T YOU FINISHED YET?! CAN'T YOU COME TO BED?!
GEE, UH, GOTTA DEADLINE TOMORROW, YOU GO ON AHEAD.
コンコン
EXCUSE ME, PLEASE!
SOMEONE, HELP ME, PLEASE!
OH, I WONDER WHO THAT COULD BE?!
ザッ

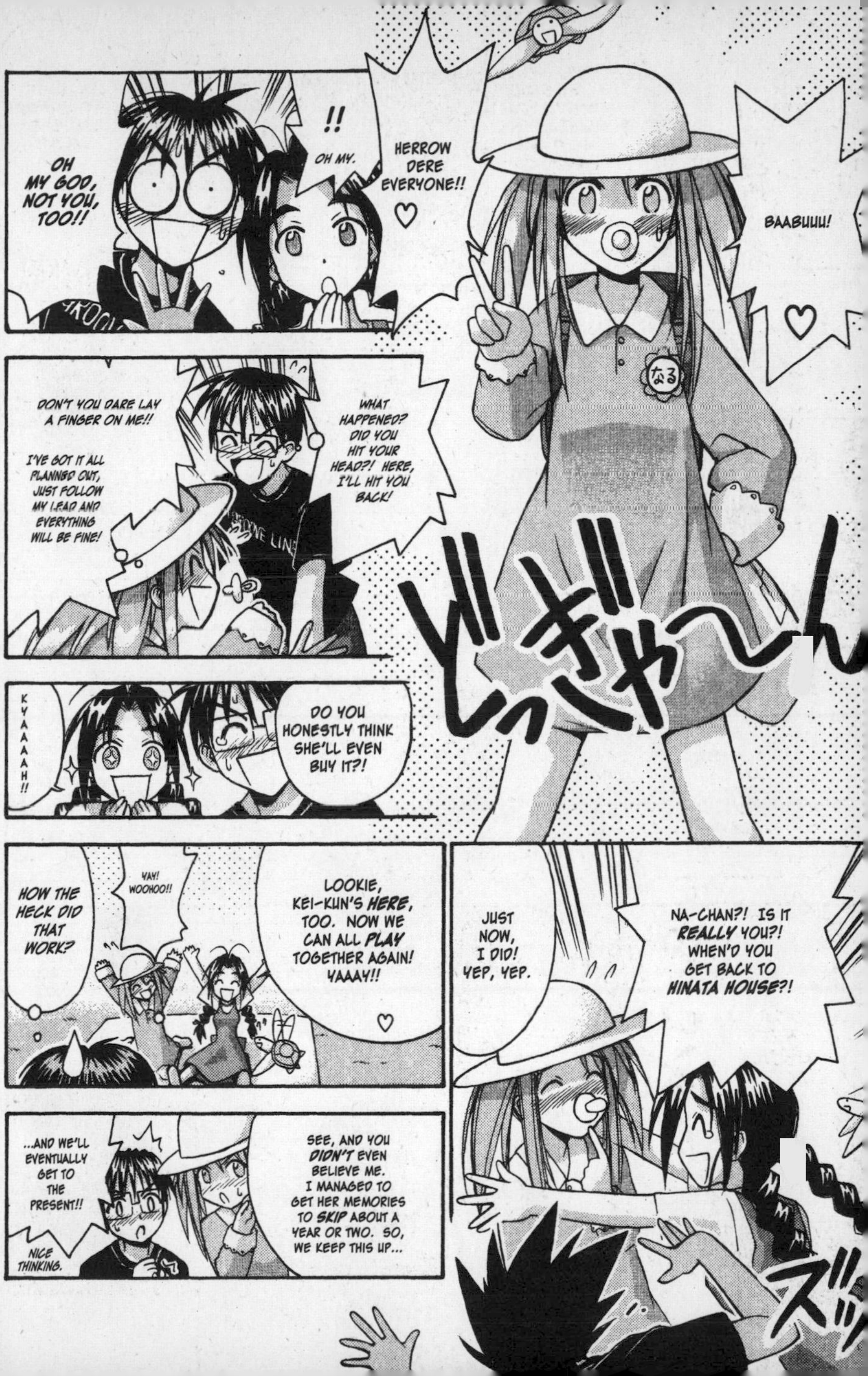
BAABUUU!
HERROW DERE EVERYONE!!
!!
OH MY.
OH MY GOD, NOT YOU, TOO!!
なる
WHAT HAPPENED? DID YOU HIT YOUR HEAD?! HERE, I'LL HIT YOU BACK!
DON'T YOU DARE LAY A FINGER ON ME!!
I'VE GOT IT ALL PLANNED OUT, JUST FOLLOW MY LEAD AND EVERYTHING WILL BE FINE!
DO YOU HONESTLY THINK SHE'LL EVEN BUY IT?!
KYAAAAAH!!
NA-CHAN?! IS IT REALLY YOU?! WHEN'D YOU GET BACK TO HINATA HOUSE?!
JUST NOW, I DID! YEP, YEP.
LOOKIE, KEI-KUN'S HERE, TOO. NOW WE CAN ALL PLAY TOGETHER AGAIN! YAAAY!!
YAY! WOOHOO!!
HOW THE HECK DID THAT WORK?
SEE, AND YOU DIDN'T EVEN BELIEVE ME. I MANAGED TO GET HER MEMORIES TO SKIP ABOUT A YEAR OR TWO. SO, WE KEEP THIS UP...
...AND WE'LL EVENTUALLY GET TO THE PRESENT!!
NICE THINKING.

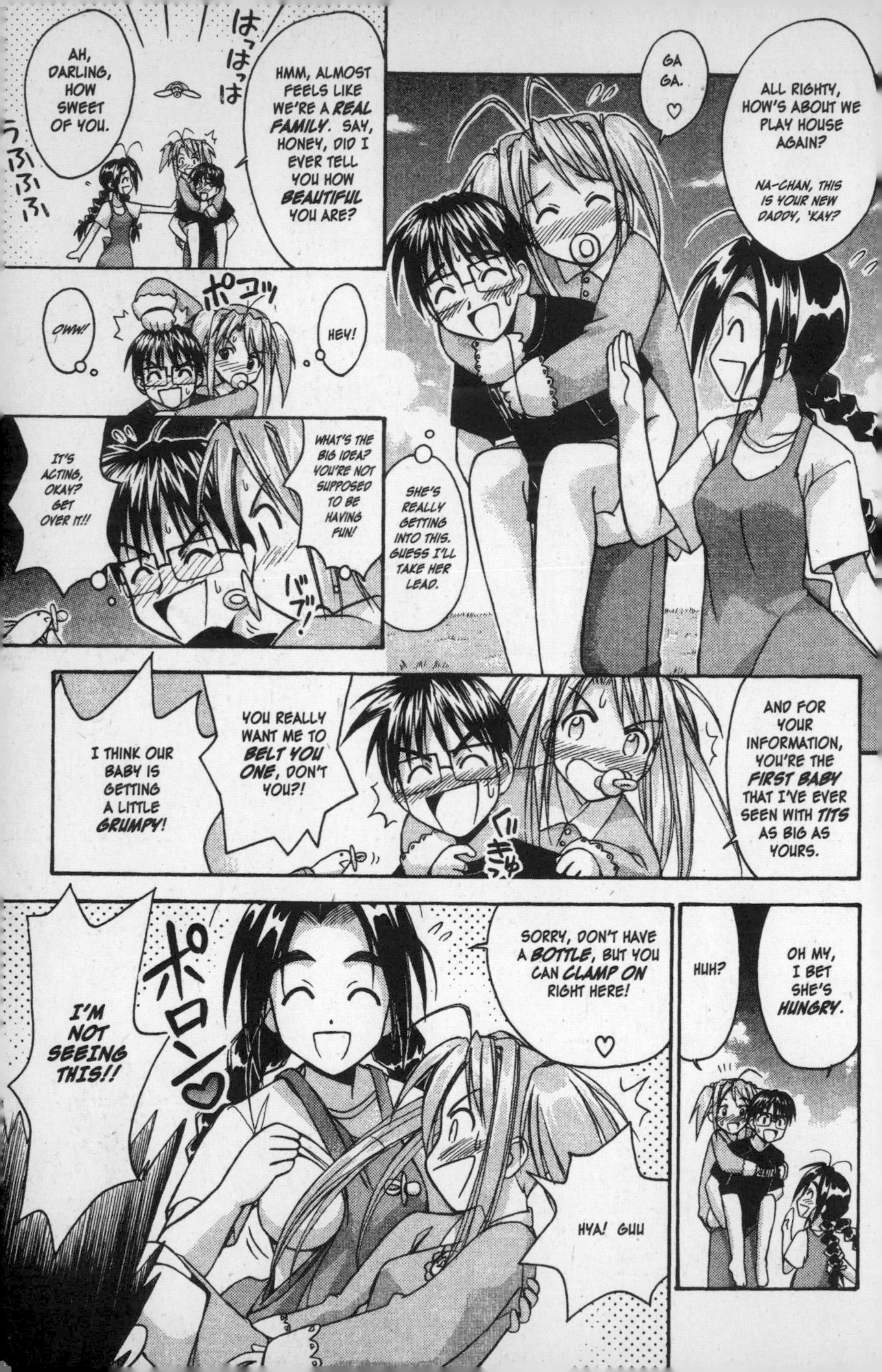

ALL RIGHTY, HOW'S ABOUT WE PLAY HOUSE AGAIN?
NA-CHAN, THIS IS YOUR NEW DADDY, 'KAY?
GA GA. ♥
SHE'S REALLY GETTING INTO THIS. GUESS I'LL TAKE HER LEAD.
はっはっは
HMM, ALMOST FEELS LIKE WE'RE A REAL FAMILY. SAY, HONEY, DID I EVER TELL YOU HOW BEAUTIFUL YOU ARE?
AH, DARLING, HOW SWEET OF YOU.
うふふふ
HEY!
ポコッ
OWW!
WHAT'S THE BIG IDEA? YOU'RE NOT SUPPOSED TO BE HAVING FUN!
IT'S ACTING, OKAY? GET OVER IT!!
バブ!
AND FOR YOUR INFORMATION, YOU'RE THE FIRST BABY THAT I'VE EVER SEEN WITH TITS AS BIG AS YOURS.
YOU REALLY WANT ME TO BELT YOU ONE, DON'T YOU?!
I THINK OUR BABY IS GETTING A LITTLE GRUMPY!
OH MY, I BET SHE'S HUNGRY.
HUH?
SORRY, DON'T HAVE A BOTTLE, BUT YOU CAN CLAMP ON RIGHT HERE!
♥
HYA! GUU
ポロン♥
I'M NOT SEEING THIS!!

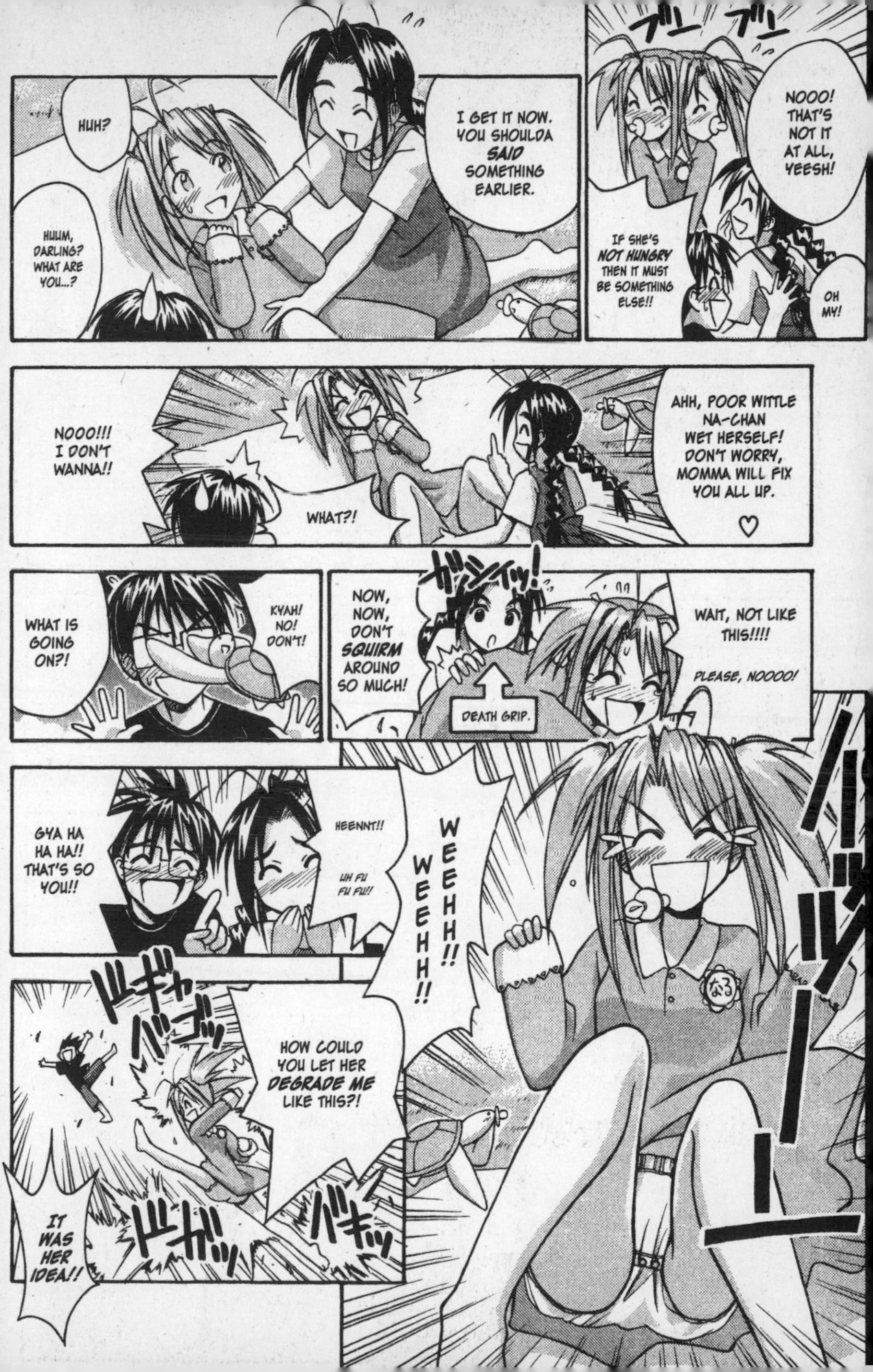
NOOO! THAT'S NOT IT AT ALL, YEESH!
IF SHE'S NOT HUNGRY THEN IT MUST BE SOMETHING ELSE!!
OH MY!
I GET IT NOW. YOU SHOULDA SAID SOMETHING EARLIER.
HUH?
HUUM, DARLING? WHAT ARE YOU...?
AHH, POOR WITTLE NA-CHAN WET HERSELF! DON'T WORRY, MOMMA WILL FIX YOU ALL UP. ♡
NOOO!!! I DON'T WANNA!!
WHAT?!
WAIT, NOT LIKE THIS!!!!
PLEASE, NOOOO!
NOW, NOW, DON'T SQUIRM AROUND SO MUCH!
DEATH GRIP.
KYAH! NO! DON'T!
WHAT IS GOING ON?!
WEEHH!! WEEHH!!
HEENNT!!
UH FU FU FU!!
GYA HA HA HA!! THAT'S SO YOU!!
HOW COULD YOU LET HER DEGRADE ME LIKE THIS?!
IT WAS HER IDEA!!

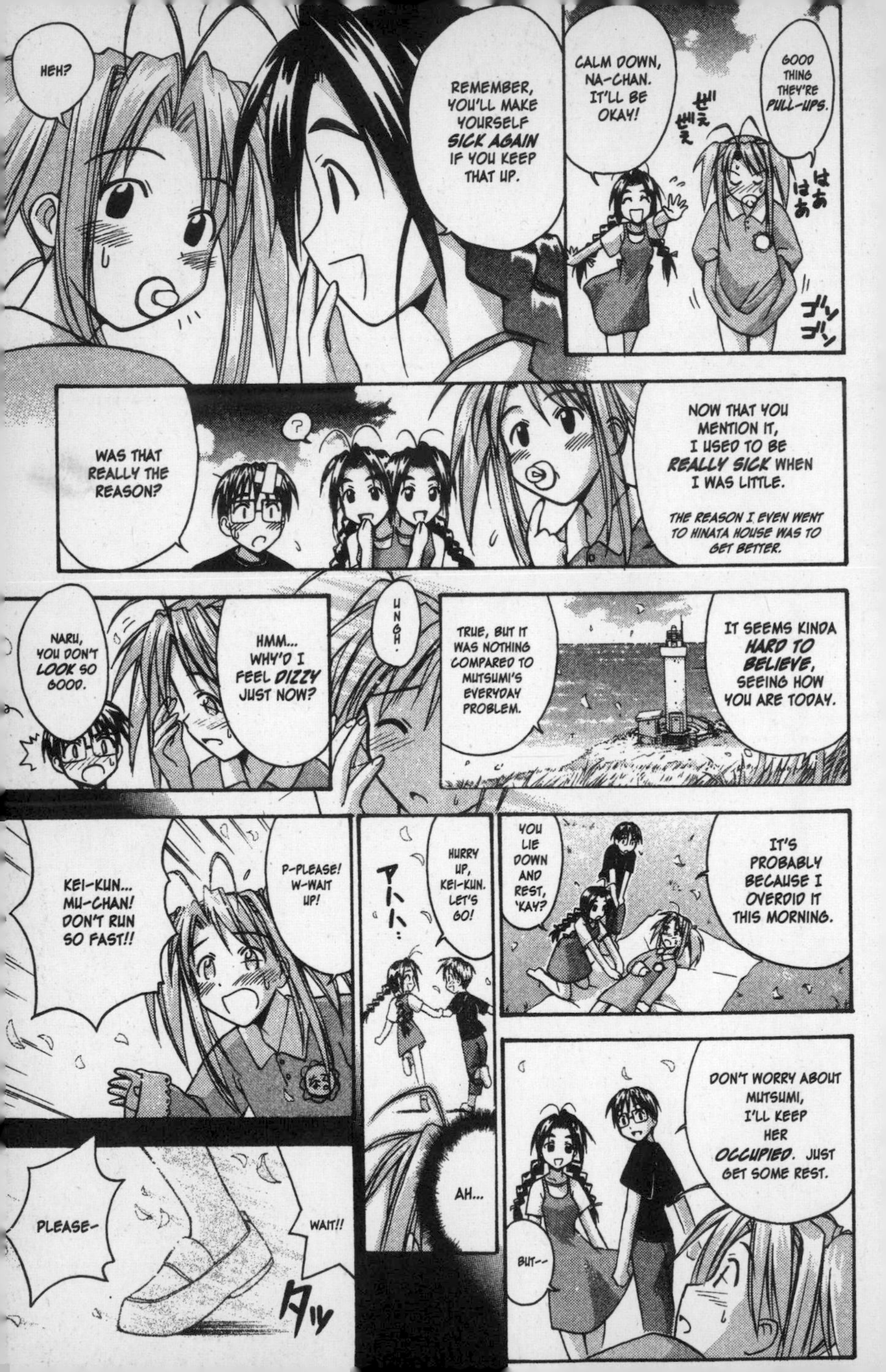
GOOD THING THEY'RE PULL-UPS.
ぜぇぜぇ
はぁはぁ
CALM DOWN, NA-CHAN. IT'LL BE OKAY!
ゴソゴソ
REMEMBER, YOU'LL MAKE YOURSELF SICK AGAIN IF YOU KEEP THAT UP.
HEH?
NOW THAT YOU MENTION IT, I USED TO BE REALLY SICK WHEN I WAS LITTLE.
THE REASON I EVEN WENT TO HINATA HOUSE WAS TO GET BETTER.
?
WAS THAT REALLY THE REASON?
IT SEEMS KINDA HARD TO BELIEVE, SEEING HOW YOU ARE TODAY.
TRUE, BUT IT WAS NOTHING COMPARED TO MUTSUMI'S EVERYDAY PROBLEM.
UNGH.
HMM... WHY'D I FEEL DIZZY JUST NOW?
NARU, YOU DON'T LOOK SO GOOD.
IT'S PROBABLY BECAUSE I OVERDID IT THIS MORNING.
YOU LIE DOWN AND REST, 'KAY?
DON'T WORRY ABOUT MUTSUMI, I'LL KEEP HER OCCUPIED. JUST GET SOME REST.
BUT--
HURRY UP, KEI-KUN. LET'S GO!
アハハ...
AH...
P-PLEASE! W-WAIT UP!
KEI-KUN... MU-CHAN! DON'T RUN SO FAST!!
WAIT!!
PLEASE-
タッ

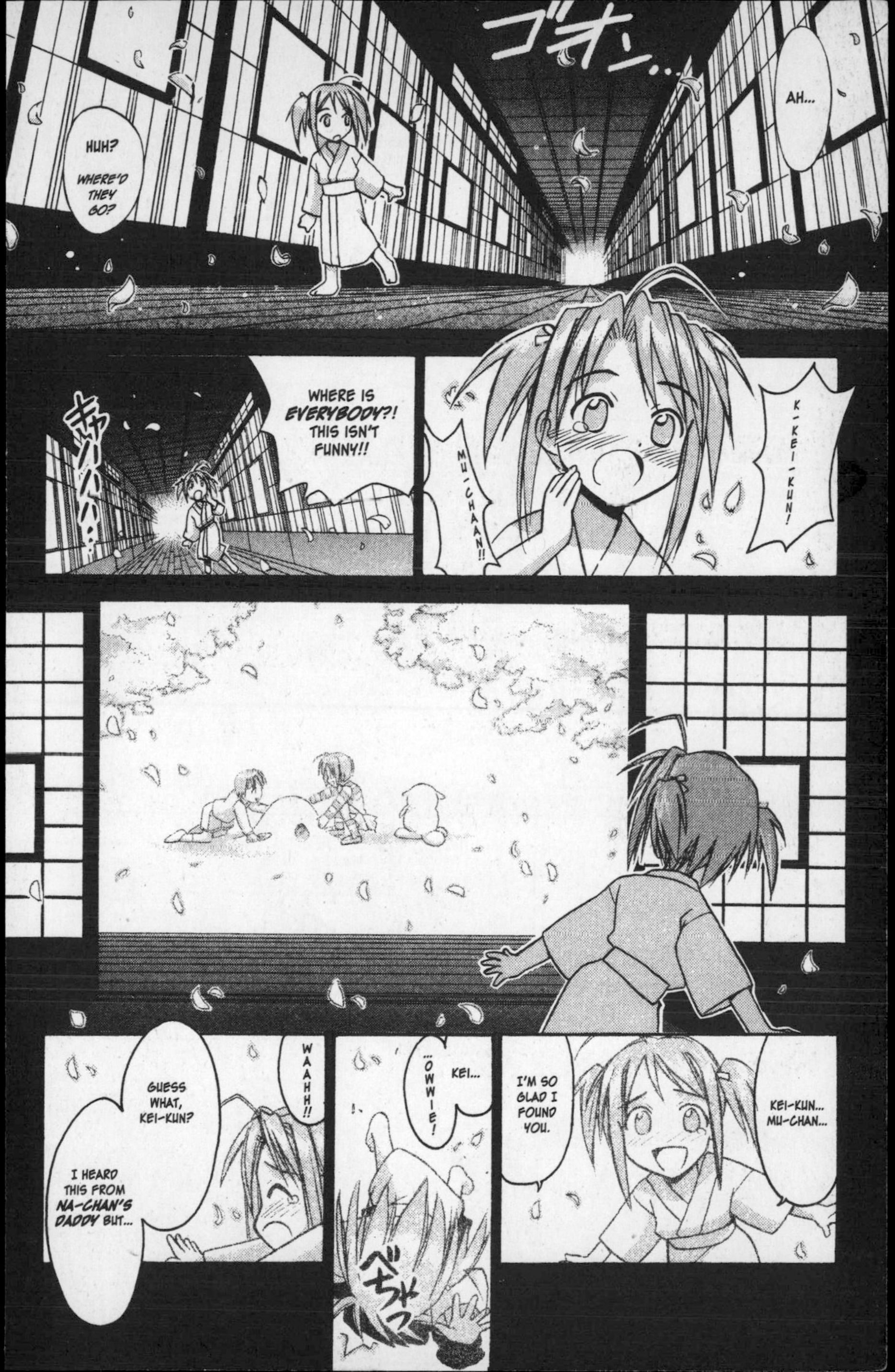
AH...
HUH? WHERE'D THEY GO?
K-KEI-KUN!
MU-CHAAN!!
WHERE IS EVERYBODY?! THIS ISN'T FUNNY!!
KEI-KUN... MU-CHAN...
I'M SO GLAD I FOUND YOU.
KEI...
...OWWIE!
WAAHH!!
GUESS WHAT, KEI-KUN?
I HEARD THIS FROM NA-CHAN'S DADDY BUT...

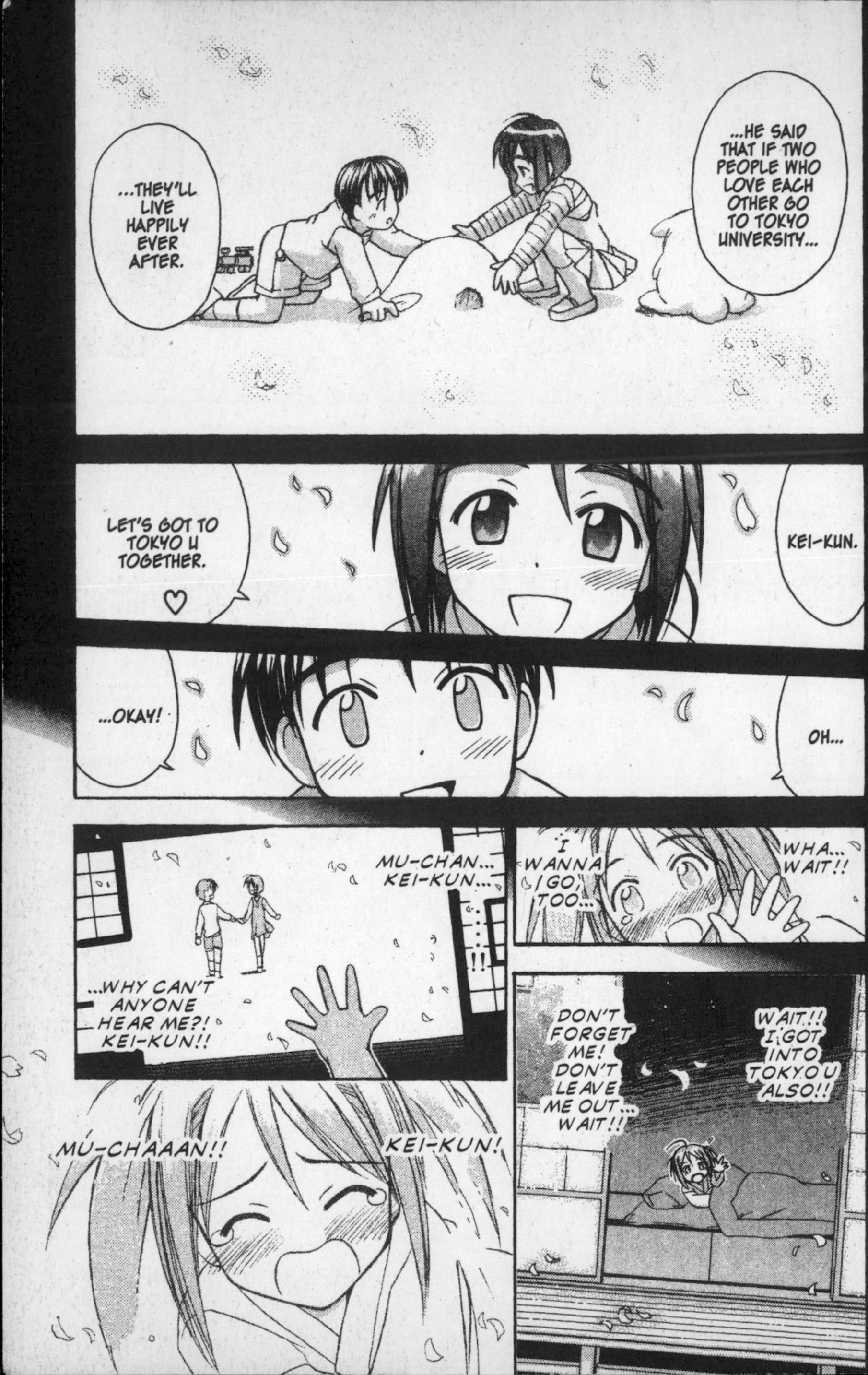
...HE SAID THAT IF TWO PEOPLE WHO LOVE EACH OTHER GO TO TOKYO UNIVERSITY...
...THEY'LL LIVE HAPPILY EVER AFTER.
KEI-KUN.
LET'S GOT TO TOKYO U TOGETHER. ♡
OH...
...OKAY!
WHA... WAIT!!
I WANNA GO, TOO...
MU-CHAN... KEI-KUN...
!!
...WHY CAN'T ANYONE HEAR ME?! KEI-KUN!!
WAIT!! I GOT INTO TOKYO U ALSO!!
DON'T FORGET ME! DON'T LEAVE ME OUT... WAIT!!
KEI-KUN!
MÚ-CHAAAN!!

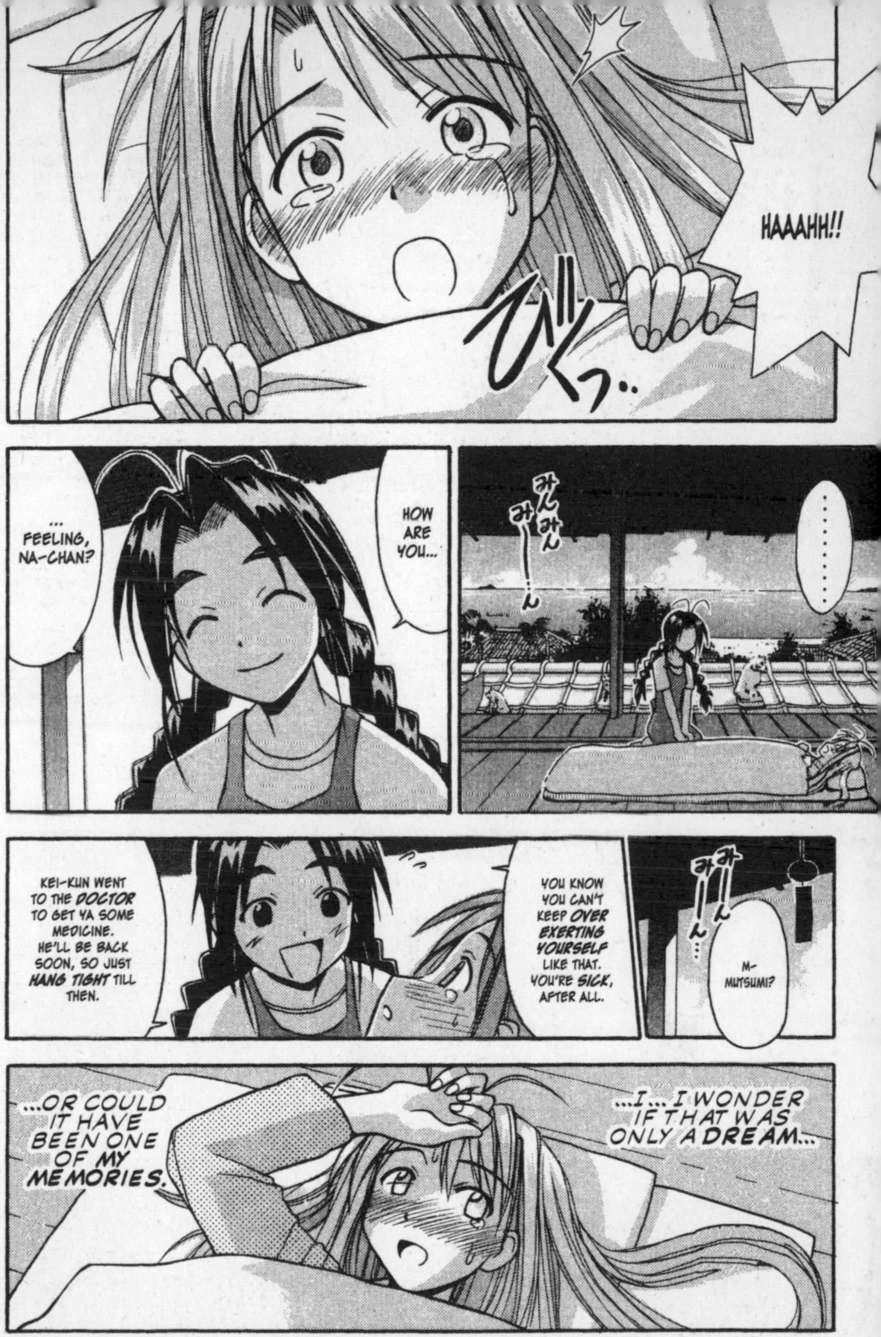
HAAAHH!!
ひくっ..
......
みんみんみーーん
HOW ARE YOU...
... FEELING, NA-CHAN?
M-MUTSUMI?
みーんみーん…
YOU KNOW YOU CAN'T KEEP OVER EXERTING YOURSELF LIKE THAT. YOU'RE SICK, AFTER ALL.
KEI-KUN WENT TO THE DOCTOR TO GET YA SOME MEDICINE. HE'LL BE BACK SOON, SO JUST HANG TIGHT TILL THEN.
...I... I WONDER IF THAT WAS ONLY A DREAM...
...OR COULD IT HAVE BEEN ONE OF MY MEMORIES.

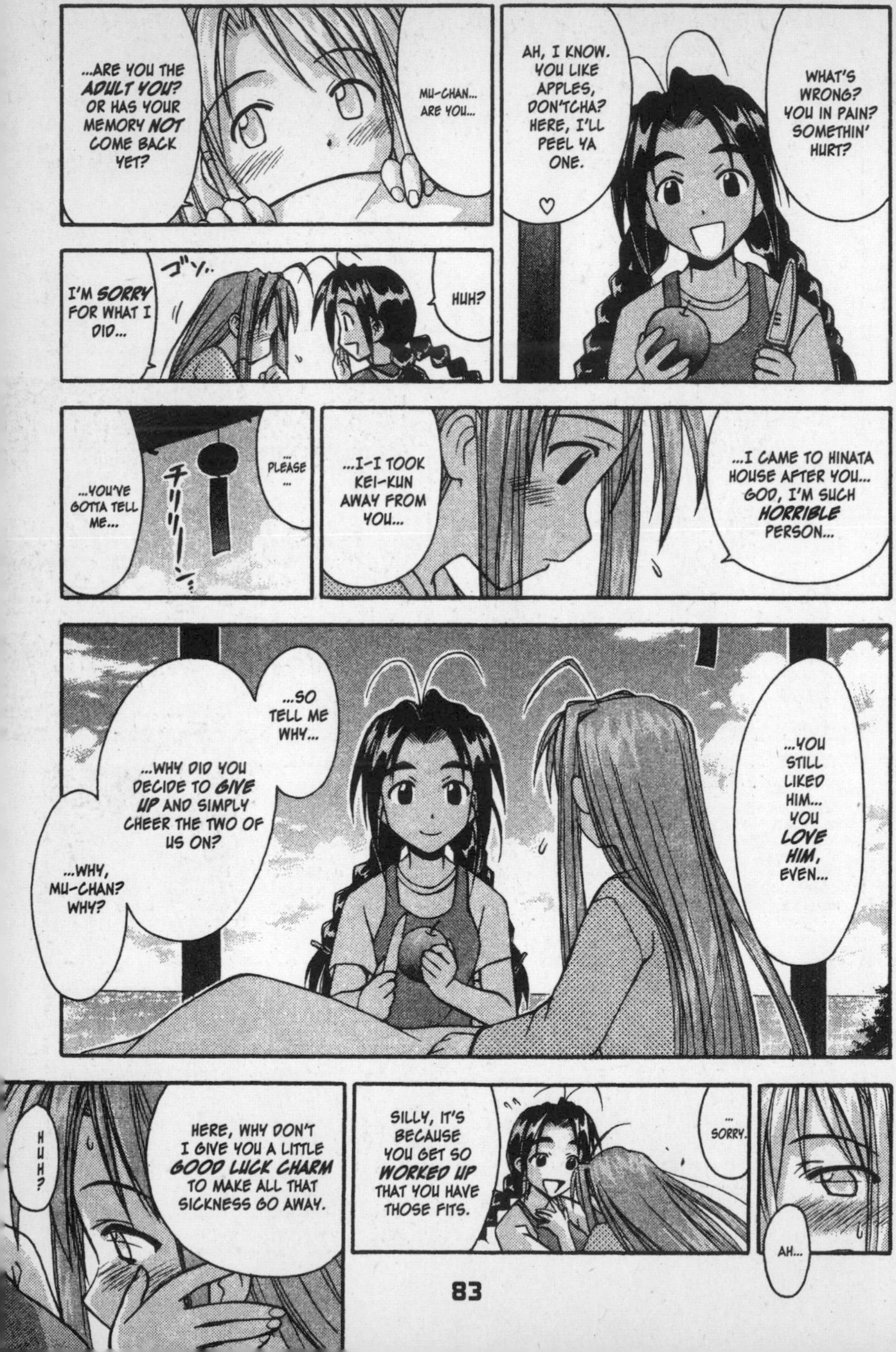
WHAT'S WRONG? YOU IN PAIN? SOMETHIN' HURT?
AH, I KNOW. YOU LIKE APPLES, DON'TCHA? HERE, I'LL PEEL YA ONE. ♡
MU-CHAN... ARE YOU...
...ARE YOU THE *ADULT YOU?* OR HAS YOUR MEMORY *NOT* COME BACK YET?
HUH?
ゴソ..
I'M *SORRY* FOR WHAT I DID...
...I CAME TO HINATA HOUSE AFTER YOU... GOD, I'M SUCH *HORRIBLE* PERSON...
...I-I TOOK KEI-KUN AWAY FROM YOU...
...PLEASE...
チリリーン
...YOU'VE GOTTA TELL ME...
...YOU STILL LIKED HIM... YOU *LOVE HIM,* EVEN...
...SO TELL ME WHY...
...WHY DID YOU DECIDE TO *GIVE UP* AND SIMPLY CHEER THE TWO OF US ON?
...WHY, MU-CHAN? WHY?
AH...
...SORRY.
SILLY, IT'S BECAUSE YOU GET SO *WORKED UP* THAT YOU HAVE THOSE FITS.
HERE, WHY DON'T I GIVE YOU A LITTLE *GOOD LUCK CHARM* TO MAKE ALL THAT SICKNESS GO AWAY.
HUH?

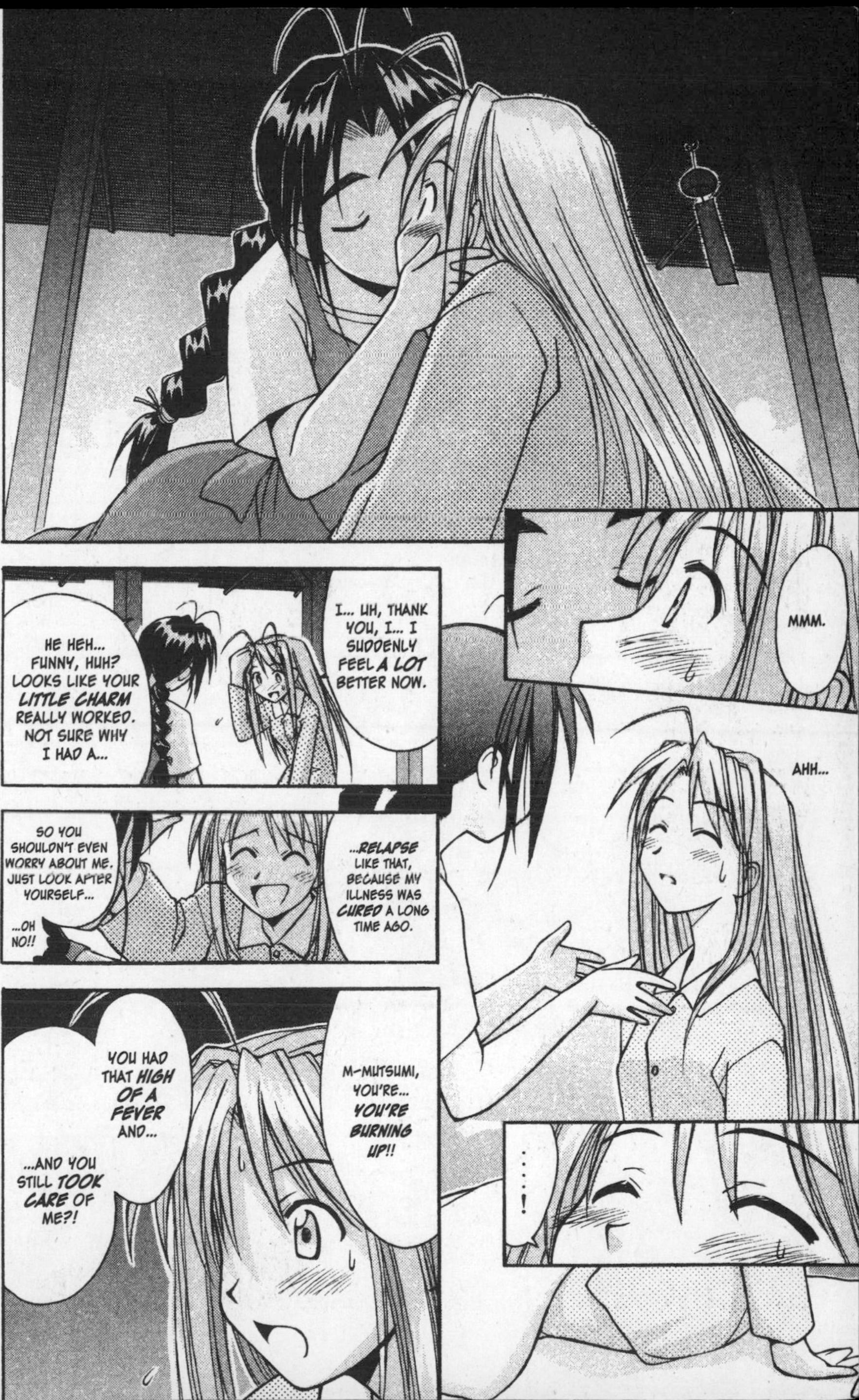
MMM.
AHH...
I... UH, THANK YOU, I... I SUDDENLY FEEL A LOT BETTER NOW.
HE HEH... FUNNY, HUH? LOOKS LIKE YOUR LITTLE CHARM REALLY WORKED. NOT SURE WHY I HAD A...
...RELAPSE LIKE THAT, BECAUSE MY ILLNESS WAS CURED A LONG TIME AGO.
SO YOU SHOULDN'T EVEN WORRY ABOUT ME. JUST LOOK AFTER YOURSELF...
...OH NO!!
....!
M-MUTSUMI, YOU'RE... YOU'RE BURNING UP!!
YOU HAD THAT HIGH OF A FEVER AND...
...AND YOU STILL TOOK CARE OF ME?!

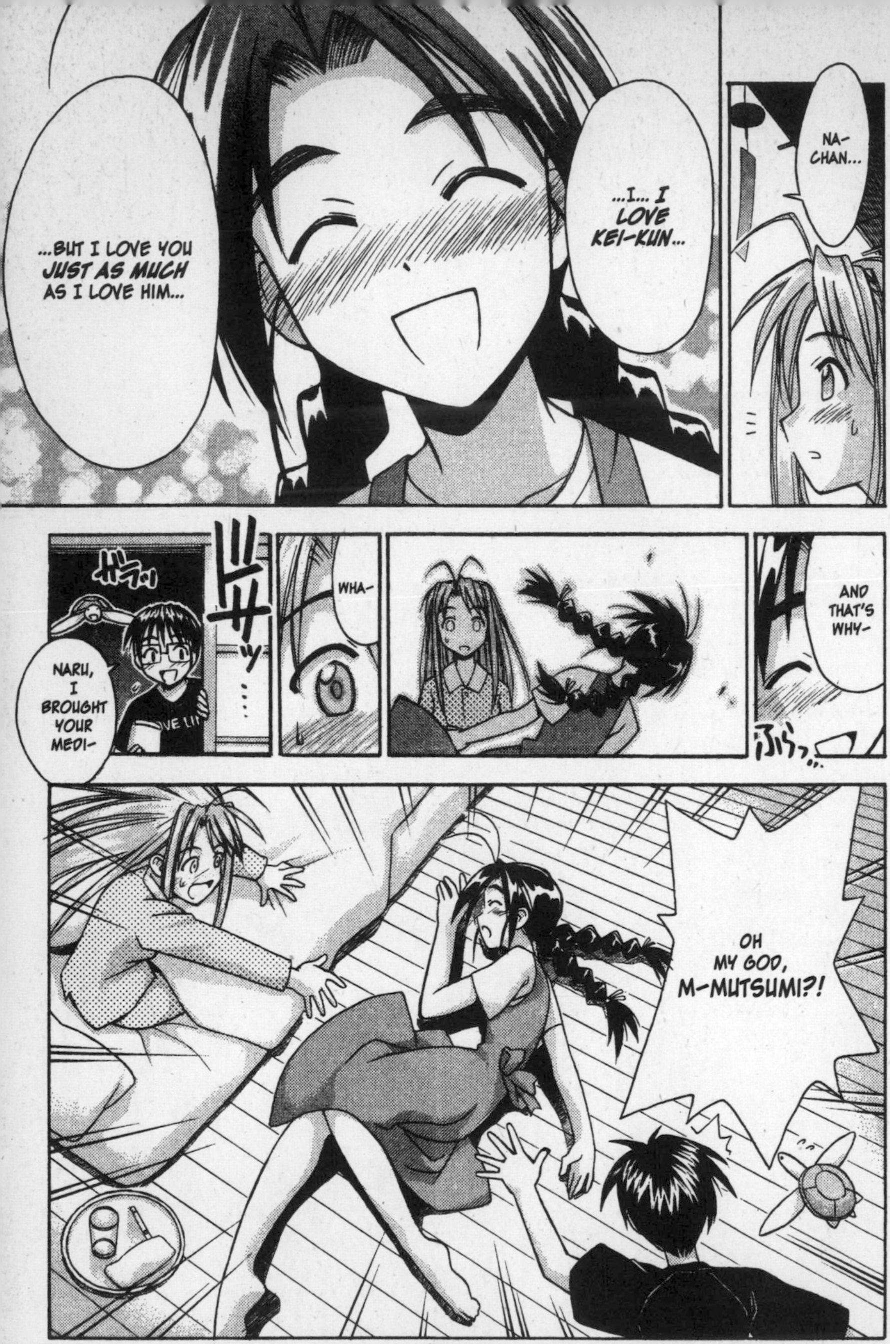
NA-CHAN...
...I... I LOVE KEI-KUN...
...BUT I LOVE YOU JUST AS MUCH AS I LOVE HIM...
AND THAT'S WHY-
ふらっ...
WHA-
NARU, I BROUGHT YOUR MEDI-
OH MY GOD, M-MUTSUMI?!

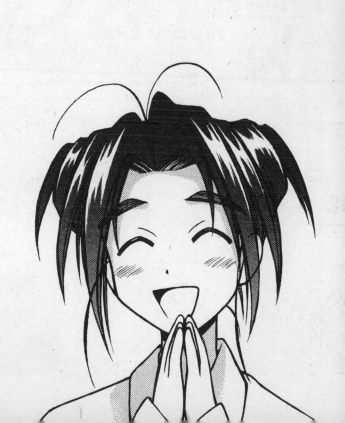

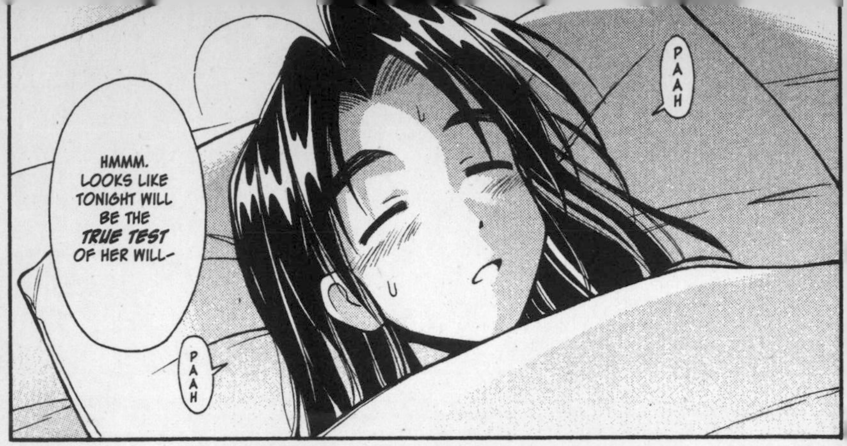
PAAH
HMMM. LOOKS LIKE TONIGHT WILL BE THE TRUE TEST OF HER WILL-
PAAH

Love Hina

HINATA.83 For Whom the Wedding Bell Tolls

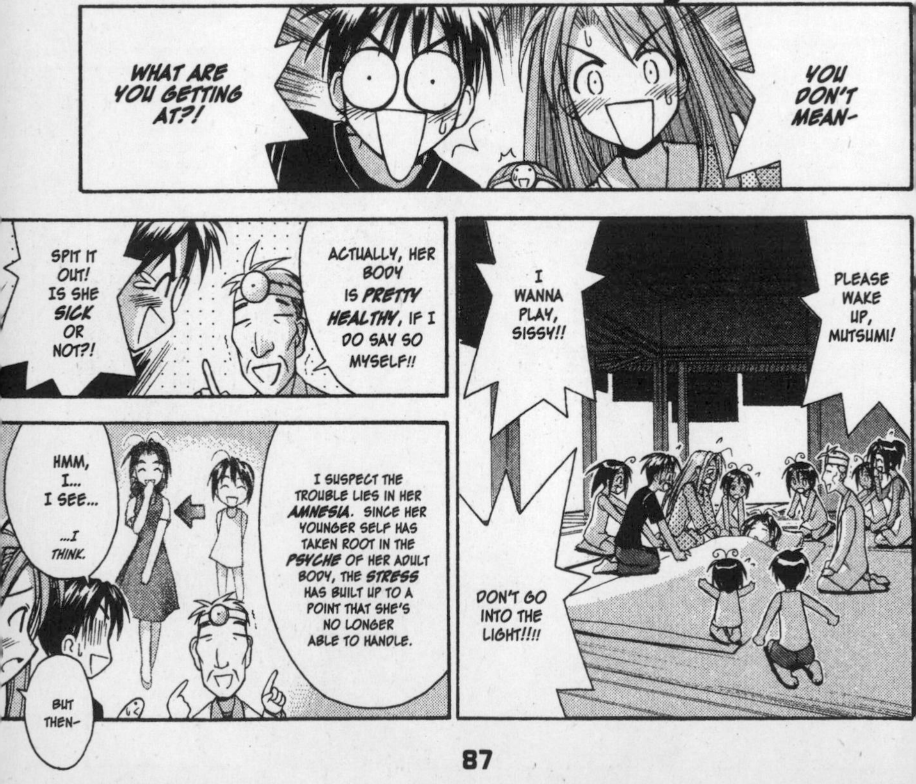
YOU DON'T MEAN-
WHAT ARE YOU GETTING AT?!
PLEASE WAKE UP, MUTSUMI!
I WANNA PLAY, SISSY!!
DON'T GO INTO THE LIGHT!!!!
ACTUALLY, HER BODY IS PRETTY HEALTHY, IF I DO SAY SO MYSELF!!
SPIT IT OUT! IS SHE SICK OR NOT?!
I SUSPECT THE TROUBLE LIES IN HER AMNESIA. SINCE HER YOUNGER SELF HAS TAKEN ROOT IN THE PSYCHE OF HER ADULT BODY, THE STRESS HAS BUILT UP TO A POINT THAT SHE'S NO LONGER ABLE TO HANDLE.
HMM, I... I SEE...
...I THINK.
BUT THEN-

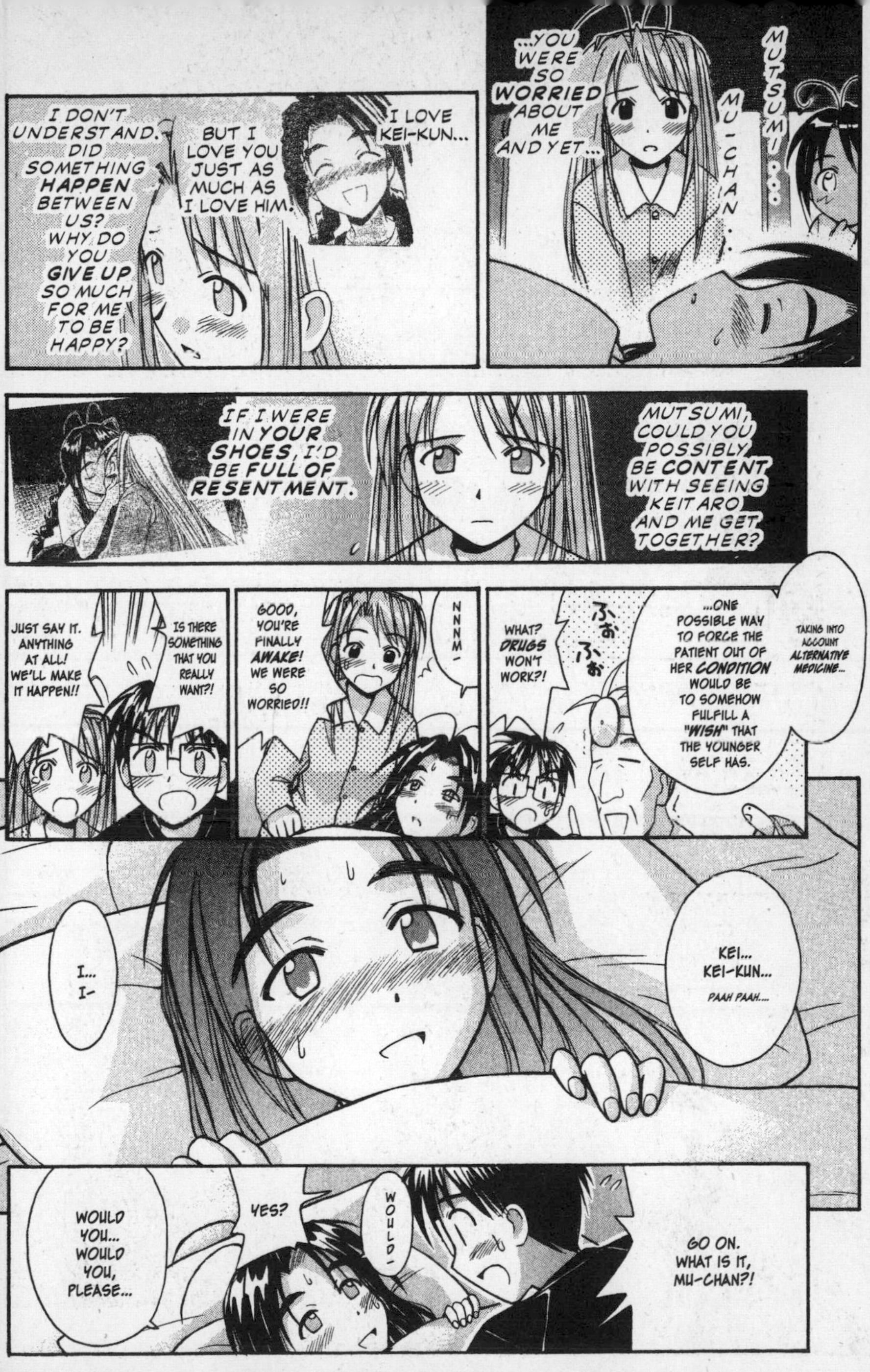
MUTSUMI... MU-CHAN...
...YOU WERE SO WORRIED ABOUT ME AND YET...
I LOVE KEI-KUN...
BUT I LOVE YOU JUST AS MUCH AS I LOVE HIM.
I DON'T UNDERSTAND. DID SOMETHING HAPPEN BETWEEN US? WHY DO YOU GIVE UP SO MUCH FOR ME TO BE HAPPY?
MUTSUMI, COULD YOU POSSIBLY BE CONTENT WITH SEEING KEITARO AND ME GET TOGETHER?
IF I WERE IN YOUR SHOES, I'D BE FULL OF RESENTMENT.
TAKING INTO ACCOUNT ALTERNATIVE MEDICINE...
...ONE POSSIBLE WAY TO FORCE THE PATIENT OUT OF HER CONDITION WOULD BE TO SOMEHOW FULFILL A "WISH" THAT THE YOUNGER SELF HAS.
ふぉ ふぉ
WHAT? DRUGS WON'T WORK?!
NNNM-
GOOD, YOU'RE FINALLY AWAKE! WE WERE SO WORRIED!!
IS THERE SOMETHING THAT YOU REALLY WANT?!
JUST SAY IT. ANYTHING AT ALL! WE'LL MAKE IT HAPPEN!!
KEI... KEI-KUN...
PAAH PAAH....
I... I-
GO ON. WHAT IS IT, MU-CHAN?!
WOULD-
YES?
WOULD YOU... WOULD YOU, PLEASE...

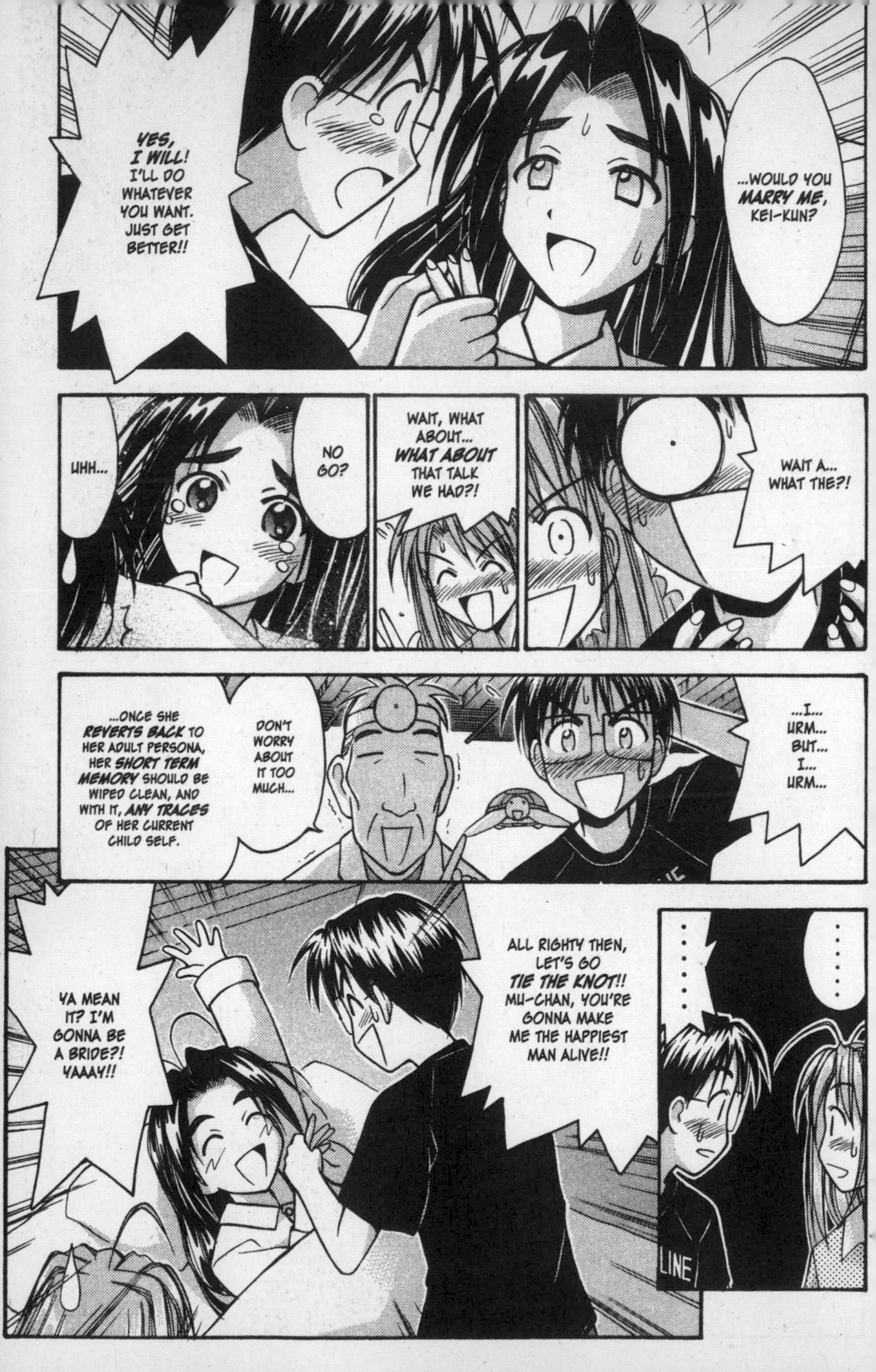
...WOULD YOU MARRY ME, KEI-KUN?
YES, I WILL! I'LL DO WHATEVER YOU WANT. JUST GET BETTER!!
WAIT A... WHAT THE?!
WAIT, WHAT ABOUT... WHAT ABOUT THAT TALK WE HAD?!
NO GO?
UHH...
...I... URM... BUT... I... URM...
DON'T WORRY ABOUT IT TOO MUCH...
...ONCE SHE REVERTS BACK TO HER ADULT PERSONA, HER SHORT TERM MEMORY SHOULD BE WIPED CLEAN, AND WITH IT, ANY TRACES OF HER CURRENT CHILD SELF.
.....
.....
LINE
ALL RIGHTY THEN, LET'S GO TIE THE KNOT!! MU-CHAN, YOU'RE GONNA MAKE ME THE HAPPIEST MAN ALIVE!!
YA MEAN IT? I'M GONNA BE A BRIDE?! YAAAY!!

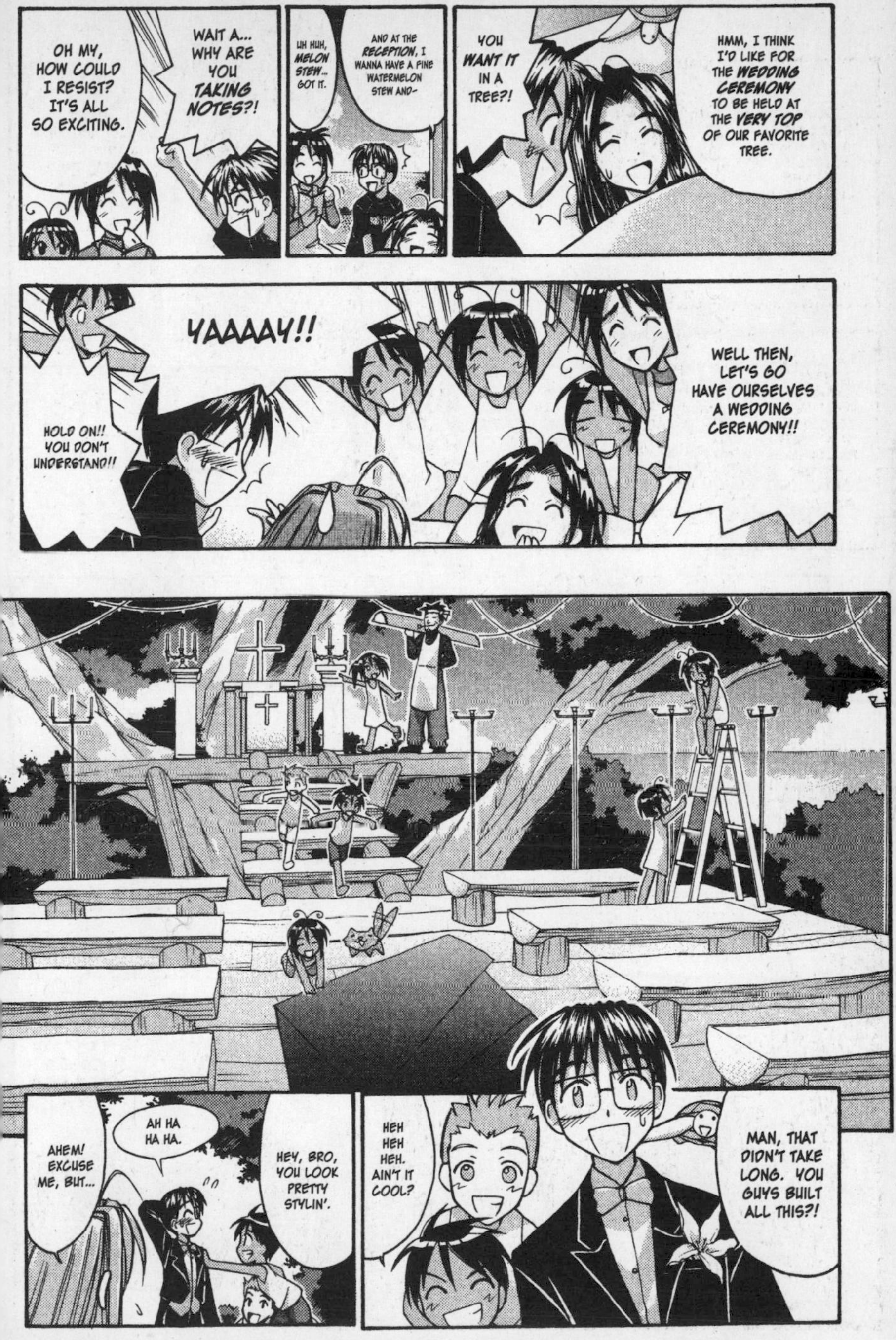
HMM, I THINK I'D LIKE FOR THE WEDDING CEREMONY TO BE HELD AT THE VERY TOP OF OUR FAVORITE TREE.
YOU WANT IT IN A TREE?!
AND AT THE RECEPTION, I WANNA HAVE A FINE WATERMELON STEW AND-
UH HUH, MELON STEW... GOT IT.
WAIT A... WHY ARE YOU TAKING NOTES?!
OH MY, HOW COULD I RESIST? IT'S ALL SO EXCITING.
WELL THEN, LET'S GO HAVE OURSELVES A WEDDING CEREMONY!!
YAAAAY!!
HOLD ON!! YOU DON'T UNDERSTAND!!
MAN, THAT DIDN'T TAKE LONG. YOU GUYS BUILT ALL THIS?!
HEH HEH HEH. AIN'T IT COOL?
HEY, BRO, YOU LOOK PRETTY STYLIN'.
AH HA HA HA.
AHEM! EXCUSE ME, BUT...

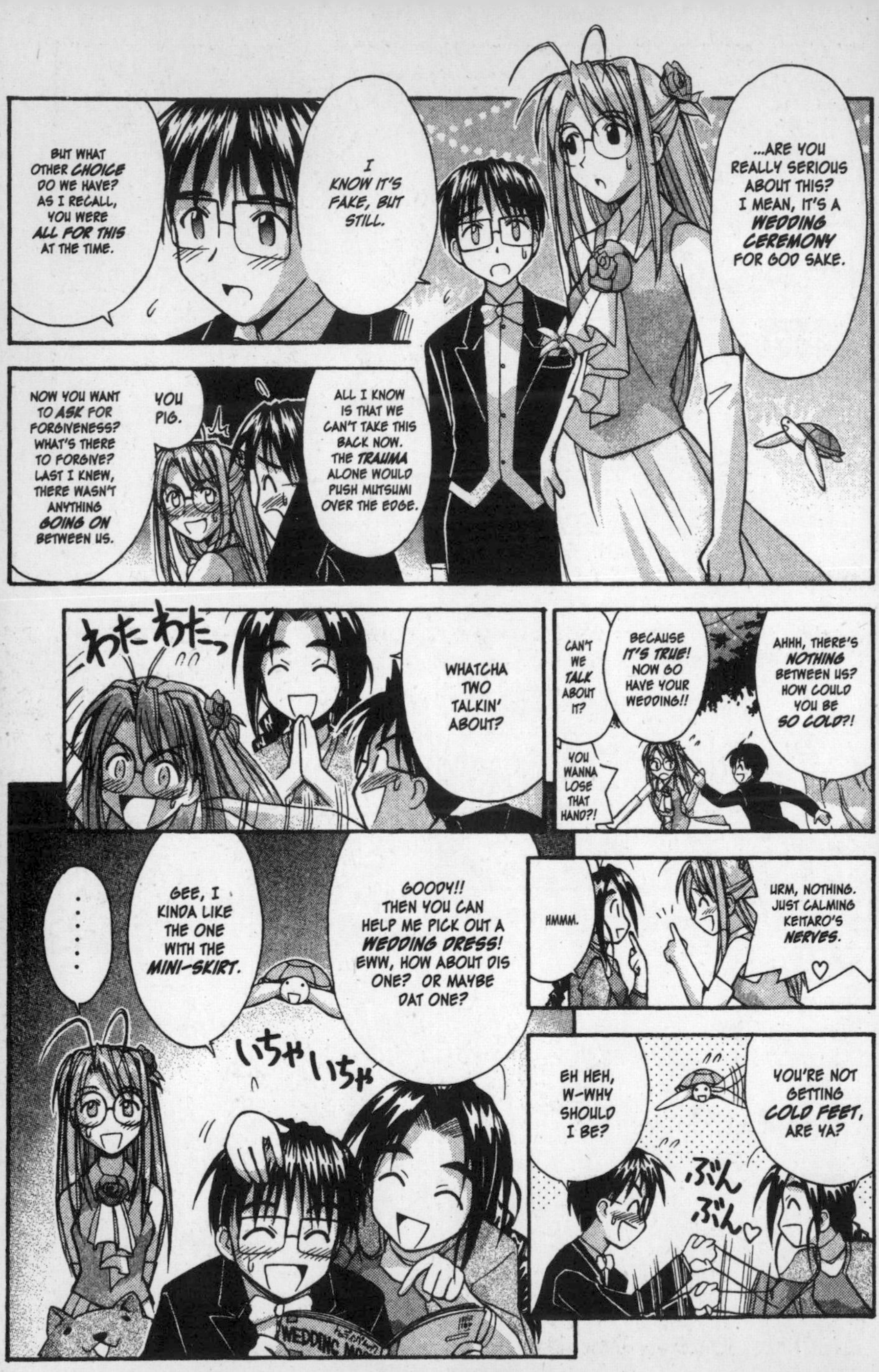
...ARE YOU REALLY SERIOUS ABOUT THIS? I MEAN, IT'S A WEDDING CEREMONY FOR GOD SAKE.
I KNOW IT'S FAKE, BUT STILL.
BUT WHAT OTHER CHOICE DO WE HAVE? AS I RECALL, YOU WERE ALL FOR THIS AT THE TIME.
ALL I KNOW IS THAT WE CAN'T TAKE THIS BACK NOW. THE TRAUMA ALONE WOULD PUSH MUTSUMI OVER THE EDGE.
YOU PIG.
NOW YOU WANT TO ASK FOR FORGIVENESS? WHAT'S THERE TO FORGIVE? LAST I KNEW, THERE WASN'T ANYTHING GOING ON BETWEEN US.
AHHH, THERE'S NOTHING BETWEEN US? HOW COULD YOU BE SO COLD?!
BECAUSE IT'S TRUE! NOW GO HAVE YOUR WEDDING!!
CAN'T WE TALK ABOUT IT?
YOU WANNA LOSE THAT HAND?!
WHATCHA TWO TALKIN' ABOUT?
わたわたっ
URM, NOTHING. JUST CALMING KEITARO'S NERVES.
HMMM.
YOU'RE NOT GETTING COLD FEET, ARE YA?
EH HEH, W-WHY SHOULD I BE?
ぶんぶん
GOODY!! THEN YOU CAN HELP ME PICK OUT A WEDDING DRESS! EWW, HOW ABOUT DIS ONE? OR MAYBE DAT ONE?
GEE, I KINDA LIKE THE ONE WITH THE MINI-SKIRT.
......
いちゃいちゃ

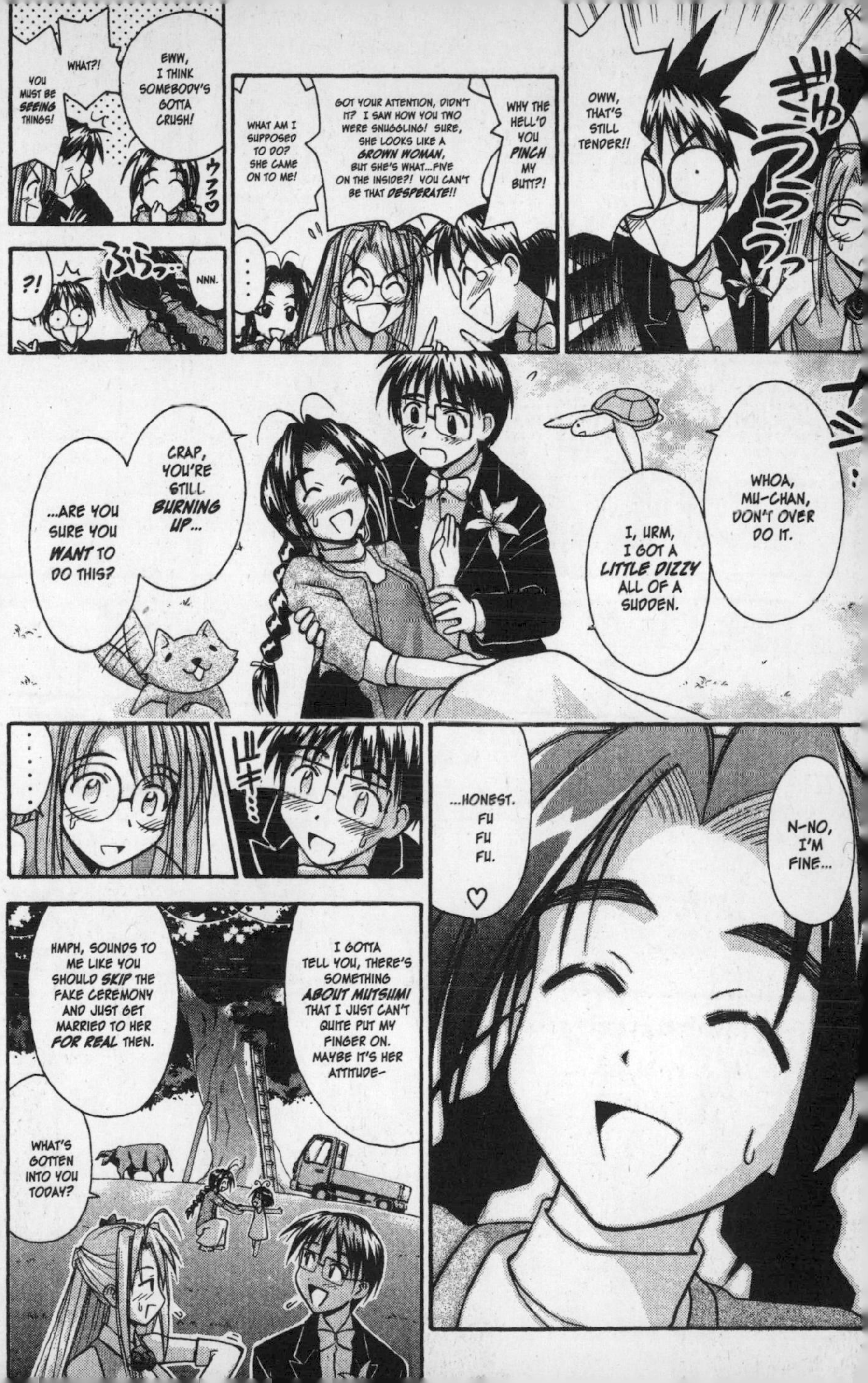
OWW, THAT'S STILL TENDER!!
WHY THE HELL'D YOU PINCH MY BUTT?!
GOT YOUR ATTENTION, DIDN'T IT? I SAW HOW YOU TWO WERE SNUGGLING! SURE, SHE LOOKS LIKE A GROWN WOMAN, BUT SHE'S WHAT...FIVE ON THE INSIDE?! YOU CAN'T BE THAT DESPERATE!!
WHAT AM I SUPPOSED TO DO? SHE CAME ON TO ME!
...
EWW, I THINK SOMEBODY'S GOTTA CRUSH!
WHAT?!
YOU MUST BE SEEING THINGS!
ウフフ♡
NNN.
ふらっ
?!
WHOA, MU-CHAN, DON'T OVER DO IT.
I, URM, I GOT A LITTLE DIZZY ALL OF A SUDDEN.
CRAP, YOU'RE STILL BURNING UP...
...ARE YOU SURE YOU WANT TO DO THIS?
N-NO, I'M FINE...
...HONEST. FU FU FU. ♡
......
I GOTTA TELL YOU, THERE'S SOMETHING ABOUT MUTSUMI THAT I JUST CAN'T QUITE PUT MY FINGER ON. MAYBE IT'S HER ATTITUDE-
HMPH, SOUNDS TO ME LIKE YOU SHOULD SKIP THE FAKE CEREMONY AND JUST GET MARRIED TO HER FOR REAL THEN.
WHAT'S GOTTEN INTO YOU TODAY?

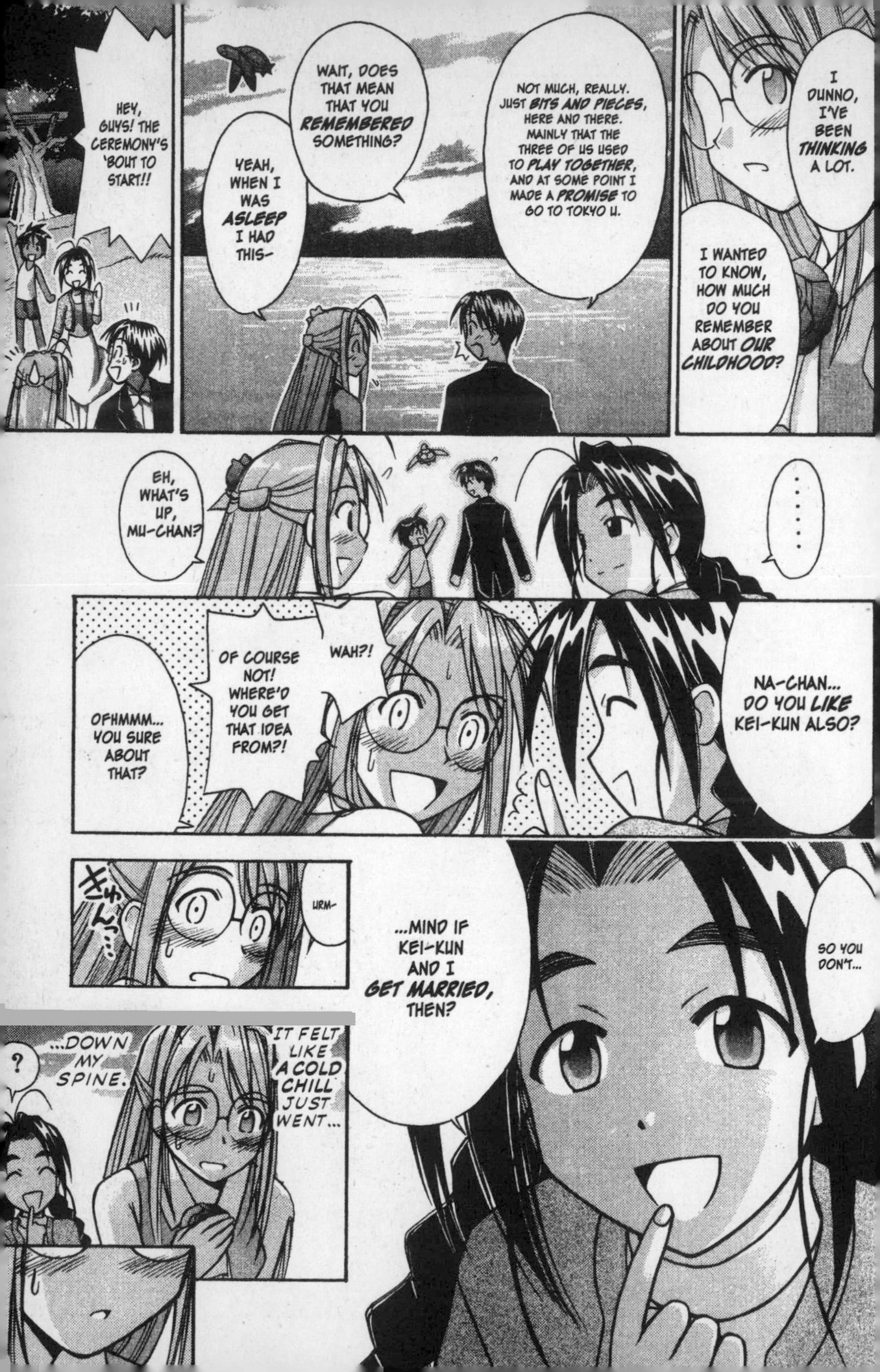
I DUNNO, I'VE BEEN THINKING A LOT.
I WANTED TO KNOW, HOW MUCH DO YOU REMEMBER ABOUT OUR CHILDHOOD?
NOT MUCH, REALLY. JUST BITS AND PIECES, HERE AND THERE. MAINLY THAT THE THREE OF US USED TO PLAY TOGETHER, AND AT SOME POINT I MADE A PROMISE TO GO TO TOKYO U.
WAIT, DOES THAT MEAN THAT YOU REMEMBERED SOMETHING?
YEAH, WHEN I WAS ASLEEP I HAD THIS-
HEY, GUYS! THE CEREMONY'S 'BOUT TO START!!
......
EH, WHAT'S UP, MU-CHAN?
NA-CHAN... DO YOU LIKE KEI-KUN ALSO?
WAH?!
OF COURSE NOT! WHERE'D YOU GET THAT IDEA FROM?!
OFHMMM... YOU SURE ABOUT THAT?
SO YOU DON'T...
...MIND IF KEI-KUN AND I GET MARRIED, THEN?
URM-
IT FELT LIKE A COLD CHILL JUST WENT...
...DOWN MY SPINE.
?

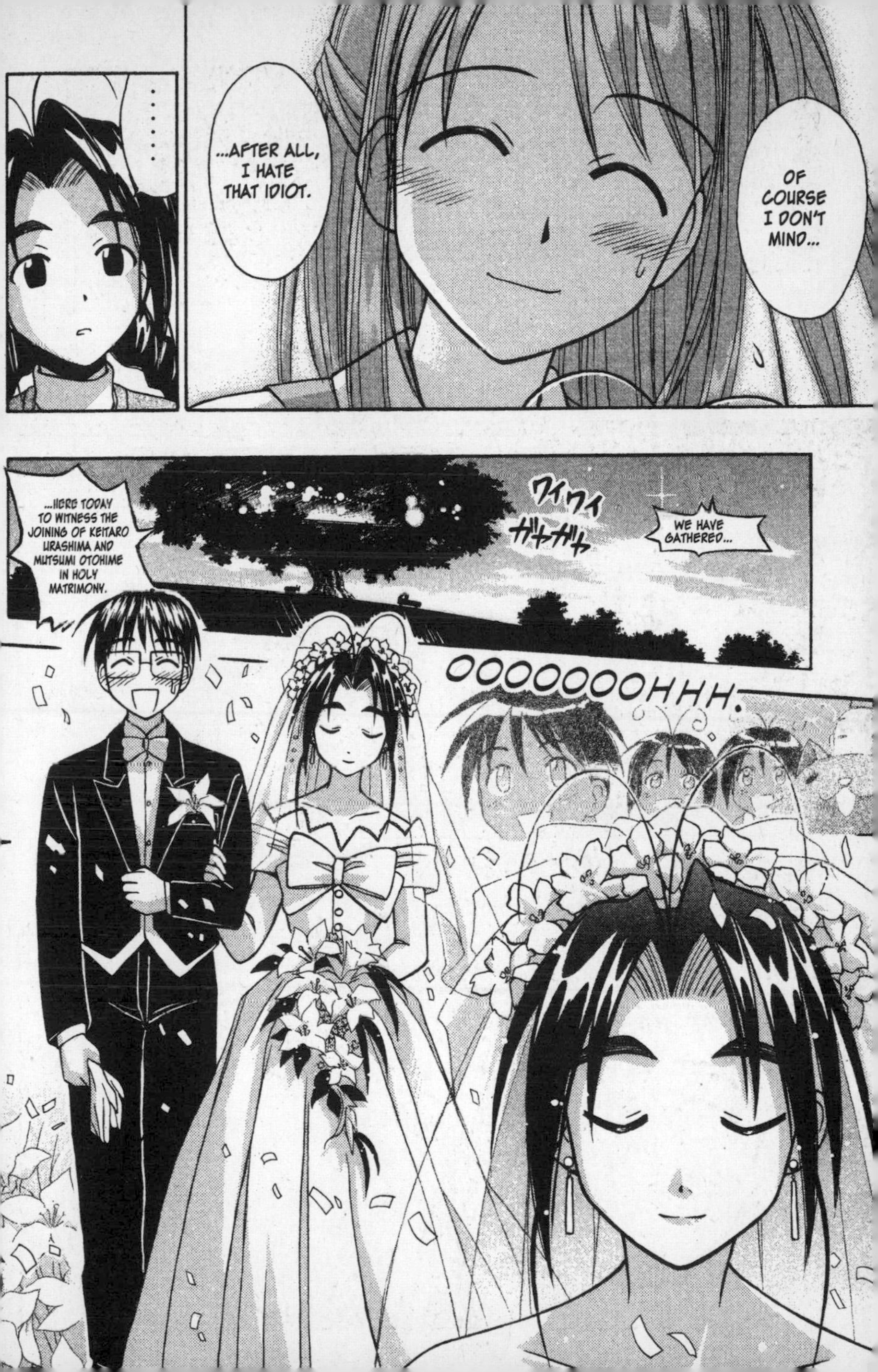
OF COURSE I DON'T MIND...
...AFTER ALL, I HATE THAT IDIOT.
......
WE HAVE GATHERED...
ワイワイ
ガヤガヤ
...HERE TODAY TO WITNESS THE JOINING OF KEITARO URASHIMA AND MUTSUMI OTOHIME IN HOLY MATRIMONY.
OOOOOOOHHH.

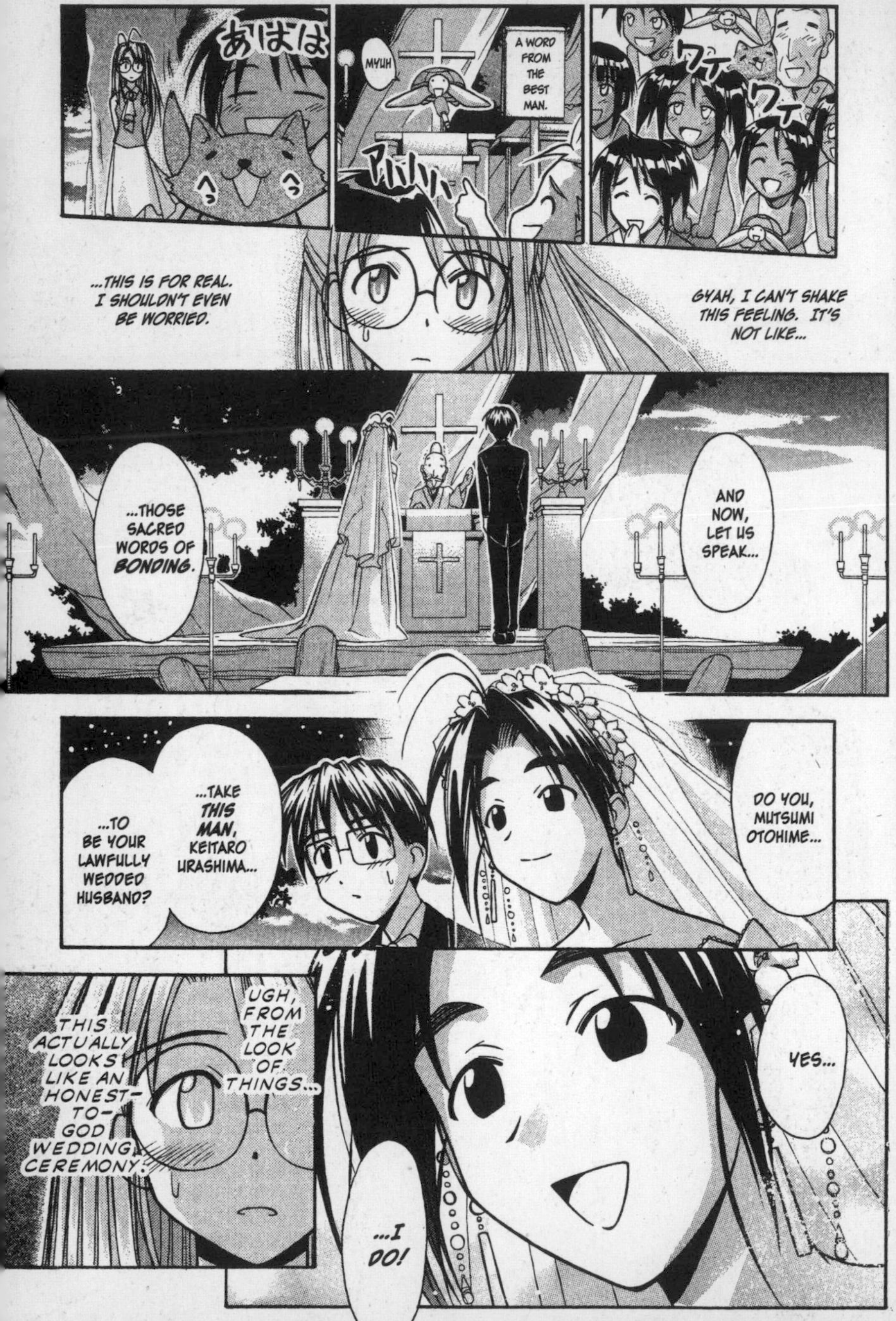
ワイワイ
MYUH
A WORD FROM THE BEST MAN.
アハハハ
あははは
へっ
へっ
GYAH, I CAN'T SHAKE THIS FEELING. IT'S NOT LIKE...
...THIS IS FOR REAL. I SHOULDN'T EVEN BE WORRIED.
AND NOW, LET US SPEAK...
...THOSE SACRED WORDS OF BONDING.
DO YOU, MUTSUMI OTOHIME...
...TAKE THIS MAN, KEITARO URASHIMA...
...TO BE YOUR LAWFULLY WEDDED HUSBAND?
YES...
...I DO!
UGH, FROM THE LOOK OF THINGS...
THIS ACTUALLY LOOKS LIKE AN HONEST-TO-GOD WEDDING CEREMONY.

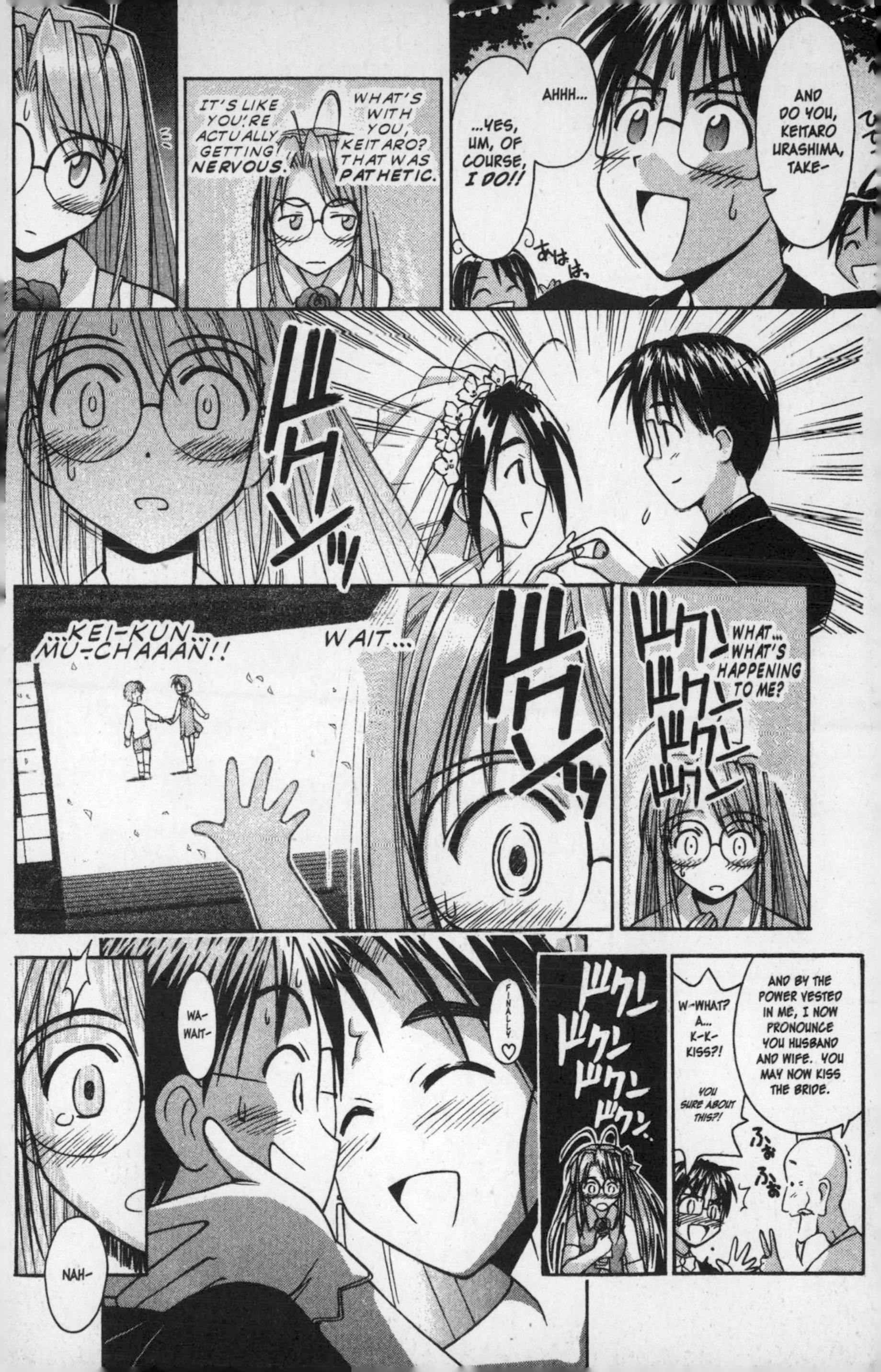
AND DO YOU, KEITARO URASHIMA, TAKE-
AHHH...
...YES, UM, OF COURSE, I DO!!
あはは
WHAT'S WITH YOU, KEITARO? THAT WAS PATHETIC.
IT'S LIKE YOU'RE ACTUALLY GETTING NERVOUS.
WHAT... WHAT'S HAPPENING TO ME?
WAIT...
...KEI-KUN... MU-CHAAAN!!
AND BY THE POWER VESTED IN ME, I NOW PRONOUNCE YOU HUSBAND AND WIFE. YOU MAY NOW KISS THE BRIDE.
W-WHAT? A... K-K-KISS?!
YOU SURE ABOUT THIS?!
FINALLY ♡
WA-WAIT-
NAH-

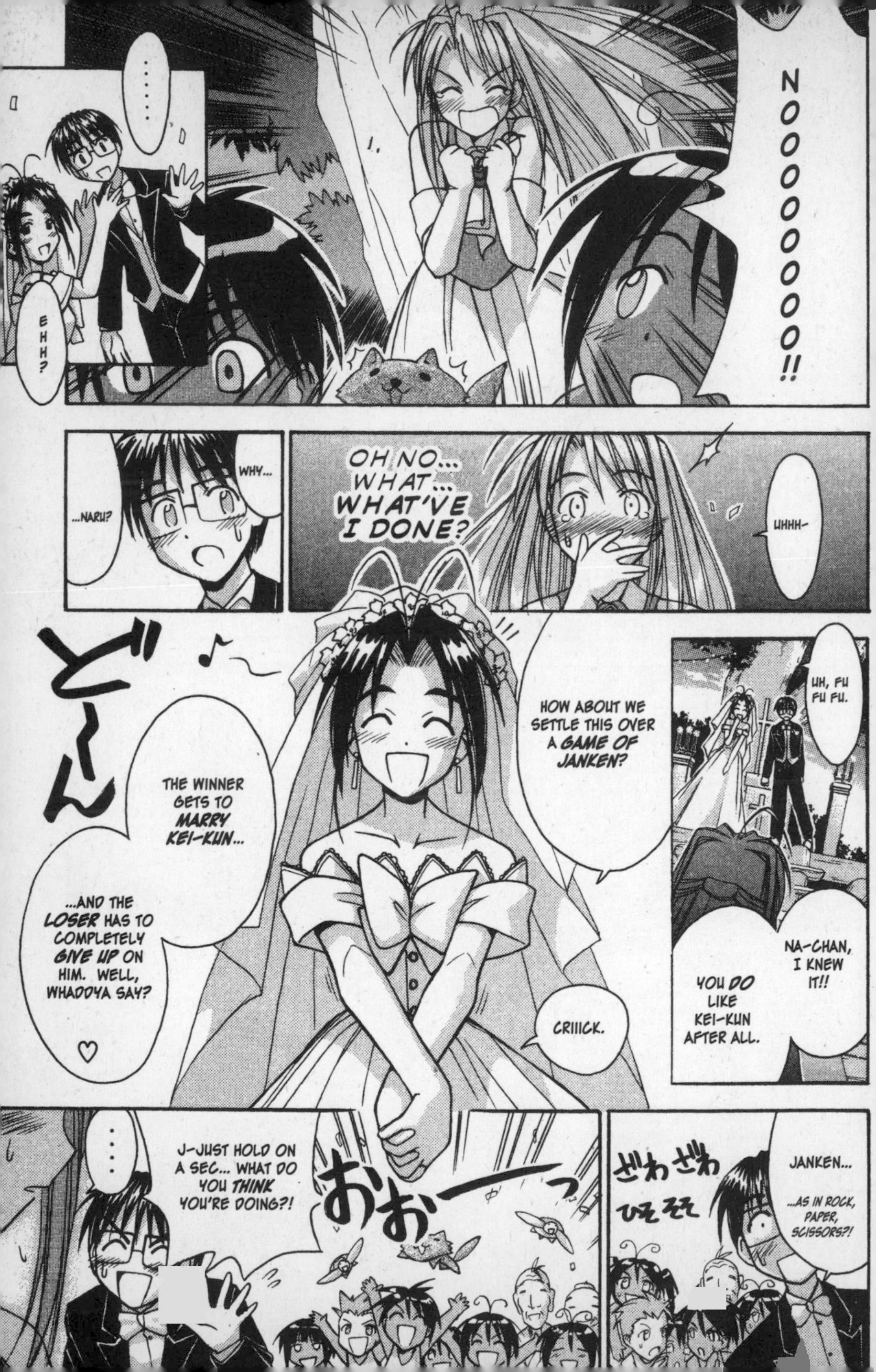
NOOOOOOOOO!!
......
EHH?
UHHH-
OH NO... WHAT... WHAT'VE I DONE?
WHY... ...NARU?
UH, FU FU FU.
NA-CHAN, I KNEW IT!!
YOU DO LIKE KEI-KUN AFTER ALL.
HOW ABOUT WE SETTLE THIS OVER A GAME OF JANKEN?
CRIIICK.
THE WINNER GETS TO MARRY KEI-KUN...
...AND THE LOSER HAS TO COMPLETELY GIVE UP ON HIM. WELL, WHADDYA SAY? ♡
どど～ん
ざわざわ ひそそそ
JANKEN...
...AS IN ROCK, PAPER, SCISSORS?!
おおーーっ
J-JUST HOLD ON A SEC... WHAT DO YOU THINK YOU'RE DOING?!
....

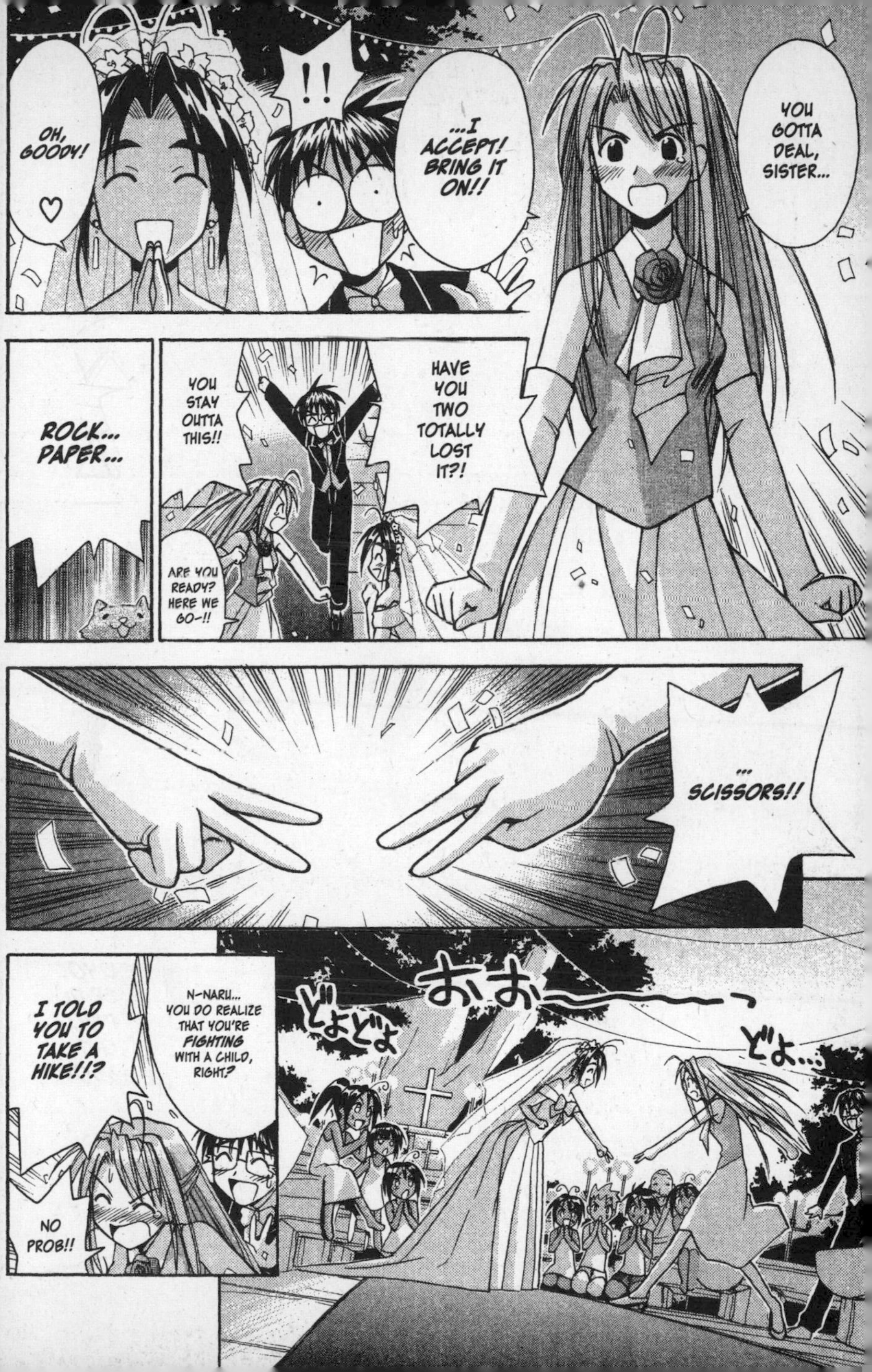

YOU GOTTA DEAL, SISTER...
!!
...I ACCEPT! BRING IT ON!!
OH, GOODY! ♡
HAVE YOU TWO TOTALLY LOST IT?!
YOU STAY OUTTA THIS!!
ARE YOU READY? HERE WE GO-!!
ROCK... PAPER...
... SCISSORS!!
どよ...
おお〜〜〜〜〜っ
どよどよ
N-NARU... YOU DO REALIZE THAT YOU'RE *FIGHTING* WITH A CHILD, RIGHT?
I TOLD YOU TO TAKE A HIKE!!!?
NO PROB!!

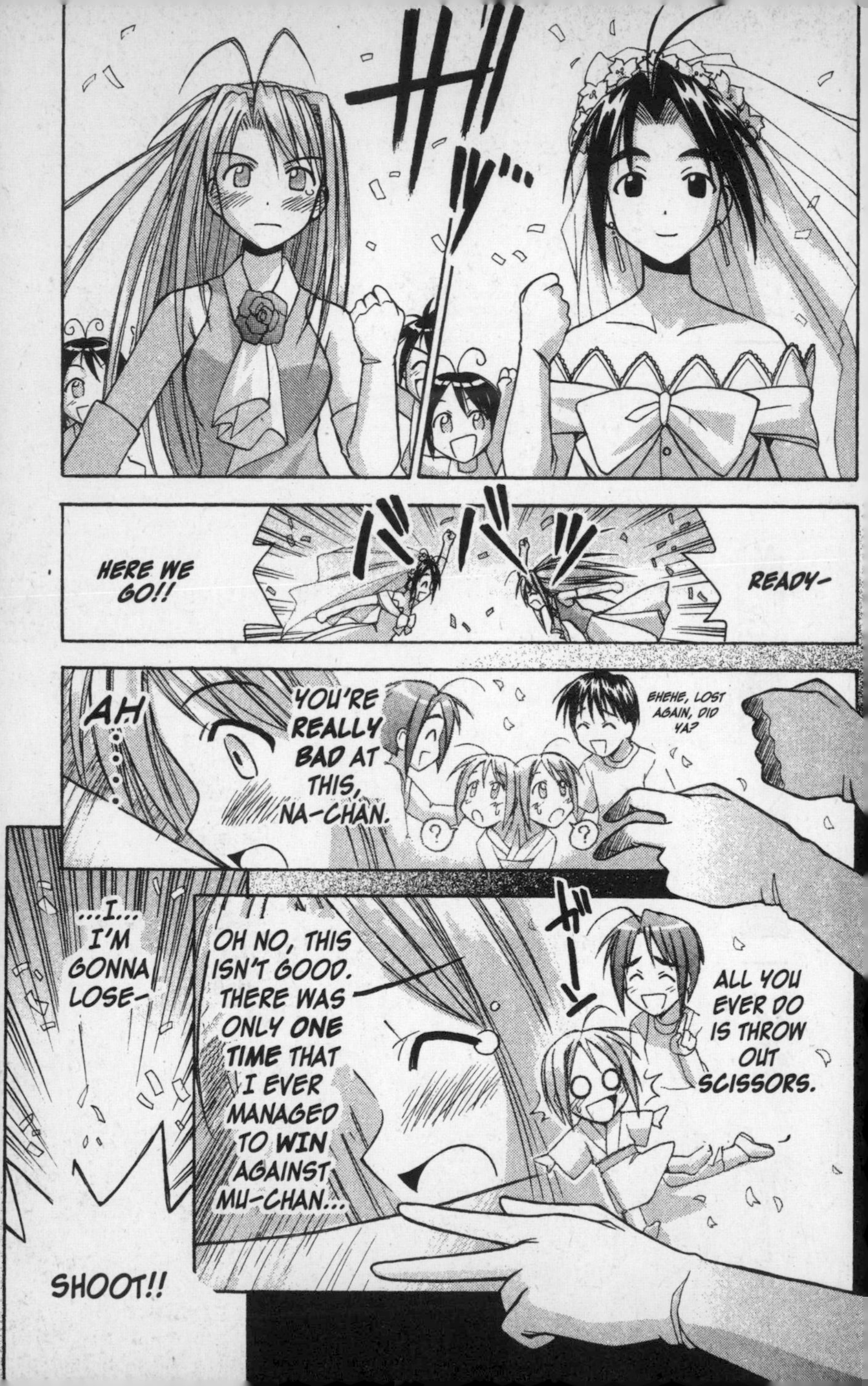
READY-
HERE WE GO!!
EHEHE, LOST AGAIN, DID YA?
YOU'RE REALLY BAD AT THIS, NA-CHAN.
AH......
ALL YOU EVER DO IS THROW OUT SCISSORS.
OH NO, THIS ISN'T GOOD. THERE WAS ONLY ONE TIME THAT I EVER MANAGED TO WIN AGAINST MU-CHAN...
...I... I'M GONNA LOSE-
SHOOT!!

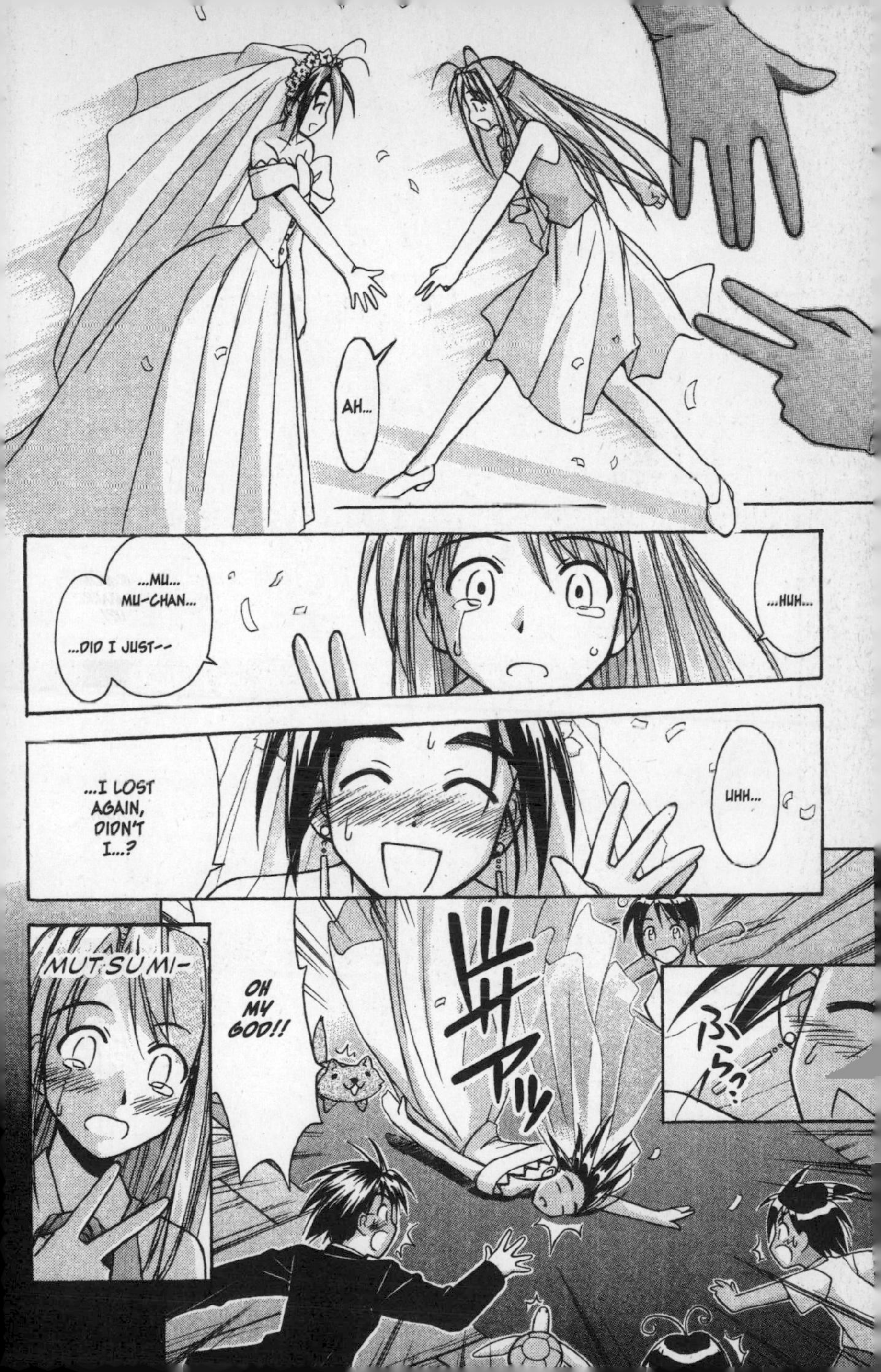
AH...
...HUH...
...MU... MU-CHAN...
...DID I JUST--
UHH...
...I LOST AGAIN, DIDN'T I...?
ふら？？
ドサァッ
OH MY GOD!!
MUTSUMI-

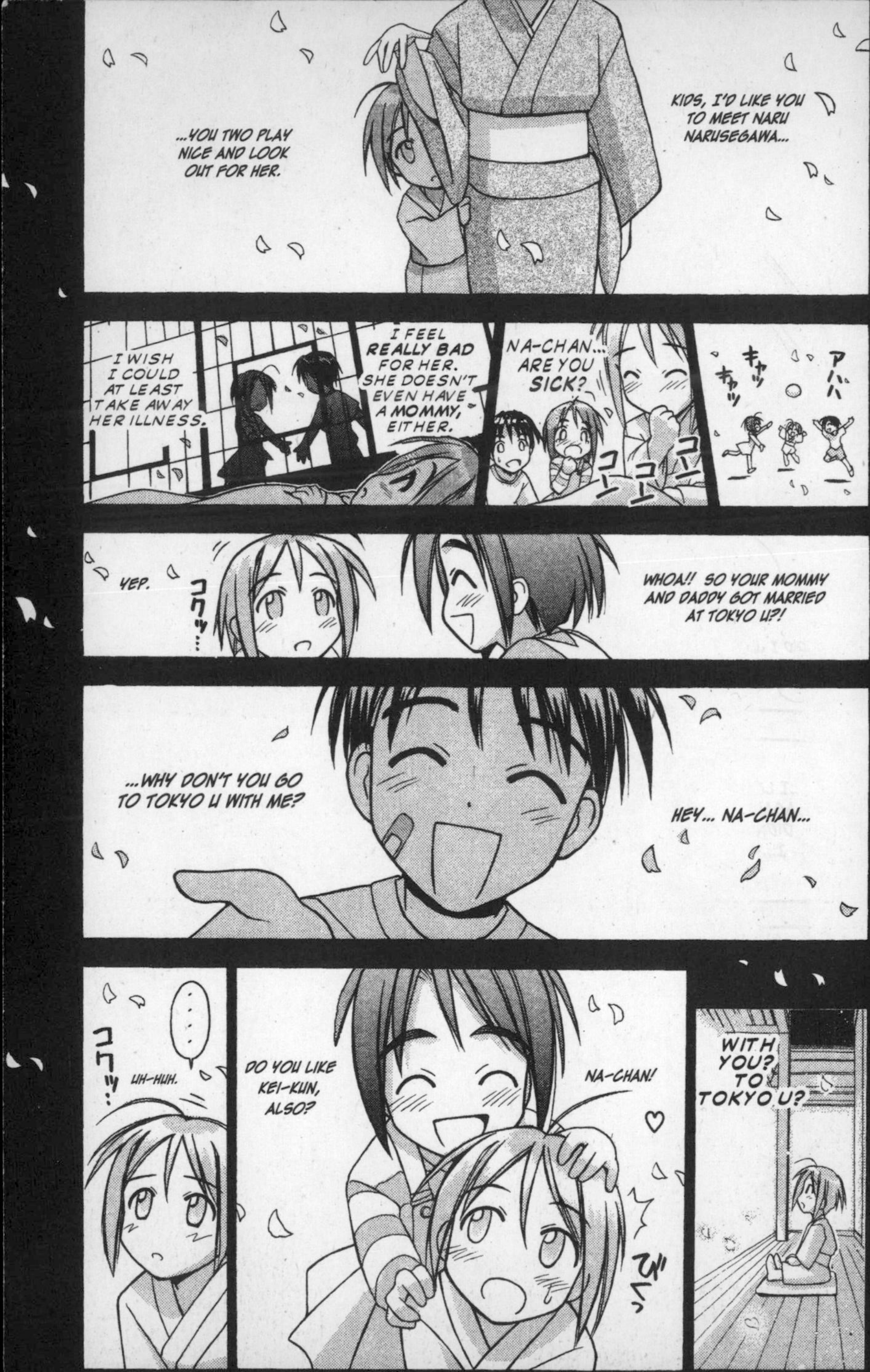
KIDS, I'D LIKE YOU TO MEET NARU NARUSEGAWA...
...YOU TWO PLAY NICE AND LOOK OUT FOR HER.
キャッ キャッ
アハハ
NA-CHAN... ARE YOU SICK?
I FEEL REALLY BAD FOR HER. SHE DOESN'T EVEN HAVE A MOMMY, EITHER.
I WISH I COULD AT LEAST TAKE AWAY HER ILLNESS.
WHOA!! SO YOUR MOMMY AND DADDY GOT MARRIED AT TOKYO U?!
YEP.
HEY... NA-CHAN...
...WHY DON'T YOU GO TO TOKYO U WITHME?
WITH YOU? TO TOKYO U?
NA-CHAN!
DO YOU LIKE KEI-KUN, ALSO?
...
UH-HUH.

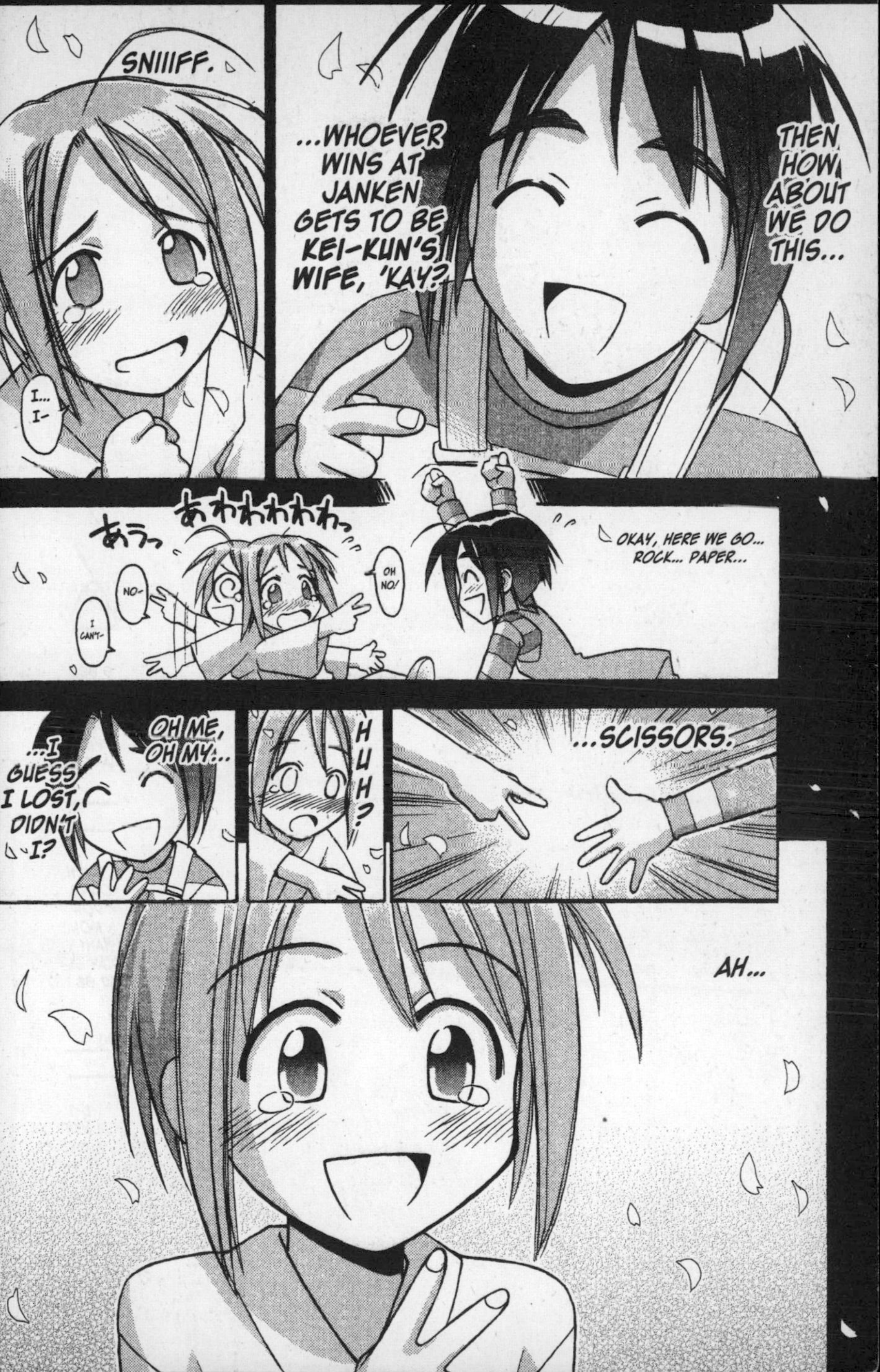
THEN HOW ABOUT WE DO THIS...
...WHOEVER WINS AT JANKEN GETS TO BE KEI-KUN'S WIFE, 'KAY?
SNIIIFF.
I... I-
OKAY, HERE WE GO... ROCK... PAPER...
OH NO!
あわわわわわっ
あうっ
NO-
I CAN'T-
...SCISSORS.
HUH?
OH ME, OH MY...
...I GUESS I LOST, DIDN'T I?
AH...

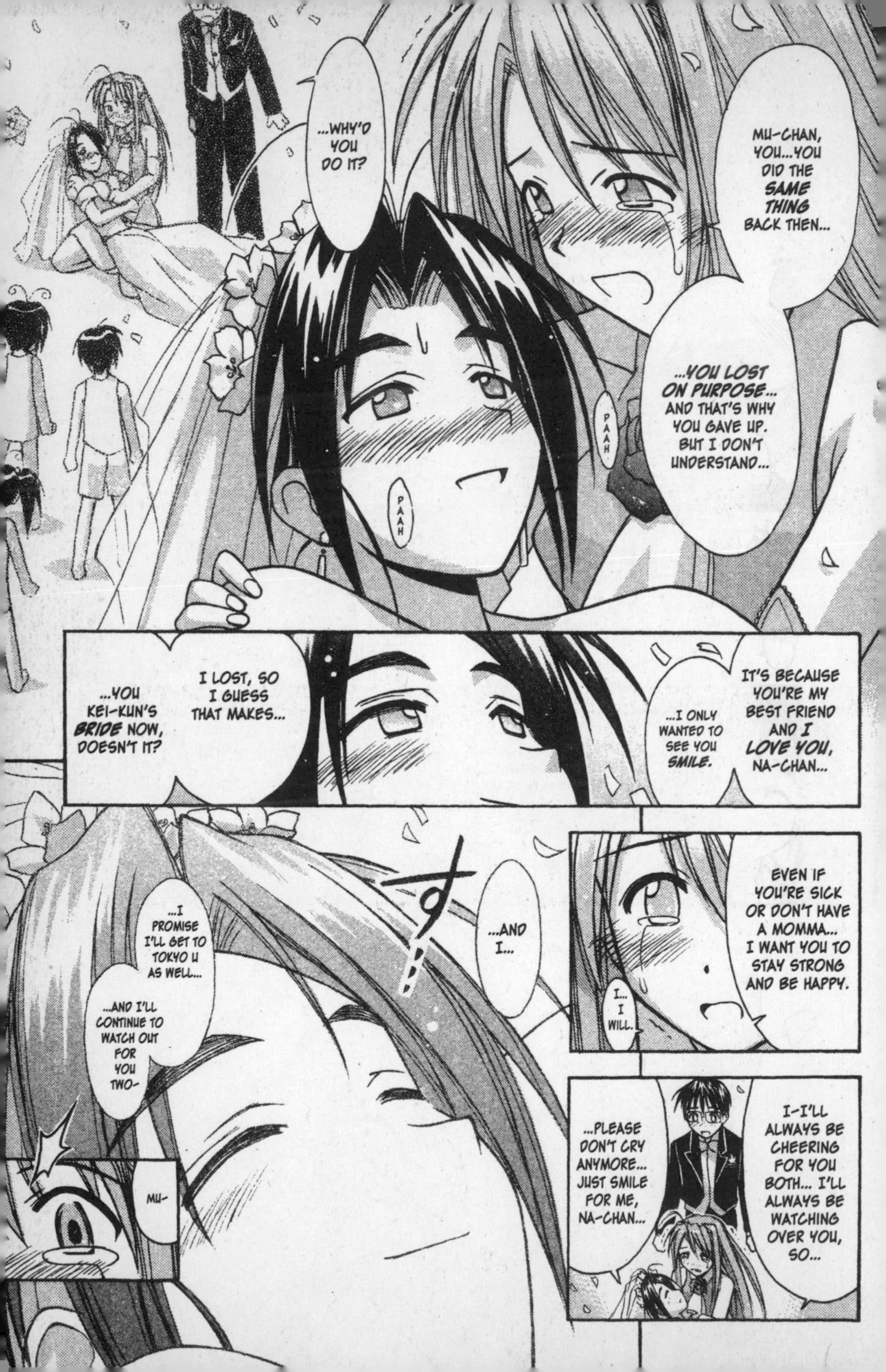
MU-CHAN, YOU...YOU DID THE SAME THING BACK THEN...
...YOU LOST ON PURPOSE... AND THAT'S WHY YOU GAVE UP. BUT I DON'T UNDERSTAND...
...WHY'D YOU DO IT?
PAAH
PAAH
IT'S BECAUSE YOU'RE MY BEST FRIEND AND I LOVE YOU, NA-CHAN...
...I ONLY WANTED TO SEE YOU SMILE.
I LOST, SO I GUESS THAT MAKES...
...YOU KEI-KUN'S BRIDE NOW, DOESN'T IT?
EVEN IF YOU'RE SICK OR DON'T HAVE A MOMMA... I WANT YOU TO STAY STRONG AND BE HAPPY.
I... I WILL.
I-I'LL ALWAYS BE CHEERING FOR YOU BOTH... I'LL ALWAYS BE WATCHING OVER YOU, SO...
...PLEASE DON'T CRY ANYMORE... JUST SMILE FOR ME, NA-CHAN...
...AND I...
...I PROMISE I'LL GET TO TOKYO U AS WELL...
...AND I'LL CONTINUE TO WATCH OUT FOR YOU TWO-
MU-

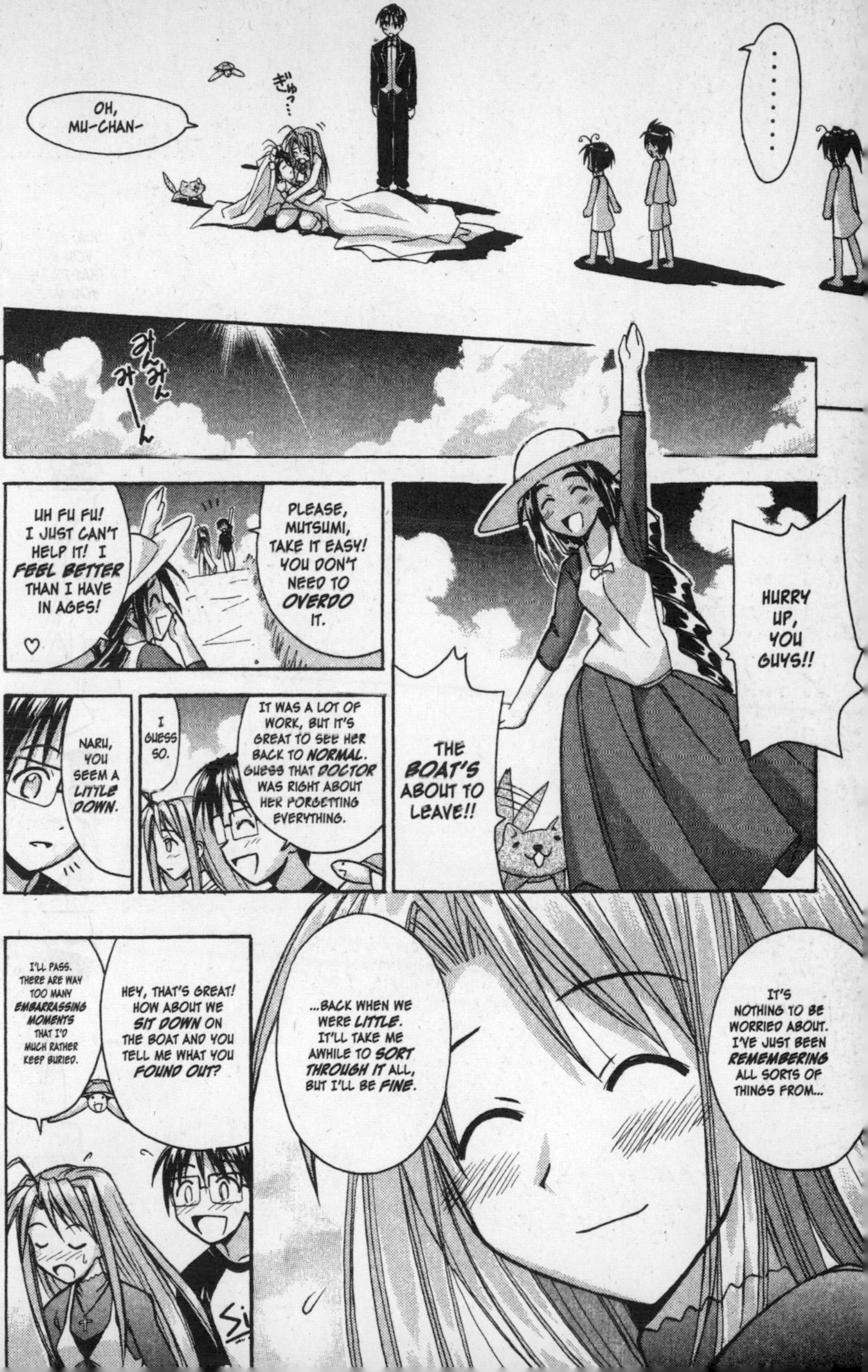

……
OH, MU-CHAN-
ぎゅっ…
みんみんみーーん
HURRY UP, YOU GUYS!!
THE BOAT'S ABOUT TO LEAVE!!
PLEASE, MUTSUMI, TAKE IT EASY! YOU DON'T NEED TO OVERDO IT.
UH FU FU! I JUST CAN'T HELP IT! I FEEL BETTER THAN I HAVE IN AGES! ♡
IT WAS A LOT OF WORK, BUT IT'S GREAT TO SEE HER BACK TO NORMAL. GUESS THAT DOCTOR WAS RIGHT ABOUT HER FORGETTING EVERYTHING.
I GUESS SO.
NARU, YOU SEEM A LITTLE DOWN.
IT'S NOTHING TO BE WORRIED ABOUT. I'VE JUST BEEN REMEMBERING ALL SORTS OF THINGS FROM...
...BACK WHEN WE WERE LITTLE. IT'LL TAKE ME AWHILE TO SORT THROUGH IT ALL, BUT I'LL BE FINE.
HEY, THAT'S GREAT! HOW ABOUT WE SIT DOWN ON THE BOAT AND YOU TELL ME WHAT YOU FOUND OUT?
I'LL PASS. THERE ARE WAY TOO MANY EMBARRASSING MOMENTS THAT I'D MUCH RATHER KEEP BURIED.

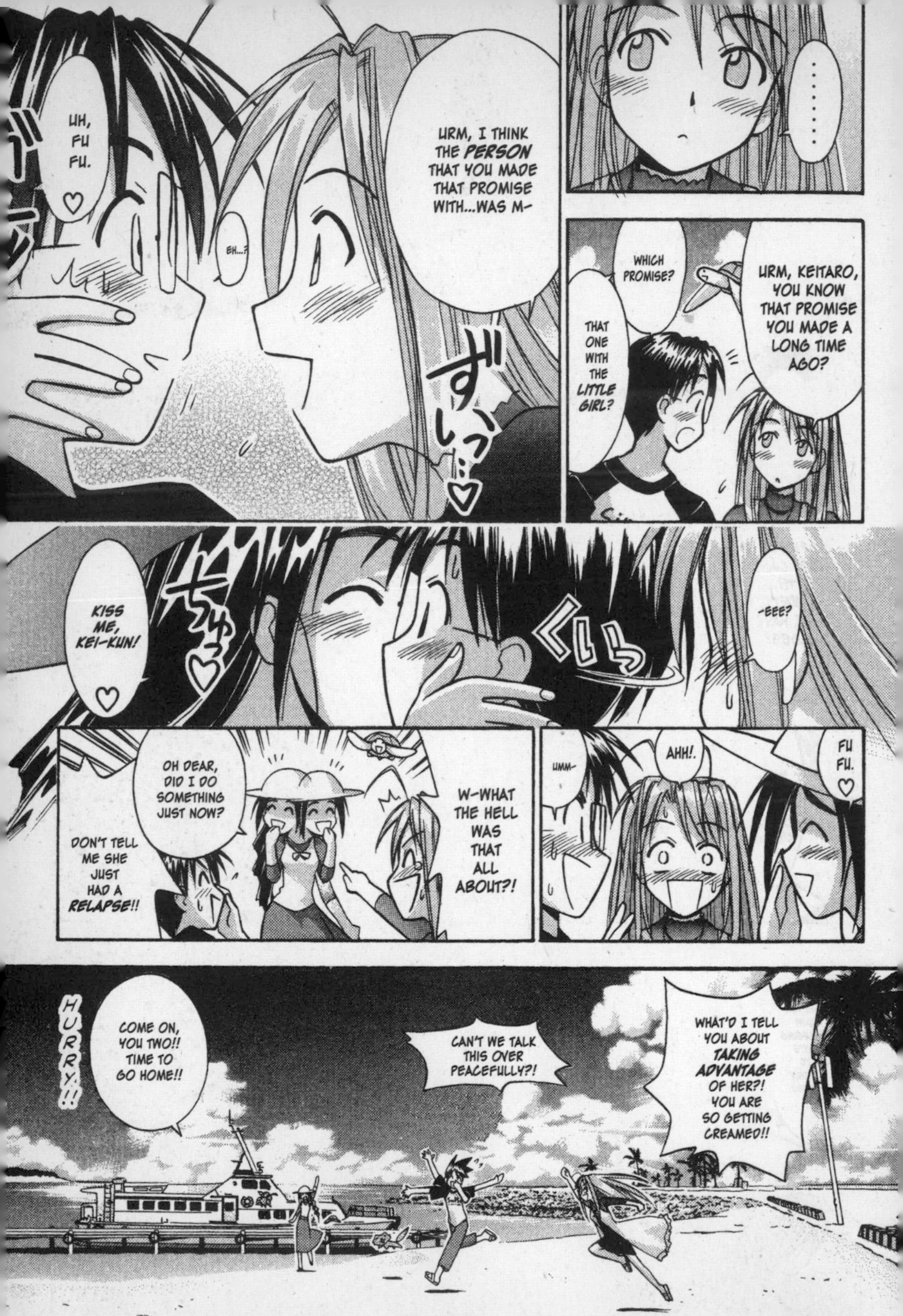
……
URM, KEITARO, YOU KNOW THAT PROMISE YOU MADE A LONG TIME AGO?
WHICH PROMISE?
THAT ONE WITH THE LITTLE GIRL?
URM, I THINK THE PERSON THAT YOU MADE THAT PROMISE WITH...WAS M-
ずいっ
EH...?
UH, FU FU. ♡
-EEE?
くらっ
ちゅっ
KISS ME, KEI-KUN! ♡
FU FU. ♡
AHH!.
UMM-
W-WHAT THE HELL WAS THAT ALL ABOUT?!
OH DEAR, DID I DO SOMETHING JUST NOW?
DON'T TELL ME SHE JUST HAD A RELAPSE!!
WHAT'D I TELL YOU ABOUT TAKING ADVANTAGE OF HER?! YOU ARE SO GETTING CREAMED!!
CAN'T WE TALK THIS OVER PEACEFULLY?!
COME ON, YOU TWO!! TIME TO GO HOME!!
HURRY!!

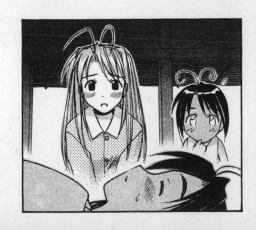

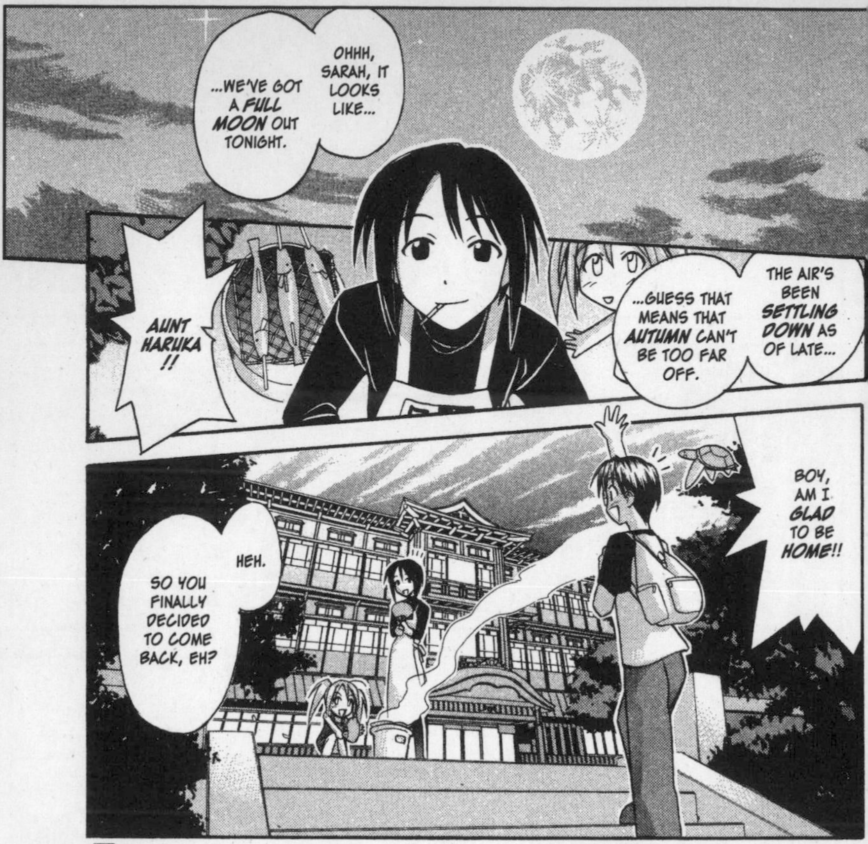
OHHH, SARAH, IT LOOKS LIKE...
...WE'VE GOT A FULL MOON OUT TONIGHT.
THE AIR'S BEEN SETTLING DOWN AS OF LATE...
...GUESS THAT MEANS THAT AUTUMN CAN'T BE TOO FAR OFF.
AUNT HARUKA!!
BOY, AM I GLAD TO BE HOME!!
HEH.
SO YOU FINALLY DECIDED TO COME BACK, EH?

Love Hina

HINATA.84 The Season of Maidens in Love

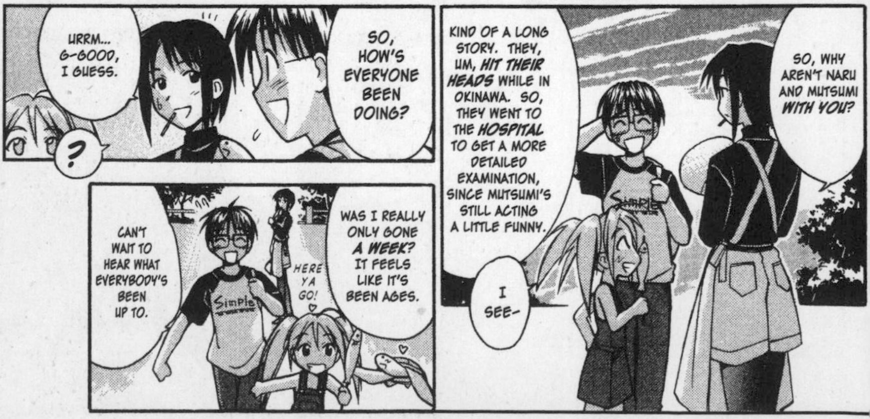
SO, WHY AREN'T NARU AND MUTSUMI WITH YOU?
KIND OF A LONG STORY. THEY, UM, HIT THEIR HEADS WHILE IN OKINAWA. SO, THEY WENT TO THE HOSPITAL TO GET A MORE DETAILED EXAMINATION, SINCE MUTSUMI'S STILL ACTING A LITTLE FUNNY.
I SEE-
SO, HOW'S EVERYONE BEEN DOING?
URRM... G-GOOD, I GUESS.
?
WAS I REALLY ONLY GONE A WEEK? IT FEELS LIKE IT'S BEEN AGES.
HERE YA GO!
CAN'T WAIT TO HEAR WHAT EVERYBODY'S BEEN UP TO.

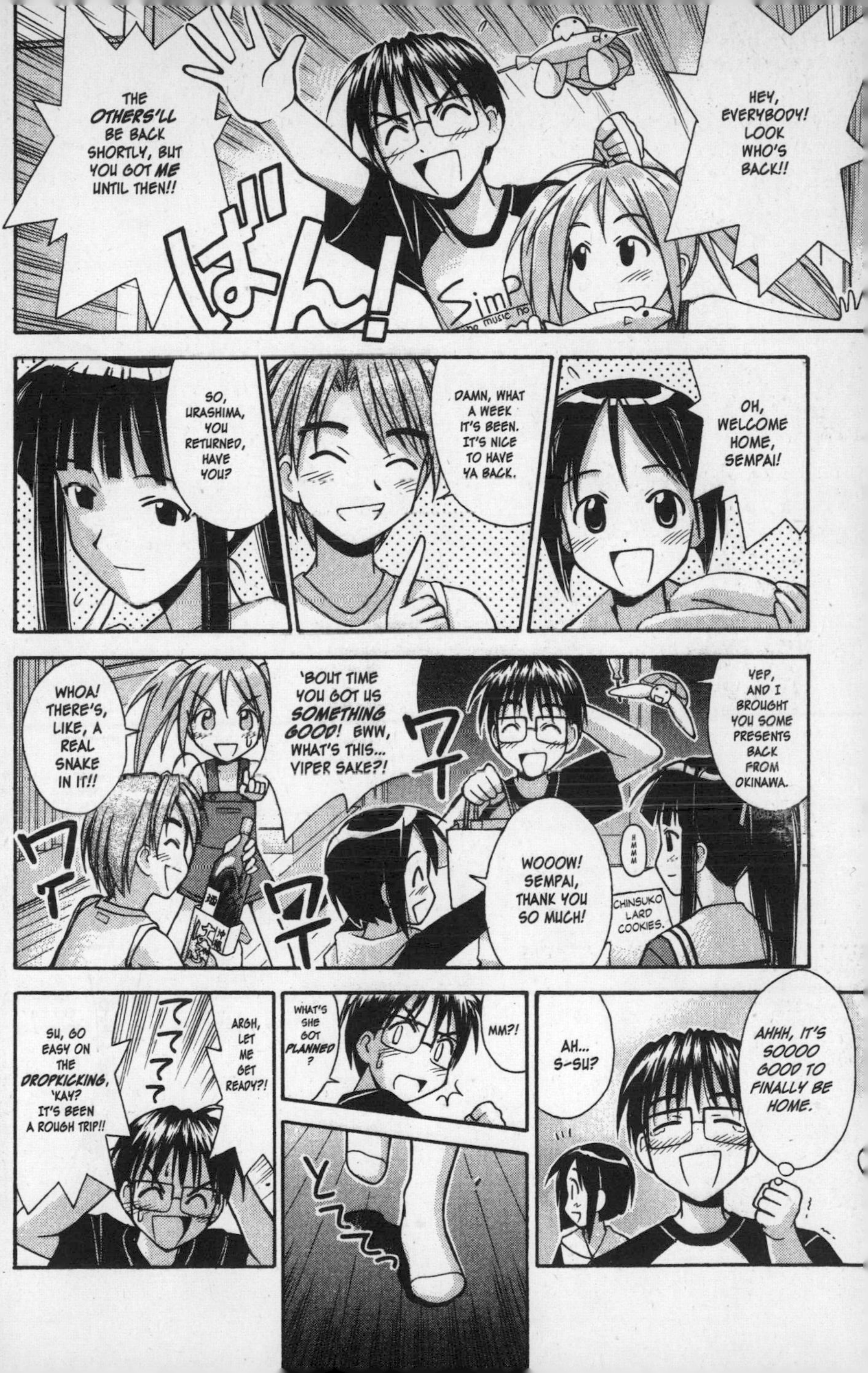
HEY, EVERYBODY! LOOK WHO'S BACK!!
THE OTHERS'LL BE BACK SHORTLY, BUT YOU GOT ME UNTIL THEN!!
ばん～！
OH, WELCOME HOME, SEMPAI!
DAMN, WHAT A WEEK IT'S BEEN. IT'S NICE TO HAVE YA BACK.
SO, URASHIMA, YOU RETURNED, HAVE YOU?
YEP, AND I BROUGHT YOU SOME PRESENTS BACK FROM OKINAWA.
HMMM
CHINSUKO LARD COOKIES.
WOOOW! SEMPAI, THANK YOU SO MUCH!
ワイ
'BOUT TIME YOU GOT US SOMETHING GOOD! EWW, WHAT'S THIS... VIPER SAKE?!
ワイ
WHOA! THERE'S, LIKE, A REAL SNAKE IN IT!!
ワイ
AHHH, IT'S SOOOO GOOD TO FINALLY BE HOME.
AH... S-SU?
MM?!
WHAT'S SHE GOT PLANNED?
ARGH, LET ME GET READY?!
てててて
SU, GO EASY ON THE DROPKICKING, 'KAY? IT'S BEEN A ROUGH TRIP!!

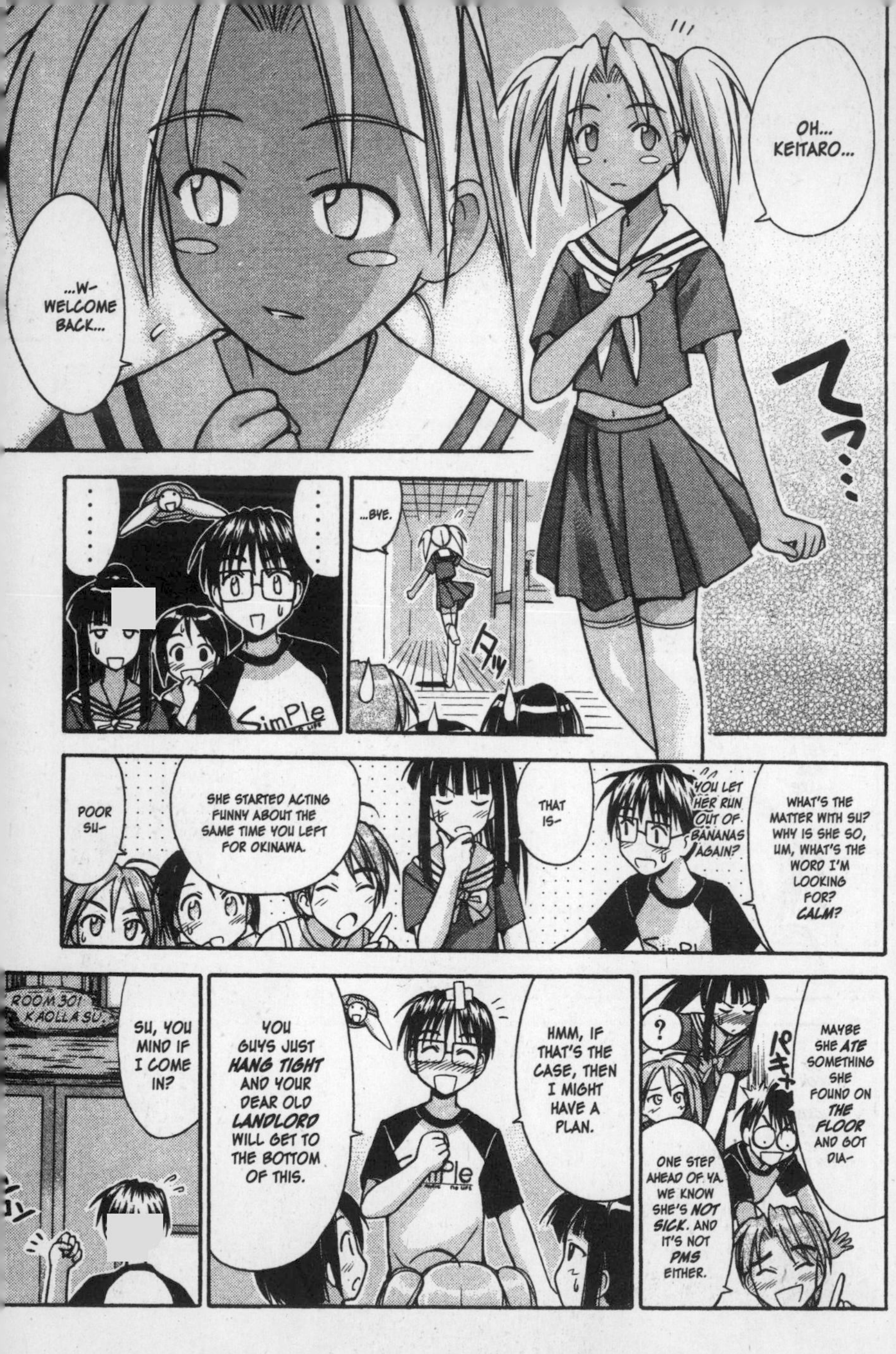

OH... KEITARO...
...W- WELCOME BACK...
...BYE.
......
......
WHAT'S THE MATTER WITH SU? WHY IS SHE SO, UM, WHAT'S THE WORD I'M LOOKING FOR? CALM?
YOU LET HER RUN OUT OF BANANAS AGAIN?
THAT IS-
SHE STARTED ACTING FUNNY ABOUT THE SAME TIME YOU LEFT FOR OKINAWA.
POOR SU-
MAYBE SHE ATE SOMETHING SHE FOUND ON THE FLOOR AND GOT DIA-
ONE STEP AHEAD OF YA. WE KNOW SHE'S NOT SICK. AND IT'S NOT PMS EITHER.
HMM, IF THAT'S THE CASE, THEN I MIGHT HAVE A PLAN.
YOU GUYS JUST HANG TIGHT AND YOUR DEAR OLD LANDLORD WILL GET TO THE BOTTOM OF THIS.
ROOM 301 KAOLLA SU
SU, YOU MIND IF I COME IN?

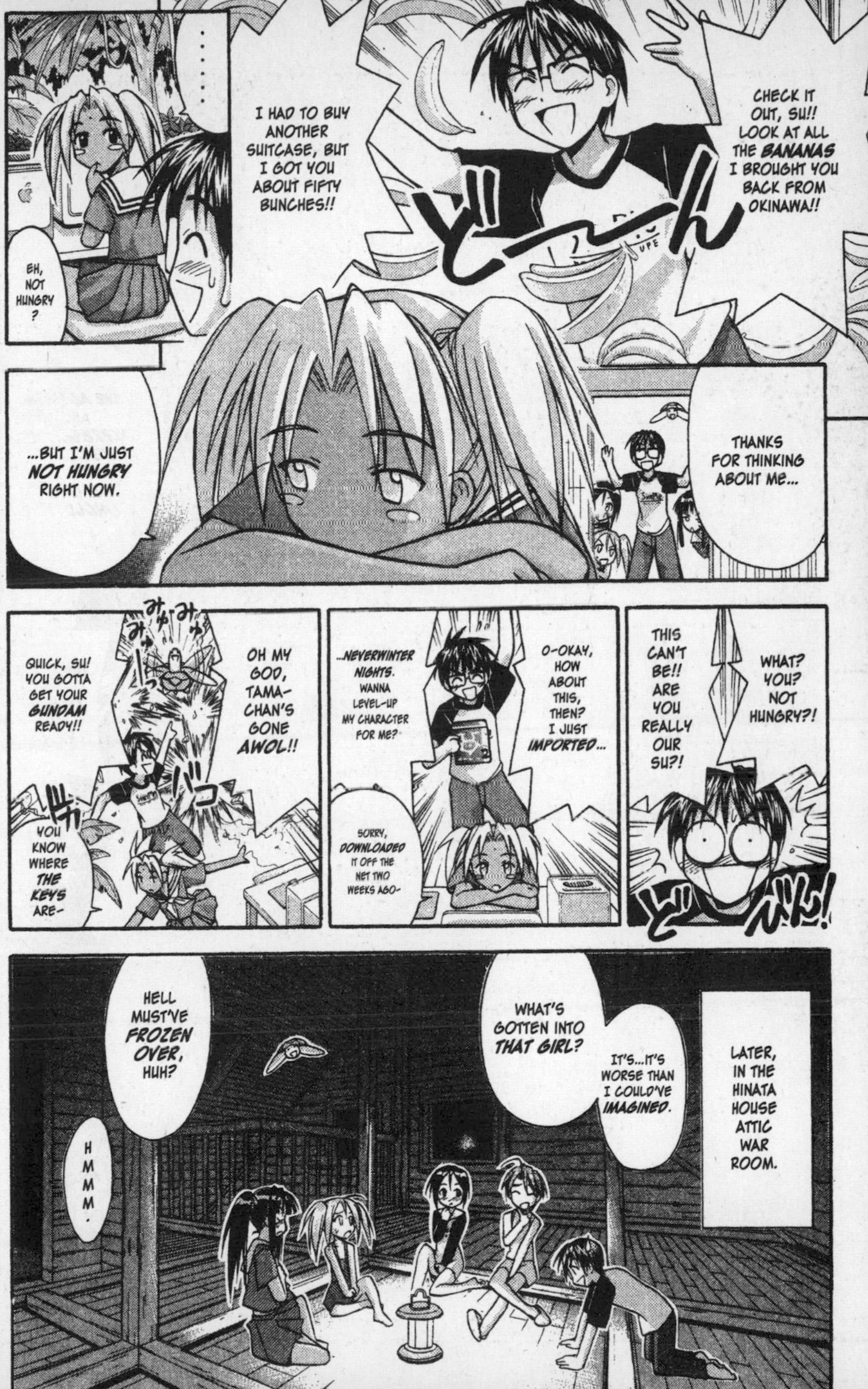
CHECK IT OUT, SU!! LOOK AT ALL THE BANANAS I BROUGHT YOU BACK FROM OKINAWA!!
I HAD TO BUY ANOTHER SUITCASE, BUT I GOT YOU ABOUT FIFTY BUNCHES!!
......
EH, NOT HUNGRY?
THANKS FOR THINKING ABOUT ME...
...BUT I'M JUST NOT HUNGRY RIGHT NOW.
WHAT? YOU? NOT HUNGRY?!
THIS CAN'T BE!! ARE YOU REALLY OUR SU?!
O-OKAY, HOW ABOUT THIS, THEN? I JUST IMPORTED...
...NEVERWINTER NIGHTS. WANNA LEVEL-UP MY CHARACTER FOR ME?
SORRY, DOWNLOADED IT OFF THE NET TWO WEEKS AGO-
OH MY GOD, TAMA-CHAN'S GONE AWOL!!
QUICK, SU! YOU GOTTA GET YOUR GUNDAM READY!!
YOU KNOW WHERE THE KEYS ARE-
LATER, IN THE HINATA HOUSE ATTIC WAR ROOM.
WHAT'S GOTTEN INTO THAT GIRL?
IT'S...IT'S WORSE THAN I COULD'VE IMAGINED.
HELL MUST'VE FROZEN OVER, HUH?
HMMM.

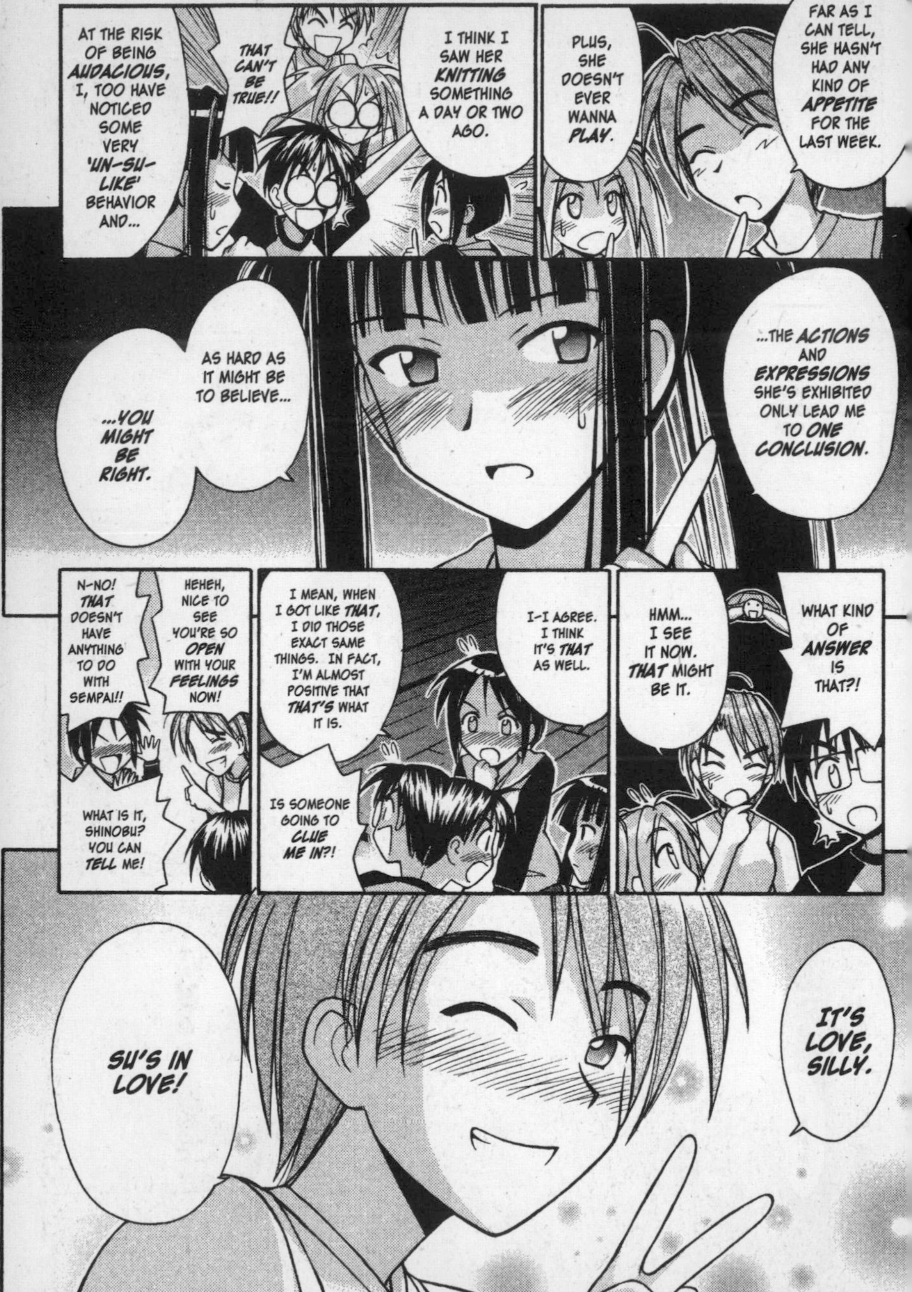
FAR AS I CAN TELL, SHE HASN'T HAD ANY KIND OF APPETITE FOR THE LAST WEEK.
PLUS, SHE DOESN'T EVER WANNA PLAY.
I THINK I SAW HER KNITTING SOMETHING A DAY OR TWO AGO.
THAT CAN'T BE TRUE!!
AT THE RISK OF BEING AUDACIOUS, I, TOO HAVE NOTICED SOME VERY 'UN-SU-LIKE' BEHAVIOR AND...
...THE ACTIONS AND EXPRESSIONS SHE'S EXHIBITED ONLY LEAD ME TO ONE CONCLUSION.
AS HARD AS IT MIGHT BE TO BELIEVE...
...YOU MIGHT BE RIGHT.
WHAT KIND OF ANSWER IS THAT?!
HMM... I SEE IT NOW. THAT MIGHT BE IT.
I-I AGREE. I THINK IT'S THAT AS WELL.
I MEAN, WHEN I GOT LIKE THAT, I DID THOSE EXACT SAME THINGS. IN FACT, I'M ALMOST POSITIVE THAT THAT'S WHAT IT IS.
IS SOMEONE GOING TO CLUE ME IN?!
HEHEH, NICE TO SEE YOU'RE SO OPEN WITH YOUR FEELINGS NOW!
N-NO! THAT DOESN'T HAVE ANYTHING TO DO WITH SEMPAI!!
WHAT IS IT, SHINOBU? YOU CAN TELL ME!
IT'S LOVE, SILLY.
SU'S IN LOVE!

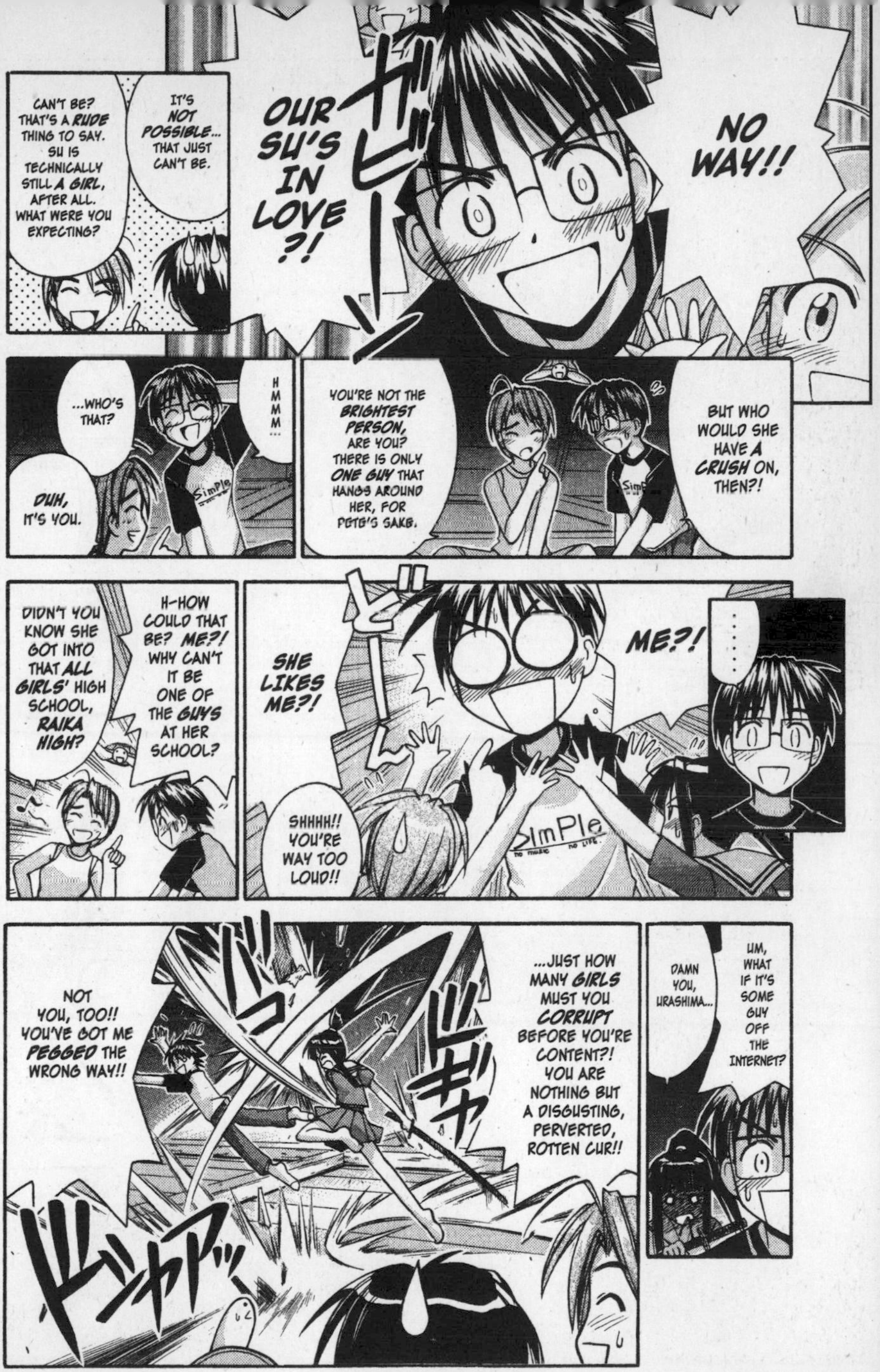
NO WAY!!
OUR SU'S IN LOVE?!
IT'S NOT POSSIBLE... THAT JUST CAN'T BE.
CAN'T BE? THAT'S A RUDE THING TO SAY. SU IS TECHNICALLY STILL A GIRL, AFTER ALL. WHAT WERE YOU EXPECTING?
BUT WHO WOULD SHE HAVE A CRUSH ON, THEN?!
YOU'RE NOT THE BRIGHTEST PERSON, ARE YOU? THERE IS ONLY ONE GUY THAT HANGS AROUND HER, FOR PETE'S SAKE.
HMMM...
...WHO'S THAT?
DUH, IT'S YOU.
......
ME?!
SHE LIKES ME?!
SHHHH!! YOU'RE WAY TOO LOUD!!
H-HOW COULD THAT BE? ME?! WHY CAN'T IT BE ONE OF THE GUYS AT HER SCHOOL?
DIDN'T YOU KNOW SHE GOT INTO THAT ALL GIRLS' HIGH SCHOOL, RAIKA HIGH?
UM, WHAT IF IT'S SOME GUY OFF THE INTERNET?
DAMN YOU, URASHIMA...
...JUST HOW MANY GIRLS MUST YOU CORRUPT BEFORE YOU'RE CONTENT?! YOU ARE NOTHING BUT A DISGUSTING, PERVERTED, ROTTEN CUR!!
NOT YOU, TOO!! YOU'VE GOT ME PEGGED THE WRONG WAY!!

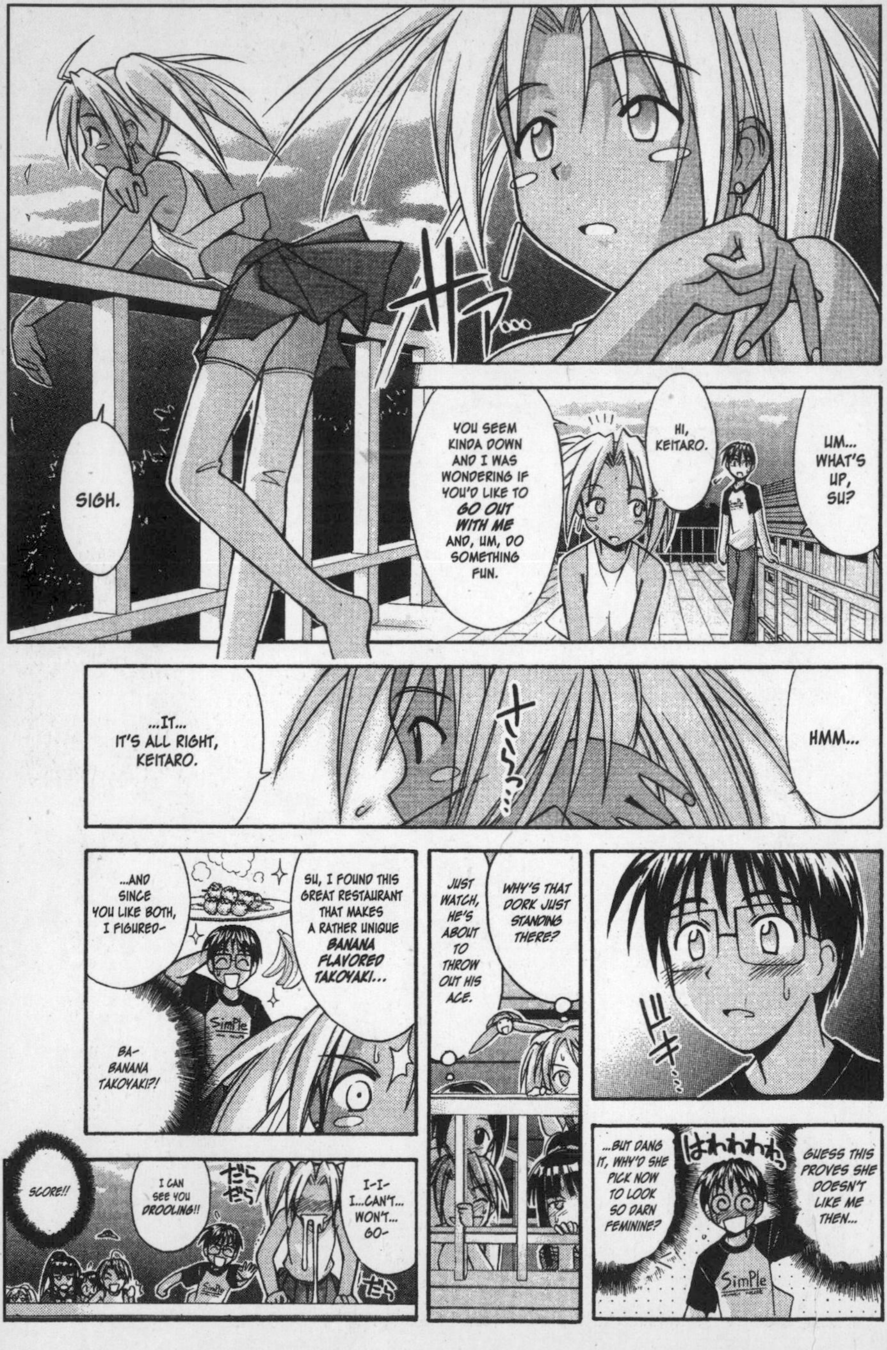
SIGH.
UM... WHAT'S UP, SU?
HI, KEITARO.
YOU SEEM KINDA DOWN AND I WAS WONDERING IF YOU'D LIKE TO GO OUT WITH ME AND, UM, DO SOMETHING FUN.
HMM...
...IT... IT'S ALL RIGHT, KEITARO.
ドキ...
WHY'S THAT DORK JUST STANDING THERE?
JUST WATCH, HE'S ABOUT TO THROW OUT HIS ACE.
SU, I FOUND THIS GREAT RESTAURANT THAT MAKES A RATHER UNIQUE BANANA FLAVORED TAKOYAKI...
...AND SINCE YOU LIKE BOTH, I FIGURED-
BA-BANANA TAKOYAKI?!
GUESS THIS PROVES SHE DOESN'T LIKE ME THEN...
はわわわわ
...BUT DANG IT, WHY'D SHE PICK NOW TO LOOK SO DARN FEMININE?
I-I- I...CAN'T... WON'T... GO-
だらだら
I CAN SEE YOU DROOLING!!
SCORE!!

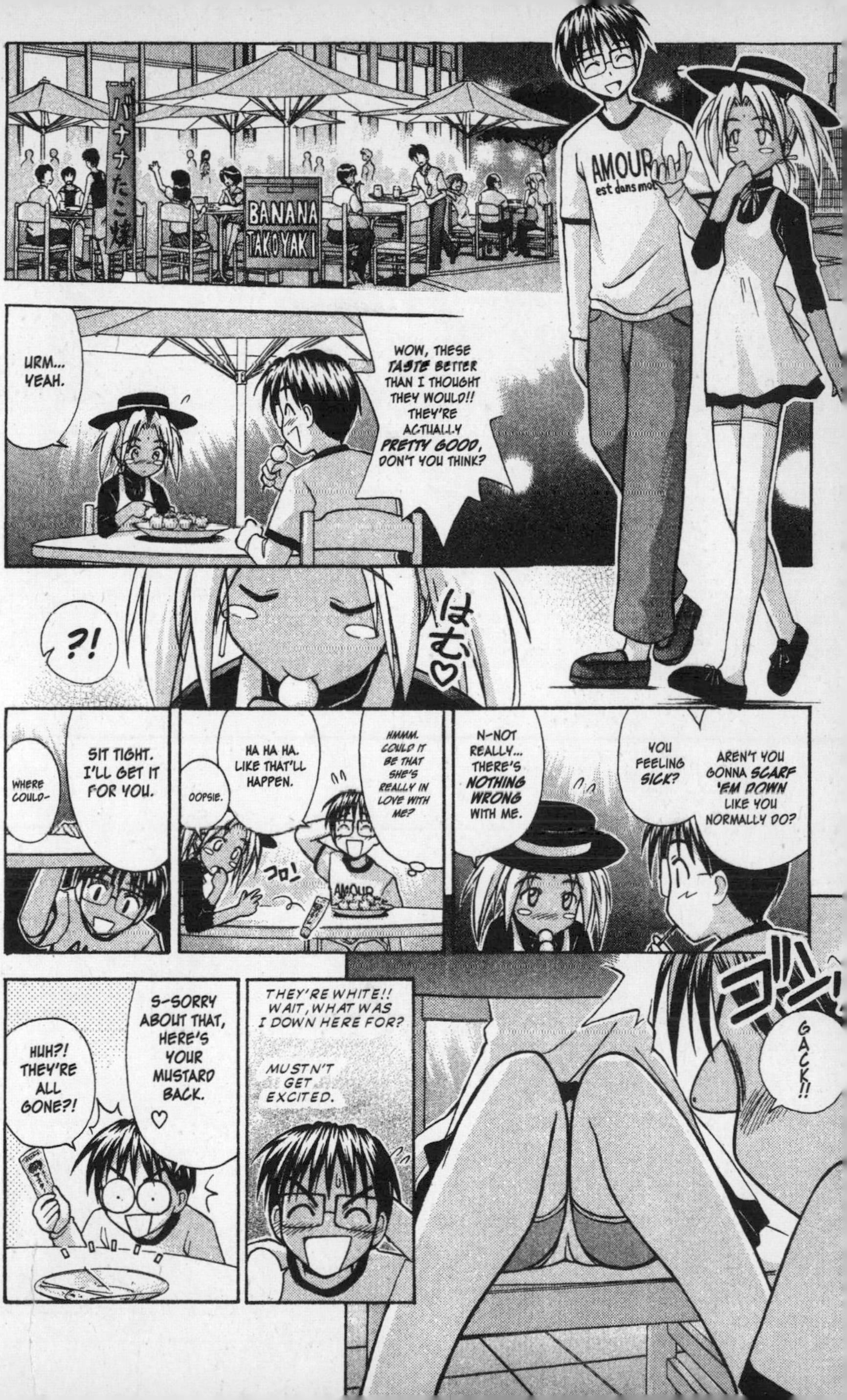
AMOUR est dans mo
バナナたこ焼
BANANA TAKOYAKI
WOW, THESE TASTE BETTER THAN I THOUGHT THEY WOULD!! THEY'RE ACTUALLY PRETTY GOOD, DON'T YOU THINK?
URM... YEAH.
はむ♡
?!
AREN'T YOU GONNA SCARF 'EM DOWN LIKE YOU NORMALLY DO?
YOU FEELING SICK?
N-NOT REALLY... THERE'S NOTHING WRONG WITH ME.
HMMM. COULD IT BE THAT SHE'S REALLY IN LOVE WITH ME?
HA HA HA. LIKE THAT'LL HAPPEN.
OOPSIE.
AMOUR
SIT TIGHT. I'LL GET IT FOR YOU.
WHERE COULD-
GACK!!
THEY'RE WHITE!! WAIT, WHAT WAS I DOWN HERE FOR?
MUSTN'T GET EXCITED.
S-SORRY ABOUT THAT, HERE'S YOUR MUSTARD BACK. ♡
HUH?! THEY'RE ALL GONE?!

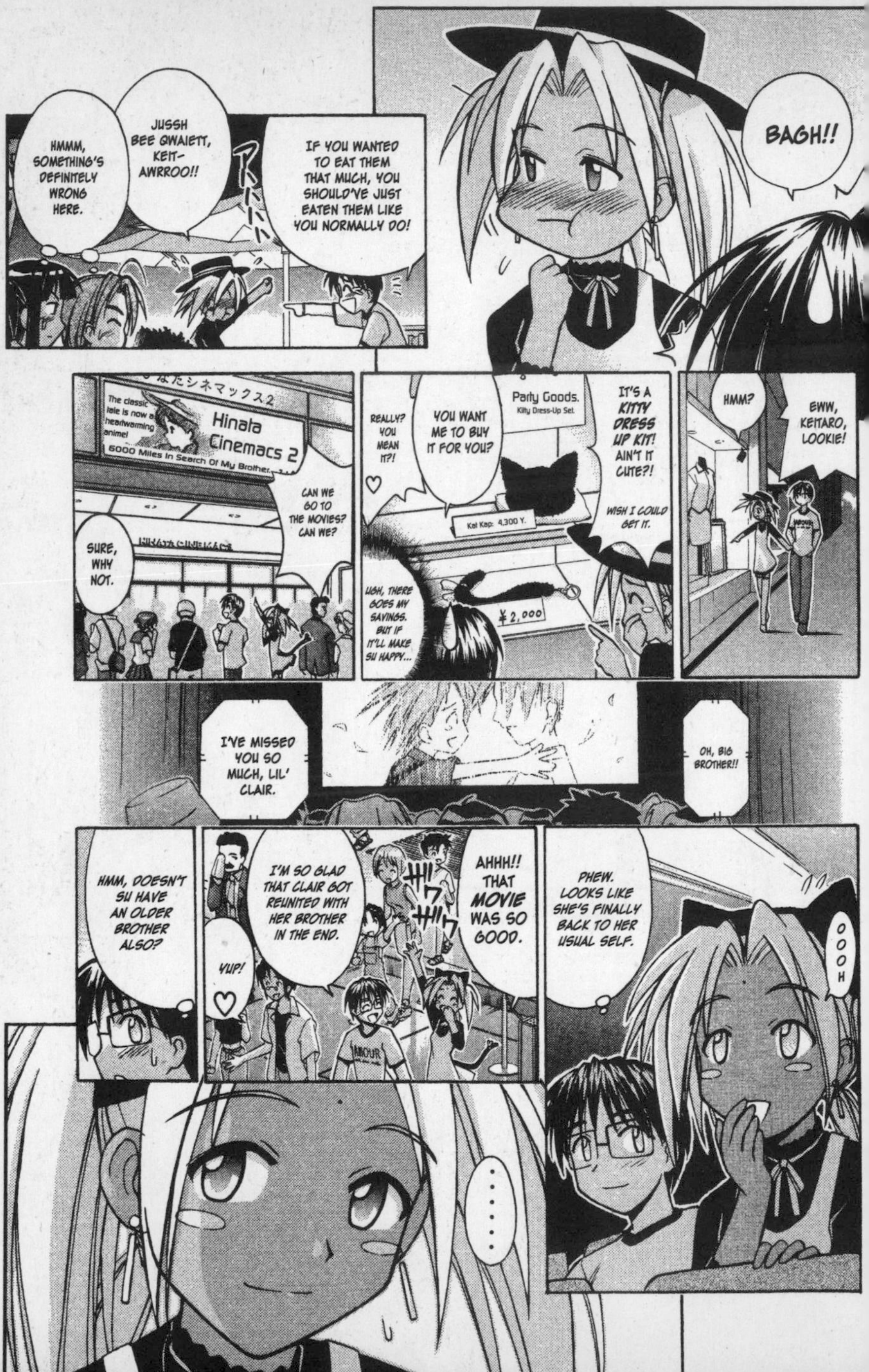
BAGH!!
IF YOU WANTED TO EAT THEM THAT MUCH, YOU SHOULD'VE JUST EATEN THEM LIKE YOU NORMALLY DO!
JUSSH BEE QWAIETT, KEIT-AWRROO!!
HMMM, SOMETHING'S DEFINITELY WRONG HERE.
EWW, KEITARO, LOOKIE!
HMM?
IT'S A KITTY DRESS UP KIT! AIN'T IT CUTE?!
Party Goods. Kitty Dress-Up Set.
WISH I COULD GET IT.
YOU WANT ME TO BUY IT FOR YOU?
REALLY? YOU MEAN IT?! ♡
Kat Kap: 4,300 Y.
¥2,000
UGH, THERE GOES MY SAVINGS. BUT IF IT'LL MAKE SU HAPPY...
Hinata Cinemacs 2
The classic tale is now a heartwarming anime!
6000 Miles In Search Of My Brother...
CAN WE GO TO THE MOVIES? CAN WE?
SURE, WHY NOT.
OH, BIG BROTHER!!
I'VE MISSED YOU SO MUCH, LIL' CLAIR.
OOOH
PHEW. LOOKS LIKE SHE'S FINALLY BACK TO HER USUAL SELF.
AHHH!! THAT MOVIE WAS SO GOOD.
I'M SO GLAD THAT CLAIR GOT REUNITED WITH HER BROTHER IN THE END.
YUP! ♡
HMM, DOESN'T SU HAVE AN OLDER BROTHER ALSO?
......

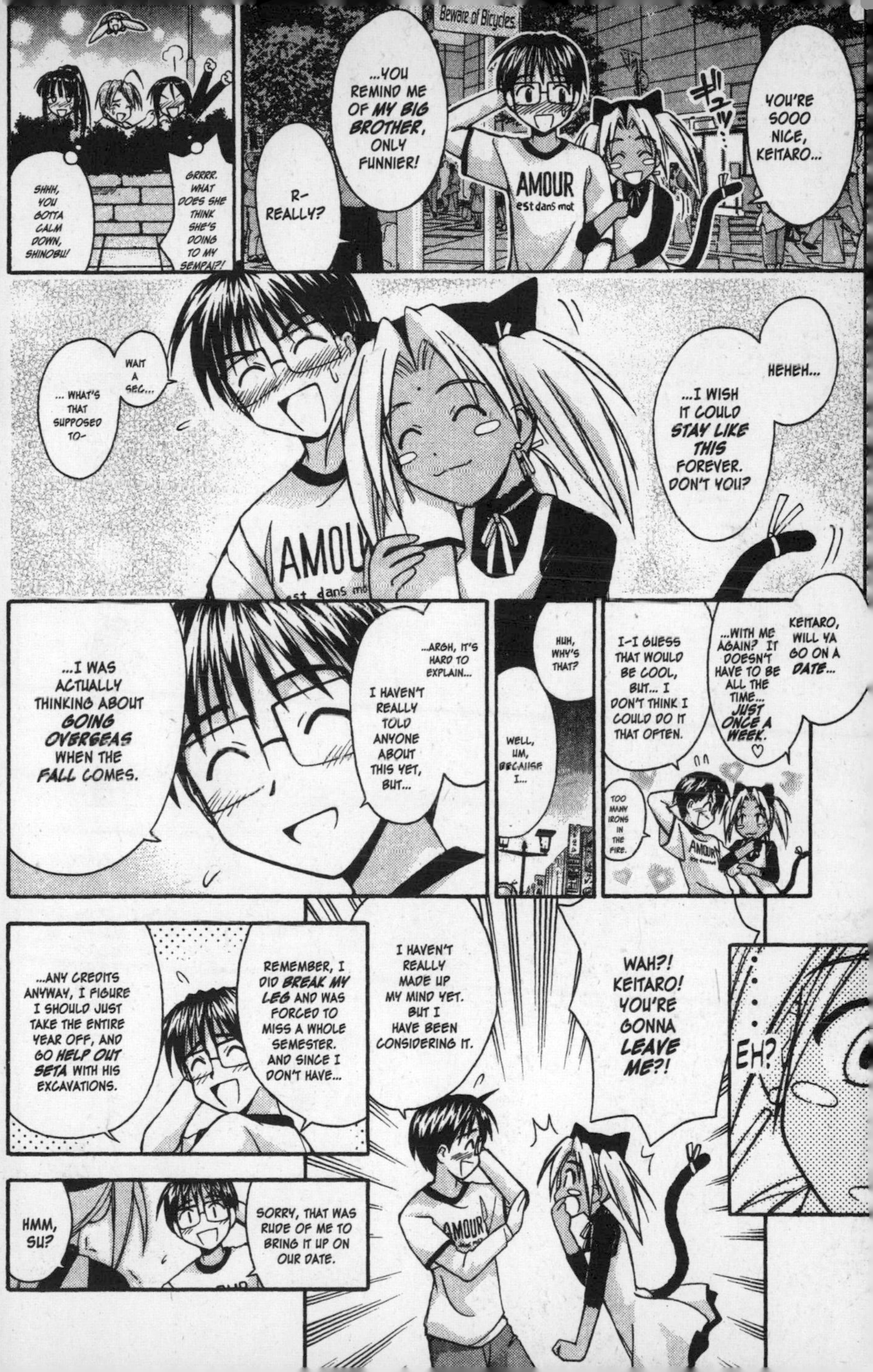
Beware of Bicycles.
YOU'RE SOOO NICE, KEITARO...
...YOU REMIND ME OF MY BIG BROTHER, ONLY FUNNIER!
R-REALLY?
GRRRR. WHAT DOES SHE THINK SHE'S DOING TO MY SEMPAI!?!
SHHH, YOU GOTTA CALM DOWN, SHINOBU!
HEHEH...
...I WISH IT COULD STAY LIKE THIS FOREVER. DON'T YOU?
WAIT A SEC...
... WHAT'S THAT SUPPOSED TO-
KEITARO, WILL YA GO ON A DATE...
...WITH ME AGAIN? IT DOESN'T HAVE TO BE ALL THE TIME... JUST ONCE A WEEK. ♡
I-I GUESS THAT WOULD BE COOL, BUT... I DON'T THINK I COULD DO IT THAT OFTEN.
TOO MANY IRONS IN THE FIRE.
HUH, WHY'S THAT?
WELL, UM, BECAUSE I...
...ARGH, IT'S HARD TO EXPLAIN...
I HAVEN'T REALLY TOLD ANYONE ABOUT THIS YET, BUT...
...I WAS ACTUALLY THINKING ABOUT GOING OVERSEAS WHEN THE FALL COMES.
EH?
WAH?! KEITARO! YOU'RE GONNA LEAVE ME?!
I HAVEN'T REALLY MADE UP MY MIND YET. BUT I HAVE BEEN CONSIDERING IT.
REMEMBER, I DID BREAK MY LEG AND WAS FORCED TO MISS A WHOLE SEMESTER. AND SINCE I DON'T HAVE...
...ANY CREDITS ANYWAY, I FIGURE I SHOULD JUST TAKE THE ENTIRE YEAR OFF, AND GO HELP OUT SETA WITH HIS EXCAVATIONS.
SORRY, THAT WAS RUDE OF ME TO BRING IT UP ON OUR DATE.
HMM, SU?

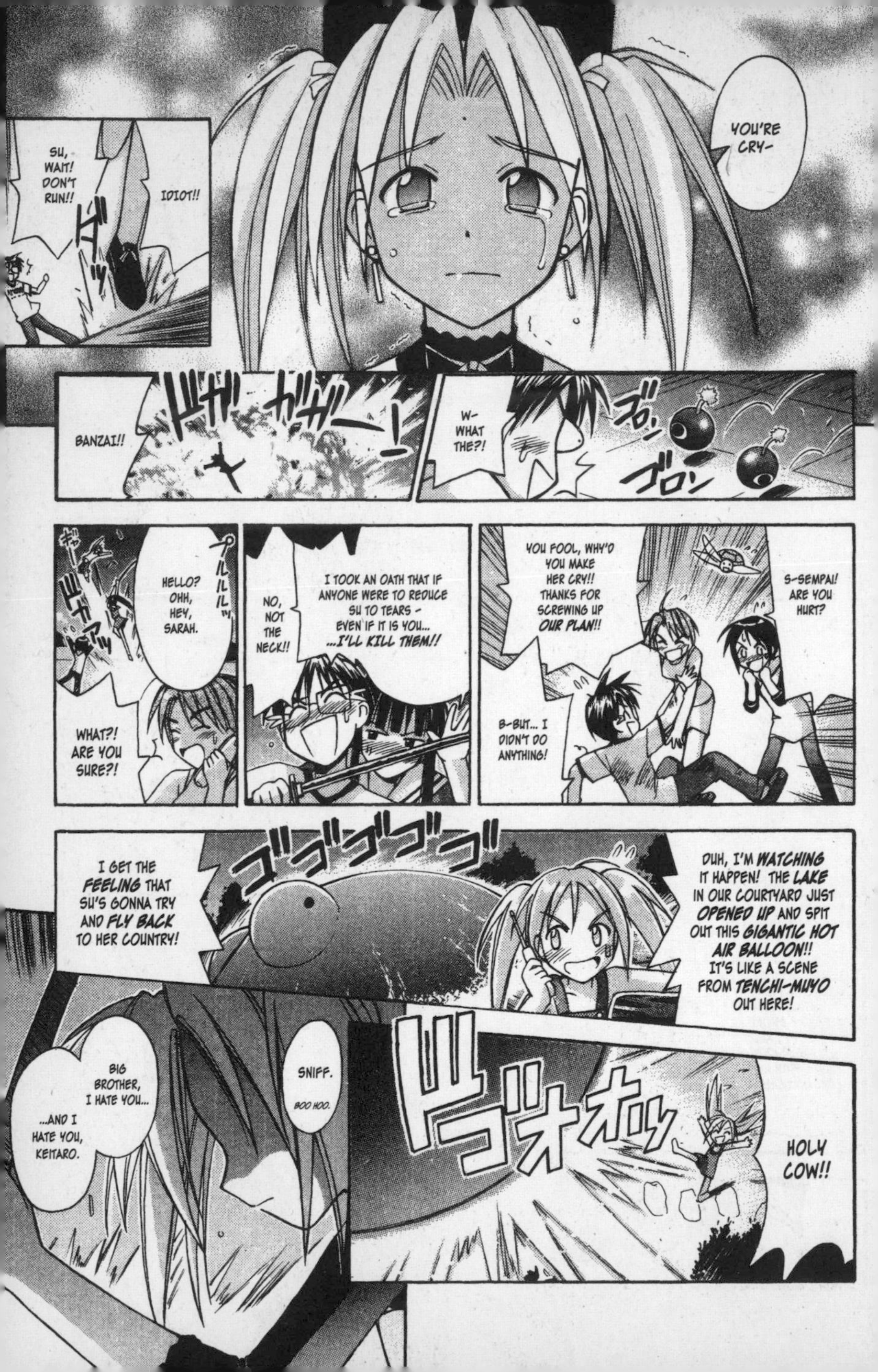
YOU'RE CRY-
SU, WAIT! DON'T RUN!!
IDIOT!!
W-WHAT THE?!
BANZAI!!
YOU FOOL, WHY'D YOU MAKE HER CRY!! THANKS FOR SCREWING UP OUR PLAN!!
S-SEMPAI! ARE YOU HURT?
B-BUT... I DIDN'T DO ANYTHING!
I TOOK AN OATH THAT IF ANYONE WERE TO REDUCE SU TO TEARS - EVEN IF IT IS YOU... ...I'LL KILL THEM!!
NO, NOT THE NECK!!
HELLO? OHH, HEY, SARAH.
WHAT?! ARE YOU SURE?!
DUH, I'M WATCHING IT HAPPEN! THE LAKE IN OUR COURTYARD JUST OPENED UP AND SPIT OUT THIS GIGANTIC HOT AIR BALLOON!! IT'S LIKE A SCENE FROM TENCHI-MUYO OUT HERE!
I GET THE FEELING THAT SU'S GONNA TRY AND FLY BACK TO HER COUNTRY!
HOLY COW!!
SNIFF.
BOO HOO.
BIG BROTHER, I HATE YOU...
...AND I HATE YOU, KEITARO.

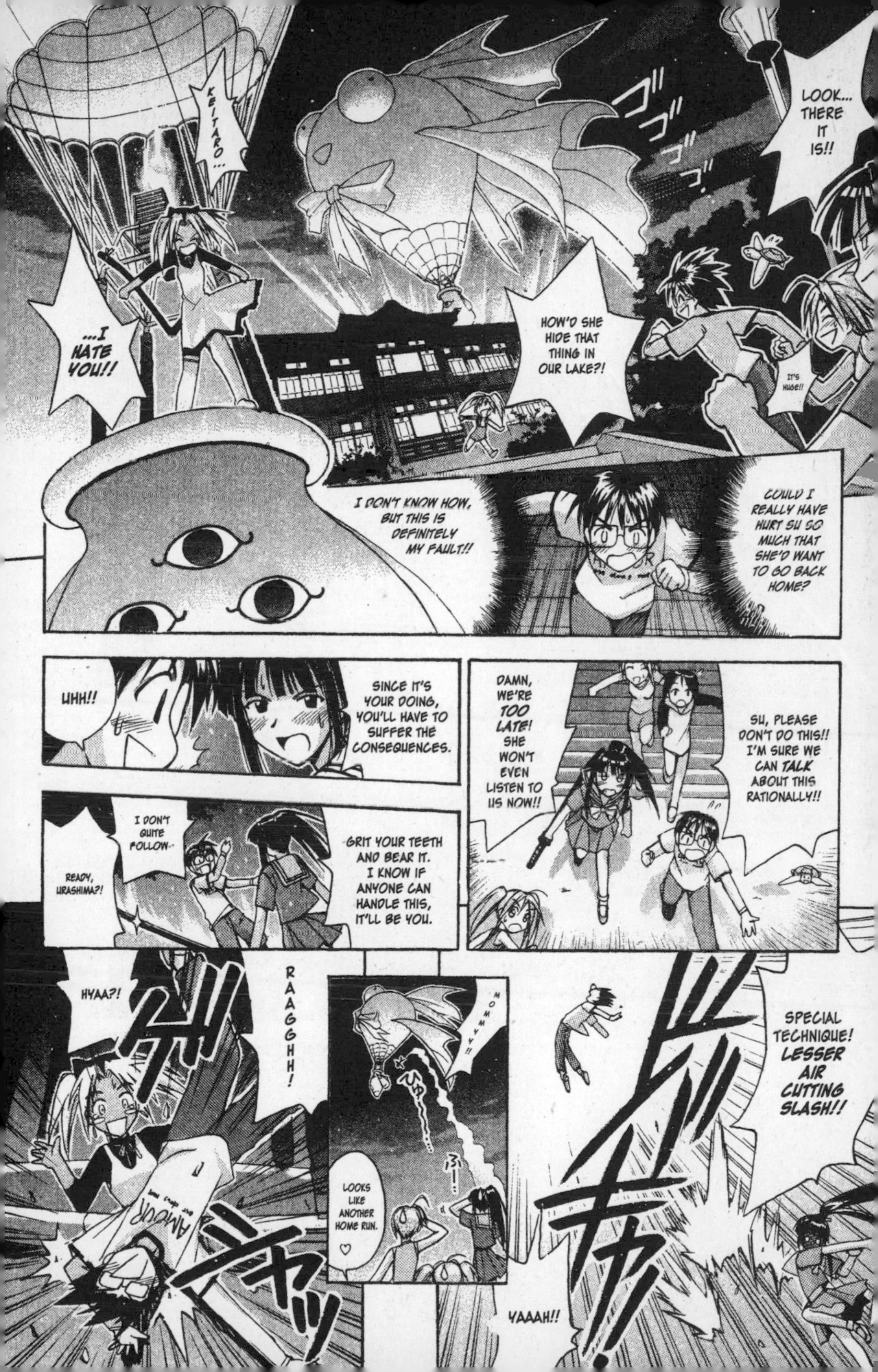
LOOK... THERE IT IS!!
IT'S HUGE!!
HOW'D SHE HIDE THAT THING IN OUR LAKE?!
KEITARO...
...I HATE YOU!!
COULD I REALLY HAVE HURT SU SO MUCH THAT SHE'D WANT TO GO BACK HOME?
I DON'T KNOW HOW, BUT THIS IS DEFINITELY MY FAULT!!
SU, PLEASE DON'T DO THIS!! I'M SURE WE CAN TALK ABOUT THIS RATIONALLY!!
DAMN, WE'RE TOO LATE! SHE WON'T EVEN LISTEN TO US NOW!!
SINCE IT'S YOUR DOING, YOU'LL HAVE TO SUFFER THE CONSEQUENCES.
UHH!!
GRIT YOUR TEETH AND BEAR IT. I KNOW IF ANYONE CAN HANDLE THIS, IT'LL BE YOU.
I DON'T QUITE FOLLOW--
READY, URASHIMA?!
SPECIAL TECHNIQUE! LESSER AIR CUTTING SLASH!!
YAAAH!!
MOMMYYY!!
LOOKS LIKE ANOTHER HOME RUN. ♡
RAAGGHH!
HYAA?!
AMOUR

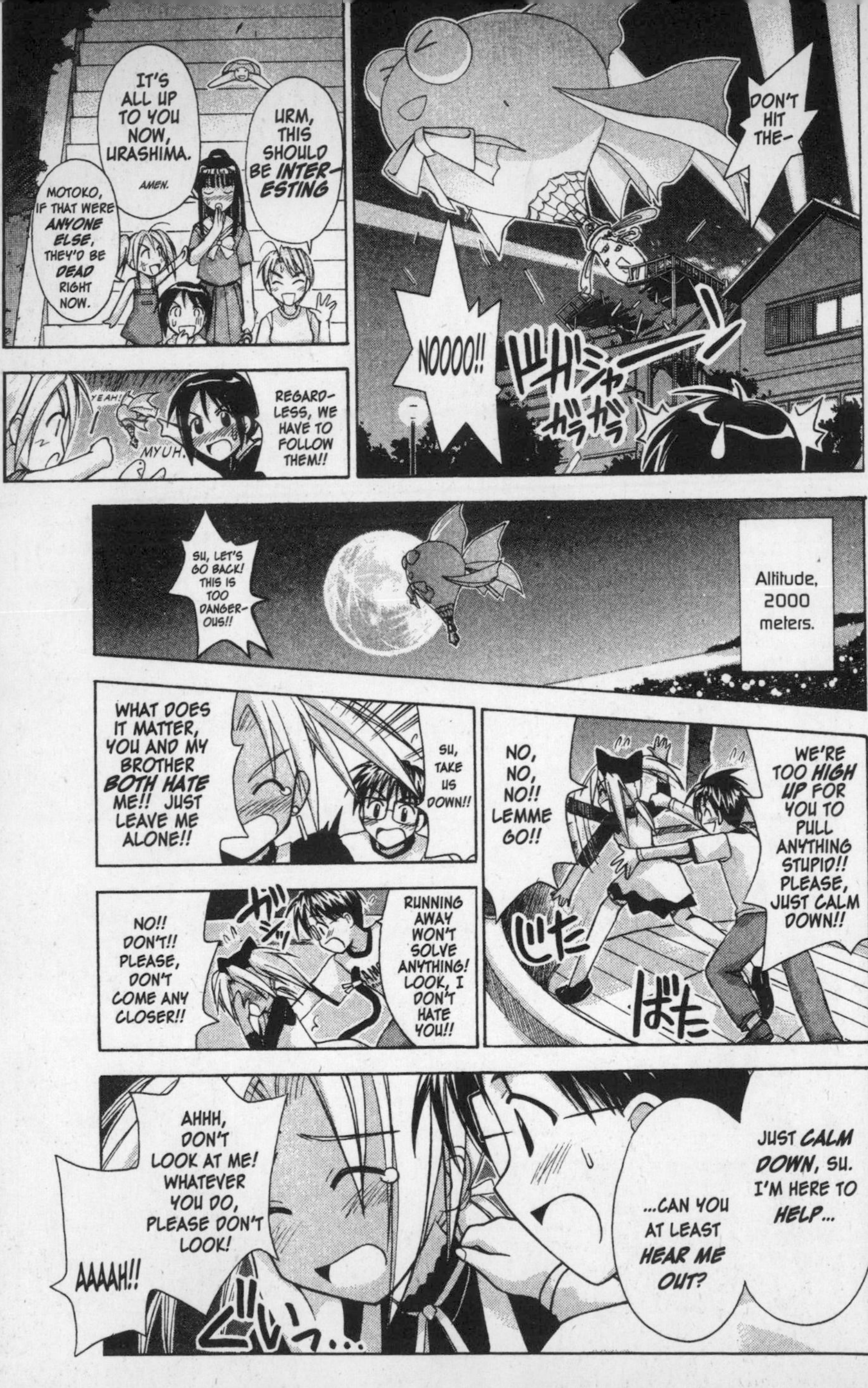
DON'T HIT THE-
NOOOO!!
ドガシャーン
ガラガラ
URM, THIS SHOULD BE *INTERESTING*
IT'S ALL UP TO YOU NOW, URASHIMA.
AMEN.
MOTOKO, IF THAT WERE *ANYONE ELSE*, THEY'D BE *DEAD* RIGHT NOW.
REGARDLESS, WE HAVE TO FOLLOW THEM!!
YEAH!
MYUH.
Altitude, 2000 meters.
SU, LET'S GO BACK! THIS IS TOO DANGEROUS!!
WE'RE TOO *HIGH UP* FOR YOU TO PULL ANYTHING STUPID!! PLEASE, JUST CALM DOWN!!
NO, NO, NO!! LEMME GO!!
じた
ばた
SU, TAKE US DOWN!!
WHAT DOES IT MATTER, YOU AND MY BROTHER *BOTH HATE* ME!! JUST LEAVE ME ALONE!!
RUNNING AWAY WON'T SOLVE ANYTHING! LOOK, I DON'T HATE YOU!!
NO!! DON'T!! PLEASE, DON'T COME ANY CLOSER!!
JUST *CALM DOWN*, SU. I'M HERE TO *HELP*...
...CAN YOU AT LEAST *HEAR ME OUT?*
AHHH, DON'T LOOK AT ME! WHATEVER YOU DO, PLEASE DON'T LOOK!
AAAAH!!
ぐいっ...

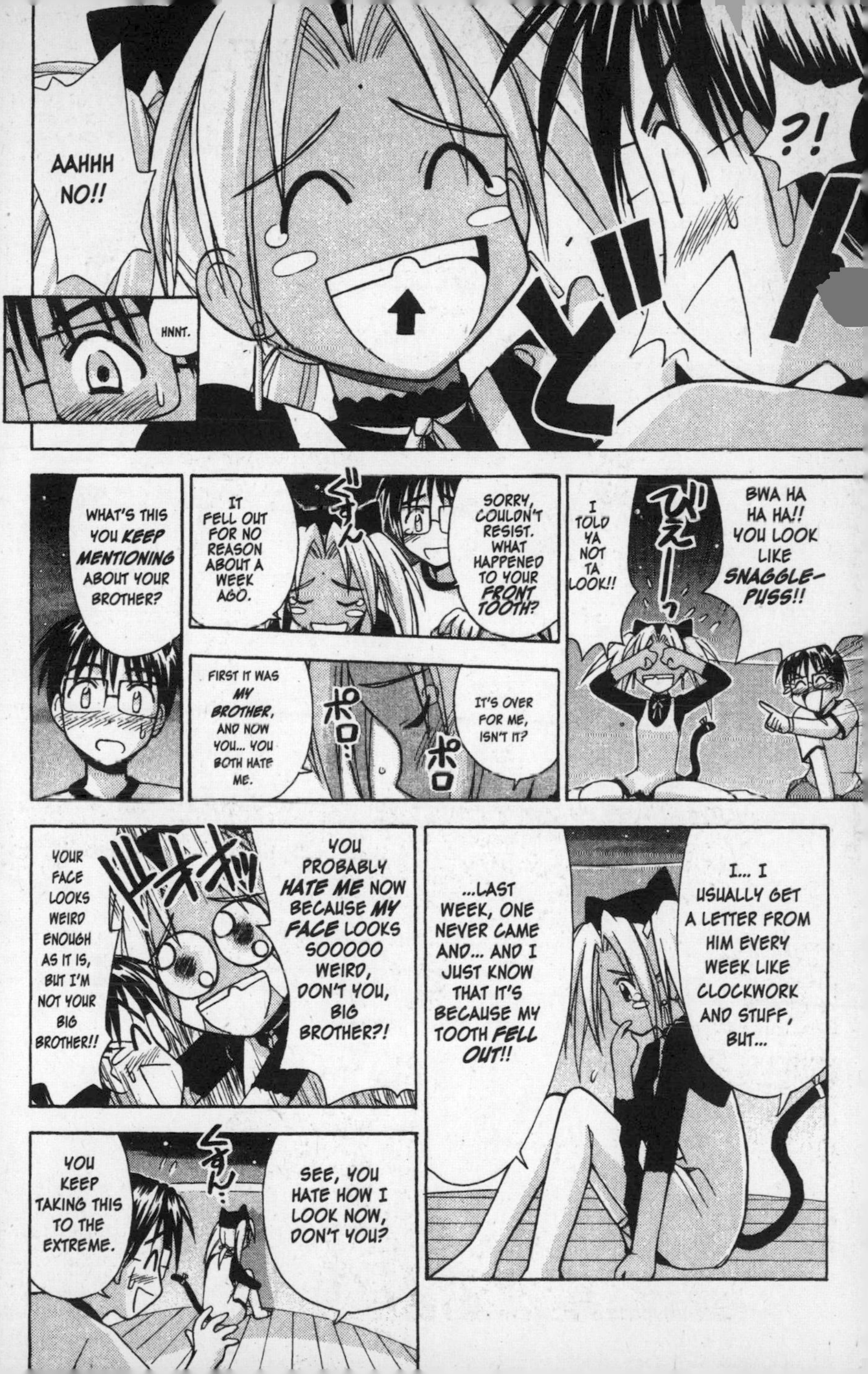
?!
AAHHH NO!!
HNNT.
BWA HA HA HA!! YOU LOOK LIKE SNAGGLE-PUSS!!
ぴえーっ
I TOLD YA NOT TA LOOK!!
SORRY, COULDN'T RESIST. WHAT HAPPENED TO YOUR FRONT TOOTH?
ぐすん
IT FELL OUT FOR NO REASON ABOUT A WEEK AGO.
IT'S OVER FOR ME, ISN'T IT?
ポロ ポロ
FIRST IT WAS MY BROTHER, AND NOW YOU... YOU BOTH HATE ME.
WHAT'S THIS YOU KEEP MENTIONING ABOUT YOUR BROTHER?
I... I USUALLY GET A LETTER FROM HIM EVERY WEEK LIKE CLOCKWORK AND STUFF, BUT...
...LAST WEEK, ONE NEVER CAME AND... AND I JUST KNOW THAT IT'S BECAUSE MY TOOTH FELL OUT!!
YOU PROBABLY HATE ME NOW BECAUSE MY FACE LOOKS SOOOOO WEIRD, DON'T YOU, BIG BROTHER?!
YOUR FACE LOOKS WEIRD ENOUGH AS IT IS, BUT I'M NOT YOUR BIG BROTHER!!
SEE, YOU HATE HOW I LOOK NOW, DON'T YOU?
くすん..
YOU KEEP TAKING THIS TO THE EXTREME.

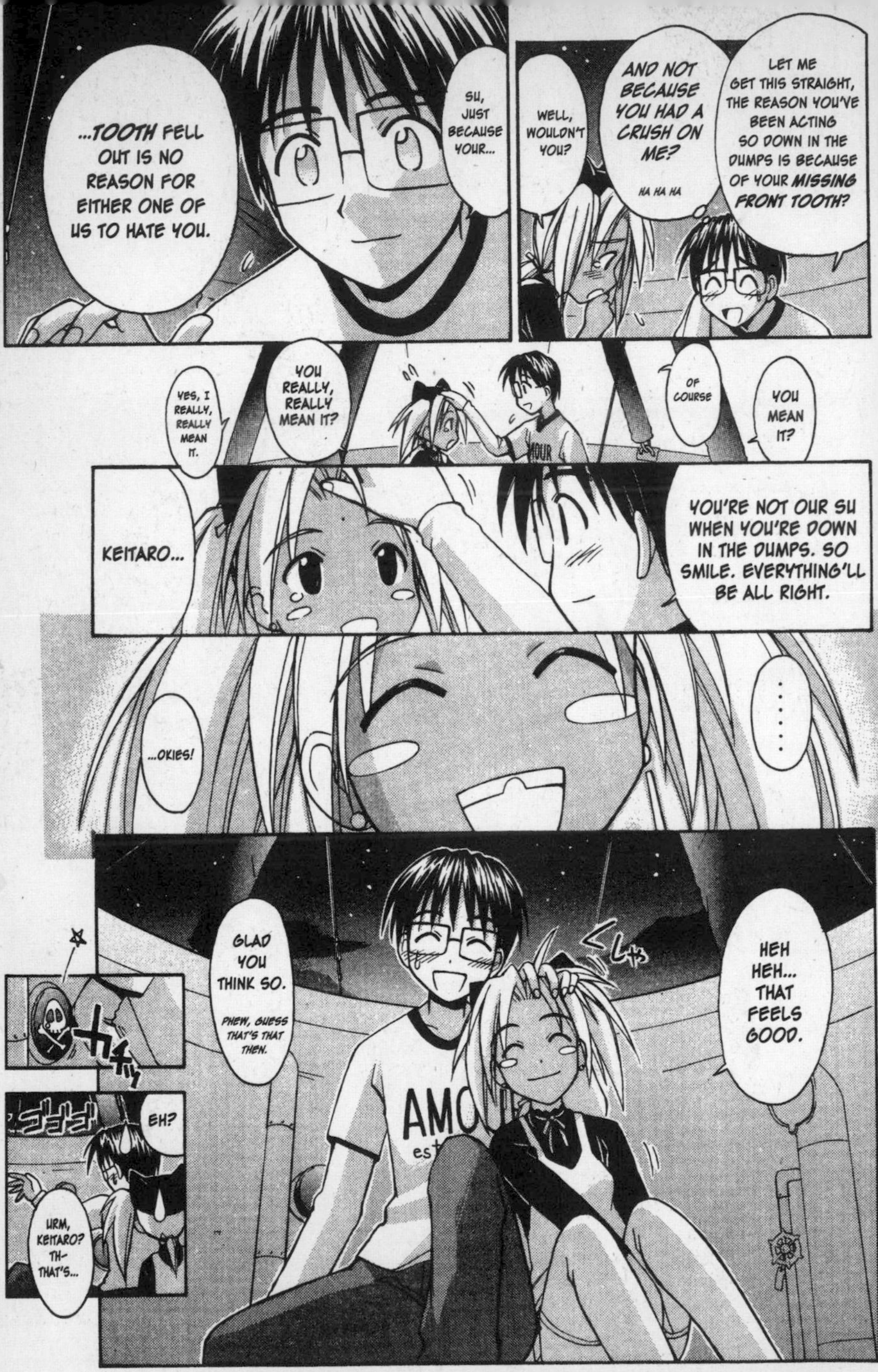
LET ME GET THIS STRAIGHT, THE REASON YOU'VE BEEN ACTING SO DOWN IN THE DUMPS IS BECAUSE OF YOUR MISSING FRONT TOOTH?
AND NOT BECAUSE YOU HAD A CRUSH ON ME?
HA HA HA
WELL, WOULDN'T YOU?
SU, JUST BECAUSE YOUR...
...TOOTH FELL OUT IS NO REASON FOR EITHER ONE OF US TO HATE YOU.
YOU MEAN IT?
OF COURSE
YOU REALLY, REALLY MEAN IT?
YES, I REALLY, REALLY MEAN IT.
YOU'RE NOT OUR SU WHEN YOU'RE DOWN IN THE DUMPS. SO SMILE. EVERYTHING'LL BE ALL RIGHT.
KEITARO...
......
...OKIES!
HEH HEH... THAT FEELS GOOD.
くしゃ
GLAD YOU THINK SO.
PHEW, GUESS THAT'S THAT THEN.
カチッ
EH?
URM, KEITARO? TH-THAT'S...

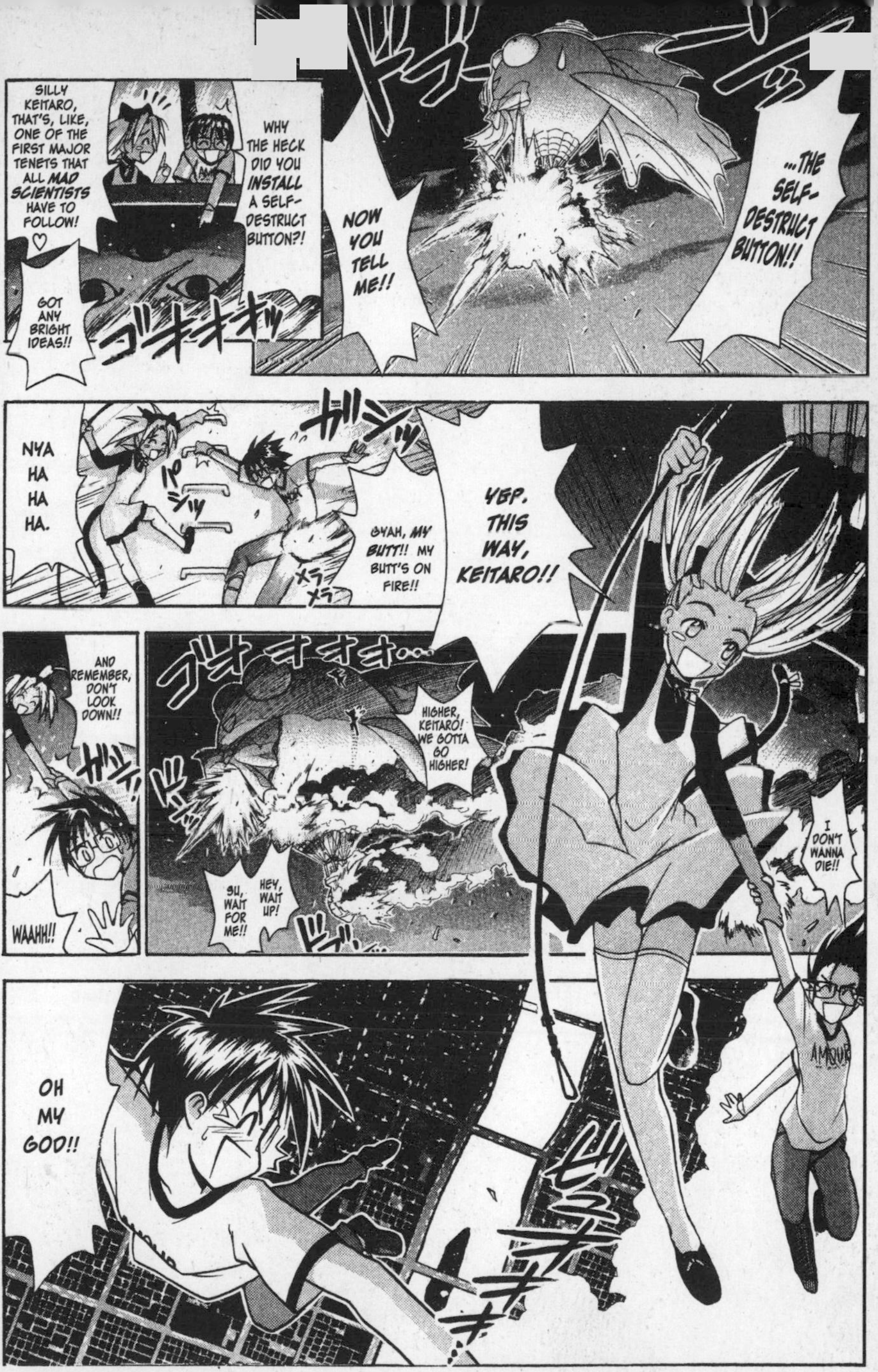
...THE SELF-DESTRUCT BUTTON!!
NOW YOU TELL ME!!
WHY THE HECK DID YOU INSTALL A SELF-DESTRUCT BUTTON?!
SILLY KEITARO, THAT'S, LIKE, ONE OF THE FIRST MAJOR TENETS THAT ALL MAD SCIENTISTS HAVE TO FOLLOW! ♡
GOT ANY BRIGHT IDEAS!!
YEP. THIS WAY, KEITARO!!
I DON'T WANNA DIE!!
AMOUR
GYAH, MY BUTT!! MY BUTT'S ON FIRE!!
NYA HA HA HA.
HIGHER, KEITARO! WE GOTTA GO HIGHER!
HEY, WAIT UP!
SU, WAIT FOR ME!!
AND REMEMBER, DON'T LOOK DOWN!!
WAAHH!!
OH MY GOD!!

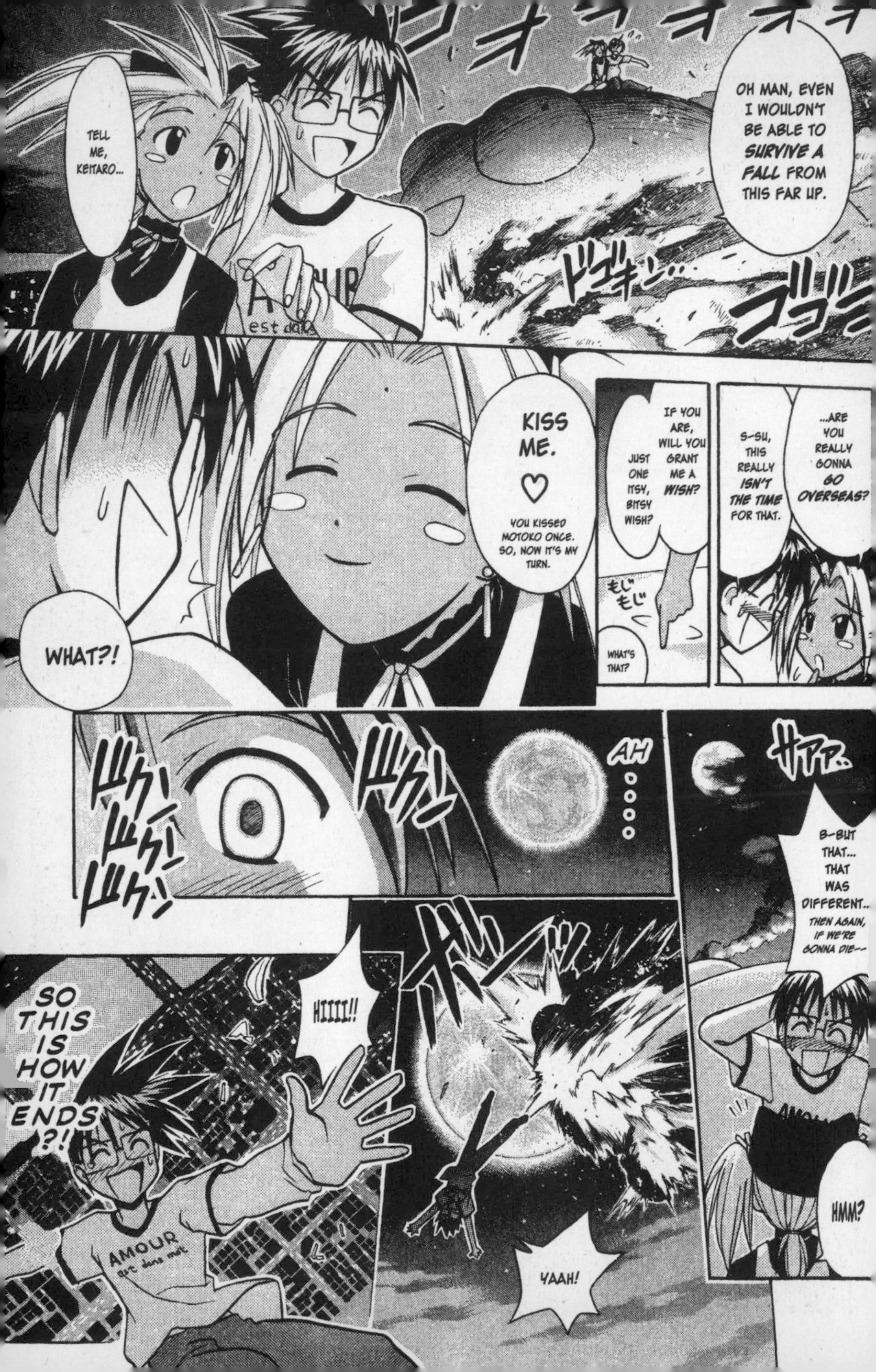

OH MAN, EVEN I WOULDN'T BE ABLE TO SURVIVE A FALL FROM THIS FAR UP.
TELL ME, KEITARO...
...ARE YOU REALLY GONNA GO OVERSEAS?
S-SU, THIS REALLY ISN'T THE TIME FOR THAT.
IF YOU ARE, WILL YOU GRANT ME A WISH?
JUST ONE ITSY, BITSY WISH?
もじもじ
WHAT'S THAT?
KISS ME. ♥
YOU KISSED MOTOKO ONCE. SO, NOW IT'S MY TURN.
WHAT?!
HAP..
B-BUT THAT... THAT WAS DIFFERENT..
THEN AGAIN, IF WE'RE GONNA DIE--
HMM?
AH OOOO
YAAH!
HIIII!!
SO THIS IS HOW IT ENDS?!

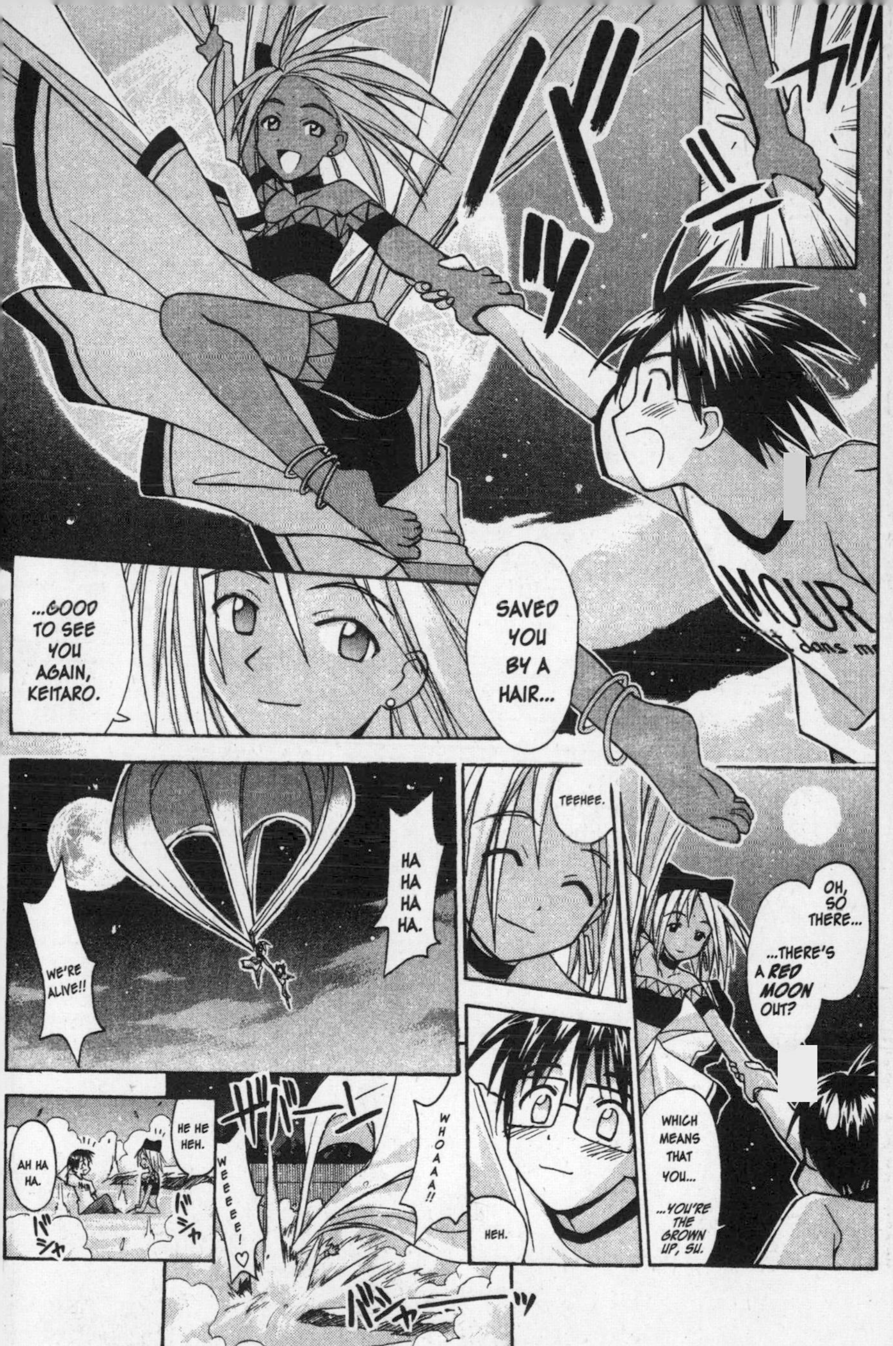
SAVED YOU BY A HAIR...
...GOOD TO SEE YOU AGAIN, KEITARO.
TEEHEE.
OH, SO THERE...
...THERE'S A RED MOON OUT?
WHICH MEANS THAT YOU...
...YOU'RE THE GROWN UP, SU.
HEH.
HA HA HA HA HA.
WE'RE ALIVE!!
WHOAAAA!!
WEEEEEE! ♡
HE HE HEH.
AH HA HA.

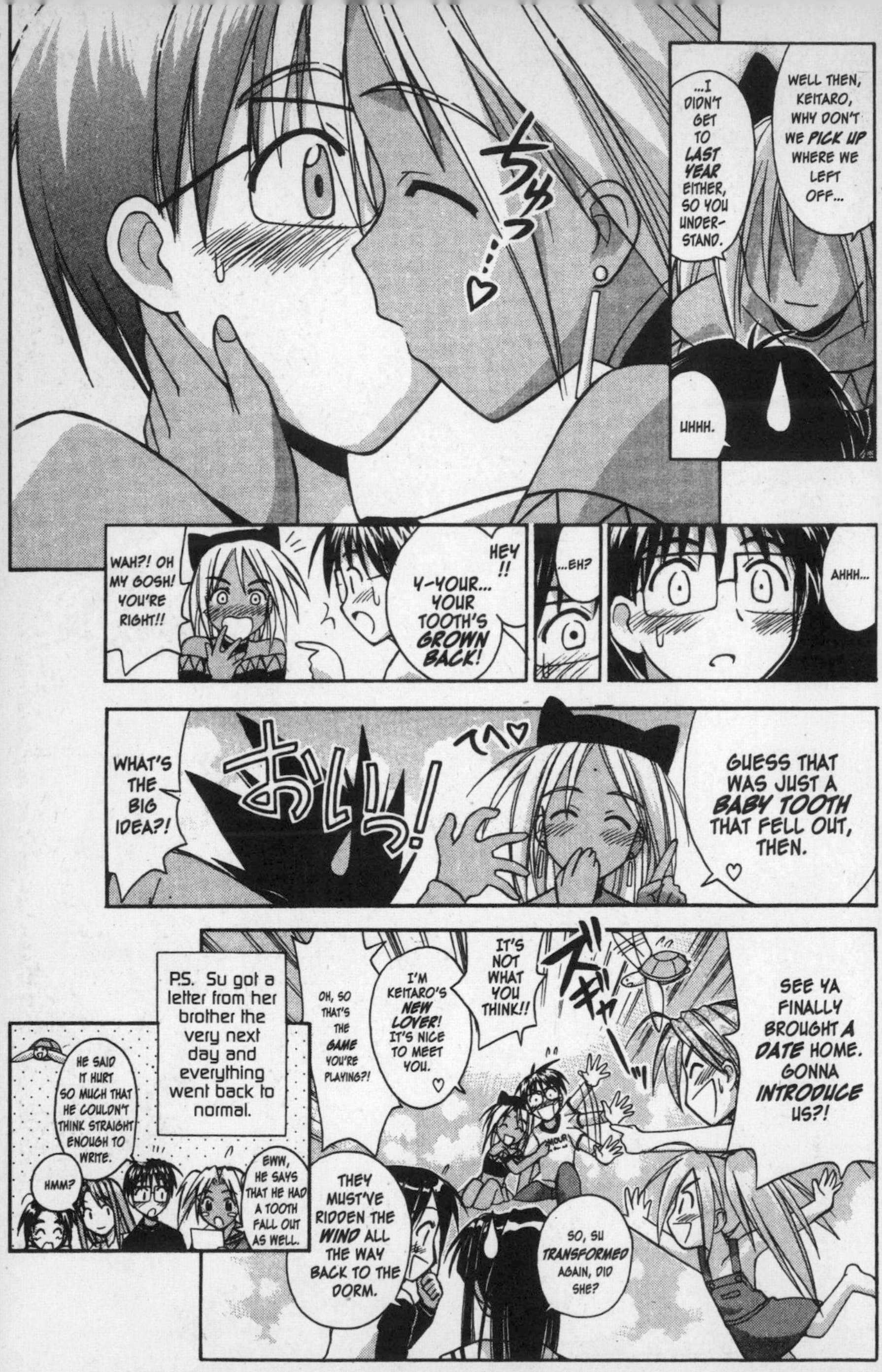
WELL THEN, KEITARO, WHY DON'T WE PICK UP WHERE WE LEFT OFF...
...I DIDN'T GET TO LAST YEAR EITHER, SO YOU UNDERSTAND.
UHHH.
ちゅっ…♡
AHHH...
...EH?
HEY!!
Y-YOUR... YOUR TOOTH'S GROWN BACK!
WAH?! OH MY GOSH! YOU'RE RIGHT!!
GUESS THAT WAS JUST A BABY TOOTH THAT FELL OUT, THEN. ♡
てへ♡
おいっ!
WHAT'S THE BIG IDEA?!
SEE YA FINALLY BROUGHT A DATE HOME. GONNA INTRODUCE US?!
ズギャーッ
IT'S NOT WHAT YOU THINK!!
I'M KEITARO'S NEW LOVER! IT'S NICE TO MEET YOU. ♡
OH, SO THAT'S THE GAME YOU'RE PLAYING?!
SO, SU TRANSFORMED AGAIN, DID SHE?
THEY MUST'VE RIDDEN THE WIND ALL THE WAY BACK TO THE DORM.
P.S. Su got a letter from her brother the very next day and everything went back to normal.
EWW, HE SAYS THAT HE HAD A TOOTH FALL OUT AS WELL.
HE SAID IT HURT SO MUCH THAT HE COULDN'T THINK STRAIGHT ENOUGH TO WRITE.
HMM?

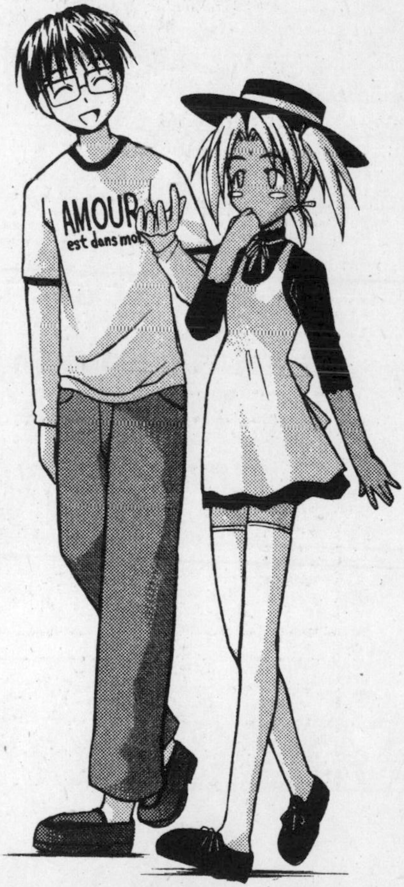
AMOUR
est dans mo

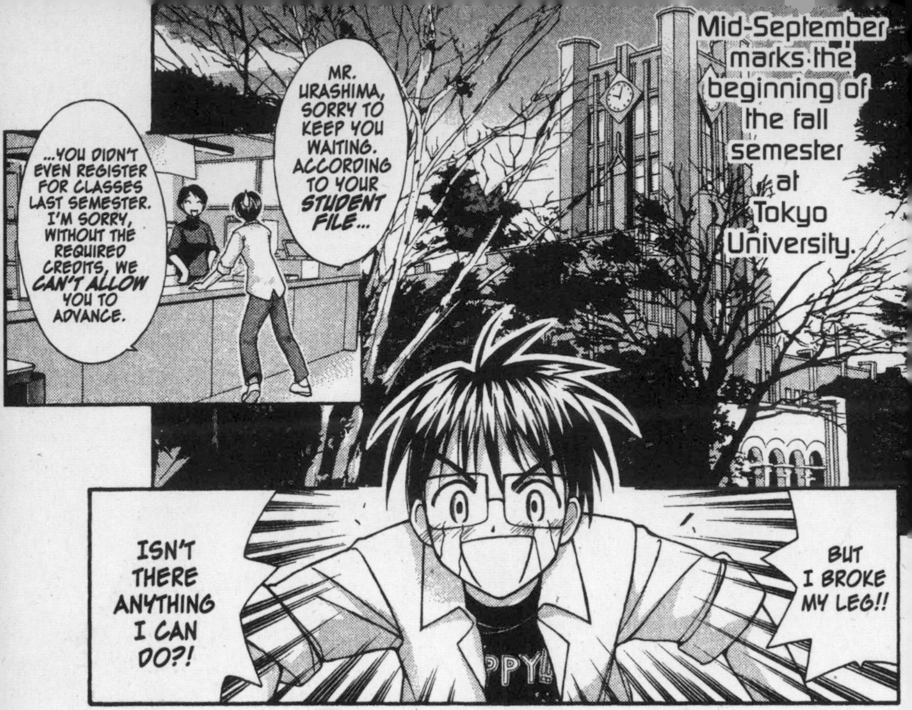
Mid-September marks the beginning of the fall semester at Tokyo University.
MR. URASHIMA, SORRY TO KEEP YOU WAITING. ACCORDING TO YOUR STUDENT FILE...
...YOU DIDN'T EVEN REGISTER FOR CLASSES LAST SEMESTER. I'M SORRY, WITHOUT THE REQUIRED CREDITS, WE CAN'T ALLOW YOU TO ADVANCE.
BUT I BROKE MY LEG!!
ISN'T THERE ANYTHING I CAN DO?!

Love Hina

HINATA.85 And When She Changed Her Attire

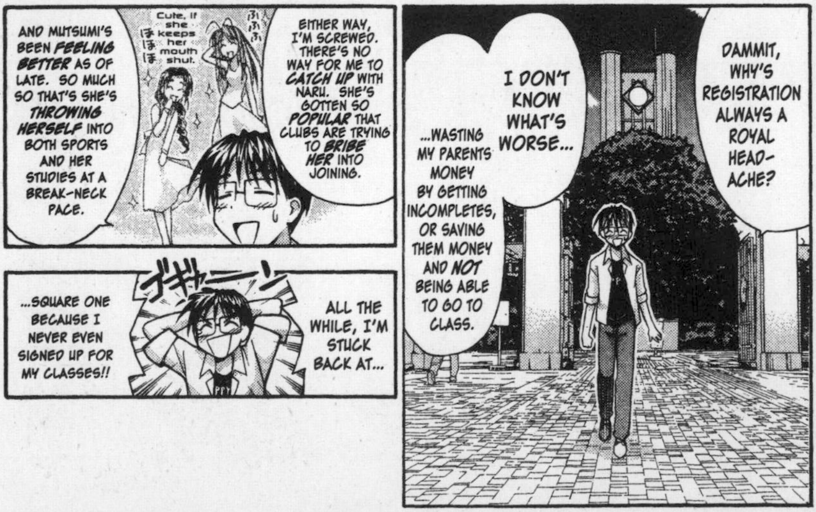
DAMMIT, WHY'S REGISTRATION ALWAYS A ROYAL HEAD-ACHE?
I DON'T KNOW WHAT'S WORSE...
...WASTING MY PARENTS MONEY BY GETTING INCOMPLETES, OR SAVING THEM MONEY AND NOT BEING ABLE TO GO TO CLASS.
EITHER WAY, I'M SCREWED. THERE'S NO WAY FOR ME TO CATCH UP WITH NARU. SHE'S GOTTEN SO POPULAR THAT CLUBS ARE TRYING TO BRIBE HER INTO JOINING.
ふふふ
Cute, if she keeps her mouth shut.
ほほほ
AND MUTSUMI'S BEEN FEELING BETTER AS OF LATE. SO MUCH SO THAT'S SHE'S THROWING HERSELF INTO BOTH SPORTS AND HER STUDIES AT A BREAK-NECK PACE.
ALL THE WHILE, I'M STUCK BACK AT...
...SQUARE ONE BECAUSE I NEVER EVEN SIGNED UP FOR MY CLASSES!!

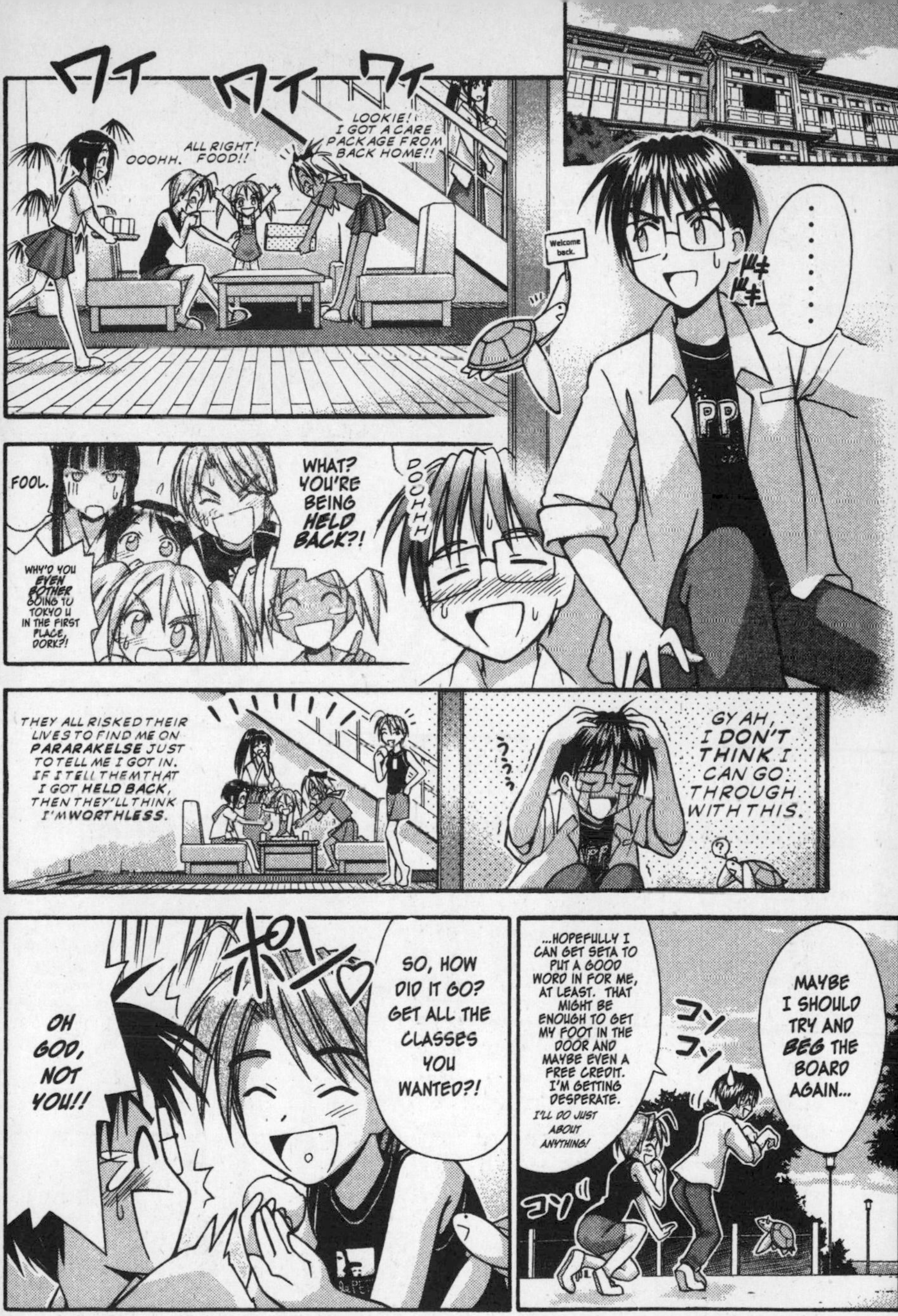
Welcome back.
……
ワイ ワイ ワイ
LOOKIE! I GOT A CARE PACKAGE FROM BACK HOME!!
ALL RIGHT! FOOD!!
OOOHH.
DOOHHH
WHAT? YOU'RE BEING HELD BACK?!
FOOL.
WHY'D YOU EVEN BOTHER GOING TO TOKYO U IN THE FIRST PLACE, DORK?!
GYAH, I DON'T THINK I CAN GO THROUGH WITH THIS.
THEY ALL RISKED THEIR LIVES TO FIND ME ON PARARAKELSE JUST TO TELL ME I GOT IN. IF I TELL THEM THAT I GOT HELD BACK, THEN THEY'LL THINK I'M WORTHLESS.
MAYBE I SHOULD TRY AND BEG THE BOARD AGAIN...
...HOPEFULLY I CAN GET SETA TO PUT A GOOD WORD IN FOR ME, AT LEAST. THAT MIGHT BE ENOUGH TO GET MY FOOT IN THE DOOR AND MAYBE EVEN A FREE CREDIT. I'M GETTING DESPERATE.
I'LL DO JUST ABOUT ANYTHING!
SO, HOW DID IT GO? GET ALL THE CLASSES YOU WANTED?!
OH GOD, NOT YOU!!

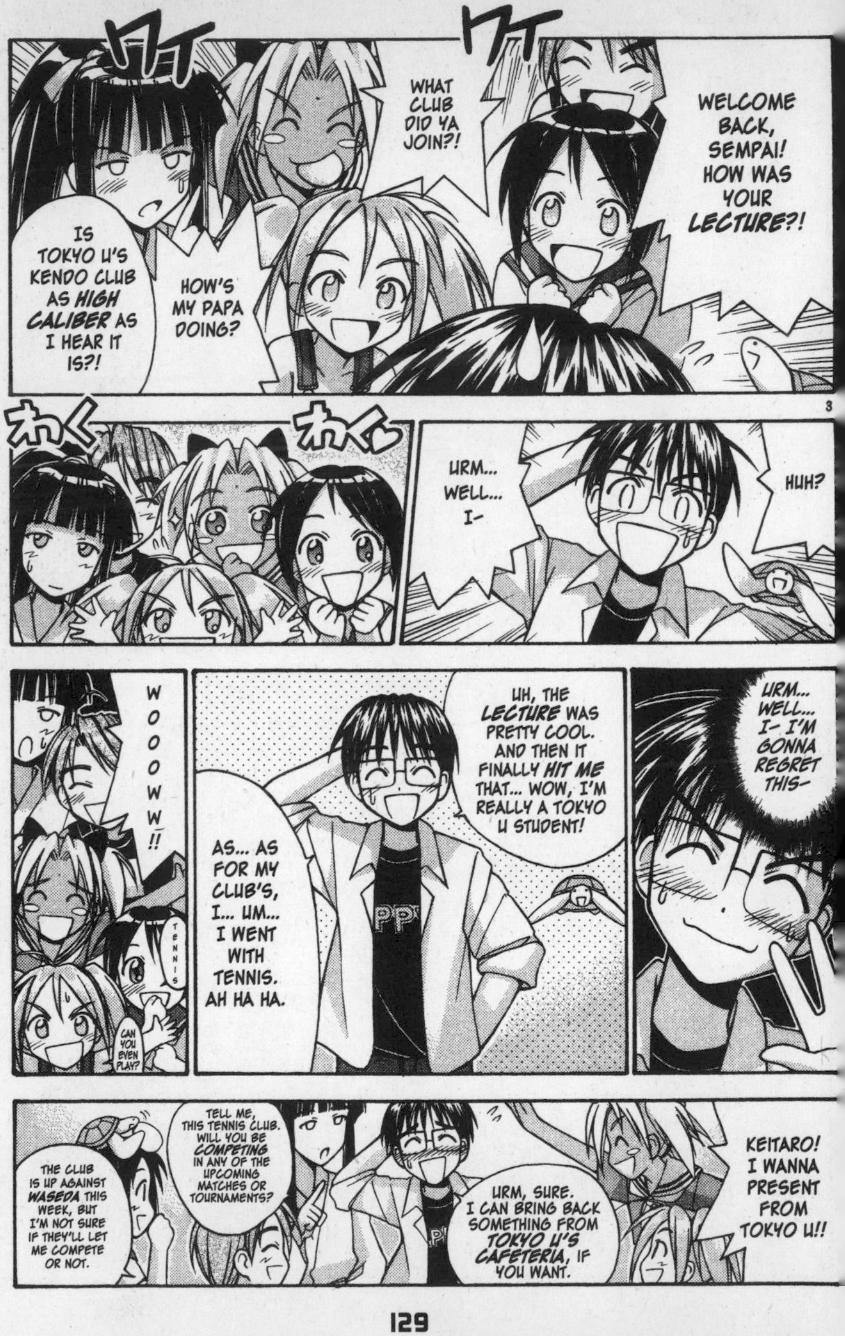
ワイ ワイ
WELCOME BACK, SEMPAI! HOW WAS YOUR LECTURE?!
WHAT CLUB DID YA JOIN?!
HOW'S MY PAPA DOING?
IS TOKYO U'S KENDO CLUB AS HIGH CALIBER AS I HEAR IT IS?!
HUH?
URM... WELL... I-
わく わく♡
URM... WELL... I- I'M GONNA REGRET THIS-
UH, THE LECTURE WAS PRETTY COOL. AND THEN IT FINALLY HIT ME THAT... WOW, I'M REALLY A TOKYO U STUDENT!
AS... AS FOR MY CLUB'S, I... UM... I WENT WITH TENNIS. AH HA HA.
WOOOOWW!!
TENNIS
CAN YOU EVEN PLAY?
KEITARO! I WANNA PRESENT FROM TOKYO U!!
URM, SURE. I CAN BRING BACK SOMETHING FROM TOKYO U'S CAFETERIA, IF YOU WANT.
TELL ME, THIS TENNIS CLUB. WILL YOU BE COMPETING IN ANY OF THE UPCOMING MATCHES OR TOURNAMENTS?
THE CLUB IS UP AGAINST WASEDA THIS WEEK, BUT I'M NOT SURE IF THEY'LL LET ME COMPETE OR NOT.

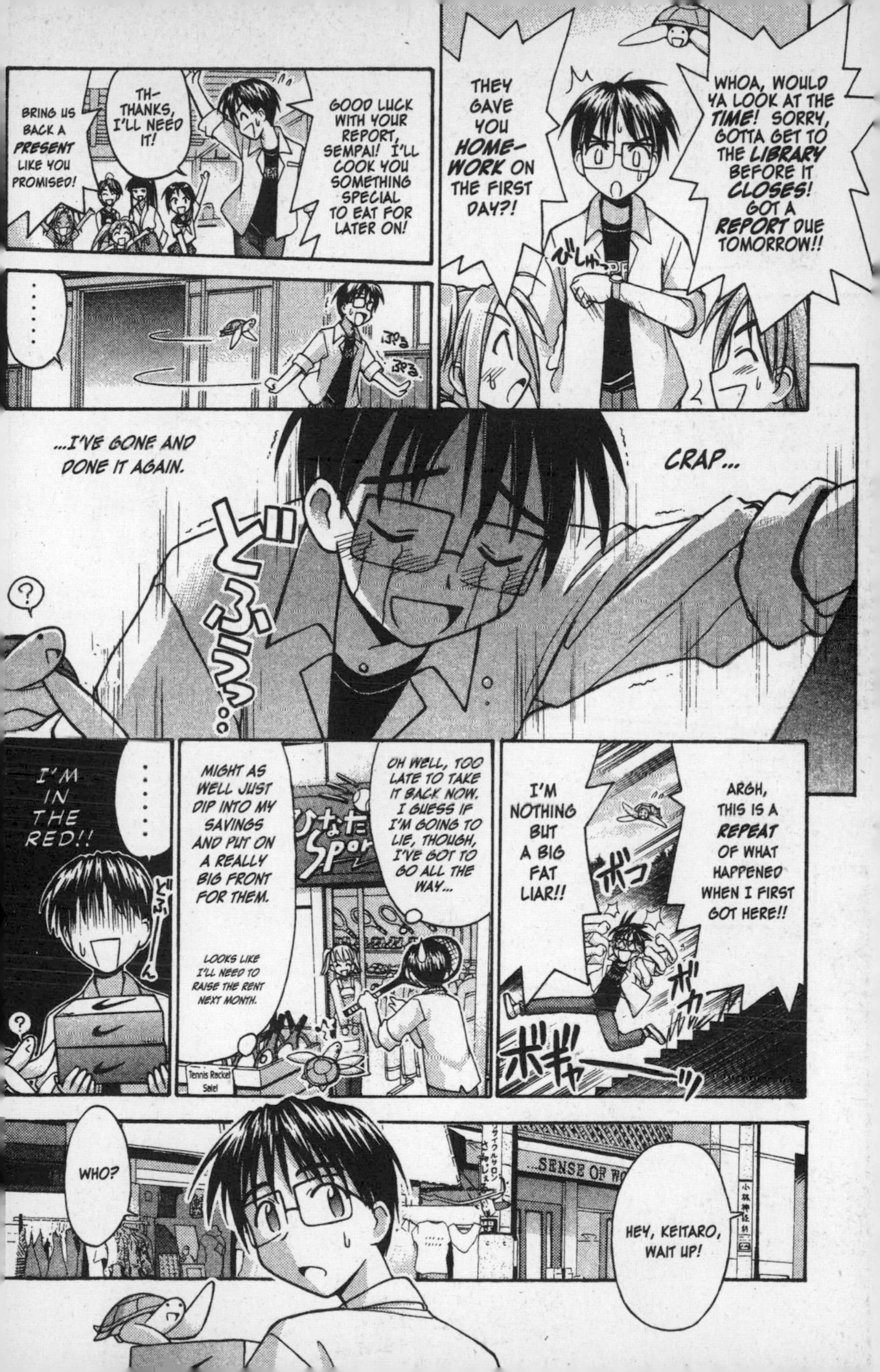

WHOA, WOULD YA LOOK AT THE TIME! SORRY, GOTTA GET TO THE LIBRARY BEFORE IT CLOSES! GOT A REPORT DUE TOMORROW!!
THEY GAVE YOU HOMEWORK ON THE FIRST DAY?!
GOOD LUCK WITH YOUR REPORT, SEMPAI! I'LL COOK YOU SOMETHING SPECIAL TO EAT FOR LATER ON!
TH-THANKS, I'LL NEED IT!
BRING US BACK A PRESENT LIKE YOU PROMISED!
......
CRAP...
...I'VE GONE AND DONE IT AGAIN.
?
ARGH, THIS IS A REPEAT OF WHAT HAPPENED WHEN I FIRST GOT HERE!!
I'M NOTHING BUT A BIG FAT LIAR!!
OH WELL, TOO LATE TO TAKE IT BACK NOW. I GUESS IF I'M GOING TO LIE, THOUGH, I'VE GOT TO GO ALL THE WAY...
MIGHT AS WELL JUST DIP INTO MY SAVINGS AND PUT ON A REALLY BIG FRONT FOR THEM.
LOOKS LIKE I'LL NEED TO RAISE THE RENT NEXT MONTH.
Tennis Racket Sale!
......
I'M IN THE RED!!
?
HEY, KEITARO, WAIT UP!
WHO?

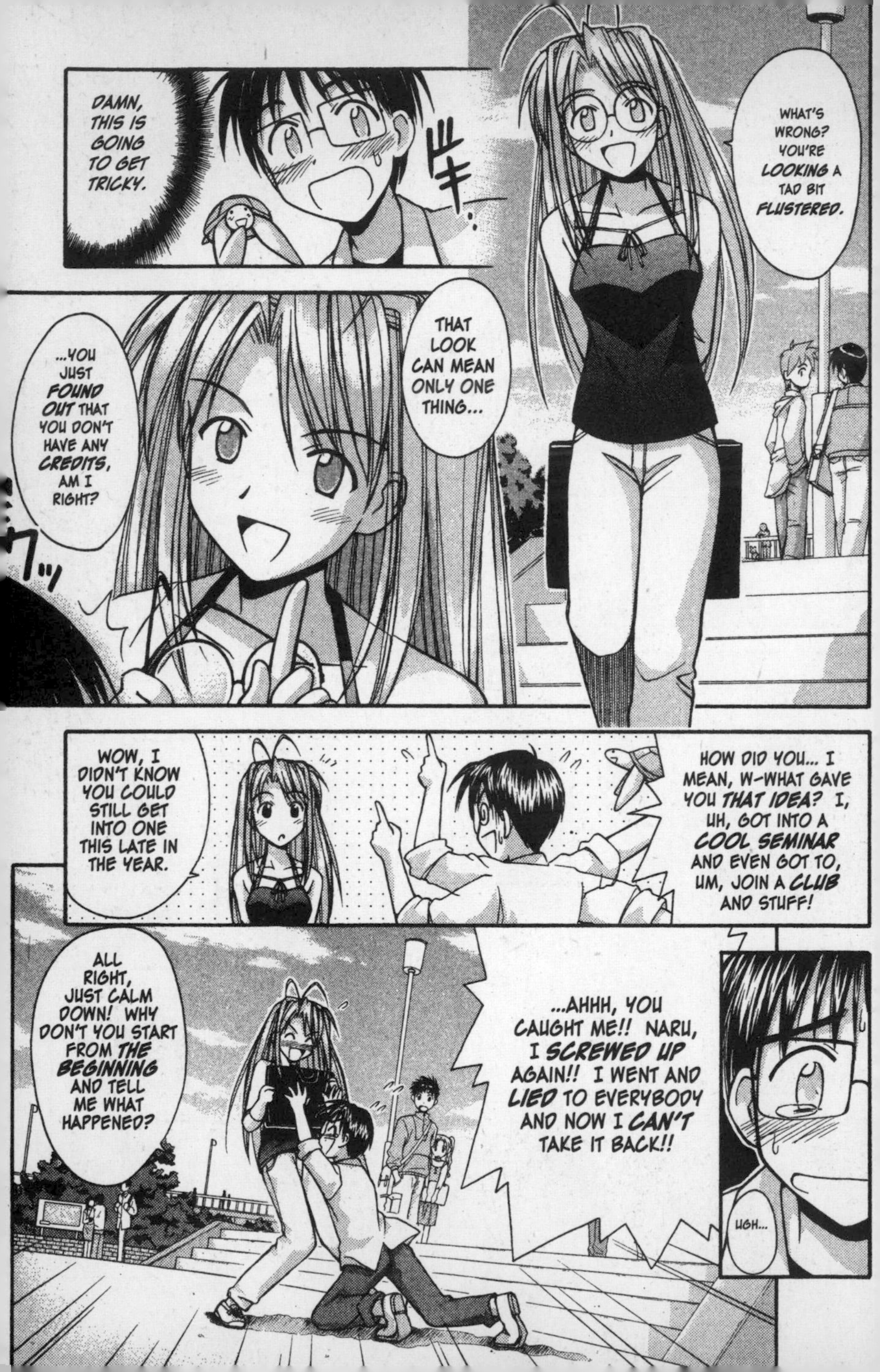
WHAT'S WRONG? YOU'RE **LOOKING** A TAD BIT **FLUSTERED.**
DAMN, THIS IS GOING TO GET TRICKY.
THAT LOOK CAN MEAN ONLY ONE THING...
...YOU JUST **FOUND OUT** THAT YOU DON'T HAVE ANY **CREDITS,** AM I RIGHT?
HOW DID YOU... I MEAN, W-WHAT GAVE YOU **THAT IDEA?** I, UH, GOT INTO A **COOL SEMINAR** AND EVEN GOT TO, UM, JOIN A **CLUB** AND STUFF!
WOW, I DIDN'T KNOW YOU COULD STILL GET INTO ONE THIS LATE IN THE YEAR.
UGH...
...AHHH, YOU CAUGHT ME!! NARU, I **SCREWED UP** AGAIN!! I WENT AND **LIED** TO EVERYBODY AND NOW I **CAN'T** TAKE IT BACK!!
ALL RIGHT, JUST CALM DOWN! WHY DON'T YOU START FROM **THE BEGINNING** AND TELL ME WHAT HAPPENED?

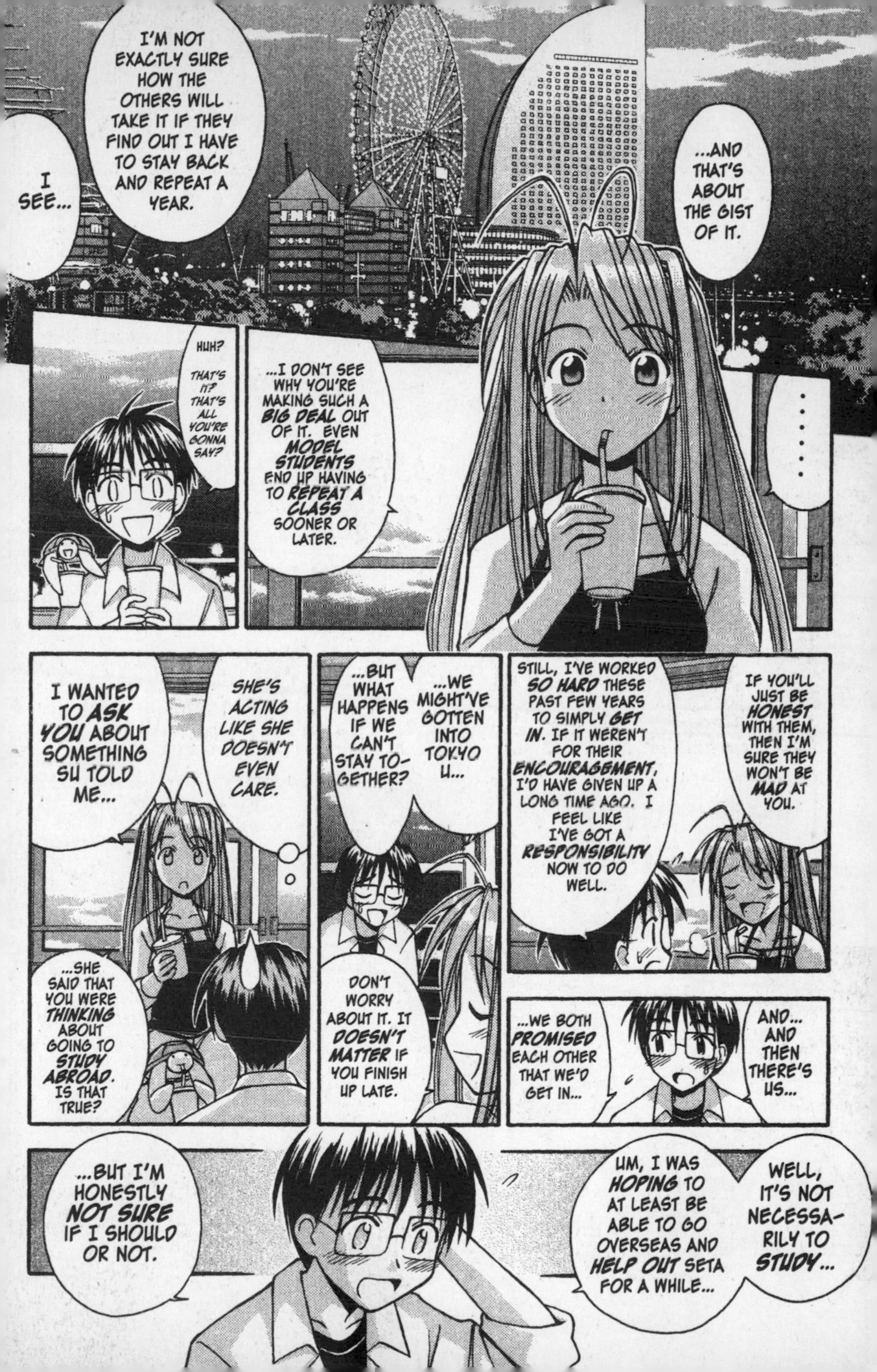
...AND THAT'S ABOUT THE GIST OF IT.
I'M NOT EXACTLY SURE HOW THE OTHERS WILL TAKE IT IF THEY FIND OUT I HAVE TO STAY BACK AND REPEAT A YEAR.
I SEE...
......
...I DON'T SEE WHY YOU'RE MAKING SUCH A BIG DEAL OUT OF IT. EVEN MODEL STUDENTS END UP HAVING TO REPEAT A CLASS SOONER OR LATER.
HUH?
THAT'S IT? THAT'S ALL YOU'RE GONNA SAY?
IF YOU'LL JUST BE HONEST WITH THEM, THEN I'M SURE THEY WON'T BE MAD AT YOU.
STILL, I'VE WORKED SO HARD THESE PAST FEW YEARS TO SIMPLY GET IN. IF IT WEREN'T FOR THEIR ENCOURAGEMENT, I'D HAVE GIVEN UP A LONG TIME AGO. I FEEL LIKE I'VE GOT A RESPONSIBILITY NOW TO DO WELL.
AND... AND THEN THERE'S US...
...WE BOTH PROMISED EACH OTHER THAT WE'D GET IN...
...WE MIGHT'VE GOTTEN INTO TOKYO U...
...BUT WHAT HAPPENS IF WE CAN'T STAY TOGETHER?
DON'T WORRY ABOUT IT. IT DOESN'T MATTER IF YOU FINISH UP LATE.
SHE'S ACTING LIKE SHE DOESN'T EVEN CARE.
I WANTED TO ASK YOU ABOUT SOMETHING SU TOLD ME...
...SHE SAID THAT YOU WERE THINKING ABOUT GOING TO STUDY ABROAD. IS THAT TRUE?
WELL, IT'S NOT NECESSARILY TO STUDY...
UM, I WAS HOPING TO AT LEAST BE ABLE TO GO OVERSEAS AND HELP OUT SETA FOR A WHILE...
...BUT I'M HONESTLY NOT SURE IF I SHOULD OR NOT.

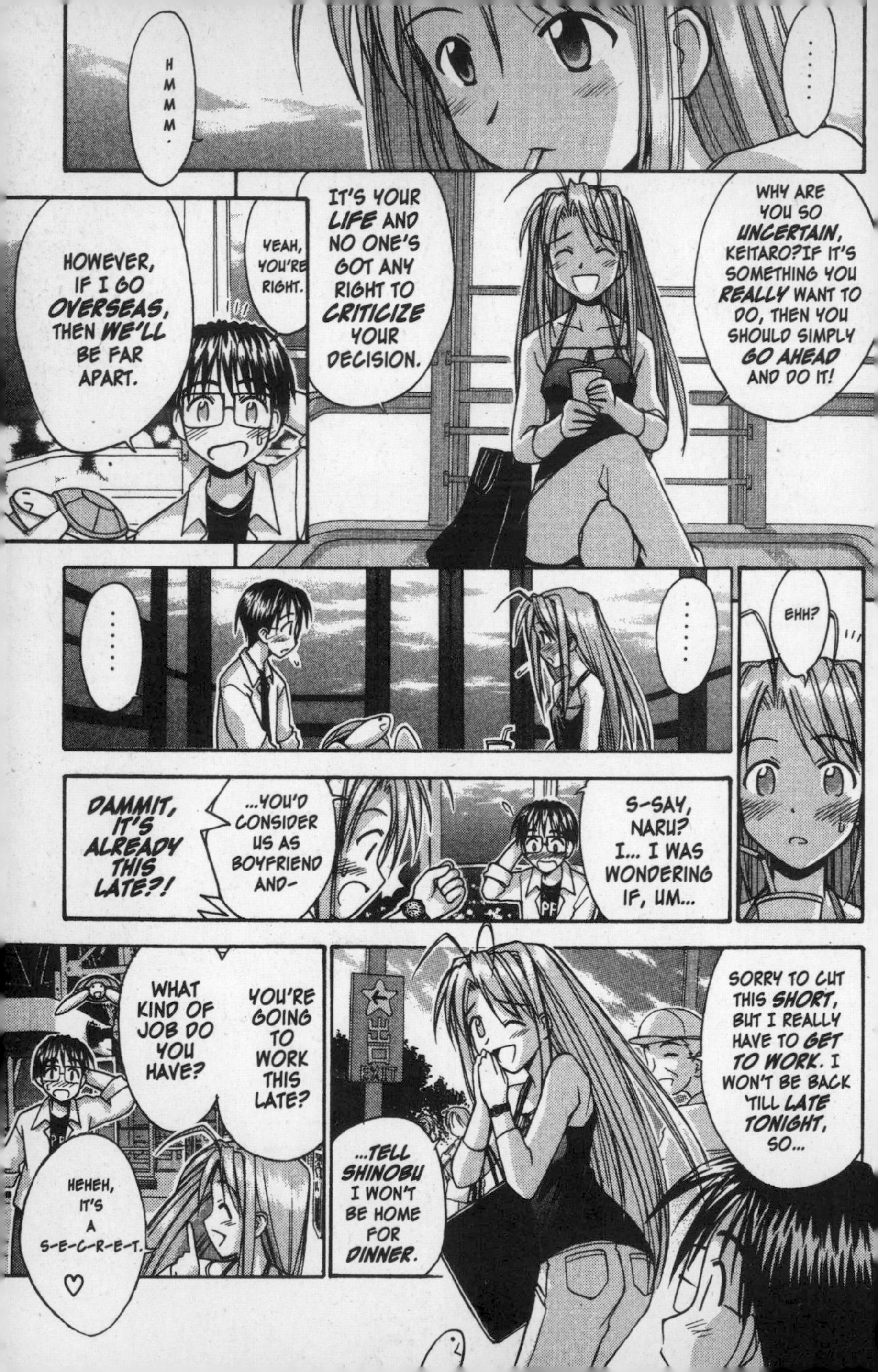
......
HMMM.
WHY ARE YOU SO UNCERTAIN, KEITARO? IF IT'S SOMETHING YOU REALLY WANT TO DO, THEN YOU SHOULD SIMPLY GO AHEAD AND DO IT!
IT'S YOUR LIFE AND NO ONE'S GOT ANY RIGHT TO CRITICIZE YOUR DECISION.
YEAH, YOU'RE RIGHT.
HOWEVER, IF I GO OVERSEAS, THEN WE'LL BE FAR APART.
EHH?
......
......
S-SAY, NARU? I... I WAS WONDERING IF, UM...
...YOU'D CONSIDER US AS BOYFRIEND AND-
DAMMIT, IT'S ALREADY THIS LATE?!
SORRY TO CUT THIS SHORT, BUT I REALLY HAVE TO GET TO WORK. I WON'T BE BACK 'TILL LATE TONIGHT, SO...
...TELL SHINOBU I WON'T BE HOME FOR DINNER.
EXIT
YOU'RE GOING TO WORK THIS LATE?
WHAT KIND OF JOB DO YOU HAVE?
HEHEH, IT'S A S-E-C-R-E-T. ♡

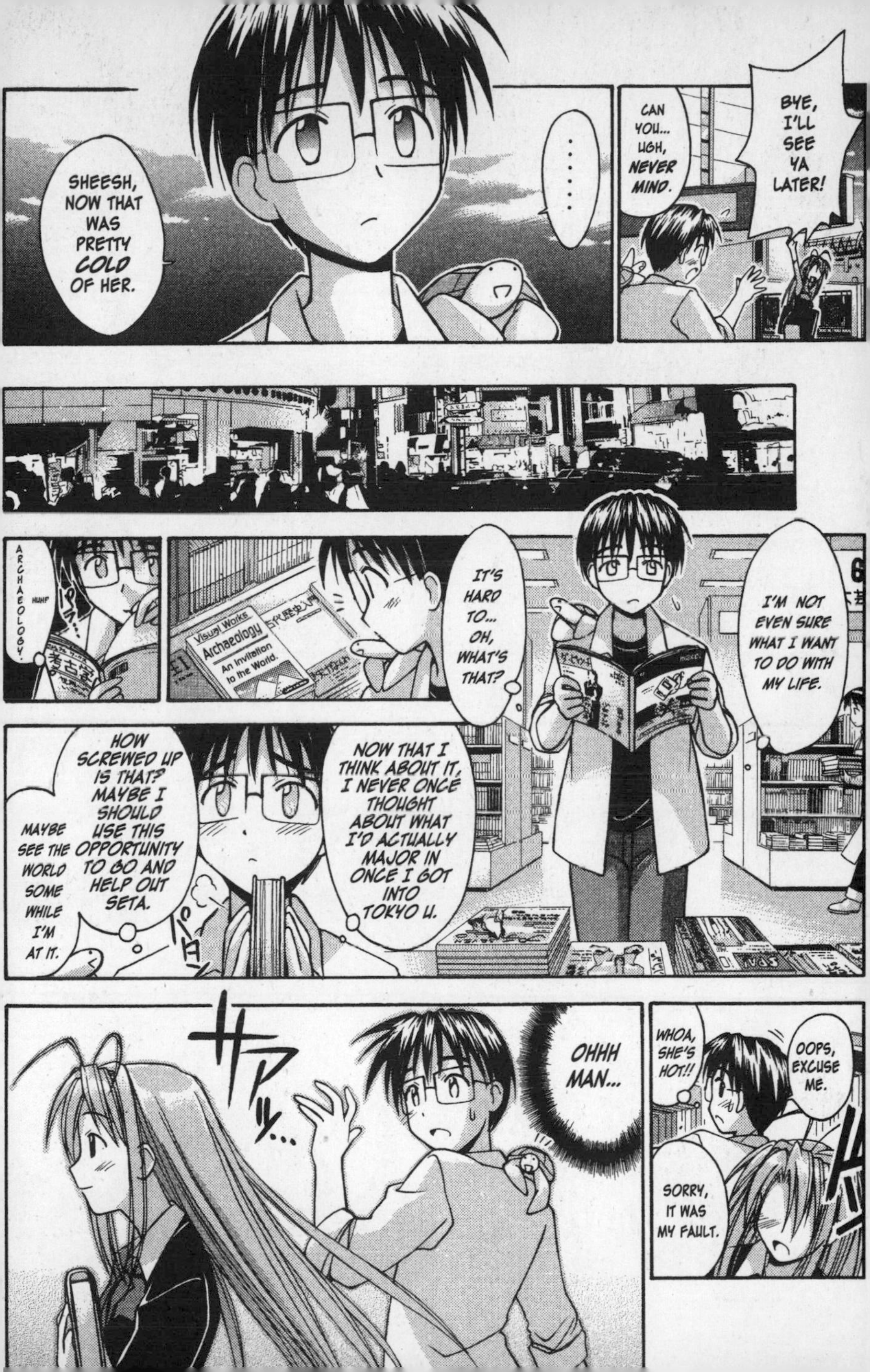

BYE, I'LL SEE YA LATER!
CAN YOU... UGH, NEVER MIND.
......
SHEESH, NOW THAT WAS PRETTY COLD OF HER.
I'M NOT EVEN SURE WHAT I WANT TO DO WITH MY LIFE.
IT'S HARD TO... OH, WHAT'S THAT?
Visual Works Archaeology An Invitation to the World.
ARCHAEOLOGY.
HUHF
NOW THAT I THINK ABOUT IT, I NEVER ONCE THOUGHT ABOUT WHAT I'D ACTUALLY MAJOR IN ONCE I GOT INTO TOKYO U.
HOW SCREWED UP IS THAT? MAYBE I SHOULD USE THIS OPPORTUNITY TO GO AND HELP OUT SETA.
MAYBE SEE THE WORLD SOME WHILE I'M AT IT.
OOPS, EXCUSE ME.
WHOA, SHE'S HOT!!
SORRY, IT WAS MY FAULT.
OHHH MAN...

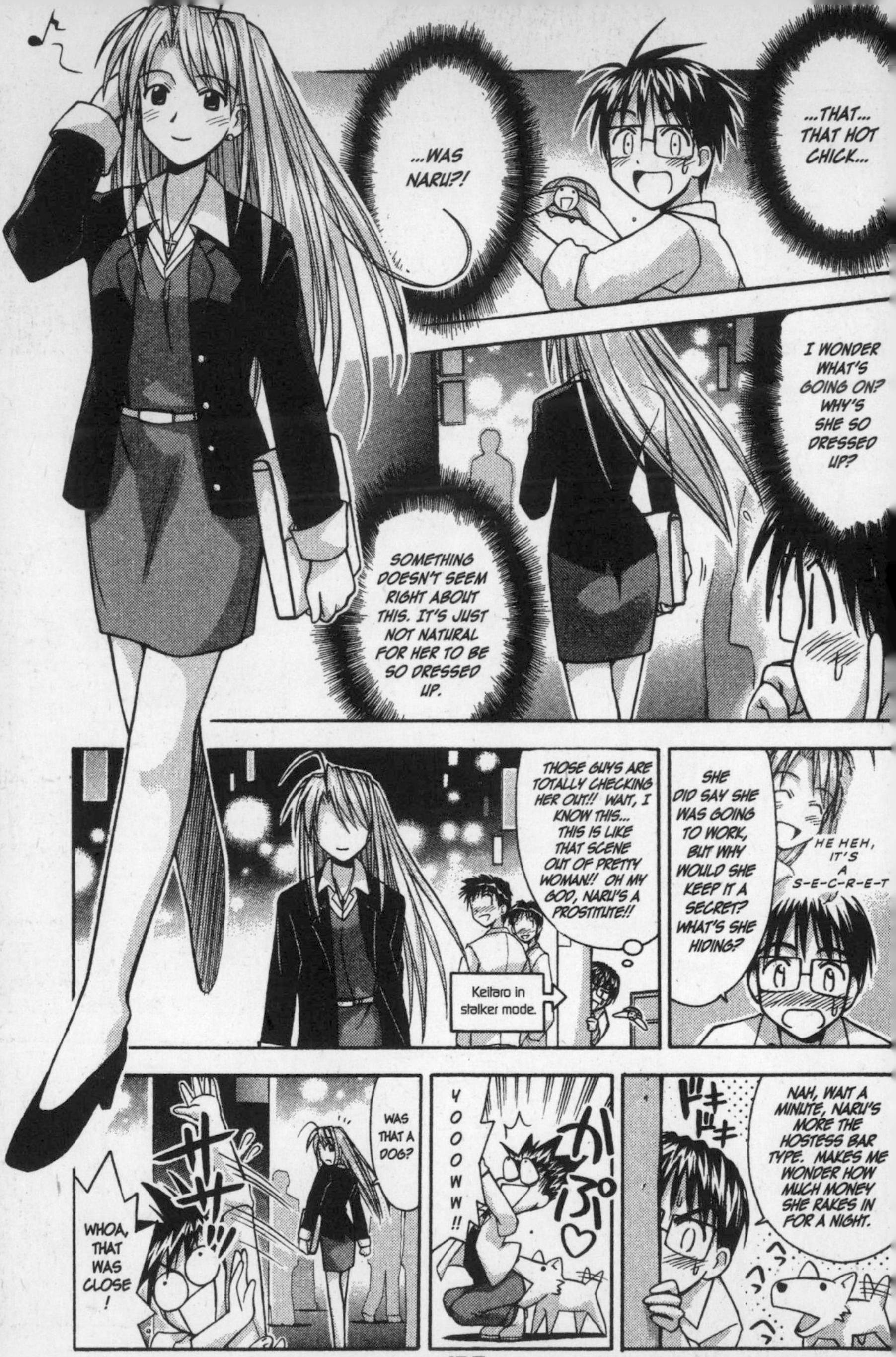
...THAT... THAT HOT CHICK...
...WAS NARU?!
I WONDER WHAT'S GOING ON? WHY'S SHE SO DRESSED UP?
SOMETHING DOESN'T SEEM RIGHT ABOUT THIS. IT'S JUST NOT NATURAL FOR HER TO BE SO DRESSED UP.
SHE DID SAY SHE WAS GOING TO WORK, BUT WHY WOULD SHE KEEP IT A SECRET? WHAT'S SHE HIDING?
HE HEH, IT'S A S-E-C-R-E-T
THOSE GUYS ARE TOTALLY CHECKING HER OUT!! WAIT, I KNOW THIS... THIS IS LIKE THAT SCENE OUT OF PRETTY WOMAN!! OH MY GOD, NARU'S A PROSTITUTE!!
Keitaro in stalker mode.
ドキドキ
NAH, WAIT A MINUTE, NARU'S MORE THE HOSTESS BAR TYPE. MAKES ME WONDER HOW MUCH MONEY SHE RAKES IN FOR A NIGHT.
YOOOOWW!!
かぷー
WAS THAT A DOG?
ササッ
WHOA, THAT WAS CLOSE!

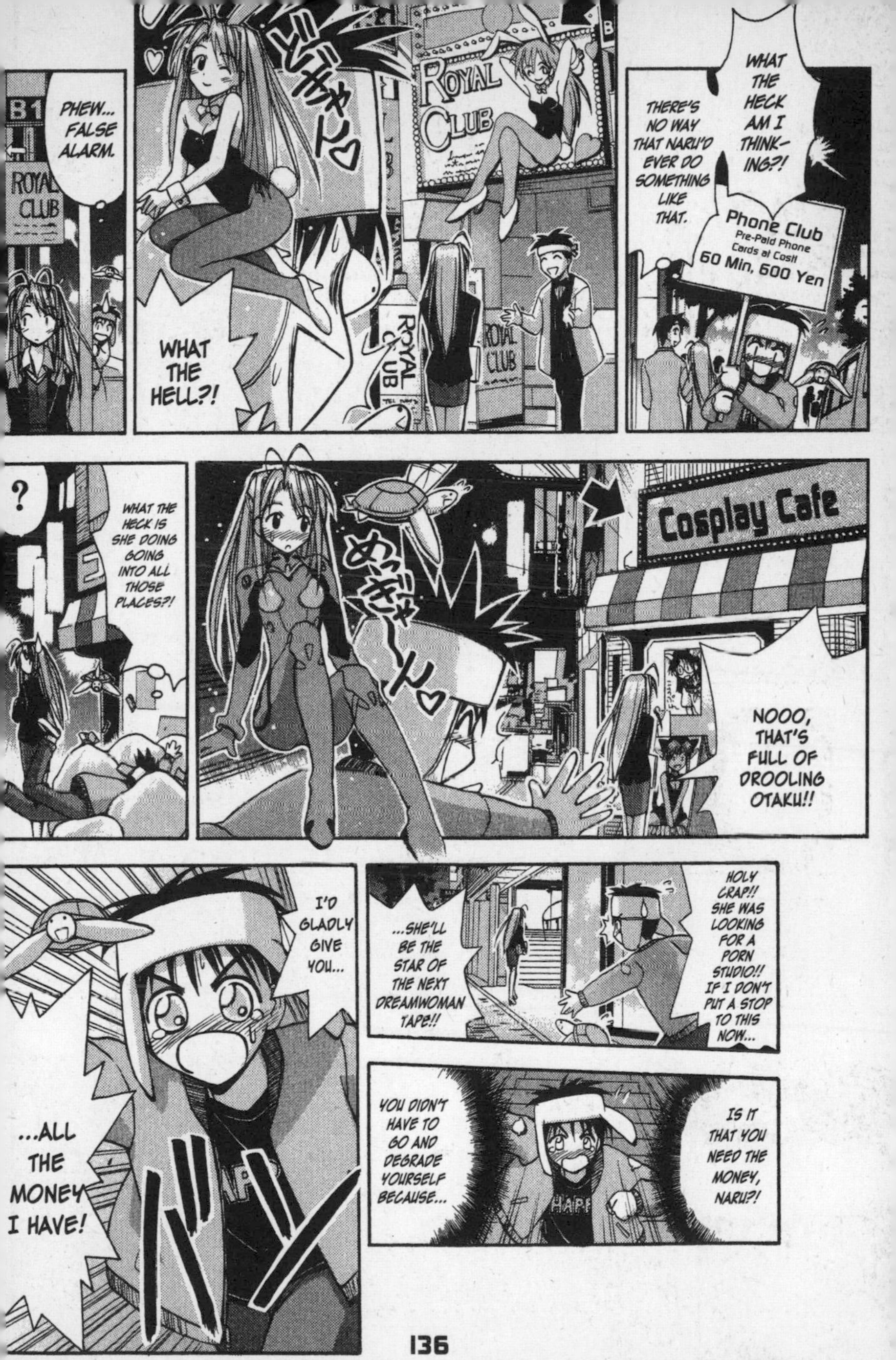
WHAT THE HECK AM I THINKING?!
THERE'S NO WAY THAT NARU'D EVER DO SOMETHING LIKE THAT.
Phone Club
Pre-Paid Phone Cards at Cost!
60 Min, 600 Yen
ROYAL CLUB
どぎゃ〜ん♡
ROYAL CLUB
ROYAL CLUB
WHAT THE HELL?!
PHEW... FALSE ALARM.
B1
ROYAL CLUB
Cosplay Cafe
めっきゃ〜ん♡
NOOO, THAT'S FULL OF DROOLING OTAKU!!
?
WHAT THE HECK IS SHE DOING GOING INTO ALL THOSE PLACES?!
HOLY CRAP!! SHE WAS LOOKING FOR A PORN STUDIO!! IF I DON'T PUT A STOP TO THIS NOW...
...SHE'LL BE THE STAR OF THE NEXT DREAMWOMAN TAPE!!
IS IT THAT YOU NEED THE MONEY, NARU?!
YOU DIDN'T HAVE TO GO AND DEGRADE YOURSELF BECAUSE...
I'D GLADLY GIVE YOU...
...ALL THE MONEY I HAVE!

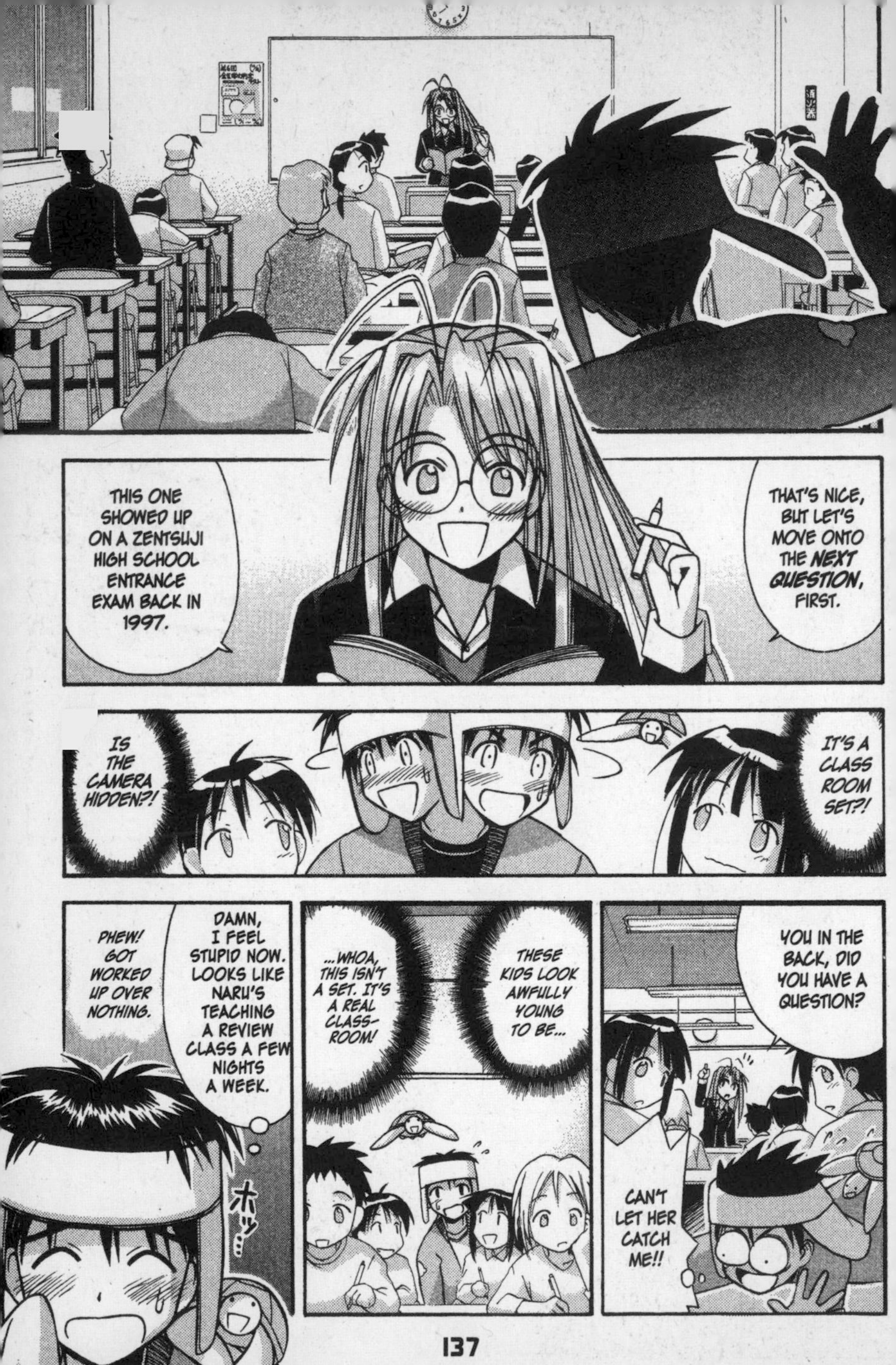
THAT'S NICE, BUT LET'S MOVE ONTO THE NEXT QUESTION, FIRST.
THIS ONE SHOWED UP ON A ZENTSUJI HIGH SCHOOL ENTRANCE EXAM BACK IN 1997.
IT'S A CLASS ROOM SET?!
IS THE CAMERA HIDDEN?!
YOU IN THE BACK, DID YOU HAVE A QUESTION?
CAN'T LET HER CATCH ME!!
THESE KIDS LOOK AWFULLY YOUNG TO BE...
...WHOA, THIS ISN'T A SET. IT'S A REAL CLASS-ROOM!
DAMN, I FEEL STUPID NOW. LOOKS LIKE NARU'S TEACHING A REVIEW CLASS A FEW NIGHTS A WEEK.
PHEW! GOT WORKED UP OVER NOTHING.
ホッ…

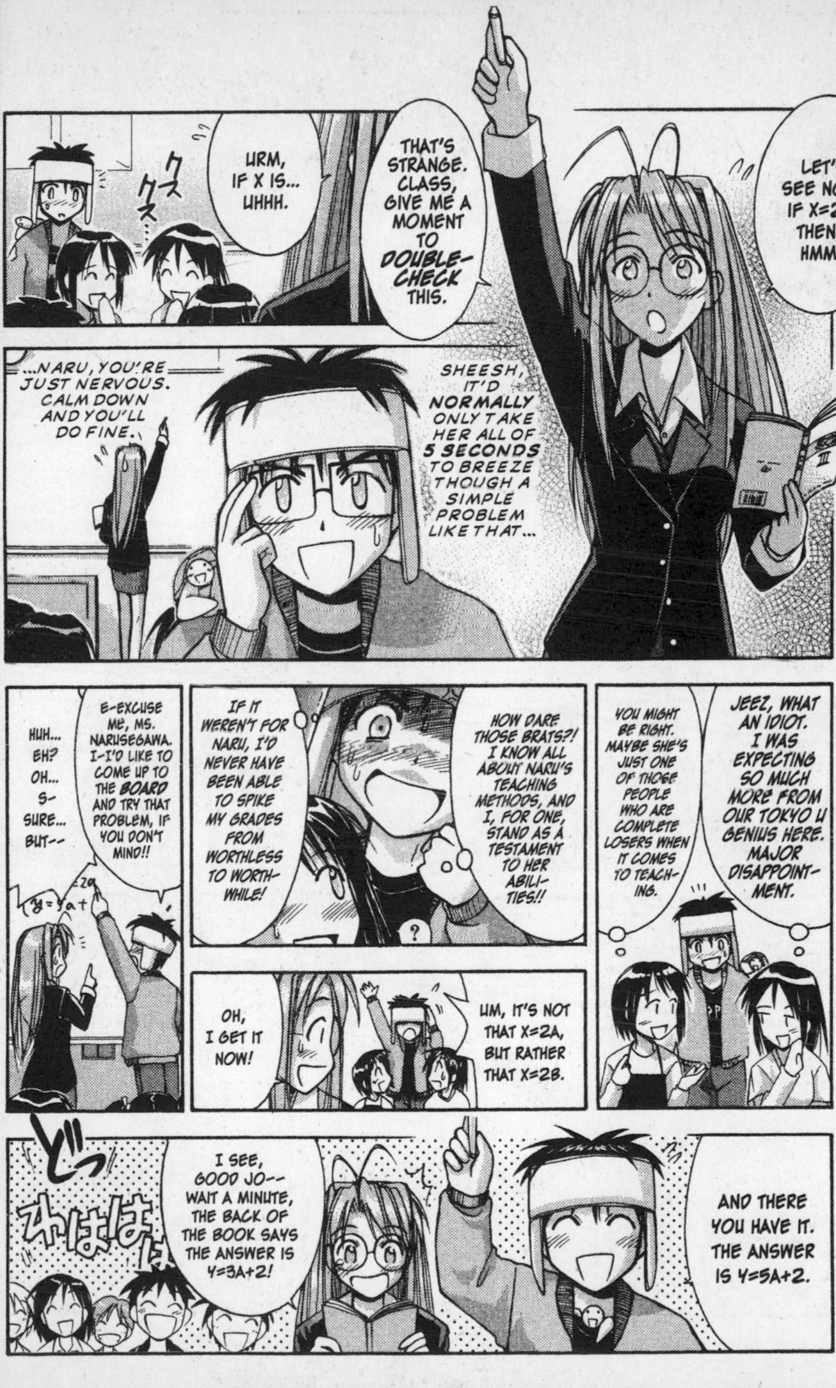
LET'S SEE NOW, IF X=2A, THEN... HMM?
THAT'S STRANGE. CLASS, GIVE ME A MOMENT TO DOUBLE-CHECK THIS.
URM, IF X IS... UHHH.
クスクス
SHEESH, IT'D NORMALLY ONLY TAKE HER ALL OF 5 SECONDS TO BREEZE THOUGH A SIMPLE PROBLEM LIKE THAT...
...NARU, YOU'RE JUST NERVOUS. CALM DOWN AND YOU'LL DO FINE.
JEEZ, WHAT AN IDIOT. I WAS EXPECTING SO MUCH MORE FROM OUR TOKYO U GENIUS HERE. MAJOR DISAPPOINTMENT.
YOU MIGHT BE RIGHT. MAYBE SHE'S JUST ONE OF THOSE PEOPLE WHO ARE COMPLETE LOSERS WHEN IT COMES TO TEACHING.
HOW DARE THOSE BRATS?! I KNOW ALL ABOUT NARU'S TEACHING METHODS, AND I, FOR ONE, STAND AS A TESTAMENT TO HER ABILITIES!!
IF IT WEREN'T FOR NARU, I'D NEVER HAVE BEEN ABLE TO SPIKE MY GRADES FROM WORTHLESS TO WORTHWHILE!
?
UM, IT'S NOT THAT X=2A, BUT RATHER THAT X=2B.
OH, I GET IT NOW!
E-EXCUSE ME, MS. NARUSEGAWA. I-I'D LIKE TO COME UP TO THE BOARD AND TRY THAT PROBLEM, IF YOU DON'T MIND!!
HUH... EH? OH... S-SURE... BUT--
AND THERE YOU HAVE IT. THE ANSWER IS Y=5A+2.
I SEE, GOOD JO-- WAIT A MINUTE, THE BACK OF THE BOOK SAYS THE ANSWER IS Y=3A+2!
どっ
わはは

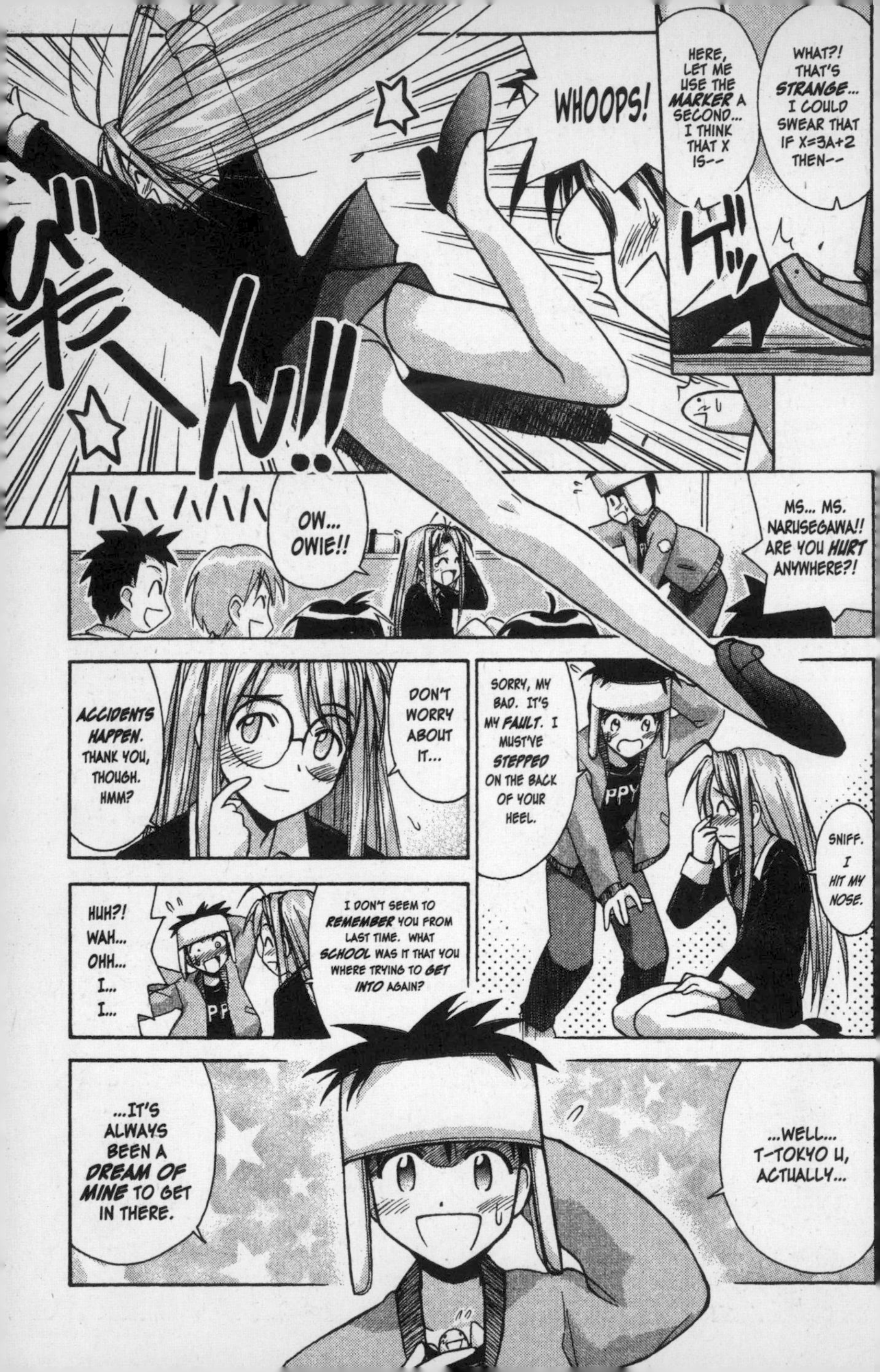
WHAT?! THAT'S STRANGE... I COULD SWEAR THAT IF X=3A+2 THEN--
HERE, LET ME USE THE MARKER A SECOND... I THINK THAT X IS--
ゲッ
WHOOPS!
MS... MS. NARUSEGAWA!! ARE YOU HURT ANYWHERE?!
OW... OWIE!!
SORRY, MY BAD. IT'S MY FAULT. I MUST'VE STEPPED ON THE BACK OF YOUR HEEL.
SNIFF. I HIT MY NOSE.
DON'T WORRY ABOUT IT...
ACCIDENTS HAPPEN. THANK YOU, THOUGH. HMM?
I DON'T SEEM TO REMEMBER YOU FROM LAST TIME. WHAT SCHOOL WAS IT THAT YOU WHERE TRYING TO GET INTO AGAIN?
HUH?! WAH... OHH... I... I...
...WELL... T-TOKYO U, ACTUALLY...
...IT'S ALWAYS BEEN A DREAM OF MINE TO GET IN THERE.

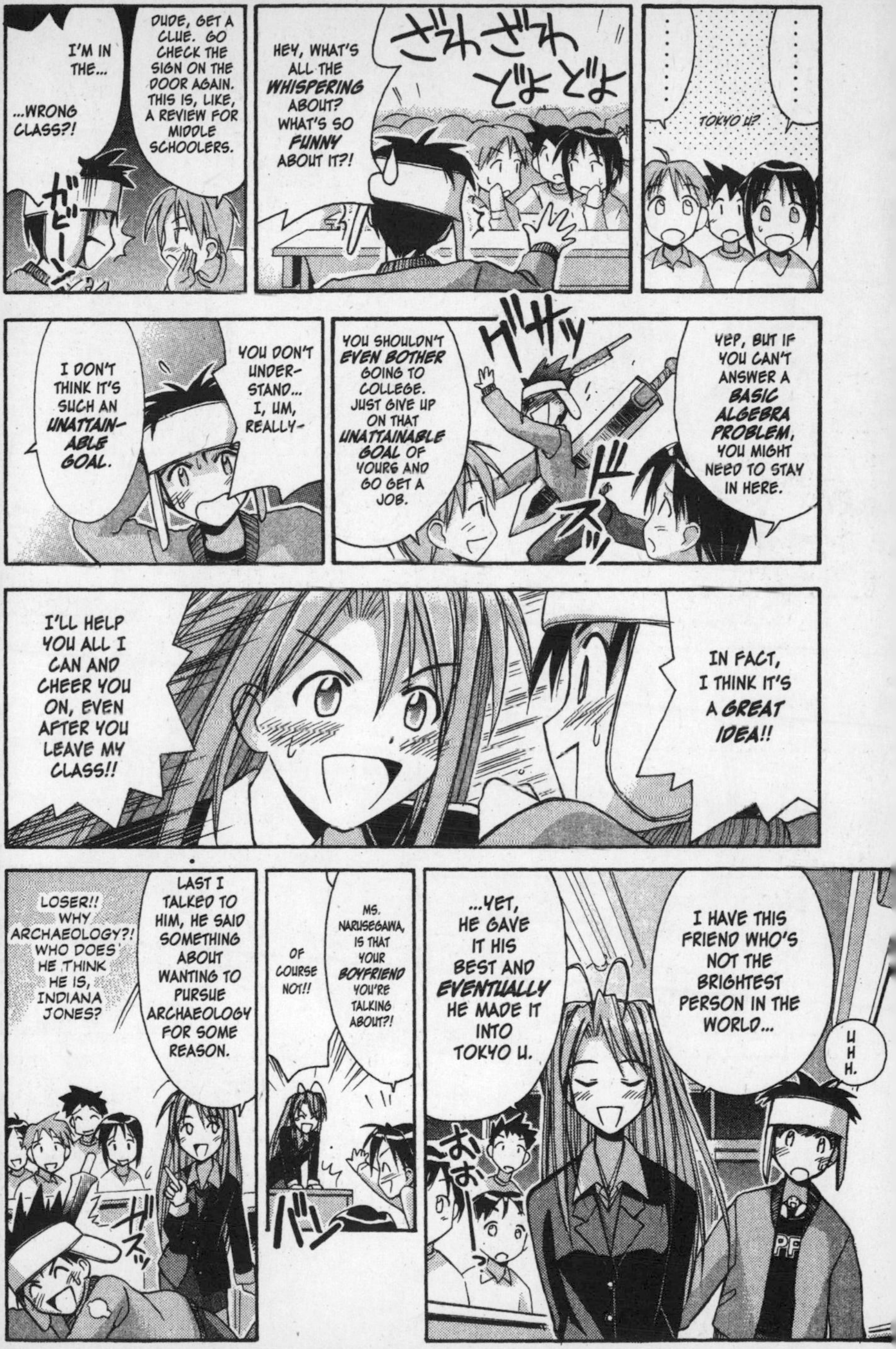
...
...
TOKYO U?
ざわざわ どよどよ
HEY, WHAT'S ALL THE WHISPERING ABOUT? WHAT'S SO FUNNY ABOUT IT?!
DUDE, GET A CLUE. GO CHECK THE SIGN ON THE DOOR AGAIN. THIS IS, LIKE, A REVIEW FOR MIDDLE SCHOOLERS.
I'M IN THE...
...WRONG CLASS?!
ガビーン
YEP, BUT IF YOU CAN'T ANSWER A BASIC ALGEBRA PROBLEM, YOU MIGHT NEED TO STAY IN HERE.
YOU SHOULDN'T EVEN BOTHER GOING TO COLLEGE. JUST GIVE UP ON THAT UNATTAINABLE GOAL OF YOURS AND GO GET A JOB.
YOU DON'T UNDERSTAND... I, UM, REALLY-
I DON'T THINK IT'S SUCH AN UNATTAINABLE GOAL.
IN FACT, I THINK IT'S A GREAT IDEA!!
I'LL HELP YOU ALL I CAN AND CHEER YOU ON, EVEN AFTER YOU LEAVE MY CLASS!!
I HAVE THIS FRIEND WHO'S NOT THE BRIGHTEST PERSON IN THE WORLD...
UHH.
...YET, HE GAVE IT HIS BEST AND EVENTUALLY HE MADE IT INTO TOKYO U.
MS. NARUSEGAWA, IS THAT YOUR BOYFRIEND YOU'RE TALKING ABOUT?!
OF COURSE NOT!!
LAST I TALKED TO HIM, HE SAID SOMETHING ABOUT WANTING TO PURSUE ARCHAEOLOGY FOR SOME REASON.
LOSER!! WHY ARCHAEOLOGY?! WHO DOES HE THINK HE IS, INDIANA JONES?

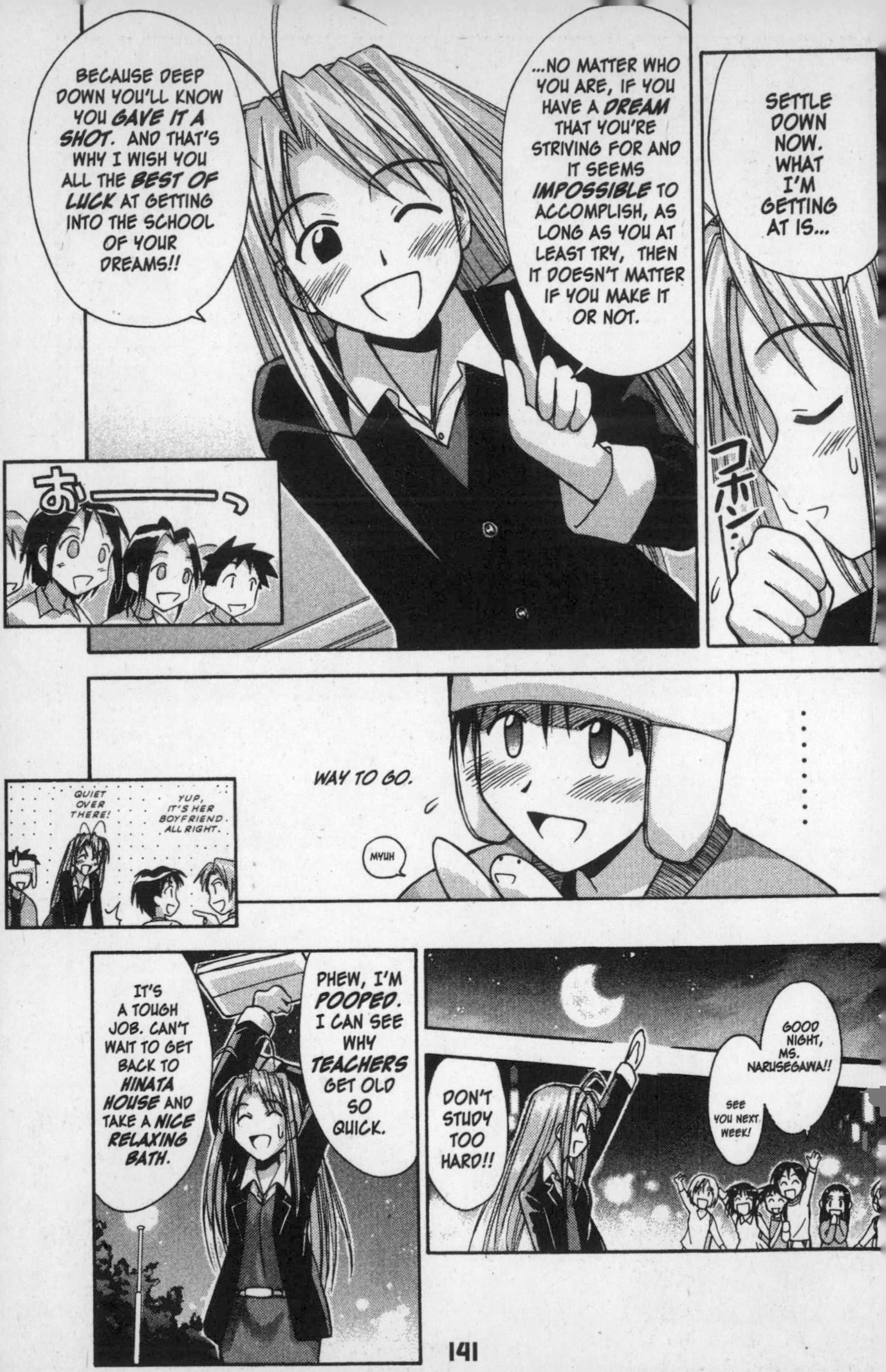
SETTLE DOWN NOW. WHAT I'M GETTING AT IS...
コホン…
...NO MATTER WHO YOU ARE, IF YOU HAVE A DREAM THAT YOU'RE STRIVING FOR AND IT SEEMS IMPOSSIBLE TO ACCOMPLISH, AS LONG AS YOU AT LEAST TRY, THEN IT DOESN'T MATTER IF YOU MAKE IT OR NOT.
BECAUSE DEEP DOWN YOU'LL KNOW YOU GAVE IT A SHOT. AND THAT'S WHY I WISH YOU ALL THE BEST OF LUCK AT GETTING INTO THE SCHOOL OF YOUR DREAMS!!
お――っ
......
WAY TO GO.
MYUH
YUP, IT'S HER BOYFRIEND ALL RIGHT.
QUIET OVER THERE!
GOOD NIGHT, MS. NARUSEGAWA!!
SEE YOU NEXT WEEK!
DON'T STUDY TOO HARD!!
PHEW, I'M POOPED. I CAN SEE WHY TEACHERS GET OLD SO QUICK.
IT'S A TOUGH JOB. CAN'T WAIT TO GET BACK TO HINATA HOUSE AND TAKE A NICE RELAXING BATH.

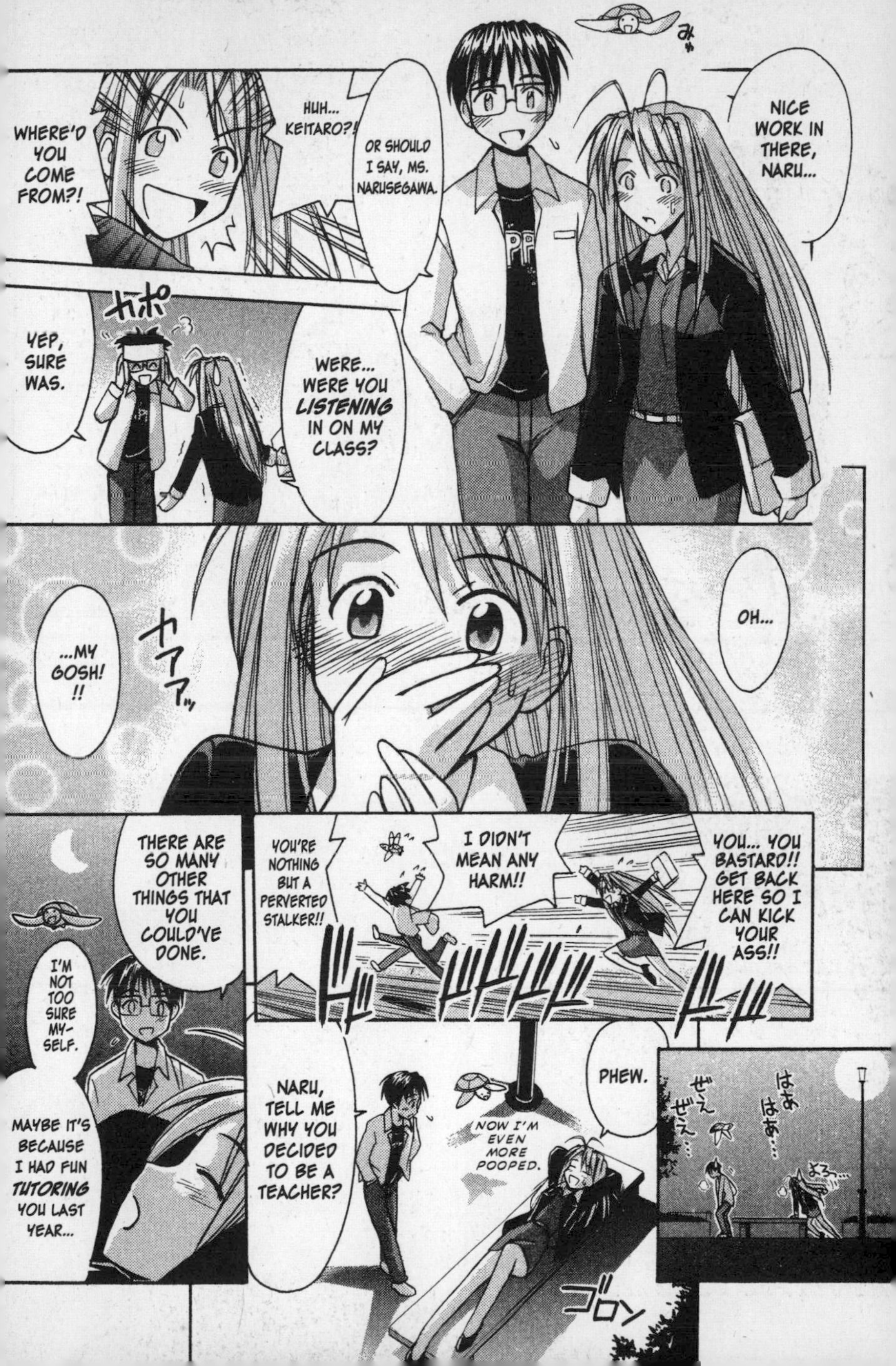
みゅ
NICE WORK IN THERE, NARU...
OR SHOULD I SAY, MS. NARUSEGAWA.
HUH... KEITARO?!
WHERE'D YOU COME FROM?!
WERE... WERE YOU LISTENING IN ON MY CLASS?
カポ
YEP, SURE WAS.
OH...
...MY GOSH! !!
ヤァァッ
YOU... YOU BASTARD!! GET BACK HERE SO I CAN KICK YOUR ASS!!
I DIDN'T MEAN ANY HARM!!
YOU'RE NOTHING BUT A PERVERTED STALKER!!
ドドドドドドドドドド
はあ はあ…
ぜえ ぜえ…
よろ…
PHEW.
NOW I'M EVEN MORE POOPED.
NARU, TELL ME WHY YOU DECIDED TO BE A TEACHER?
ゴロン
THERE ARE SO MANY OTHER THINGS THAT YOU COULD'VE DONE.
I'M NOT TOO SURE MY-SELF.
MAYBE IT'S BECAUSE I HAD FUN TUTORING YOU LAST YEAR...

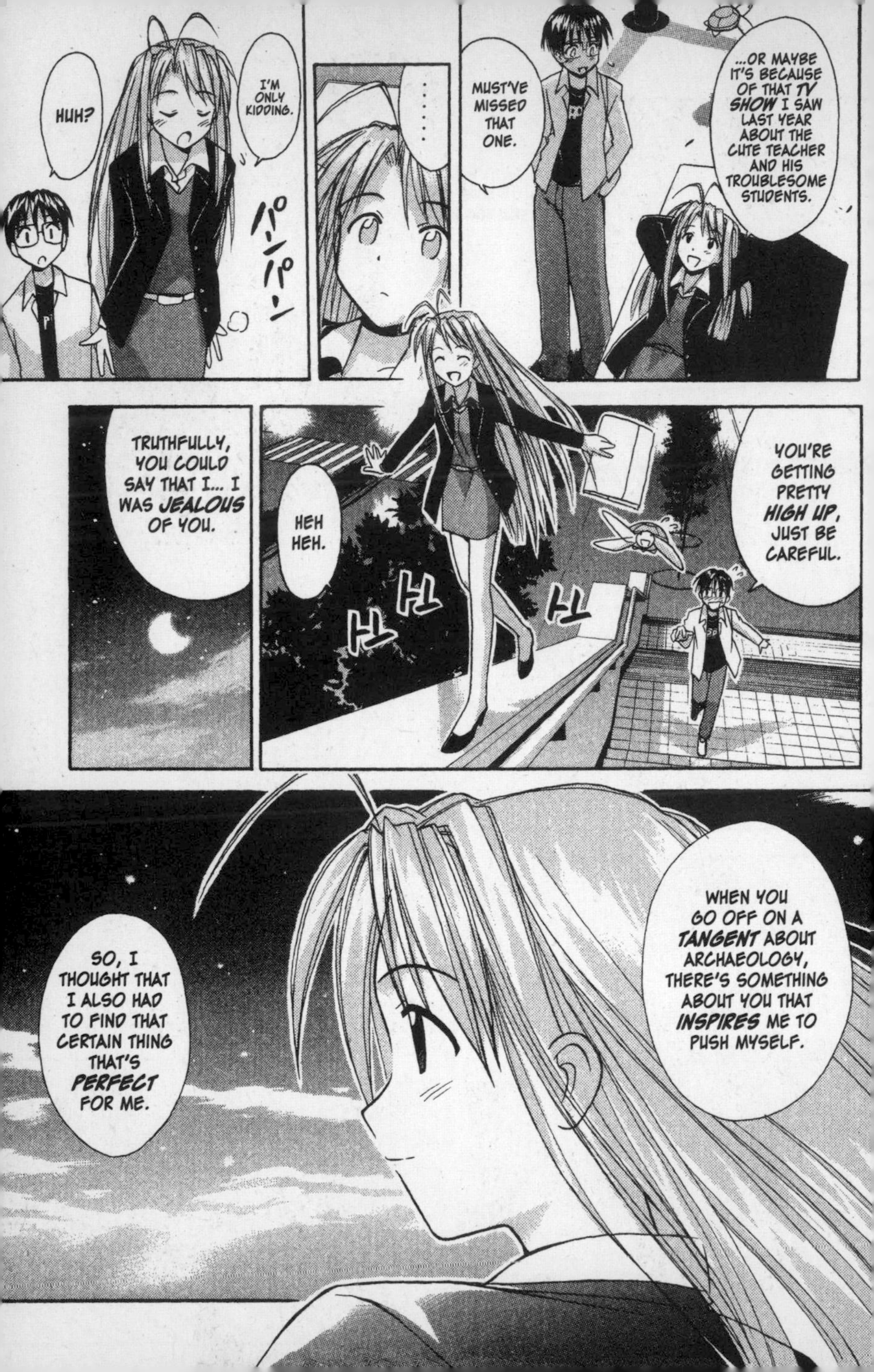
...OR MAYBE IT'S BECAUSE OF THAT TV SHOW I SAW LAST YEAR ABOUT THE CUTE TEACHER AND HIS TROUBLESOME STUDENTS.
MUST'VE MISSED THAT ONE.
......
I'M ONLY KIDDING.
HUH?
パンパン
YOU'RE GETTING PRETTY HIGH UP, JUST BE CAREFUL.
HEH HEH.
TRUTHFULLY, YOU COULD SAY THAT I... I WAS JEALOUS OF YOU.
WHEN YOU GO OFF ON A TANGENT ABOUT ARCHAEOLOGY, THERE'S SOMETHING ABOUT YOU THAT INSPIRES ME TO PUSH MYSELF.
SO, I THOUGHT THAT I ALSO HAD TO FIND THAT CERTAIN THING THAT'S PERFECT FOR ME.

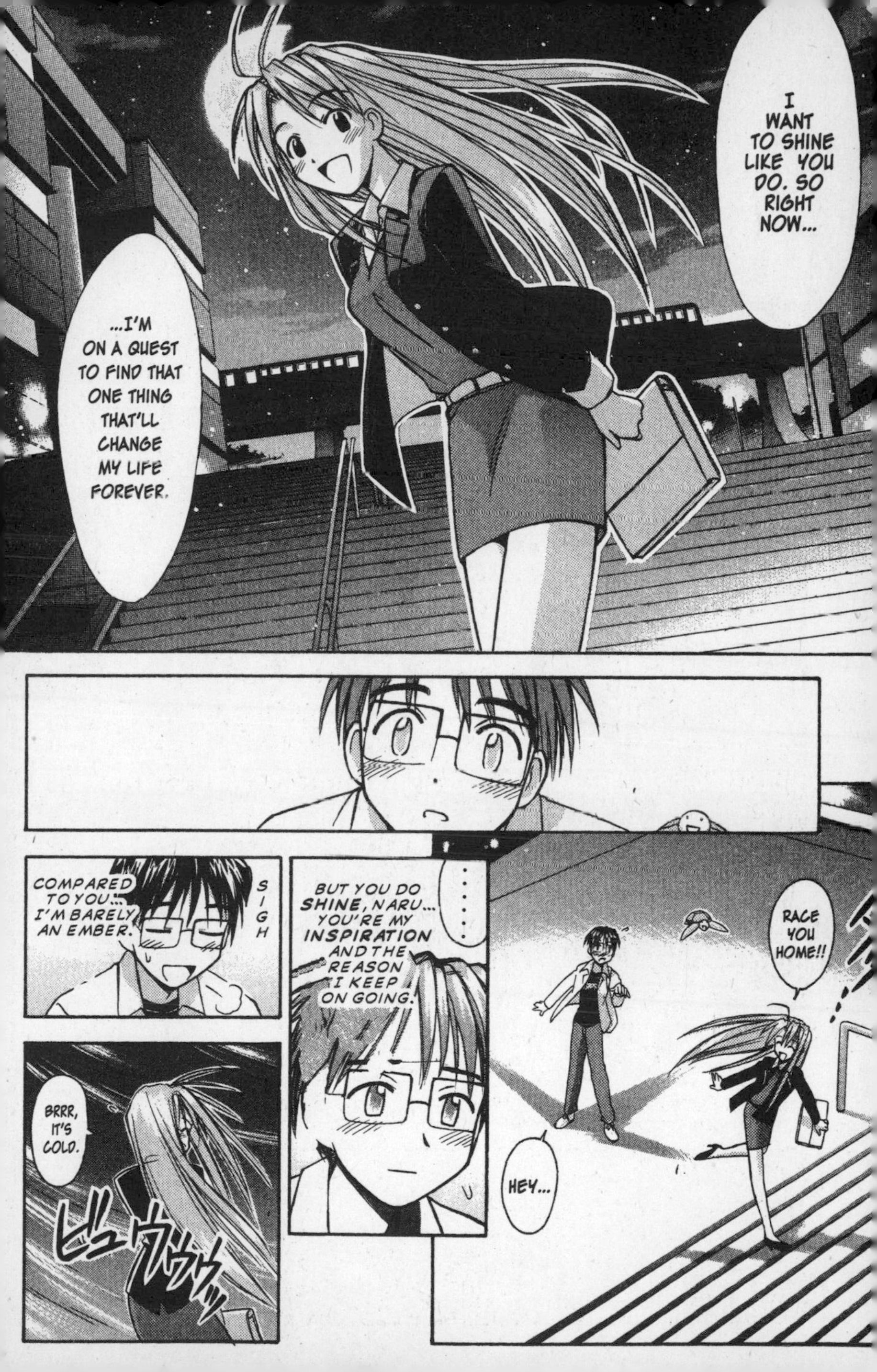
I WANT TO SHINE LIKE YOU DO. SO RIGHT NOW...
...I'M ON A QUEST TO FIND THAT ONE THING THAT'LL CHANGE MY LIFE FOREVER.
RACE YOU HOME!!
HEY...
......
BUT YOU DO SHINE, NARU... YOU'RE MY INSPIRATION AND THE REASON I KEEP ON GOING.
COMPARED TO YOU... I'M BARELY AN EMBER.
SIGH
BRRR, IT'S COLD.
ビュウウウッ

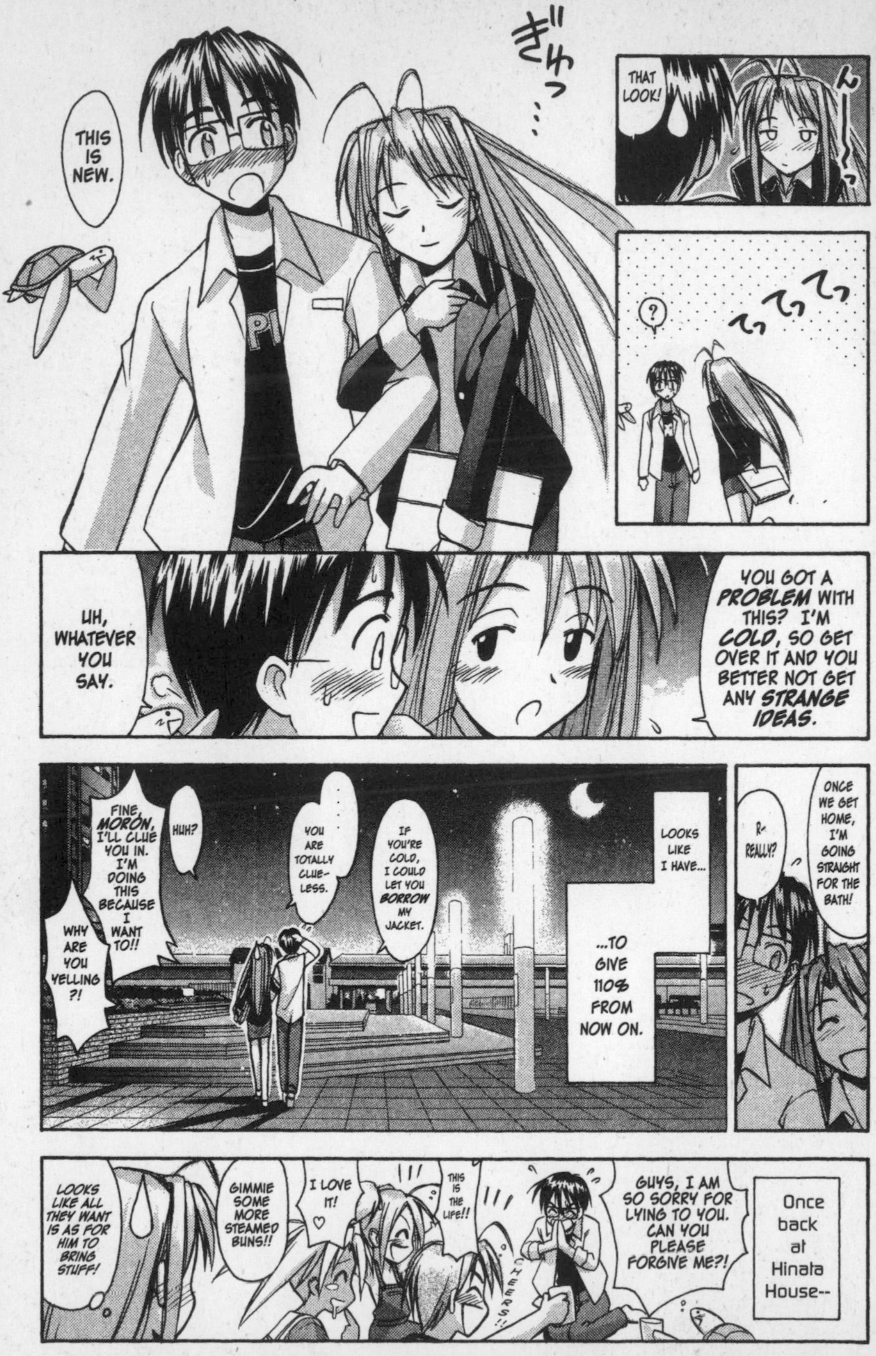
んー～っ
THAT LOOK!
てっ てっ てっ てっ
?
ぎゅっ
THIS IS NEW.
YOU GOT A PROBLEM WITH THIS? I'M COLD, SO GET OVER IT AND YOU BETTER NOT GET ANY STRANGE IDEAS.
UH, WHATEVER YOU SAY.
ONCE WE GET HOME, I'M GOING STRAIGHT FOR THE BATH!
R-REALLY?
LOOKS LIKE I HAVE...
...TO GIVE 110% FROM NOW ON.
IF YOU'RE COLD, I COULD LET YOU BORROW MY JACKET.
...
YOU ARE TOTALLY CLUELESS.
HUH?
FINE, MORON, I'LL CLUE YOU IN. I'M DOING THIS BECAUSE I WANT TO!!
WHY ARE YOU YELLING?!
Once back at Hinata House--
GUYS, I AM SO SORRY FOR LYING TO YOU. CAN YOU PLEASE FORGIVE ME?!
CHEERS!!
THIS IS THE LIFE!!
I LOVE IT!
GIMMIE SOME MORE STEAMED BUNS!!
LOOKS LIKE ALL THEY WANT IS AS FOR HIM TO BRING STUFF!

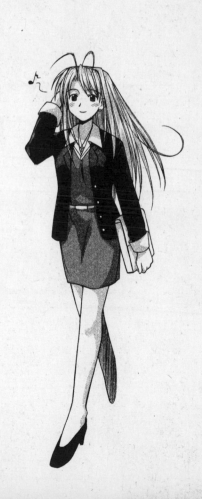

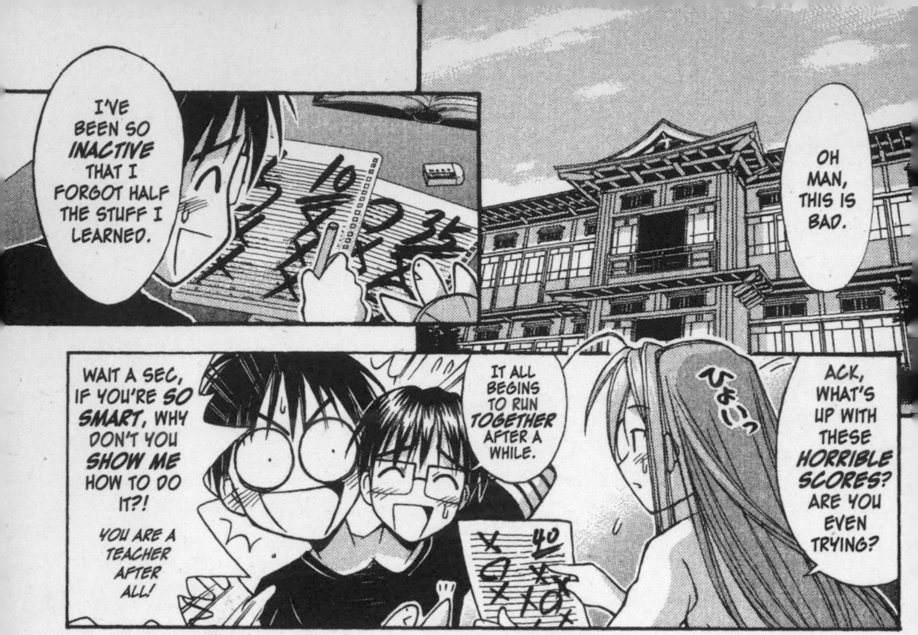
OH MAN, THIS IS BAD.
I'VE BEEN SO INACTIVE THAT I FORGOT HALF THE STUFF I LEARNED.
ひよいっ
ACK, WHAT'S UP WITH THESE HORRIBLE SCORES? ARE YOU EVEN TRYING?
IT ALL BEGINS TO RUN TOGETHER AFTER A WHILE.
WAIT A SEC, IF YOU'RE SO SMART, WHY DON'T YOU SHOW ME HOW TO DO IT?!
YOU ARE A TEACHER AFTER ALL!

Love Hina

HINATA.86 I Miss You (A Week Later)

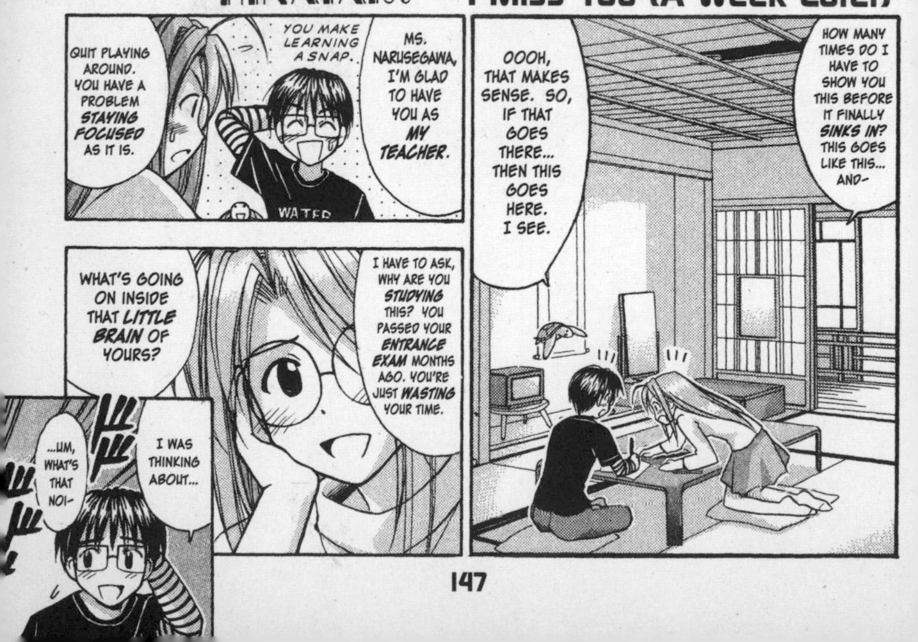
HOW MANY TIMES DO I HAVE TO SHOW YOU THIS BEFORE IT FINALLY SINKS IN? THIS GOES LIKE THIS... AND-
OOOH, THAT MAKES SENSE. SO, IF THAT GOES THERE... THEN THIS GOES HERE. I SEE.
MS. NARUSEGAWA, I'M GLAD TO HAVE YOU AS MY TEACHER.
YOU MAKE LEARNING A SNAP.
QUIT PLAYING AROUND. YOU HAVE A PROBLEM STAYING FOCUSED AS IT IS.
WATER
I HAVE TO ASK, WHY ARE YOU STUDYING THIS? YOU PASSED YOUR ENTRANCE EXAM MONTHS AGO. YOU'RE JUST WASTING YOUR TIME.
WHAT'S GOING ON INSIDE THAT LITTLE BRAIN OF YOURS?
I WAS THINKING ABOUT...
...UM, WHAT'S THAT NOI-

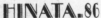

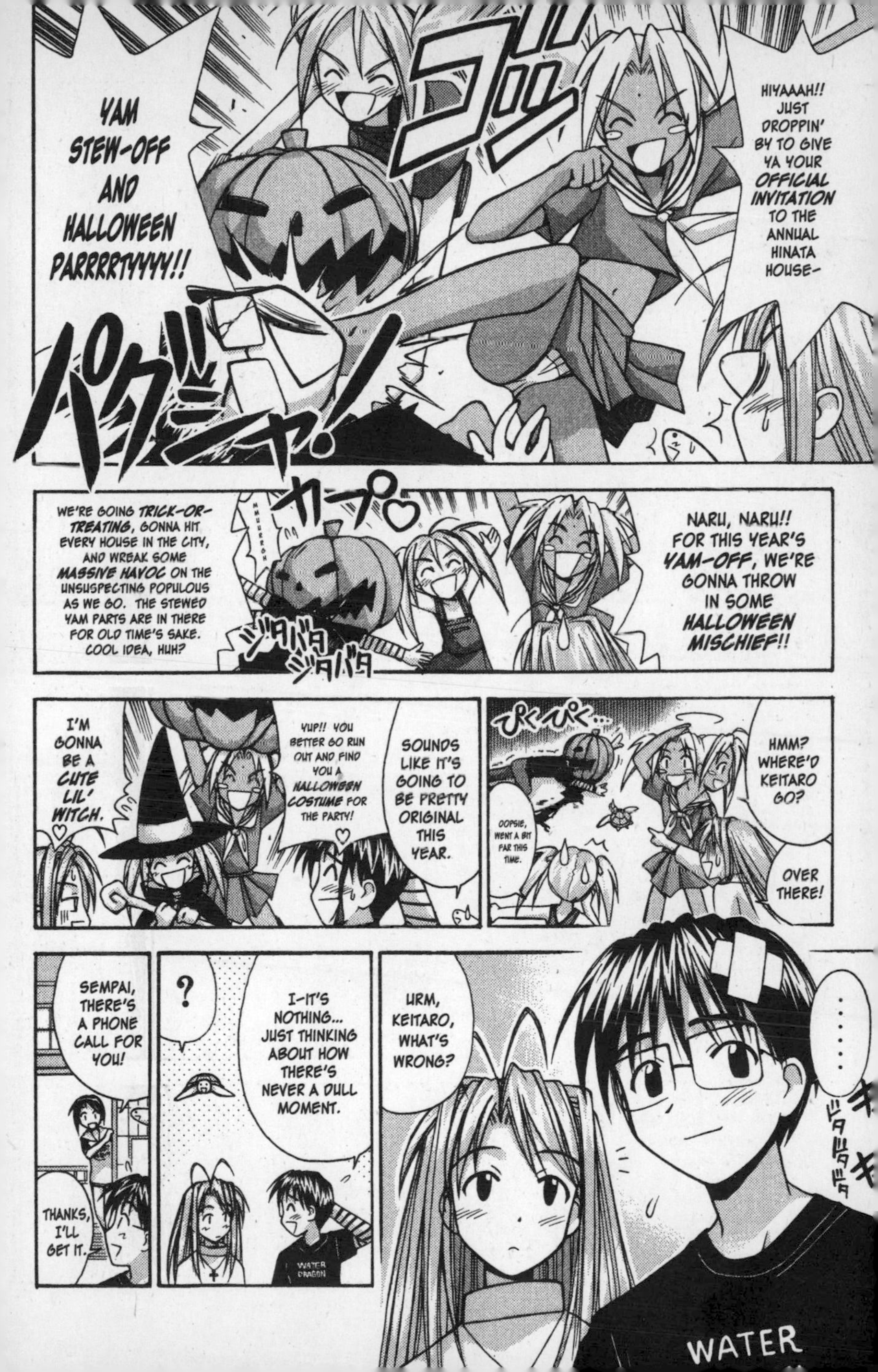

HIYAAAH!! JUST DROPPIN' BY TO GIVE YA YOUR OFFICIAL INVITATION TO THE ANNUAL HINATA HOUSE-
YAM STEW-OFF AND HALLOWEEN PARRRRTYYYY!!
NARU, NARU!! FOR THIS YEAR'S YAM-OFF, WE'RE GONNA THROW IN SOME HALLOWEEN MISCHIEF!!
カプ♡
MMURRGH
WE'RE GOING TRICK-OR-TREATING, GONNA HIT EVERY HOUSE IN THE CITY, AND WREAK SOME MASSIVE HAVOC ON THE UNSUSPECTING POPULOUS AS WE GO. THE STEWED YAM PARTS ARE IN THERE FOR OLD TIME'S SAKE. COOL IDEA, HUH?
ジタバタ ジタバタ
ぴくぴく…
HMM? WHERE'D KEITARO GO?
OVER THERE!
OOPSIE, WENT A BIT FAR THIS TIME.
SOUNDS LIKE IT'S GOING TO BE PRETTY ORIGINAL THIS YEAR.
YUP!! YOU BETTER GO RUN OUT AND FIND YOU A HALLOWEEN COSTUME FOR THE PARTY!
I'M GONNA BE A CUTE LIL' WITCH.
......
ジタバタ
URM, KEITARO, WHAT'S WRONG?
WATER
I-IT'S NOTHING... JUST THINKING ABOUT HOW THERE'S NEVER A DULL MOMENT.
?
WATER DRAGON
SEMPAI, THERE'S A PHONE CALL FOR YOU!
THANKS, I'LL GET IT.

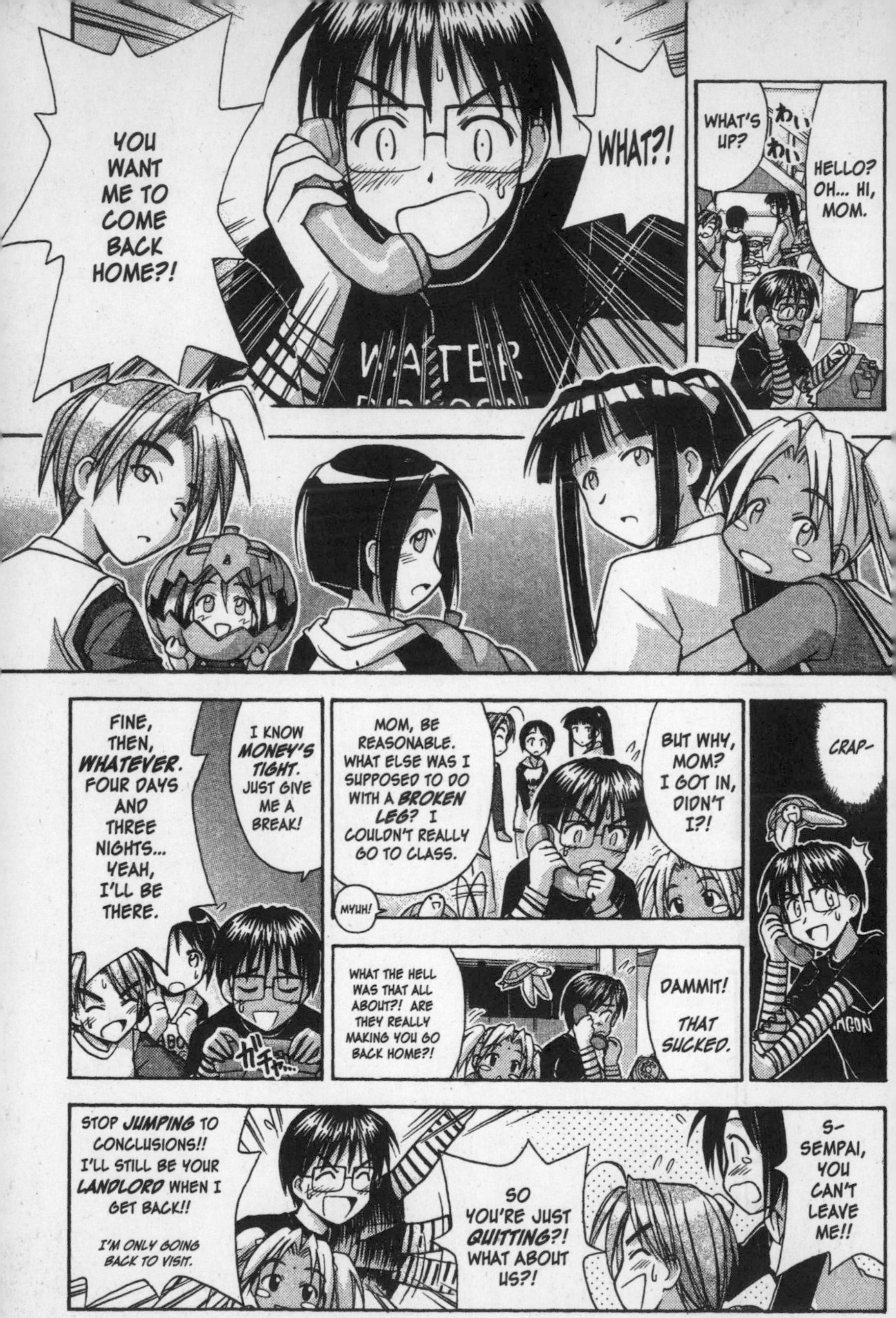
HELLO? OH... HI, MOM.
WHAT'S UP?
わい わい
WHAT?!
YOU WANT ME TO COME BACK HOME?!
WATER
CRAP-
BUT WHY, MOM? I GOT IN, DIDN'T I?!
MOM, BE REASONABLE. WHAT ELSE WAS I SUPPOSED TO DO WITH A BROKEN LEG? I COULDN'T REALLY GO TO CLASS.
MYUH!
DAMMIT! THAT SUCKED.
WHAT THE HELL WAS THAT ALL ABOUT?! ARE THEY REALLY MAKING YOU GO BACK HOME?!
I KNOW MONEY'S TIGHT. JUST GIVE ME A BREAK!
FINE, THEN, WHATEVER. FOUR DAYS AND THREE NIGHTS... YEAH, I'LL BE THERE.
ガチャ...
S-SEMPAI, YOU CAN'T LEAVE ME!!
SO YOU'RE JUST QUITTING?! WHAT ABOUT US?!
STOP JUMPING TO CONCLUSIONS!! I'LL STILL BE YOUR LANDLORD WHEN I GET BACK!!
I'M ONLY GOING BACK TO VISIT.

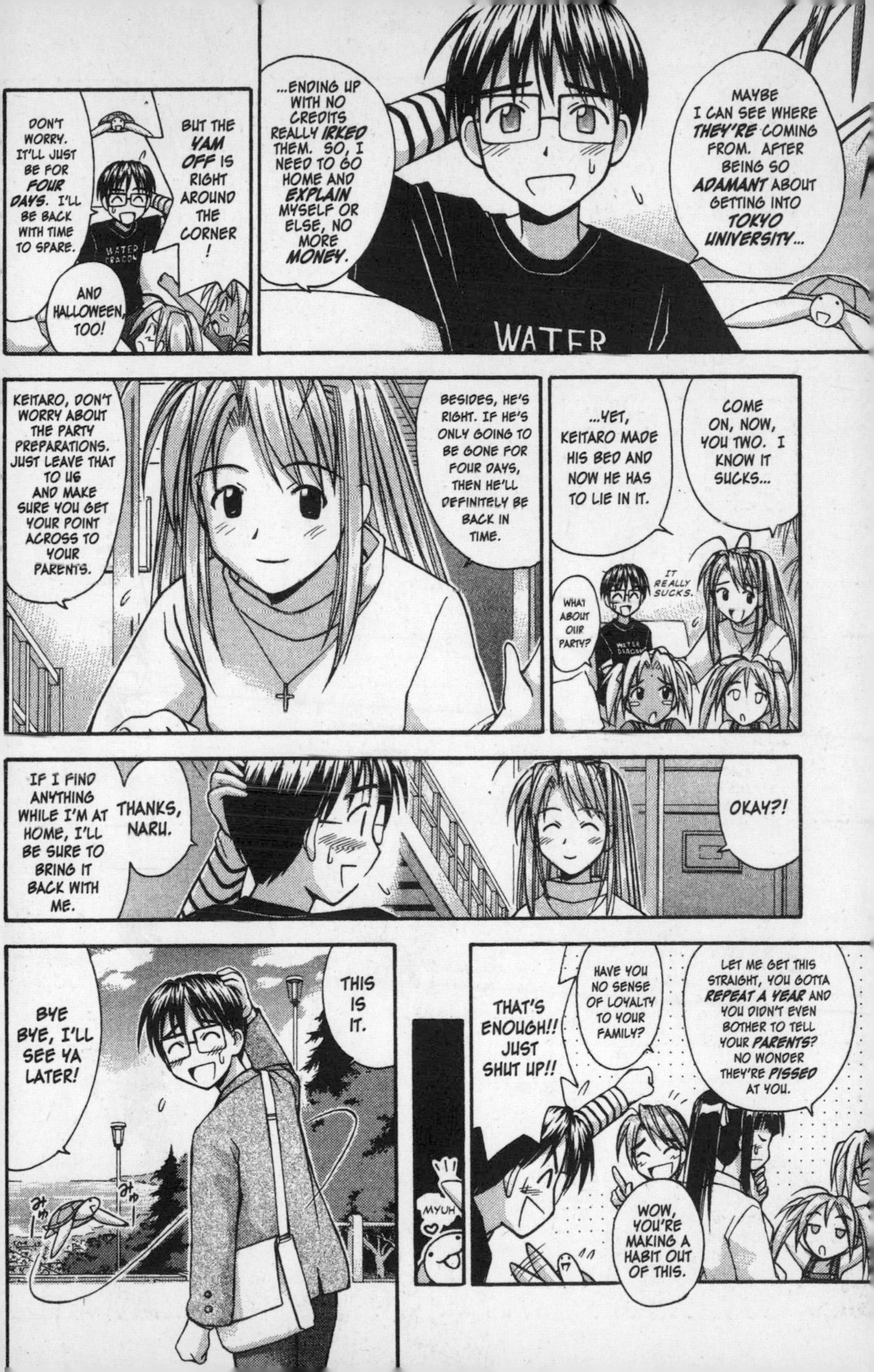
MAYBE I CAN SEE WHERE THEY'RE COMING FROM. AFTER BEING SO ADAMANT ABOUT GETTING INTO TOKYO UNIVERSITY...
...ENDING UP WITH NO CREDITS REALLY IRKED THEM. SO, I NEED TO GO HOME AND EXPLAIN MYSELF OR ELSE, NO MORE MONEY.
WATER
BUT THE YAM OFF IS RIGHT AROUND THE CORNER!
DON'T WORRY. IT'LL JUST BE FOR FOUR DAYS. I'LL BE BACK WITH TIME TO SPARE.
AND HALLOWEEN, TOO!
COME ON, NOW, YOU TWO. I KNOW IT SUCKS...
...YET, KEITARO MADE HIS BED AND NOW HE HAS TO LIE IN IT.
IT REALLY SUCKS.
WHAT ABOUT OUR PARTY?
BESIDES, HE'S RIGHT. IF HE'S ONLY GOING TO BE GONE FOR FOUR DAYS, THEN HE'LL DEFINITELY BE BACK IN TIME.
KEITARO, DON'T WORRY ABOUT THE PARTY PREPARATIONS. JUST LEAVE THAT TO US AND MAKE SURE YOU GET YOUR POINT ACROSS TO YOUR PARENTS.
OKAY?!
THANKS, NARU.
IF I FIND ANYTHING WHILE I'M AT HOME, I'LL BE SURE TO BRING IT BACK WITH ME.
LET ME GET THIS STRAIGHT, YOU GOTTA REPEAT A YEAR AND YOU DIDN'T EVEN BOTHER TO TELL YOUR PARENTS? NO WONDER THEY'RE PISSED AT YOU.
HAVE YOU NO SENSE OF LOYALTY TO YOUR FAMILY?
THAT'S ENOUGH!! JUST SHUT UP!!
WOW, YOU'RE MAKING A HABIT OUT OF THIS.
MYUH
THIS IS IT.
BYE BYE, I'LL SEE YA LATER!
みゅ
みゅ

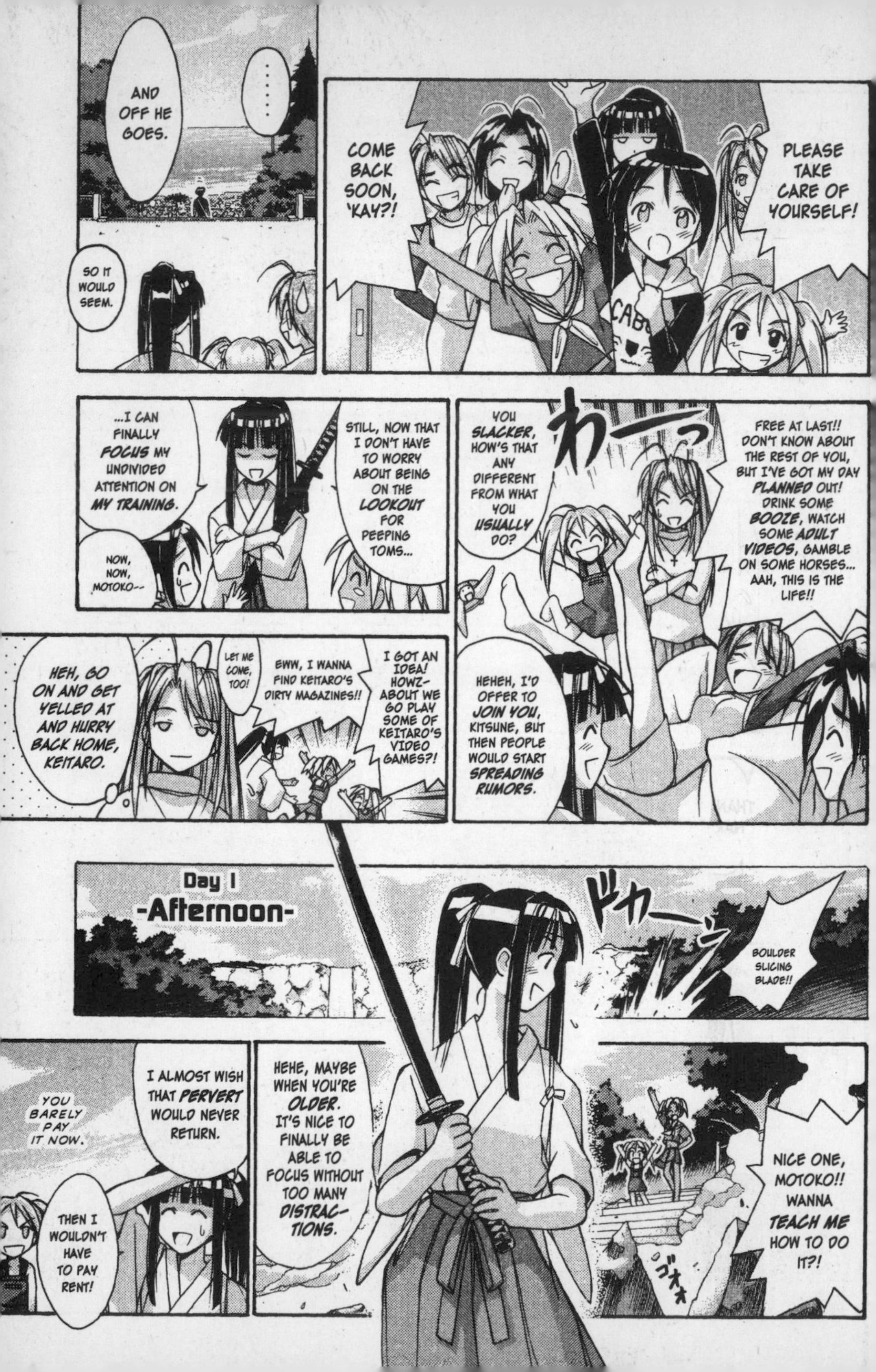
PLEASE TAKE CARE OF YOURSELF!
COME BACK SOON, 'KAY?!
......
AND OFF HE GOES.
SO IT WOULD SEEM.
FREE AT LAST!! DON'T KNOW ABOUT THE REST OF YOU, BUT I'VE GOT MY DAY PLANNED OUT! DRINK SOME BOOZE, WATCH SOME ADULT VIDEOS, GAMBLE ON SOME HORSES... AAH, THIS IS THE LIFE!!
わーっ
YOU SLACKER, HOW'S THAT ANY DIFFERENT FROM WHAT YOU USUALLY DO?
HEHEH, I'D OFFER TO JOIN YOU, KITSUNE, BUT THEN PEOPLE WOULD START SPREADING RUMORS.
STILL, NOW THAT I DON'T HAVE TO WORRY ABOUT BEING ON THE LOOKOUT FOR PEEPING TOMS...
...I CAN FINALLY FOCUS MY UNDIVIDED ATTENTION ON MY TRAINING.
NOW, NOW, MOTOKO--
I GOT AN IDEA! HOWZ-ABOUT WE GO PLAY SOME OF KEITARO'S VIDEO GAMES?!
EWW, I WANNA FIND KEITARO'S DIRTY MAGAZINES!!
LET ME COME, TOO!
HEH, GO ON AND GET YELLED AT AND HURRY BACK HOME, KEITARO.
ドカーン
BOULDER SLICING BLADE!!
Day 1
-Afternoon-
NICE ONE, MOTOKO!! WANNA TEACH ME HOW TO DO IT?!
ゴオオ
HEHE, MAYBE WHEN YOU'RE OLDER. IT'S NICE TO FINALLY BE ABLE TO FOCUS WITHOUT TOO MANY DISTRACTIONS.
I ALMOST WISH THAT PERVERT WOULD NEVER RETURN.
THEN I WOULDN'T HAVE TO PAY RENT!
YOU BARELY PAY IT NOW.

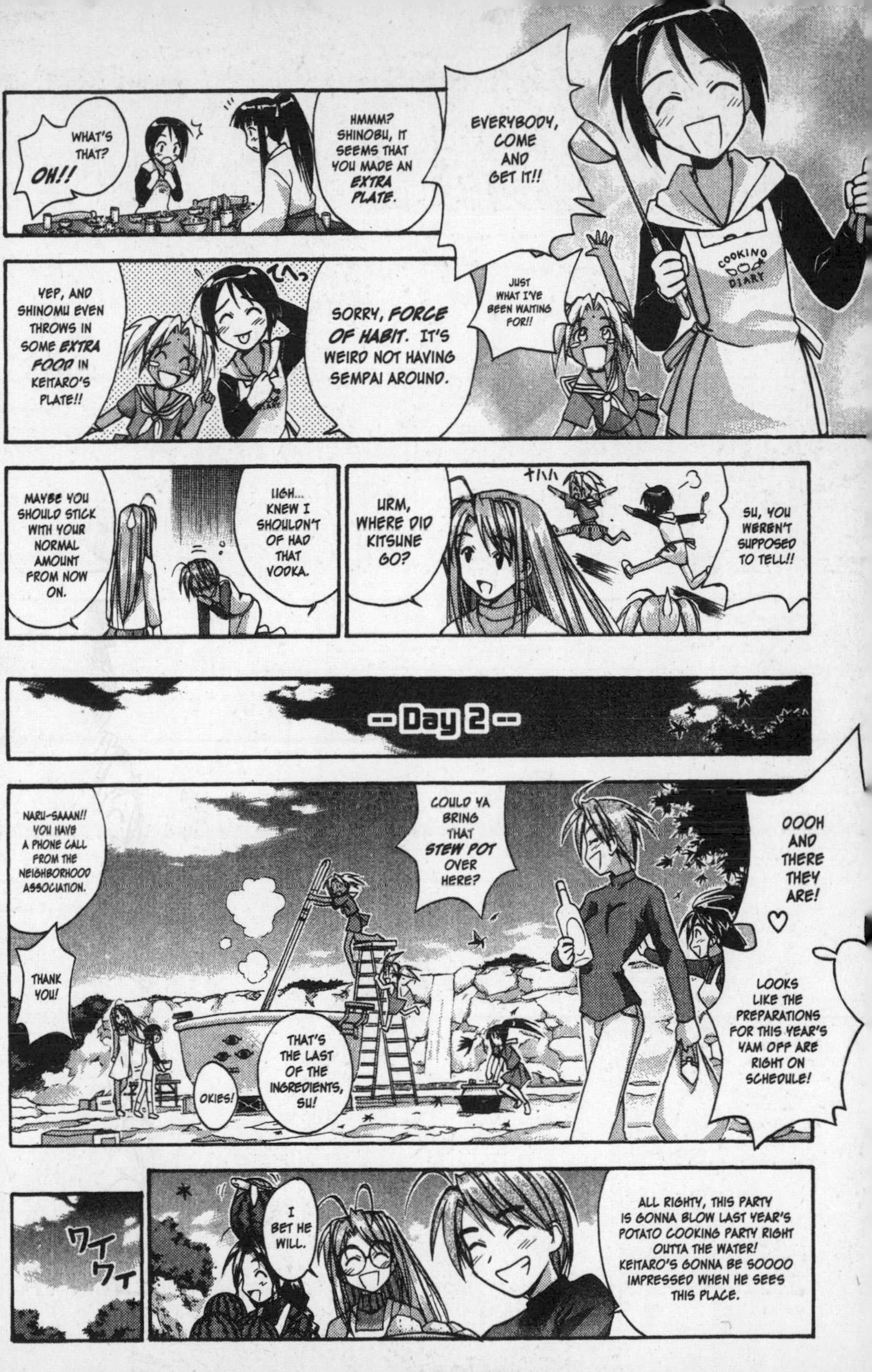
EVERYBODY, COME AND GET IT!!
JUST WHAT I'VE BEEN WAITING FOR!!
HMMM? SHINOBU, IT SEEMS THAT YOU MADE AN EXTRA PLATE.
WHAT'S THAT? OH!!
SORRY, FORCE OF HABIT. IT'S WEIRD NOT HAVING SEMPAI AROUND.
YEP, AND SHINOMU EVEN THROWS IN SOME EXTRA FOOD IN KEITARO'S PLATE!!
SU, YOU WEREN'T SUPPOSED TO TELL!!
ナハハ
URM, WHERE DID KITSUNE GO?
UGH... KNEW I SHOULDN'T OF HAD THAT VODKA.
MAYBE YOU SHOULD STICK WITH YOUR NORMAL AMOUNT FROM NOW ON.
-- Day 2 --
OOOH AND THERE THEY ARE! ♡
LOOKS LIKE THE PREPARATIONS FOR THIS YEAR'S YAM OFF ARE RIGHT ON SCHEDULE!
COULD YA BRING THAT STEW POT OVER HERE?
THAT'S THE LAST OF THE INGREDIENTS, SU!
OKIES!
NARU-SAAAN!! YOU HAVE A PHONE CALL FROM THE NEIGHBORHOOD ASSOCIATION.
THANK YOU!
ALL RIGHTY, THIS PARTY IS GONNA BLOW LAST YEAR'S POTATO COOKING PARTY RIGHT OUTTA THE WATER! KEITARO'S GONNA BE SOOOO IMPRESSED WHEN HE SEES THIS PLACE.
I BET HE WILL.
ワイワイ

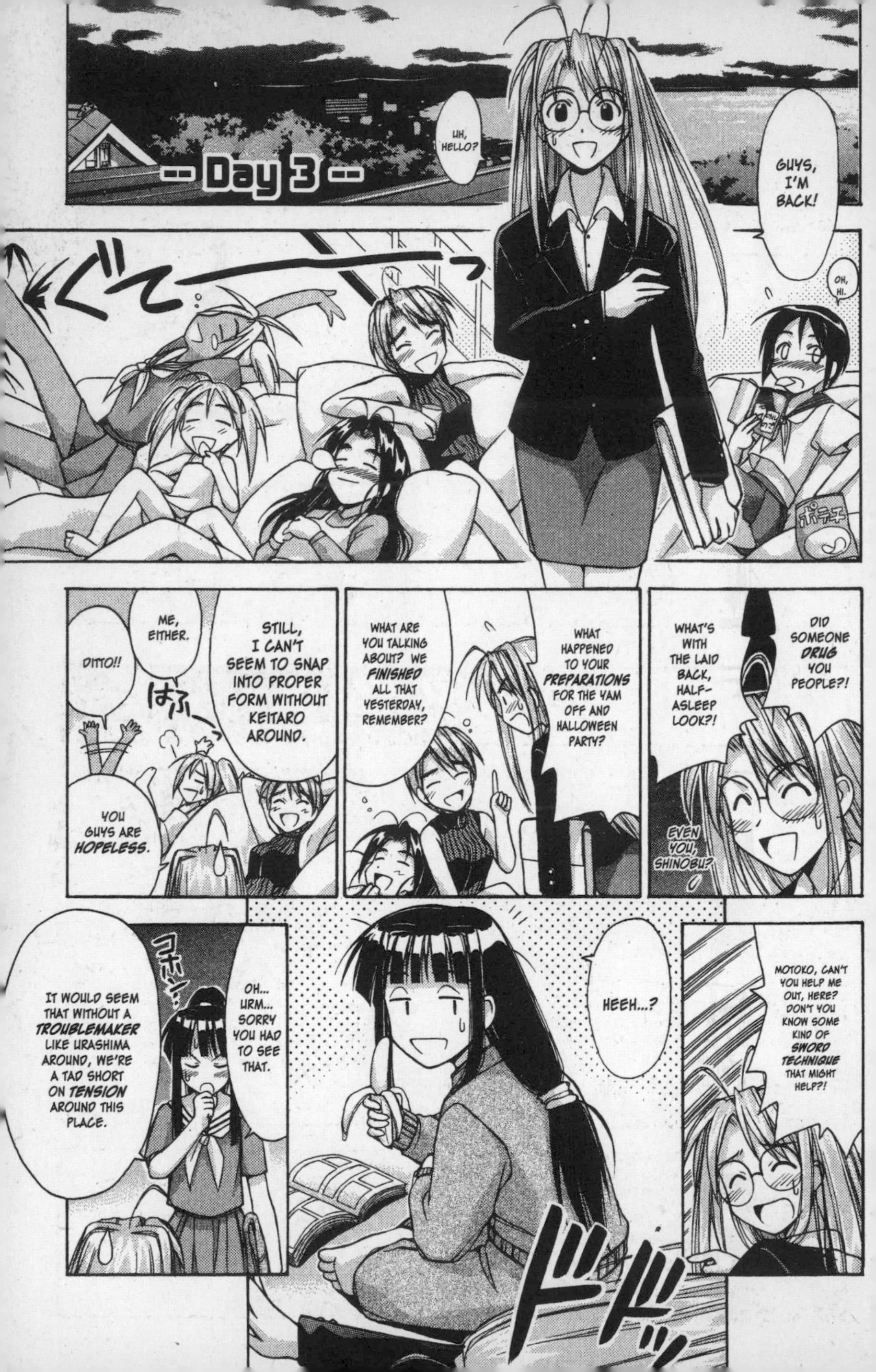
-- Day 3 --
GUYS, I'M BACK!
UH, HELLO?
OH, HI.
ぐでーーっ
DID SOMEONE DRUG YOU PEOPLE?!
WHAT'S WITH THE LAID BACK, HALF-ASLEEP LOOK?!
EVEN YOU, SHINOBU?
WHAT HAPPENED TO YOUR PREPARATIONS FOR THE YAM OFF AND HALLOWEEN PARTY?
WHAT ARE YOU TALKING ABOUT? WE FINISHED ALL THAT YESTERDAY, REMEMBER?
STILL, I CAN'T SEEM TO SNAP INTO PROPER FORM WITHOUT KEITARO AROUND.
ME, EITHER.
はふ〜
DITTO!!
YOU GUYS ARE HOPELESS.
MOTOKO, CAN'T YOU HELP ME OUT, HERE? DON'T YOU KNOW SOME KIND OF SWORD TECHNIQUE THAT MIGHT HELP?!
HEEH...?
ドドッ
OH... URM... SORRY YOU HAD TO SEE THAT.
コホン
IT WOULD SEEM THAT WITHOUT A TROUBLEMAKER LIKE URASHIMA AROUND, WE'RE A TAD SHORT ON TENSION AROUND THIS PLACE.

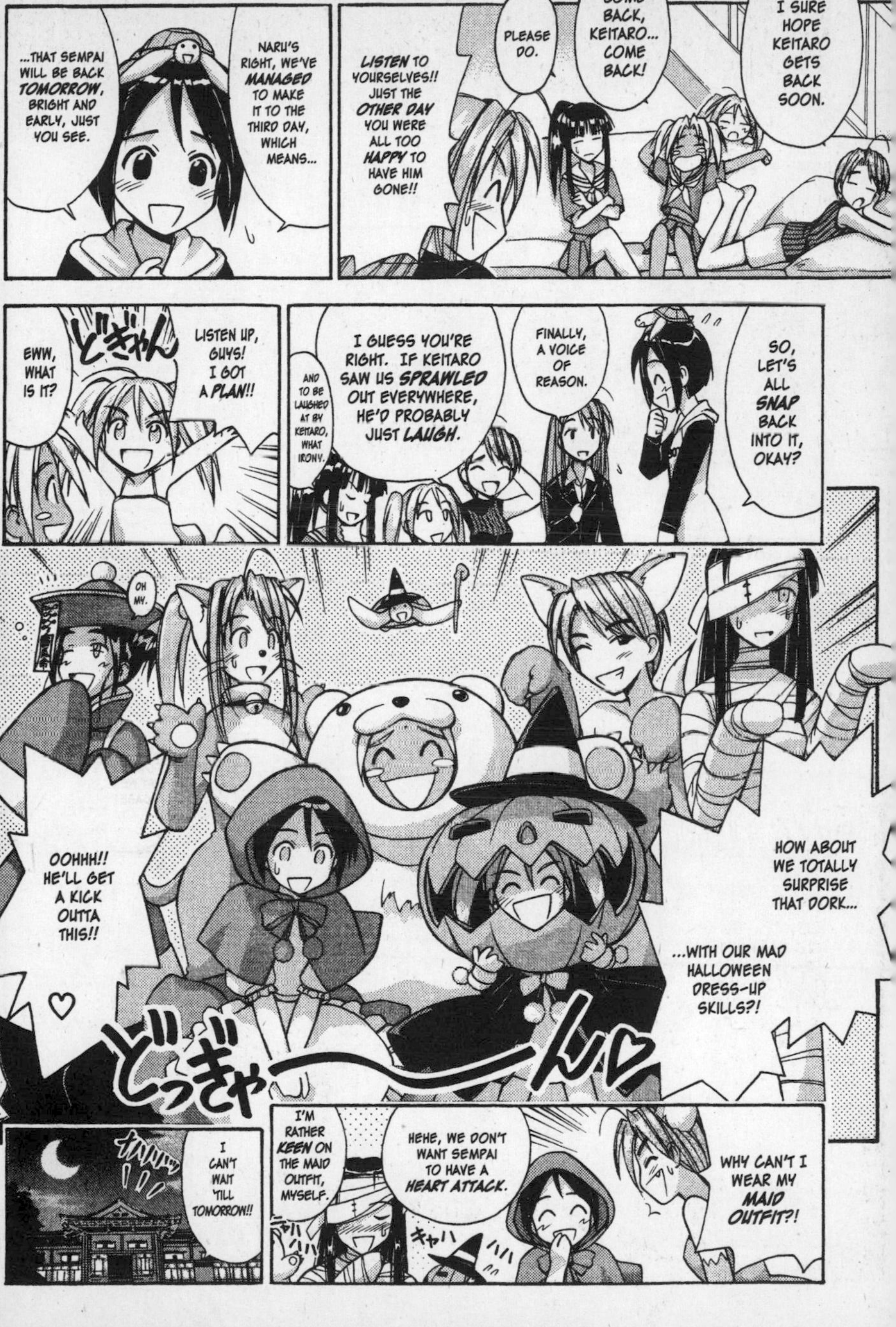
I SURE HOPE KEITARO GETS BACK SOON.
COME BACK, KEITARO... COME BACK!
PLEASE DO.
LISTEN TO YOURSELVES!! JUST THE OTHER DAY YOU WERE ALL TOO HAPPY TO HAVE HIM GONE!!
NARU'S RIGHT, WE'VE MANAGED TO MAKE IT TO THE THIRD DAY, WHICH MEANS...
...THAT SEMPAI WILL BE BACK TOMORROW, BRIGHT AND EARLY, JUST YOU SEE.
SO, LET'S ALL SNAP BACK INTO IT, OKAY?
FINALLY, A VOICE OF REASON.
I GUESS YOU'RE RIGHT. IF KEITARO SAW US SPRAWLED OUT EVERYWHERE, HE'D PROBABLY JUST LAUGH.
AND TO BE LAUGHED AT BY KEITARO, WHAT IRONY.
LISTEN UP, GUYS! I GOT A PLAN!!
どぎゃん
EWW, WHAT IS IT?
HOW ABOUT WE TOTALLY SURPRISE THAT DORK...
...WITH OUR MAD HALLOWEEN DRESS-UP SKILLS?!
OH MY.
OOHHH!! HE'LL GET A KICK OUTTA THIS!!
どっぎゃーーん♡
WHY CAN'T I WEAR MY MAID OUTFIT?!
HEHE, WE DON'T WANT SEMPAI TO HAVE A HEART ATTACK.
キャハ
I'M RATHER KEEN ON THE MAID OUTFIT, MYSELF.
I CAN'T WAIT 'TILL TOMORROW!!

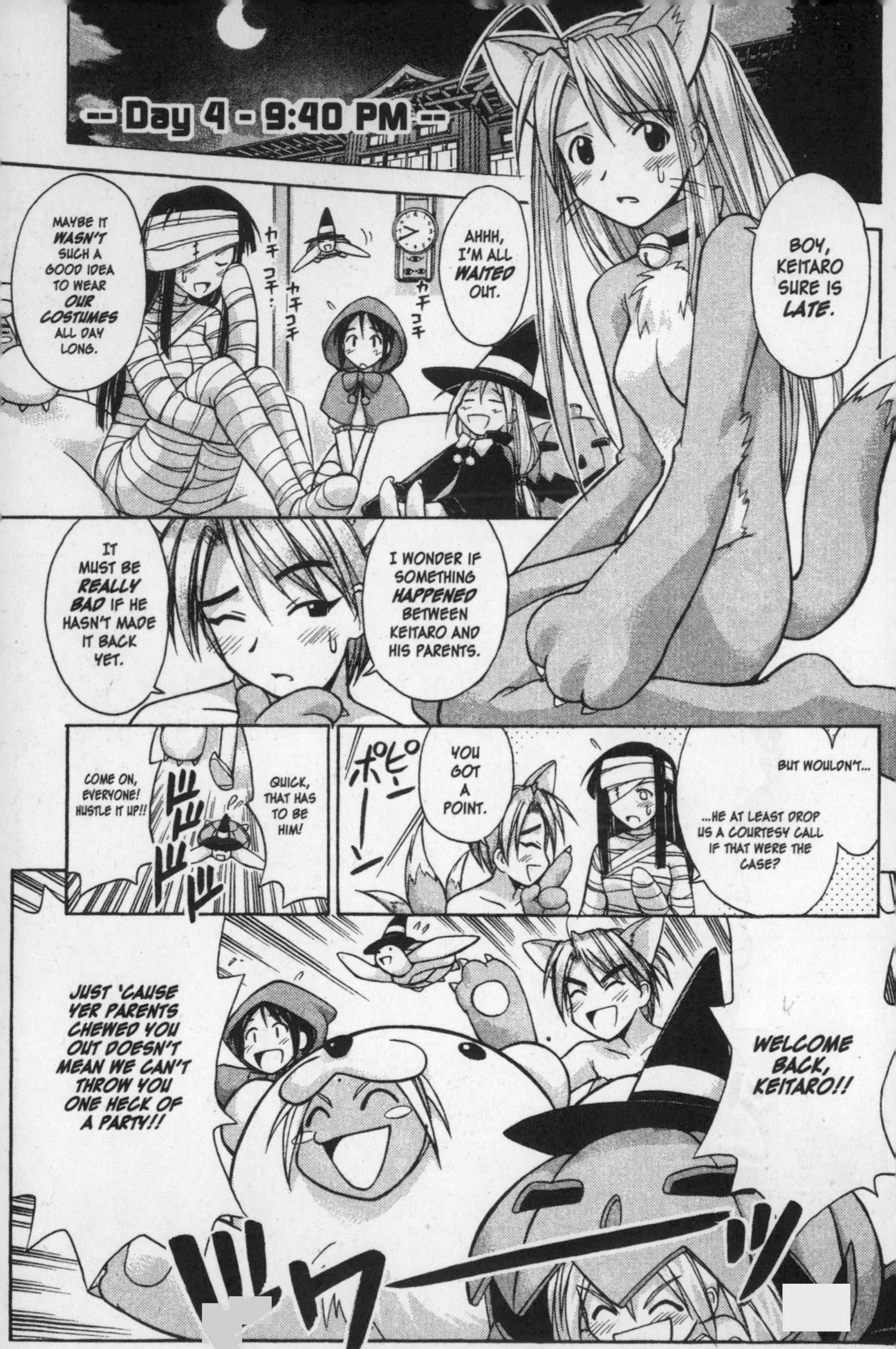
-- Day 4 - 9:40 PM --
BOY, KEITARO SURE IS LATE.
AHHH, I'M ALL WAITED OUT.
カチコチ
カチコチ
カチコチ…
MAYBE IT WASN'T SUCH A GOOD IDEA TO WEAR OUR COSTUMES ALL DAY LONG.
I WONDER IF SOMETHING HAPPENED BETWEEN KEITARO AND HIS PARENTS.
IT MUST BE REALLY BAD IF HE HASN'T MADE IT BACK YET.
BUT WOULDN'T...
...HE AT LEAST DROP US A COURTESY CALL IF THAT WERE THE CASE?
YOU GOT A POINT.
ポピーン
QUICK, THAT HAS TO BE HIM!
COME ON, EVERYONE! HUSTLE IT UP!!
WELCOME BACK, KEITARO!!
JUST 'CAUSE YER PARENTS CHEWED YOU OUT DOESN'T MEAN WE CAN'T THROW YOU ONE HECK OF A PARTY!!

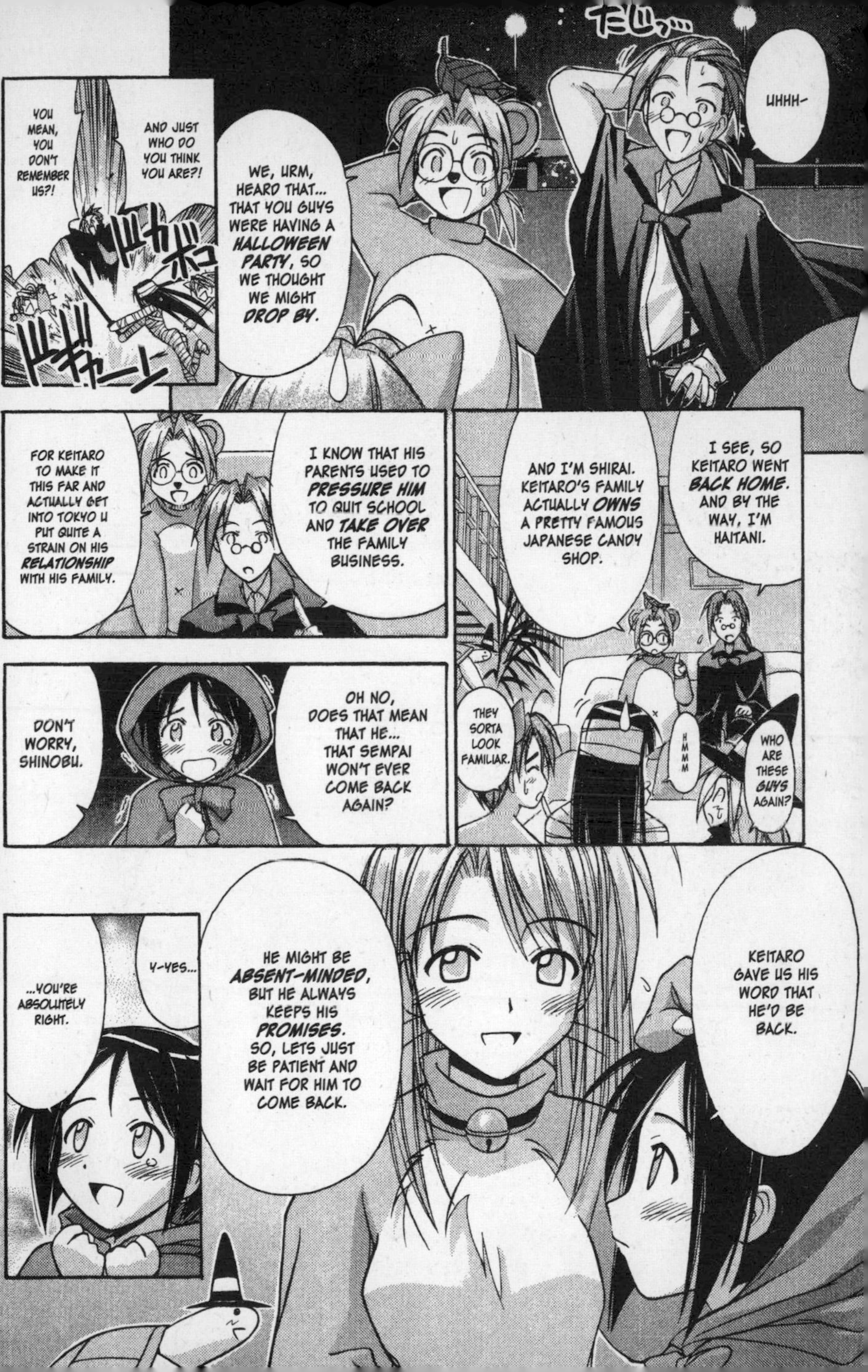
UHHH-
WE, URM, HEARD THAT... THAT YOU GUYS WERE HAVING A HALLOWEEN PARTY, SO WE THOUGHT WE MIGHT DROP BY.
AND JUST WHO DO YOU THINK YOU ARE?!
YOU MEAN, YOU DON'T REMEMBER US?!
I SEE, SO KEITARO WENT BACK HOME. AND BY THE WAY, I'M HAITANI.
AND I'M SHIRAI. KEITARO'S FAMILY ACTUALLY OWNS A PRETTY FAMOUS JAPANESE CANDY SHOP.
WHO ARE THESE GUYS AGAIN?
HMMM
THEY SORTA LOOK FAMILIAR.
I KNOW THAT HIS PARENTS USED TO PRESSURE HIM TO QUIT SCHOOL AND TAKE OVER THE FAMILY BUSINESS.
FOR KEITARO TO MAKE IT THIS FAR AND ACTUALLY GET INTO TOKYO U PUT QUITE A STRAIN ON HIS RELATIONSHIP WITH HIS FAMILY.
OH NO, DOES THAT MEAN THAT HE... THAT SEMPAI WON'T EVER COME BACK AGAIN?
DON'T WORRY, SHINOBU.
KEITARO GAVE US HIS WORD THAT HE'D BE BACK.
HE MIGHT BE ABSENT-MINDED, BUT HE ALWAYS KEEPS HIS PROMISES. SO, LETS JUST BE PATIENT AND WAIT FOR HIM TO COME BACK.
Y-YES...
...YOU'RE ABSOLUTELY RIGHT.

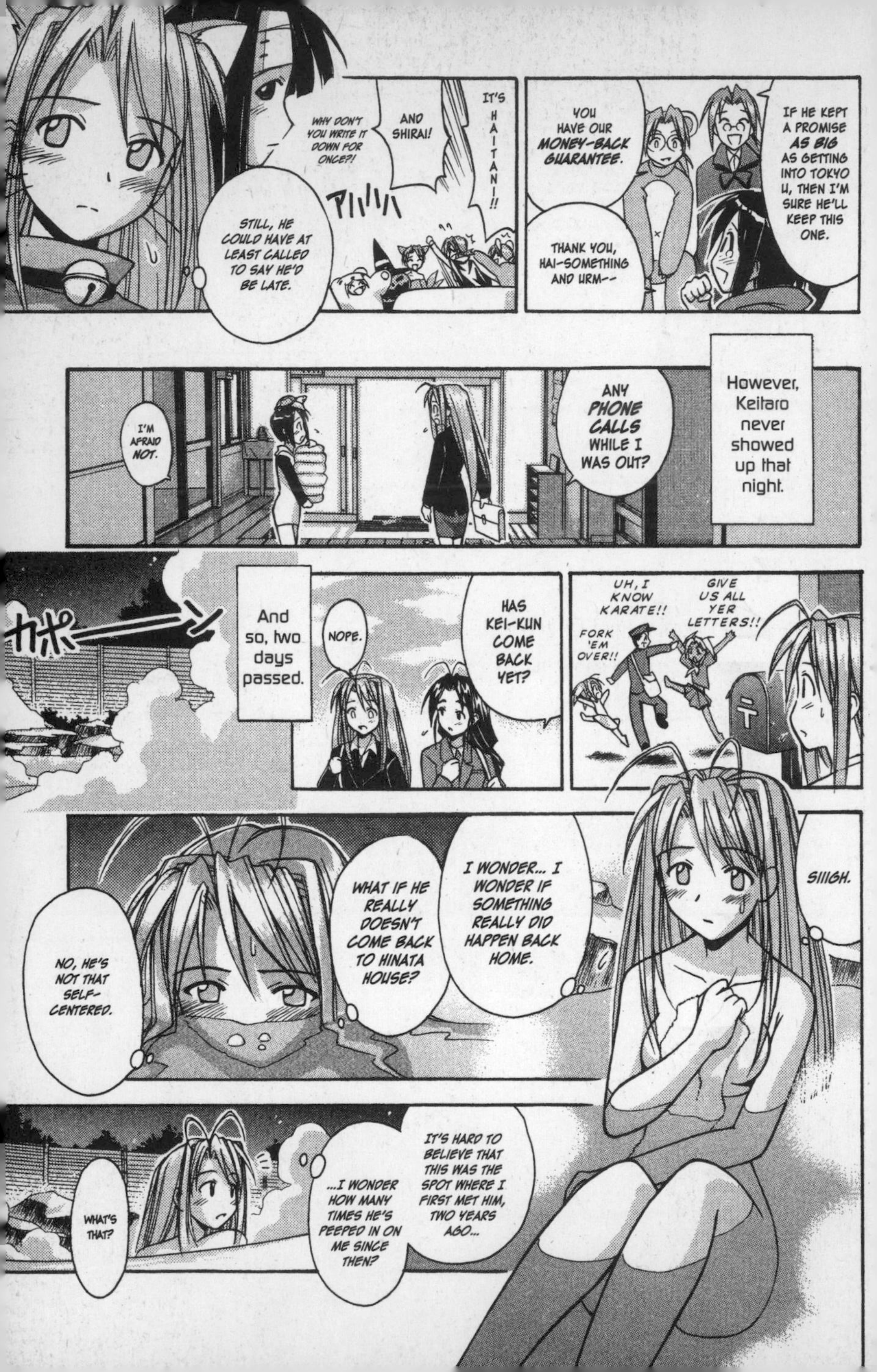
IF HE KEPT A PROMISE AS BIG AS GETTING INTO TOKYO U, THEN I'M SURE HE'LL KEEP THIS ONE.
YOU HAVE OUR MONEY-BACK GUARANTEE.
THANK YOU, HAI-SOMETHING AND URM--
IT'S HAITANI!!
AND SHIRAI!
WHY DON'T YOU WRITE IT DOWN FOR ONCE?!
アハハハ
STILL, HE COULD HAVE AT LEAST CALLED TO SAY HE'D BE LATE.
However, Keitaro never showed up that night.
ANY PHONE CALLS WHILE I WAS OUT?
I'M AFRAID NOT.
GIVE US ALL YER LETTERS!!
UH, I KNOW KARATE!!
FORK 'EM OVER!!
HAS KEI-KUN COME BACK YET?
NOPE.
And so, two days passed.
カポーン
SIIIGH.
I WONDER... I WONDER IF SOMETHING REALLY DID HAPPEN BACK HOME.
WHAT IF HE REALLY DOESN'T COME BACK TO HINATA HOUSE?
NO, HE'S NOT THAT SELF-CENTERED.
IT'S HARD TO BELIEVE THAT THIS WAS THE SPOT WHERE I FIRST MET HIM, TWO YEARS AGO...
...I WONDER HOW MANY TIMES HE'S PEEPED IN ON ME SINCE THEN?
WHAT'S THAT?

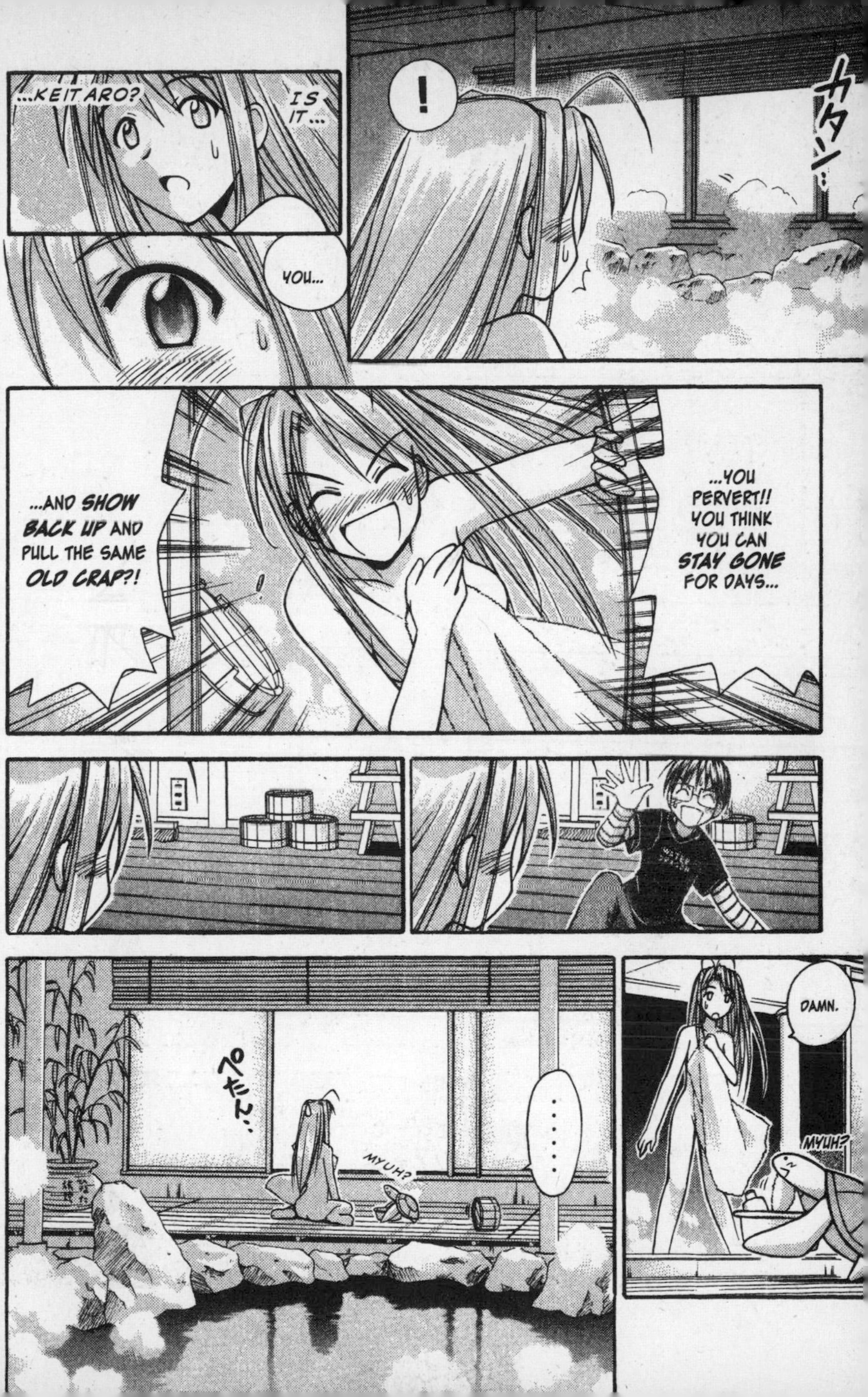

カタン…
!
IS IT...
...KEITARO?
YOU...
...YOU PERVERT!! YOU THINK YOU CAN STAY GONE FOR DAYS...
...AND SHOW BACK UP AND PULL THE SAME OLD CRAP?!
DAMN.
MYUH?
......
ぺたん…
MYUH?

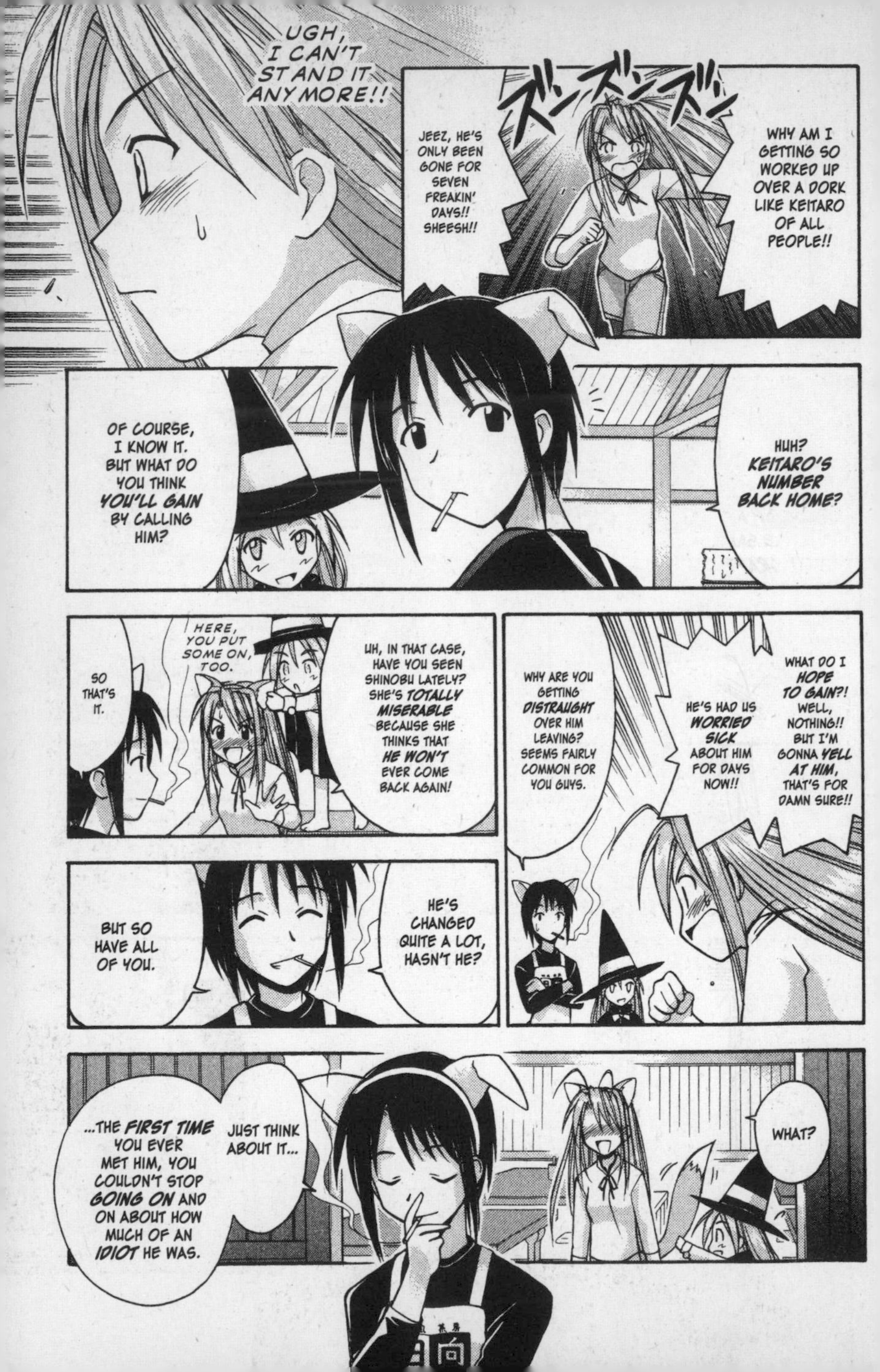
ズンズンズン
WHY AM I GETTING SO WORKED UP OVER A DORK LIKE KEITARO OF ALL PEOPLE!!
JEEZ, HE'S ONLY BEEN GONE FOR SEVEN FREAKIN' DAYS!! SHEESH!!
UGH, I CAN'T STAND IT ANYMORE!!
HUH? KEITARO'S NUMBER BACK HOME?
OF COURSE, I KNOW IT. BUT WHAT DO YOU THINK YOU'LL GAIN BY CALLING HIM?
WHAT DO I HOPE TO GAIN?! WELL, NOTHING!! BUT I'M GONNA YELL AT HIM, THAT'S FOR DAMN SURE!!
HE'S HAD US WORRIED SICK ABOUT HIM FOR DAYS NOW!!
WHY ARE YOU GETTING DISTRAUGHT OVER HIM LEAVING? SEEMS FAIRLY COMMON FOR YOU GUYS.
UH, IN THAT CASE, HAVE YOU SEEN SHINOBU LATELY? SHE'S TOTALLY MISERABLE BECAUSE SHE THINKS THAT HE WON'T EVER COME BACK AGAIN!
HERE, YOU PUT SOME ON, TOO.
SO THAT'S IT.
HE'S CHANGED QUITE A LOT, HASN'T HE?
BUT SO HAVE ALL OF YOU.
WHAT?
JUST THINK ABOUT IT...
...THE FIRST TIME YOU EVER MET HIM, YOU COULDN'T STOP GOING ON AND ON ABOUT HOW MUCH OF AN IDIOT HE WAS.

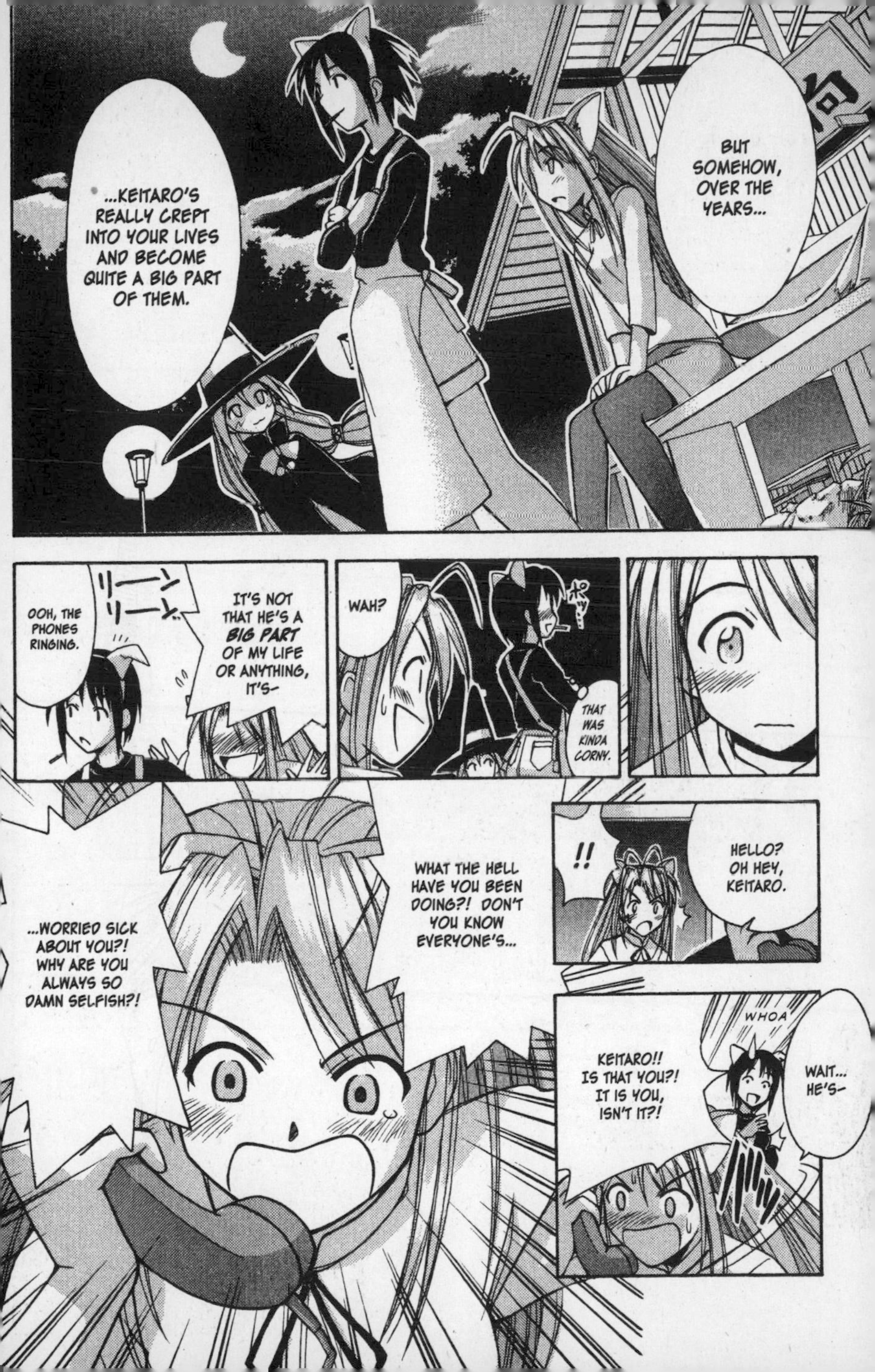
BUT SOMEHOW, OVER THE YEARS...
...KEITARO'S REALLY CREPT INTO YOUR LIVES AND BECOME QUITE A BIG PART OF THEM.
WAH?
THAT WAS KINDA CORNY.
IT'S NOT THAT HE'S A BIG PART OF MY LIFE OR ANYTHING, IT'S-
リーン リーン
OOH, THE PHONES RINGING.
HELLO? OH HEY, KEITARO.
!!
WAIT... HE'S-
WHOA
KEITARO!! IS THAT YOU?! IT IS YOU, ISN'T IT?!
WHAT THE HELL HAVE YOU BEEN DOING?! DON'T YOU KNOW EVERYONE'S...
...WORRIED SICK ABOUT YOU?! WHY ARE YOU ALWAYS SO DAMN SELFISH?!

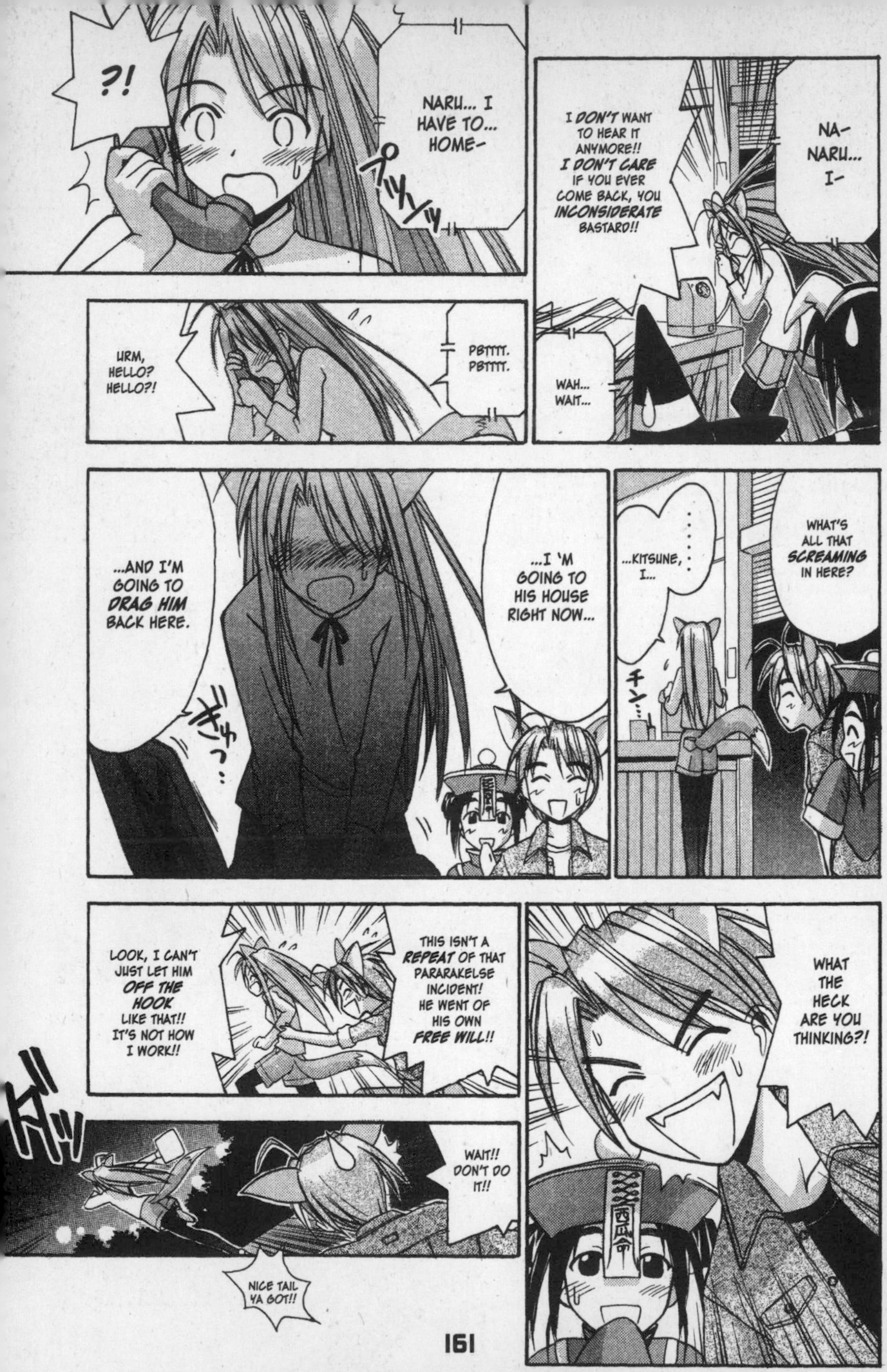
NA-NARU... I-
I DON'T WANT TO HEAR IT ANYMORE!! I DON'T CARE IF YOU EVER COME BACK, YOU INCONSIDERATE BASTARD!!
WAH... WAIT...
NARU... I HAVE TO... HOME-
?!
PBTTTT. PBTTTT.
URM, HELLO? HELLO?!
WHAT'S ALL THAT SCREAMING IN HERE?
......
...KITSUNE, I...
...I 'M GOING TO HIS HOUSE RIGHT NOW...
...AND I'M GOING TO DRAG HIM BACK HERE.
WHAT THE HECK ARE YOU THINKING?!
THIS ISN'T A REPEAT OF THAT PARARAKELSE INCIDENT! HE WENT OF HIS OWN FREE WILL!!
LOOK, I CAN'T JUST LET HIM OFF THE HOOK LIKE THAT!! IT'S NOT HOW I WORK!!
WAIT!! DON'T DO IT!!
NICE TAIL YA GOT!!

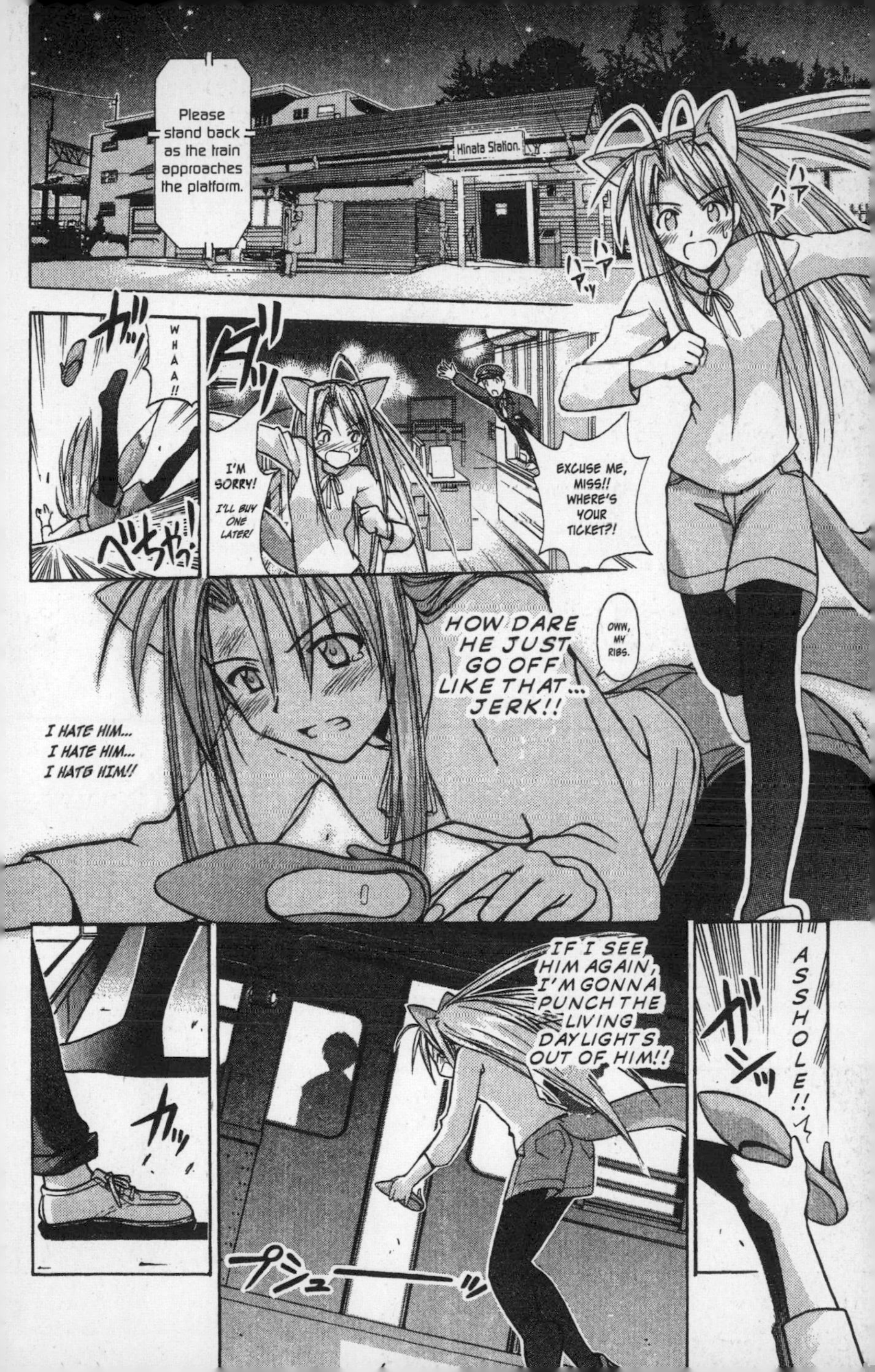
Please stand back as the train approaches the platform.
Hinata Station.
ハァ ハァ ハァ ハァッ
ダッ
EXCUSE ME, MISS!! WHERE'S YOUR TICKET?!
I'M SORRY!
I'LL BUY ONE LATER!
ガッ
WHAAA!!
べちゃっ
OWW, MY RIBS.
HOW DARE HE JUST GO OFF LIKE THAT... JERK!!
I HATE HIM... I HATE HIM... I HATE HIM!!
ASSHOLE!!
ガシッ
IF I SEE HIM AGAIN, I'M GONNA PUNCH THE LIVING DAYLIGHTS OUT OF HIM!!
プシューーーッ
カッ

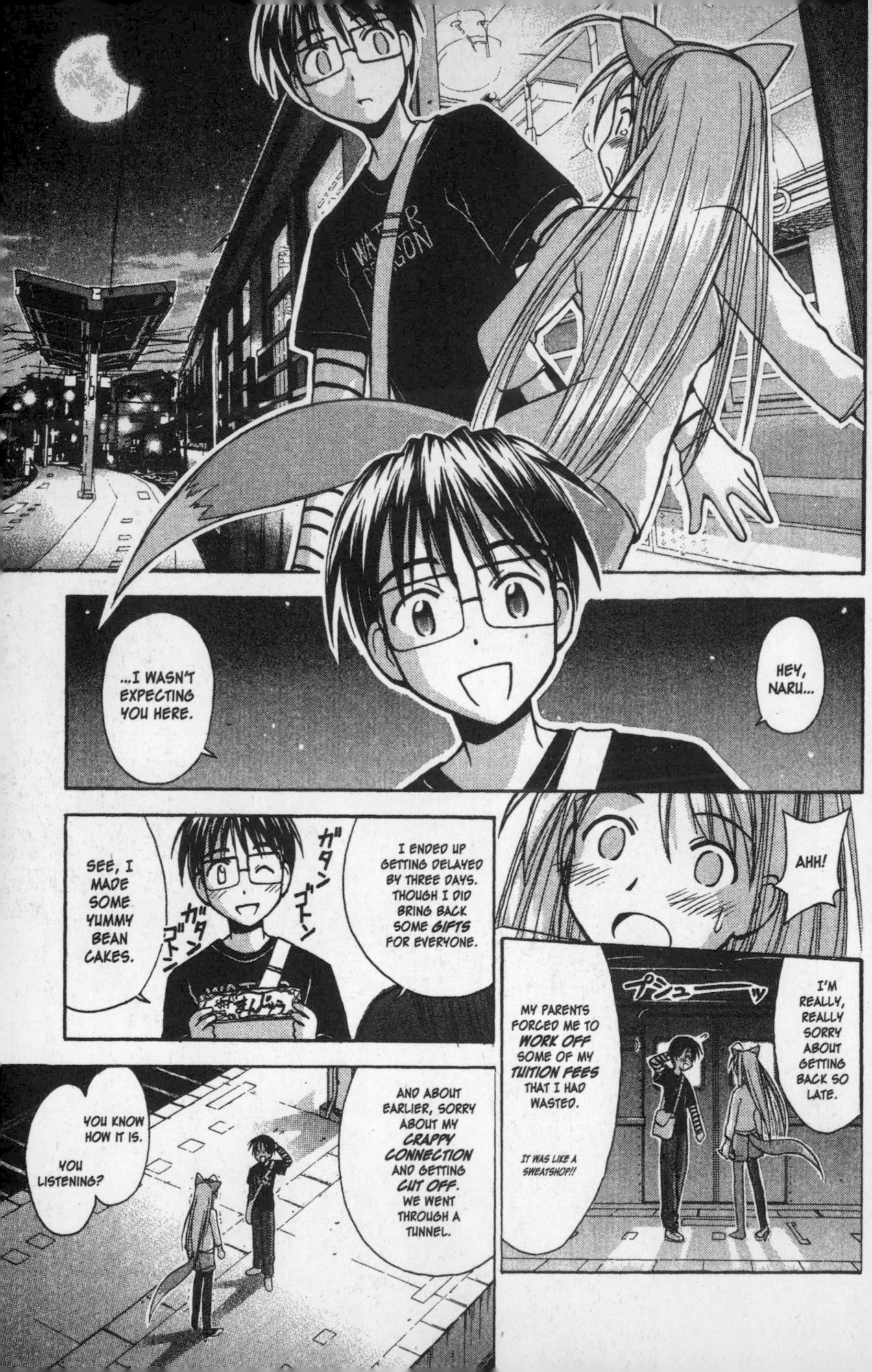
HEY, NARU...
...I WASN'T EXPECTING YOU HERE.
AHH!
ガタン ゴトン
ガタン ゴトン
I ENDED UP GETTING DELAYED BY THREE DAYS. THOUGH I DID BRING BACK SOME *GIFTS* FOR EVERYONE.
SEE, I MADE SOME YUMMY BEAN CAKES.
プシューッ
I'M REALLY, REALLY SORRY ABOUT GETTING BACK SO LATE.
MY PARENTS FORCED ME TO *WORK OFF* SOME OF MY *TUITION FEES* THAT I HAD WASTED.
IT WAS LIKE A SWEATSHOP!!
AND ABOUT EARLIER, SORRY ABOUT MY *CRAPPY CONNECTION* AND GETTING *CUT OFF*. WE WENT THROUGH A TUNNEL.
YOU KNOW HOW IT IS.
YOU LISTENING?

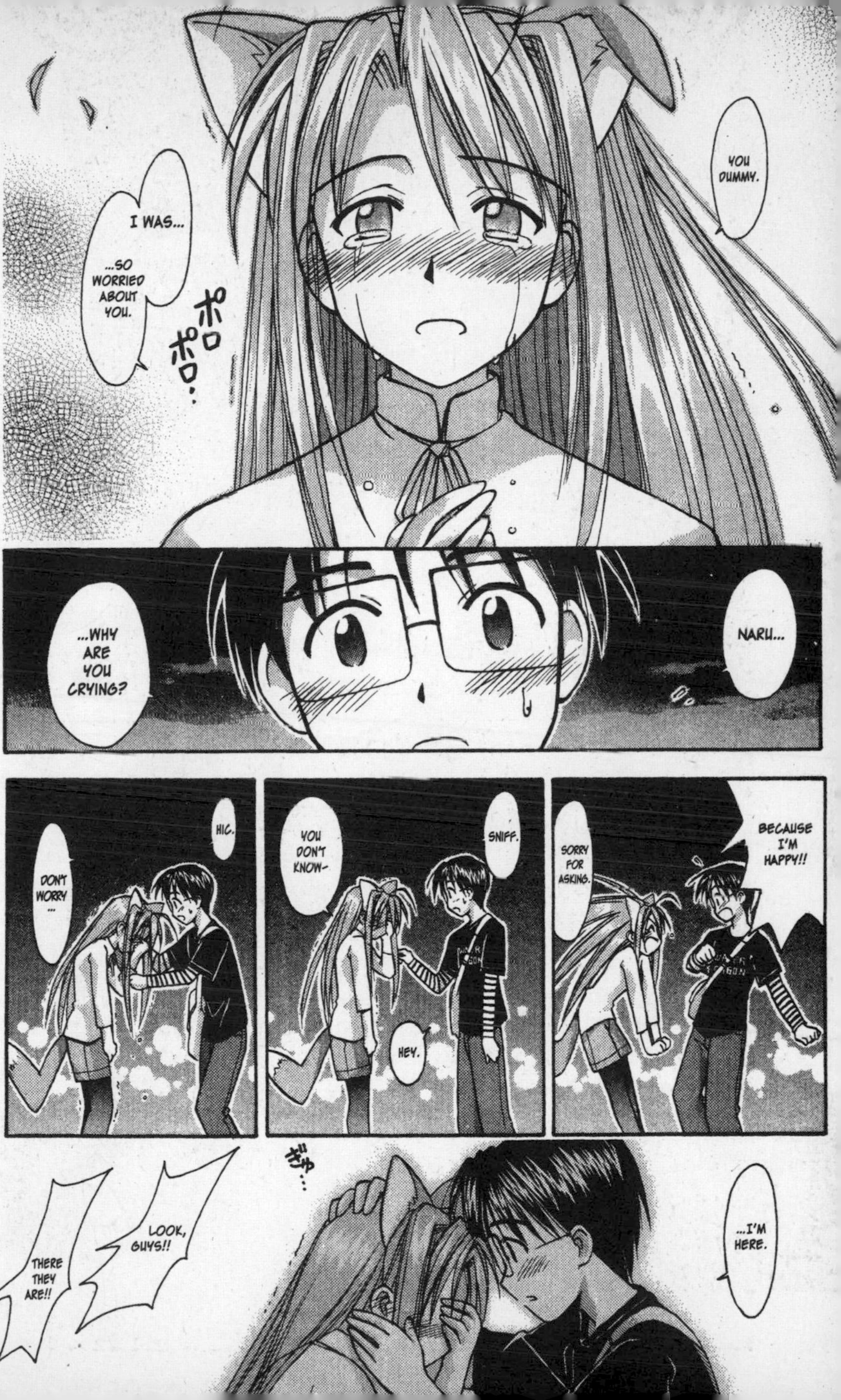
YOU DUMMY.
I WAS...
...SO WORRIED ABOUT YOU.
ポロポロ…
NARU...
...WHY ARE YOU CRYING?
BECAUSE I'M HAPPY!!
SORRY FOR ASKING.
SNIFF.
YOU DON'T KNOW-
HEY.
HIC.
DON'T WORRY ...
...I'M HERE.
ぎゅ…
LOOK, GUYS!!
THERE THEY ARE!!

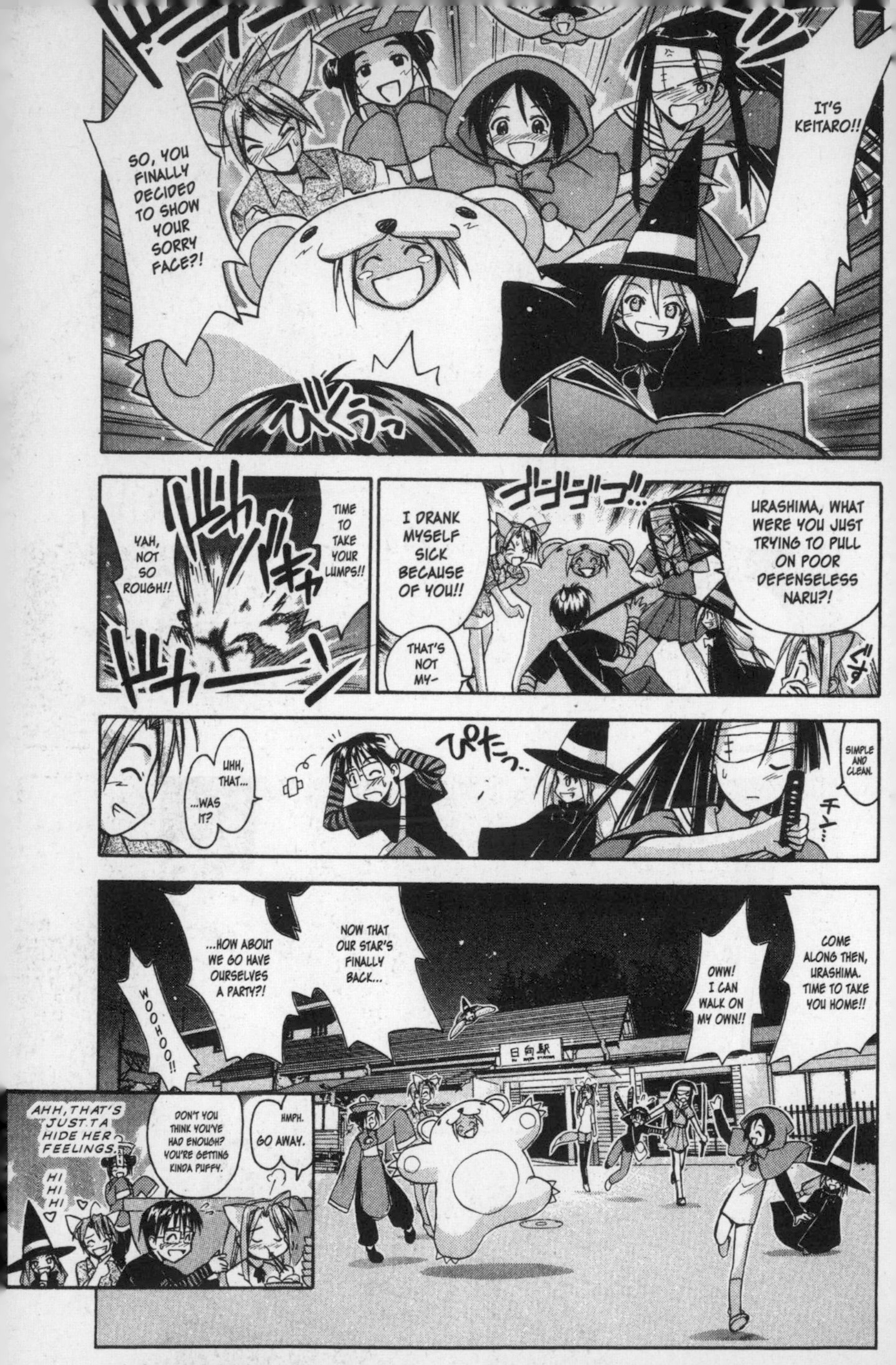
IT'S KEITARO!!
SO, YOU FINALLY DECIDED TO SHOW YOUR SORRY FACE?!
URASHIMA, WHAT WERE YOU JUST TRYING TO PULL ON POOR DEFENSELESS NARU?!
I DRANK MYSELF SICK BECAUSE OF YOU!!
THAT'S NOT MY-
TIME TO TAKE YOUR LUMPS!!
YAH, NOT SO ROUGH!!
SIMPLE AND CLEAN.
UHH, THAT...
...WAS IT?
COME ALONG THEN, URASHIMA. TIME TO TAKE YOU HOME!!
OWW! I CAN WALK ON MY OWN!!
NOW THAT OUR STAR'S FINALLY BACK...
...HOW ABOUT WE GO HAVE OURSELVES A PARTY?!
WOOHOO!!
日向駅
HMPH. GO AWAY.
DON'T YOU THINK YOU'VE HAD ENOUGH? YOU'RE GETTING KINDA PUFFY.
AHH, THAT'S JUST TA HIDE HER FEELINGS.
HI HI HI

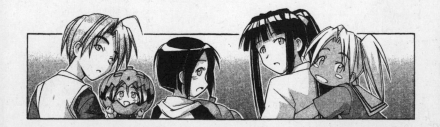

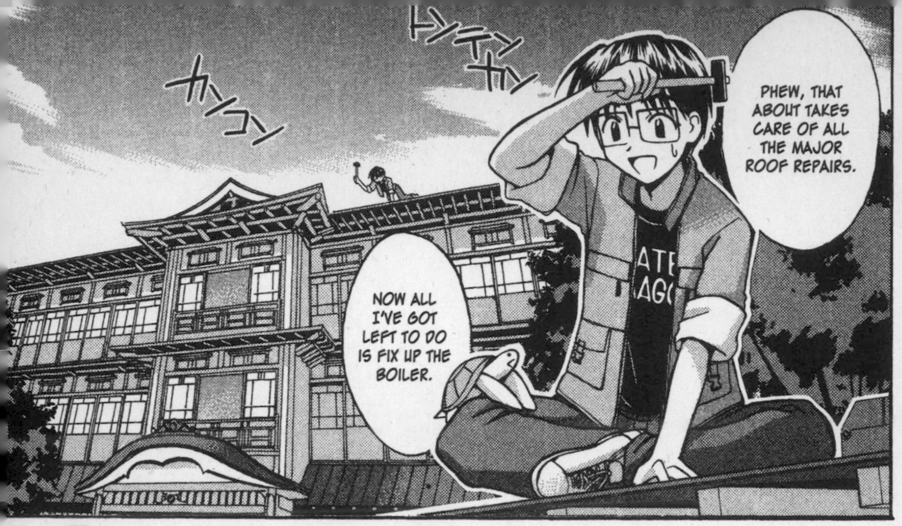
トンテンカン
カンコン
PHEW, THAT ABOUT TAKES CARE OF ALL THE MAJOR ROOF REPAIRS.
NOW ALL I'VE GOT LEFT TO DO IS FIX UP THE BOILER.

Love Hina

HINATA.87 Zen and the Art of Coming Out

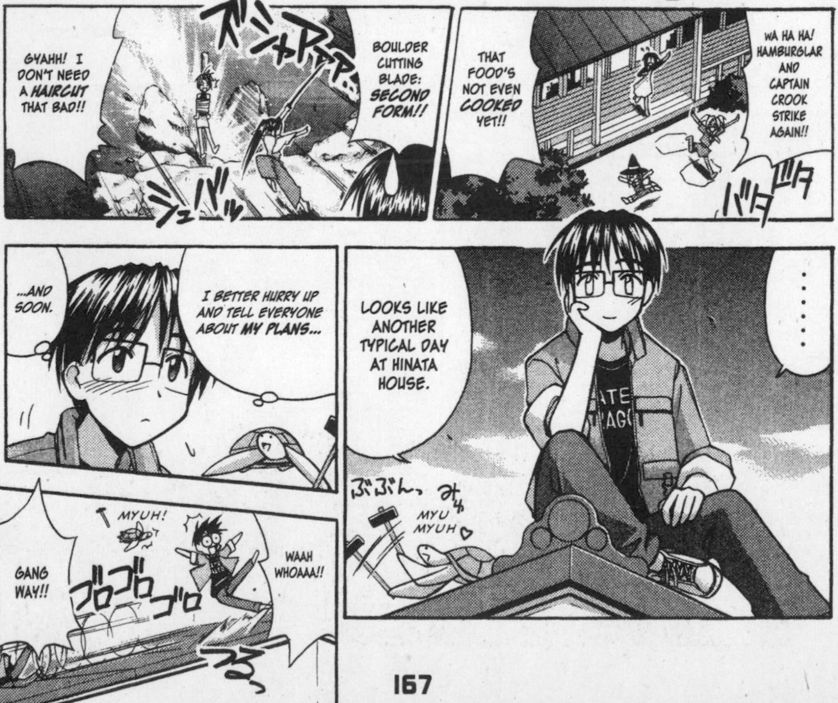
WA HA HA! HAMBURGLAR AND CAPTAIN CROOK STRIKE AGAIN!!
THAT FOOD'S NOT EVEN COOKED YET!!
BOULDER CUTTING BLADE: SECOND FORM!!
GYAHH! I DON'T NEED A HAIRCUT THAT BAD!!
......
LOOKS LIKE ANOTHER TYPICAL DAY AT HINATA HOUSE.
MYU MYUH
I BETTER HURRY UP AND TELL EVERYONE ABOUT MY PLANS...
...AND SOON.
WAAH WHOAAA!!
MYUH!
GANG WAY!!

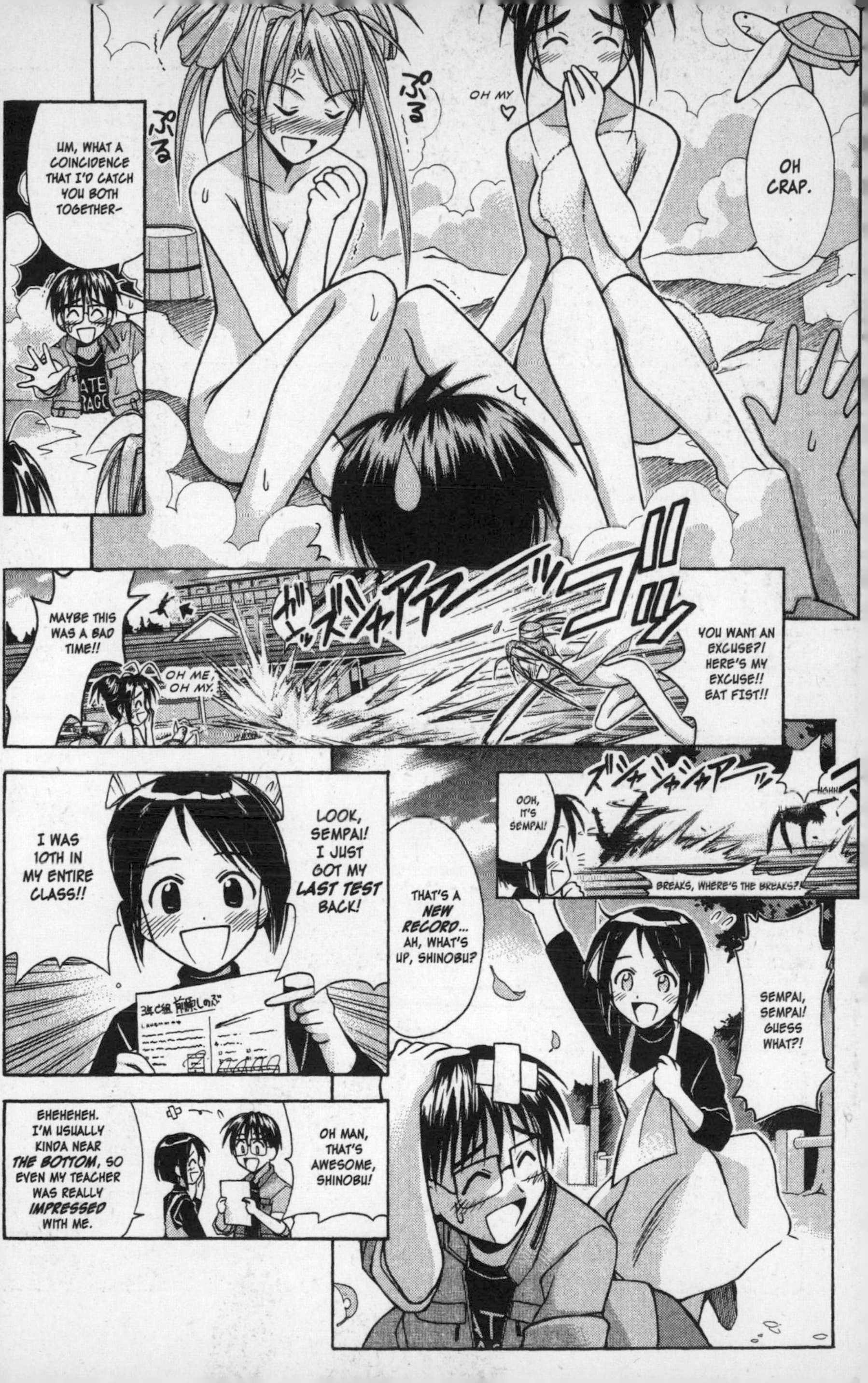
OH CRAP.
OH MY ♡
ぷる
ぷる
UM, WHAT A COINCIDENCE THAT I'D CATCH YOU BOTH TOGETHER-
YOU WANT AN EXCUSE?! HERE'S MY EXCUSE!! EAT FIST!!
ゴッ
ズシャアーッ
MAYBE THIS WAS A BAD TIME!!
OH ME, OH MY.
ズシャシャアーッ
OOH, IT'S SEMPAI!
BREAKS, WHERE'S THE BREAKS?!
SEMPAI, SEMPAI! GUESS WHAT?!
THAT'S A *NEW RECORD*... AH, WHAT'S UP, SHINOBU?
LOOK, SEMPAI! I JUST GOT MY *LAST TEST* BACK!
I WAS 10TH IN MY ENTIRE CLASS!!
3年C組 前原しのぶ
OH MAN, THAT'S AWESOME, SHINOBU!
EHEHEHEH. I'M USUALLY KINDA NEAR *THE BOTTOM*, SO EVEN MY TEACHER WAS REALLY *IMPRESSED* WITH ME.

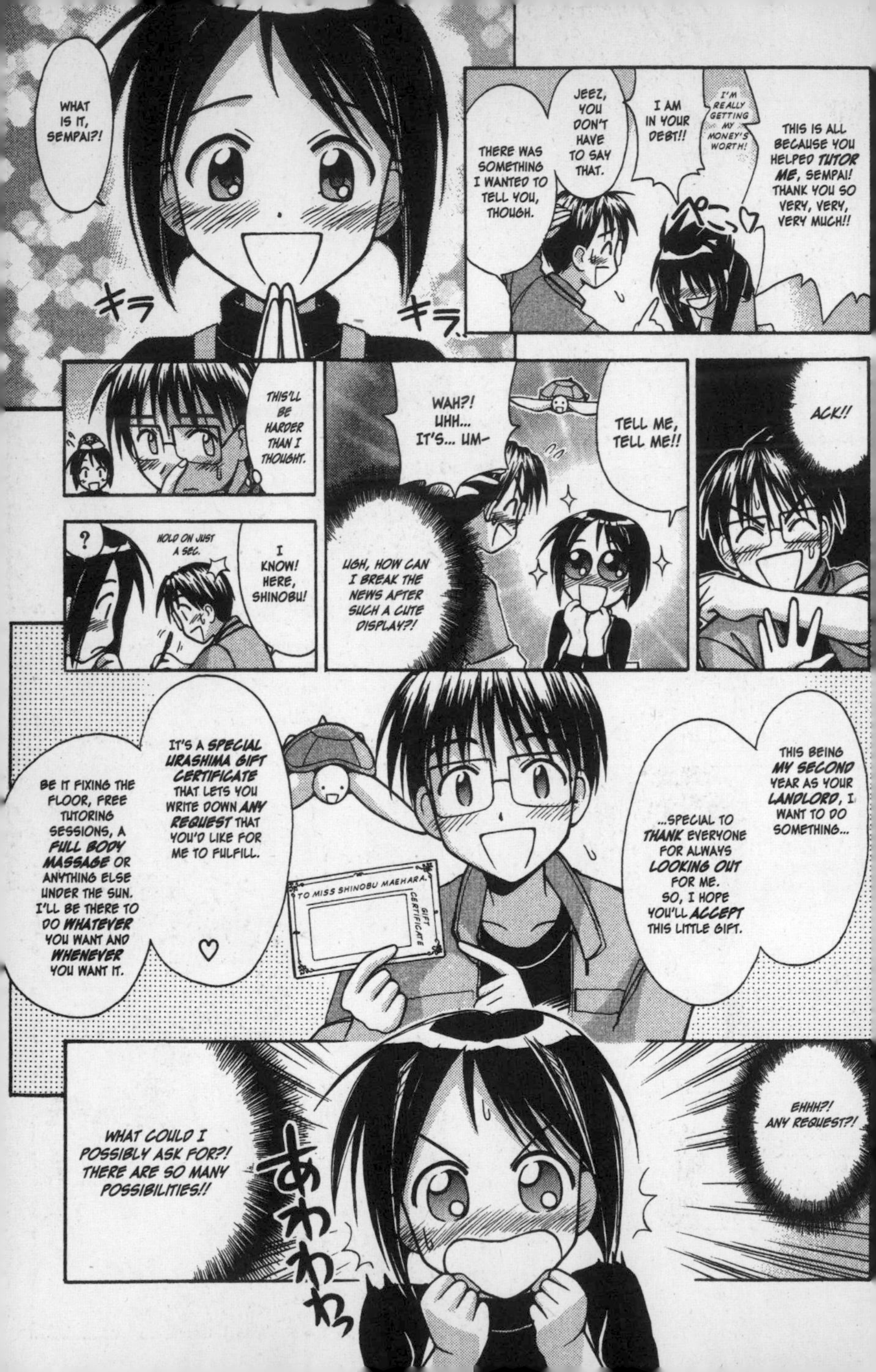
THIS IS ALL BECAUSE YOU HELPED TUTOR ME, SEMPAI! THANK YOU SO VERY, VERY, VERY MUCH!!
I'M REALLY GETTING MY MONEY'S WORTH!
I AM IN YOUR DEBT!!
JEEZ, YOU DON'T HAVE TO SAY THAT.
THERE WAS SOMETHING I WANTED TO TELL YOU, THOUGH.
WHAT IS IT, SEMPAI?!
キラ
キラ
ACK!!
TELL ME, TELL ME!!
WAH?! UHH... IT'S... UM-
UGH, HOW CAN I BREAK THE NEWS AFTER SUCH A CUTE DISPLAY?!
THIS'LL BE HARDER THAN I THOUGHT.
I KNOW! HERE, SHINOBU!
HOLD ON JUST A SEC.
?
THIS BEING MY SECOND YEAR AS YOUR LANDLORD, I WANT TO DO SOMETHING...
...SPECIAL TO THANK EVERYONE FOR ALWAYS LOOKING OUT FOR ME. SO, I HOPE YOU'LL ACCEPT THIS LITTLE GIFT.
TO MISS SHINOBU MAEHARA.
GIFT CERTIFICATE
IT'S A SPECIAL URASHIMA GIFT CERTIFICATE THAT LETS YOU WRITE DOWN ANY REQUEST THAT YOU'D LIKE FOR ME TO FULFILL.
BE IT FIXING THE FLOOR, FREE TUTORING SESSIONS, A FULL BODY MASSAGE OR ANYTHING ELSE UNDER THE SUN. I'LL BE THERE TO DO WHATEVER YOU WANT AND WHENEVER YOU WANT IT.
EHHH?! ANY REQUEST?!
あわわわ
WHAT COULD I POSSIBLY ASK FOR?! THERE ARE SO MANY POSSIBILITIES!!

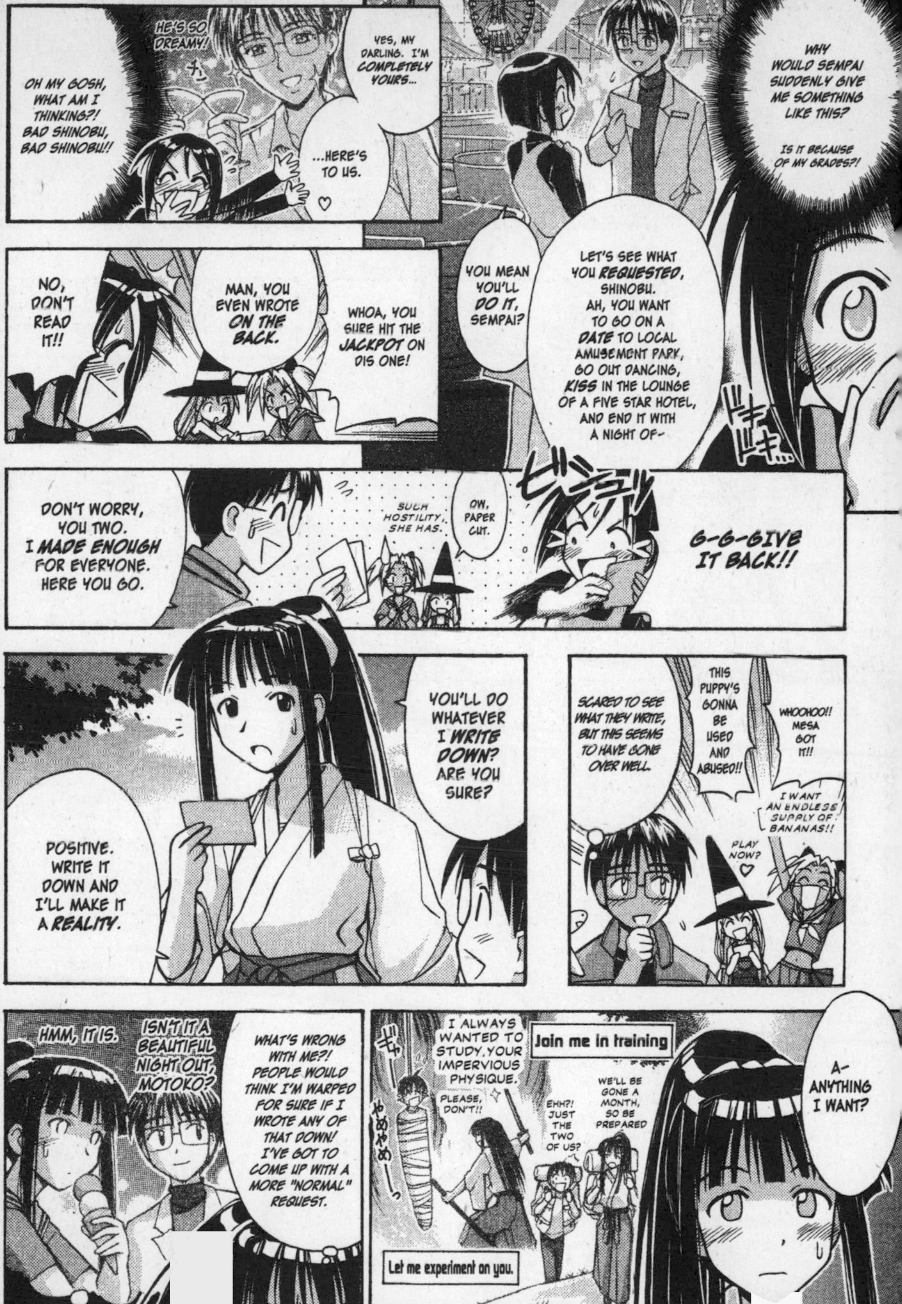

WHY WOULD SEMPAI SUDDENLY GIVE ME SOMETHING LIKE THIS?
IS IT BECAUSE OF MY GRADES?!
YES, MY DARLING. I'M COMPLETELY YOURS...
...HERE'S TO US. ♡
HE'S SO DREAMY!
OH MY GOSH, WHAT AM I THINKING?! BAD SHINOBU, BAD SHINOBU!!
LET'S SEE WHAT YOU REQUESTED, SHINOBU. AH, YOU WANT TO GO ON A DATE TO LOCAL AMUSEMENT PARK, GO OUT DANCING, KISS IN THE LOUNGE OF A FIVE STAR HOTEL, AND END IT WITH A NIGHT OF-
YOU MEAN YOU'LL DO IT, SEMPAI?
WHOA, YOU SURE HIT THE JACKPOT ON DIS ONE!
MAN, YOU EVEN WROTE ON THE BACK.
NO, DON'T READ IT!!
G-G-GIVE IT BACK!!
OW, PAPER CUT.
SUCH HOSTILITY, SHE HAS.
DON'T WORRY, YOU TWO. I MADE ENOUGH FOR EVERYONE. HERE YOU GO.
WHOOHOO!! MESA GOT IT!!
THIS PUPPY'S GONNA BE USED AND ABUSED!!
SCARED TO SEE WHAT THEY WRITE, BUT THIS SEEMS TO HAVE GONE OVER WELL.
I WANT AN ENDLESS SUPPLY OF BANANAS!!
PLAY NOW? ♡
YOU'LL DO WHATEVER I WRITE DOWN? ARE YOU SURE?
POSITIVE. WRITE IT DOWN AND I'LL MAKE IT A REALITY.
A- ANYTHING I WANT?
Join me in training
WE'LL BE GONE A MONTH, SO BE PREPARED
EHH?! JUST THE TWO OF US?
I ALWAYS WANTED TO STUDY YOUR IMPERVIOUS PHYSIQUE.
PLEASE, DON'T!!
Let me experiment on you.
WHAT'S WRONG WITH ME?! PEOPLE WOULD THINK I'M WARPED FOR SURE IF I WROTE ANY OF THAT DOWN! I'VE GOT TO COME UP WITH A MORE "NORMAL" REQUEST.
ISN'T IT A BEAUTIFUL NIGHT OUT, MOTOKO?
HMM, IT IS.
A 24 Hour Date

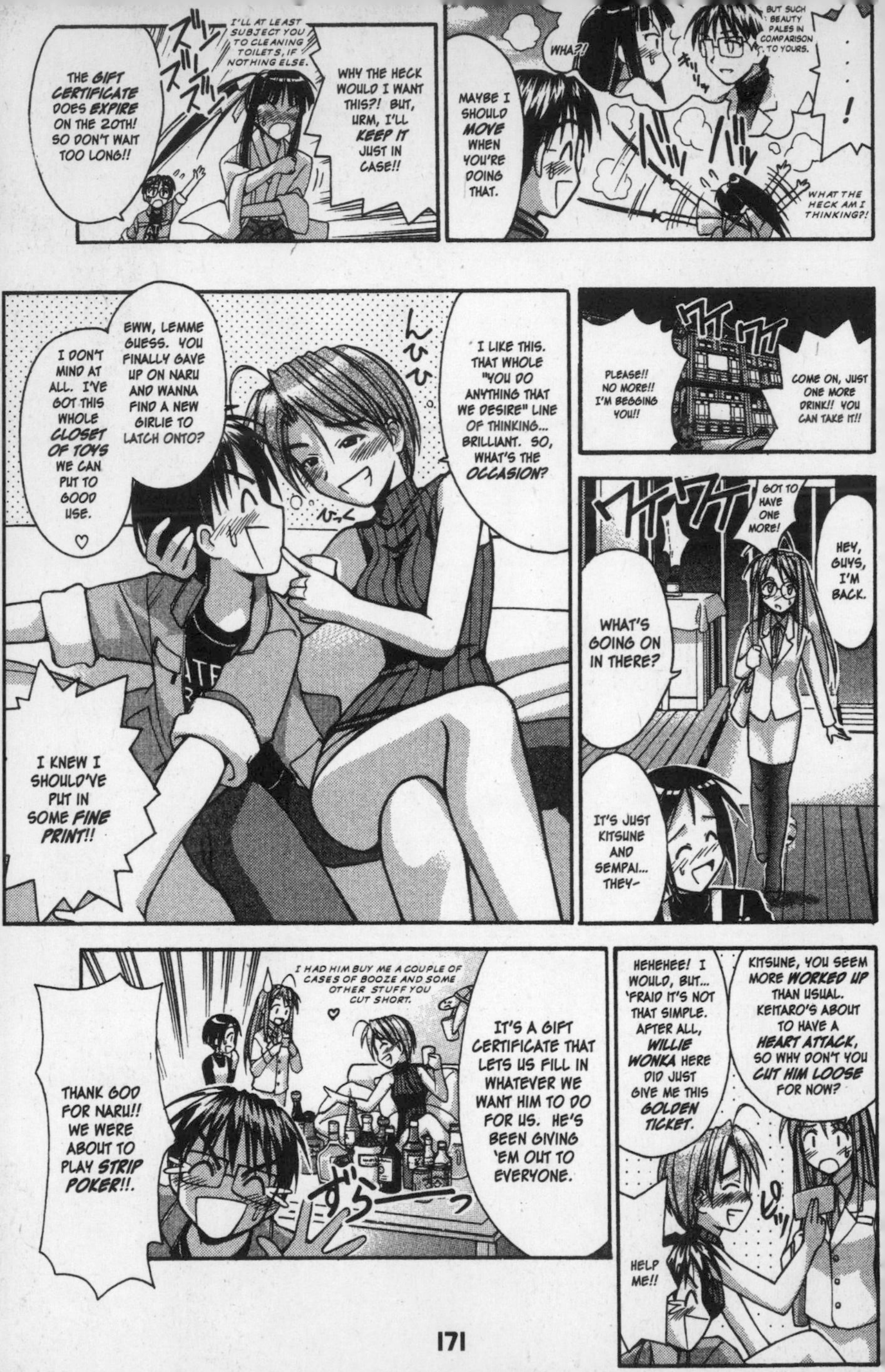
BUT SUCH BEAUTY PALES IN COMPARISON TO YOURS.
WHA?!
MAYBE I SHOULD MOVE WHEN YOU'RE DOING THAT.
WHAT THE HECK AM I THINKING?!
WHY THE HECK WOULD I WANT THIS?! BUT, URM, I'LL KEEP IT JUST IN CASE!!
I'LL AT LEAST SUBJECT YOU TO CLEANING TOILETS, IF NOTHING ELSE.
THE GIFT CERTIFICATE DOES EXPIRE ON THE 20TH! SO DON'T WAIT TOO LONG!!
COME ON, JUST ONE MORE DRINK!! YOU CAN TAKE IT!!
PLEASE!! NO MORE!! I'M BEGGING YOU!!
GOT TO HAVE ONE MORE!
HEY, GUYS, I'M BACK.
WHAT'S GOING ON IN THERE?
IT'S JUST KITSUNE AND SEMPAI... THEY-
I LIKE THIS. THAT WHOLE "YOU DO ANYTHING THAT WE DESIRE" LINE OF THINKING... BRILLIANT. SO, WHAT'S THE OCCASION?
EWW, LEMME GUESS. YOU FINALLY GAVE UP ON NARU AND WANNA FIND A NEW GIRLIE TO LATCH ONTO?
I DON'T MIND AT ALL. I'VE GOT THIS WHOLE CLOSET OF TOYS WE CAN PUT TO GOOD USE. ♡
I KNEW I SHOULD'VE PUT IN SOME FINE PRINT!!
KITSUNE, YOU SEEM MORE WORKED UP THAN USUAL. KEITARO'S ABOUT TO HAVE A HEART ATTACK, SO WHY DON'T YOU CUT HIM LOOSE FOR NOW?
HEHEHEE! I WOULD, BUT... 'FRAID IT'S NOT THAT SIMPLE. AFTER ALL, WILLIE WONKA HERE DID JUST GIVE ME THIS GOLDEN TICKET.
HELP ME!!
IT'S A GIFT CERTIFICATE THAT LETS US FILL IN WHATEVER WE WANT HIM TO DO FOR US. HE'S BEEN GIVING 'EM OUT TO EVERYONE.
I HAD HIM BUY ME A COUPLE OF CASES OF BOOZE AND SOME OTHER STUFF YOU CUT SHORT. ♡
THANK GOD FOR NARU!! WE WERE ABOUT TO PLAY STRIP POKER!!.

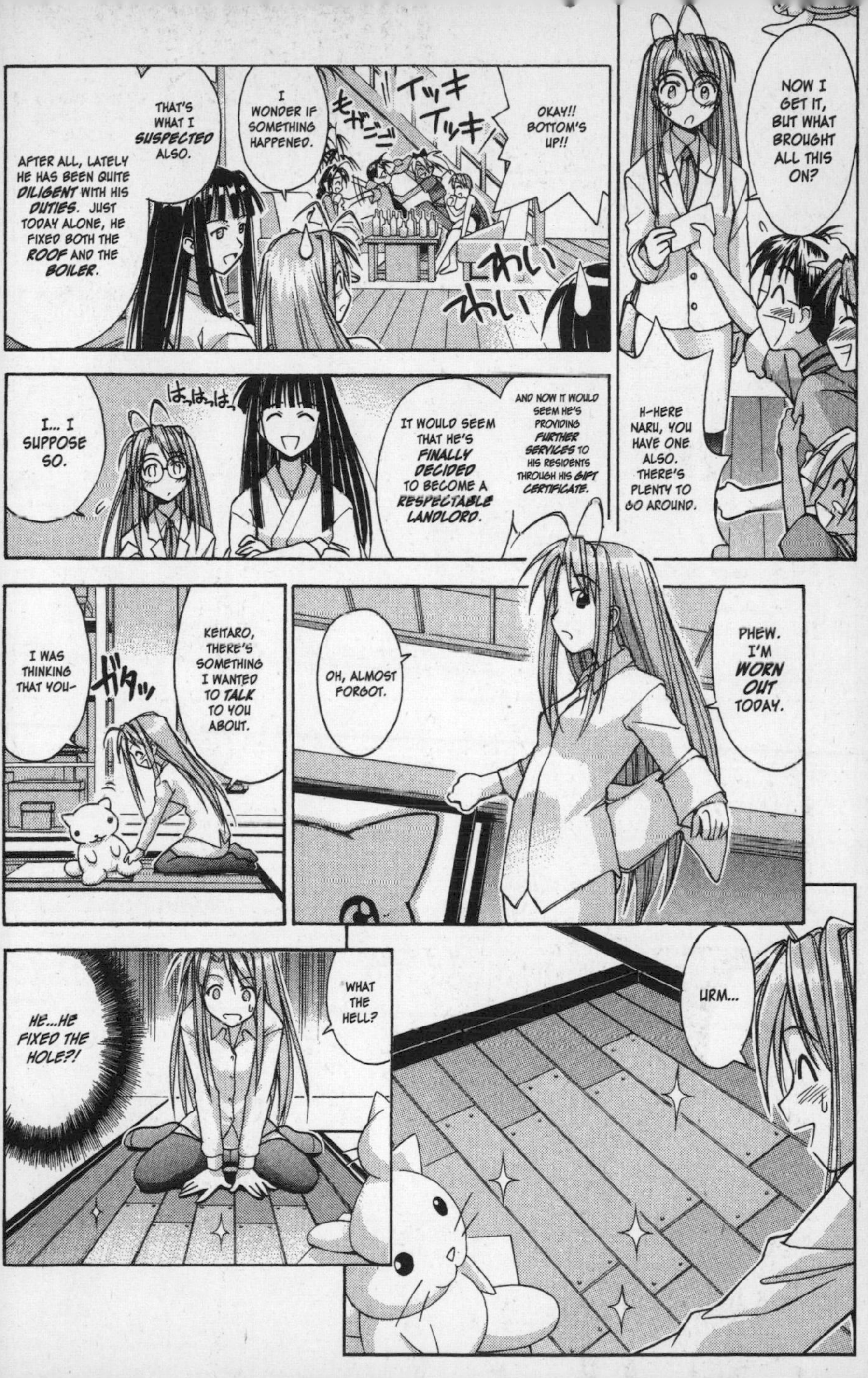
NOW I GET IT, BUT WHAT BROUGHT ALL THIS ON?
H-HERE NARU, YOU HAVE ONE ALSO. THERE'S PLENTY TO GO AROUND.
OKAY!! BOTTOM'S UP!!
イッキ イッキ
I WONDER IF SOMETHING HAPPENED.
THAT'S WHAT I SUSPECTED ALSO.
AFTER ALL, LATELY HE HAS BEEN QUITE DILIGENT WITH HIS DUTIES. JUST TODAY ALONE, HE FIXED BOTH THE ROOF AND THE BOILER.
わい わい
AND NOW IT WOULD SEEM HE'S PROVIDING FURTHER SERVICES TO HIS RESIDENTS THROUGH HIS GIFT CERTIFICATE.
IT WOULD SEEM THAT HE'S FINALLY DECIDED TO BECOME A RESPECTABLE LANDLORD.
はっはっは
I... I SUPPOSE SO.
PHEW. I'M WORN OUT TODAY.
OH, ALMOST FORGOT.
KEITARO, THERE'S SOMETHING I WANTED TO TALK TO YOU ABOUT.
ガタッ
I WAS THINKING THAT YOU-
URM...
WHAT THE HELL?
HE...HE FIXED THE HOLE?!

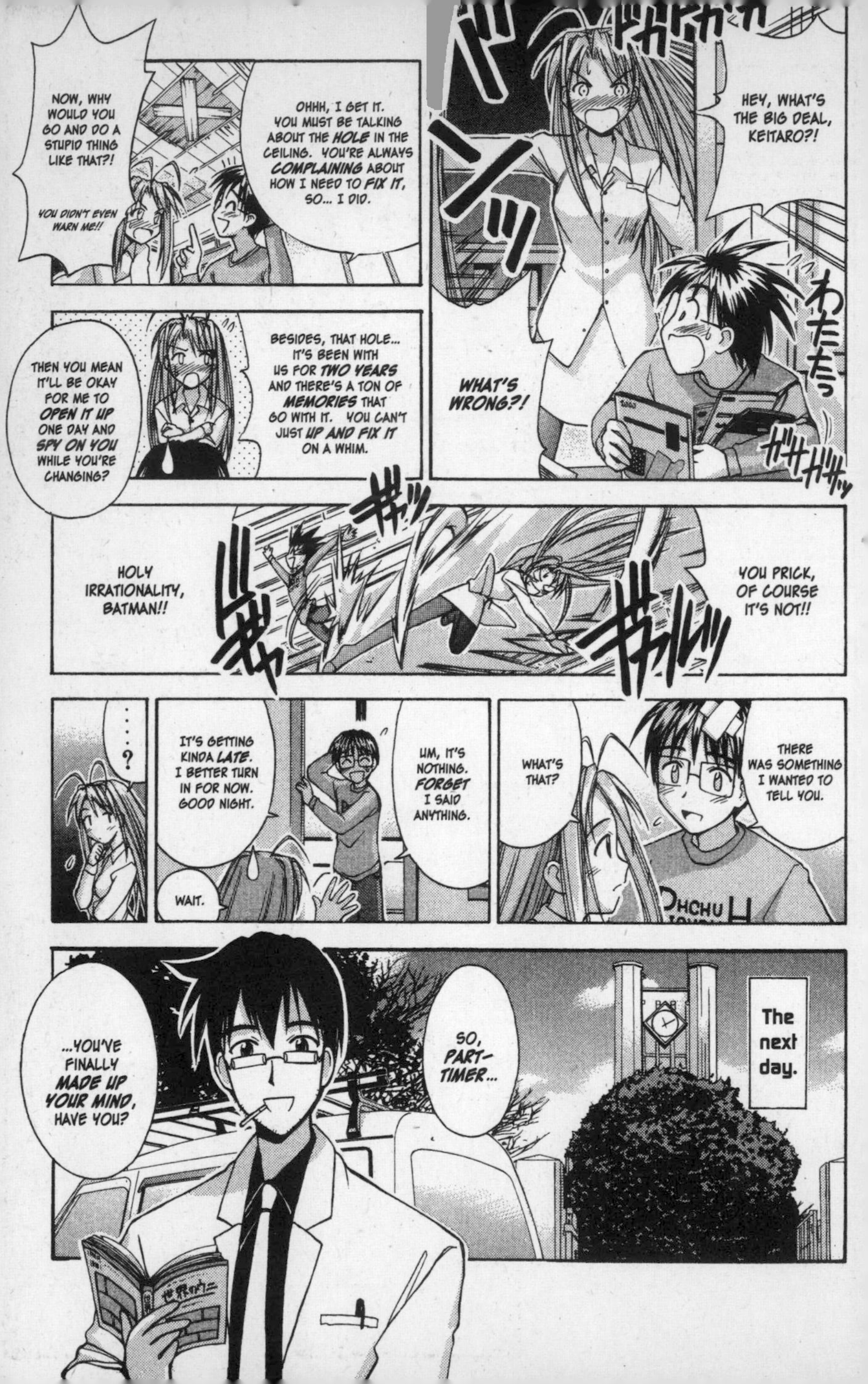
HEY, WHAT'S THE BIG DEAL, KEITARO?!
WHAT'S WRONG?!
OHHH, I GET IT. YOU MUST BE TALKING ABOUT THE HOLE IN THE CEILING. YOU'RE ALWAYS COMPLAINING ABOUT HOW I NEED TO FIX IT, SO... I DID.
NOW, WHY WOULD YOU GO AND DO A STUPID THING LIKE THAT?!
YOU DIDN'T EVEN WARN ME!!
BESIDES, THAT HOLE... IT'S BEEN WITH US FOR TWO YEARS AND THERE'S A TON OF MEMORIES THAT GO WITH IT. YOU CAN'T JUST UP AND FIX IT ON A WHIM.
THEN YOU MEAN IT'LL BE OKAY FOR ME TO OPEN IT UP ONE DAY AND SPY ON YOU WHILE YOU'RE CHANGING?
YOU PRICK, OF COURSE IT'S NOT!!
HOLY IRRATIONALITY, BATMAN!!
THERE WAS SOMETHING I WANTED TO TELL YOU.
WHAT'S THAT?
UM, IT'S NOTHING. FORGET I SAID ANYTHING.
IT'S GETTING KINDA LATE. I BETTER TURN IN FOR NOW. GOOD NIGHT.
WAIT.
....?
The next day.
SO, PART-TIMER...
...YOU'VE FINALLY MADE UP YOUR MIND, HAVE YOU?
世界のウニ

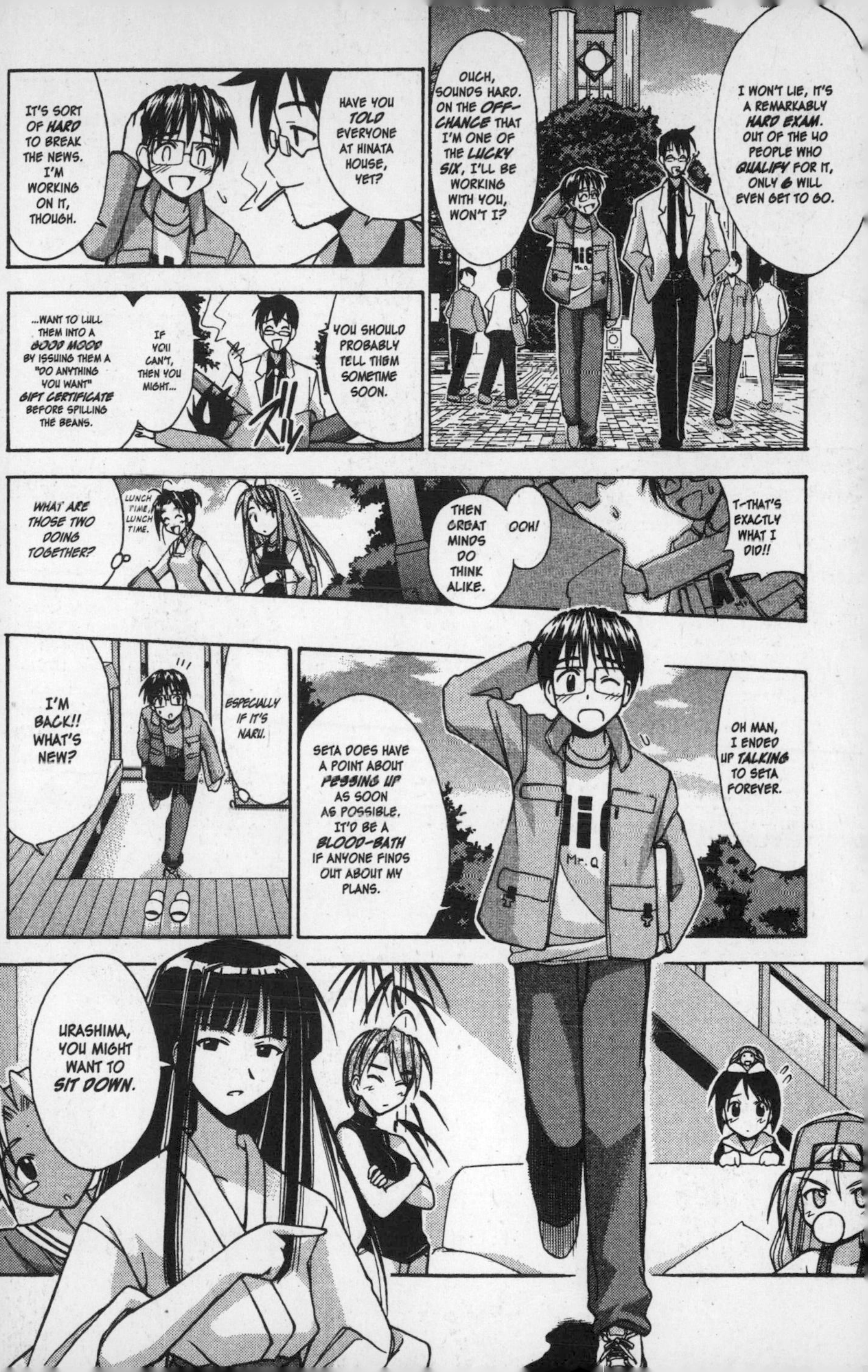
I WON'T LIE, IT'S A REMARKABLY **HARD EXAM**. OUT OF THE 40 PEOPLE WHO **QUALIFY** FOR IT, ONLY 6 WILL EVEN GET TO GO.
OUCH, SOUNDS HARD. ON THE **OFF-CHANCE** THAT I'M ONE OF THE **LUCKY SIX**, I'LL BE WORKING WITH YOU, WON'T I?
HAVE YOU **TOLD** EVERYONE AT HINATA HOUSE, YET?
IT'S SORT OF **HARD** TO BREAK THE NEWS. I'M WORKING ON IT, THOUGH.
YOU SHOULD PROBABLY TELL THEM SOMETIME SOON.
IF YOU CAN'T, THEN YOU MIGHT...
...WANT TO LULL THEM INTO A **GOOD MOOD** BY ISSUING THEM A "DO ANYTHING YOU WANT" **GIFT CERTIFICATE** BEFORE SPILLING THE BEANS.
T-THAT'S EXACTLY WHAT I DID!!
OOH!
THEN GREAT MINDS DO THINK ALIKE.
LUNCH TIME, LUNCH TIME.
WHAT ARE THOSE TWO DOING TOGETHER?
OH MAN, I ENDED UP **TALKING** TO SETA FOREVER.
SETA DOES HAVE A POINT ABOUT **FESSING UP** AS SOON AS POSSIBLE. IT'D BE A **BLOOD-BATH** IF ANYONE FINDS OUT ABOUT MY PLANS.
ESPECIALLY IF IT'S NARU.
I'M BACK!! WHAT'S NEW?
URASHIMA, YOU MIGHT WANT TO **SIT DOWN**.

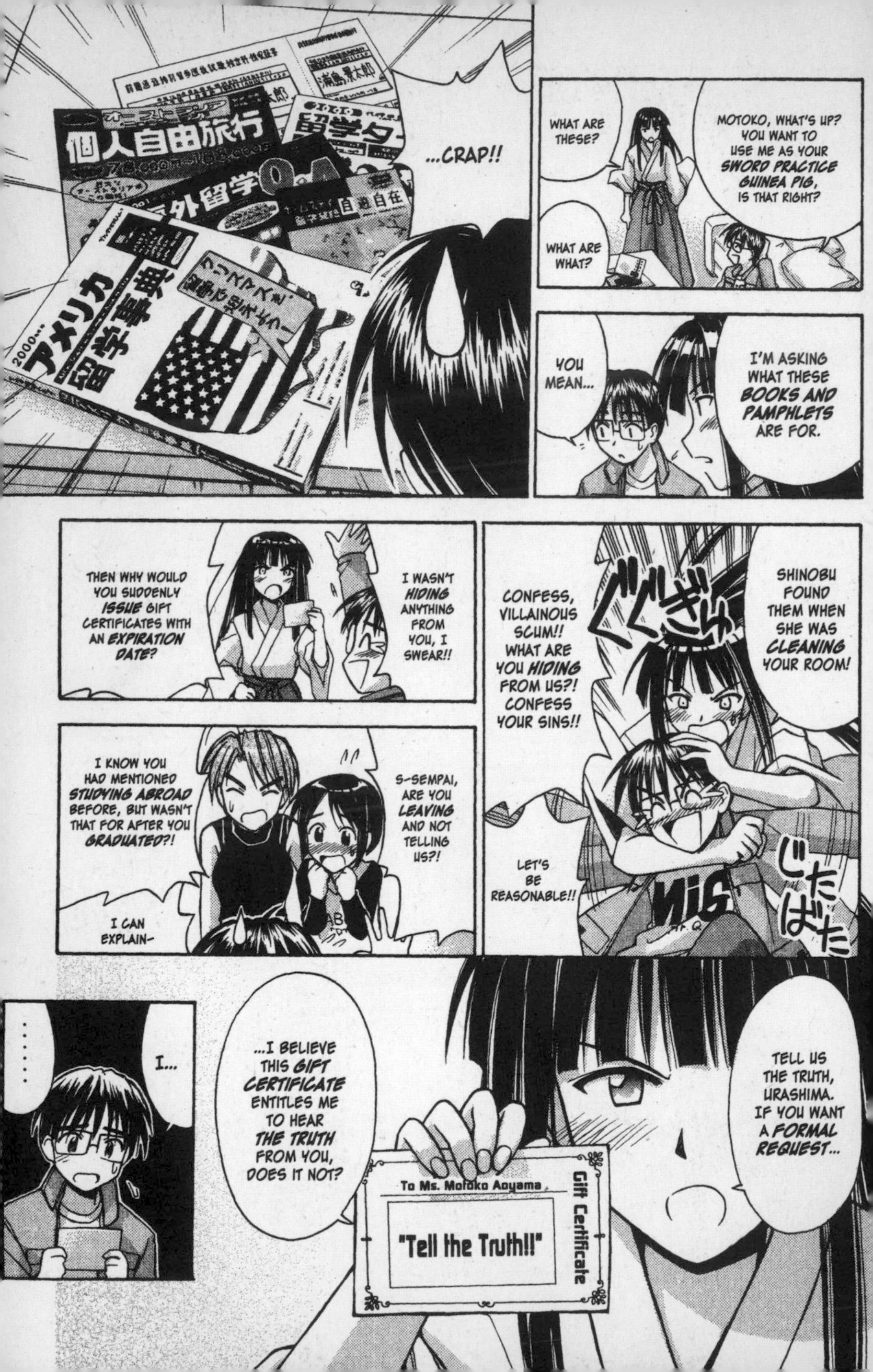

MOTOKO, WHAT'S UP? YOU WANT TO USE ME AS YOUR *SWORD PRACTICE GUINEA PIG*, IS THAT RIGHT?
WHAT ARE THESE?
WHAT ARE WHAT?
I'M ASKING WHAT THESE *BOOKS AND PAMPHLETS* ARE FOR.
YOU MEAN...
個人自由旅行
2000...
アメリカ留学事典
...CRAP!!
SHINOBU FOUND THEM WHEN SHE WAS *CLEANING* YOUR ROOM!
CONFESS, VILLAINOUS SCUM!! WHAT ARE YOU *HIDING* FROM US?! CONFESS YOUR SINS!!
じたばた
LET'S BE REASONABLE!!
I WASN'T *HIDING* ANYTHING FROM YOU, I SWEAR!!
THEN WHY WOULD YOU SUDDENLY *ISSUE* GIFT CERTIFICATES WITH AN *EXPIRATION DATE*?
S-SEMPAI, ARE YOU *LEAVING* AND NOT TELLING US?!
I KNOW YOU HAD MENTIONED *STUDYING ABROAD* BEFORE, BUT WASN'T THAT FOR AFTER YOU *GRADUATED*?!
I CAN EXPLAIN-
TELL US THE TRUTH, URASHIMA. IF YOU WANT A *FORMAL REQUEST*...
...I BELIEVE THIS *GIFT CERTIFICATE* ENTITLES ME TO HEAR *THE TRUTH* FROM YOU, DOES IT NOT?
To Ms. Motoko Aoyama
Gift Certificate
"Tell the Truth!!"
......
I...

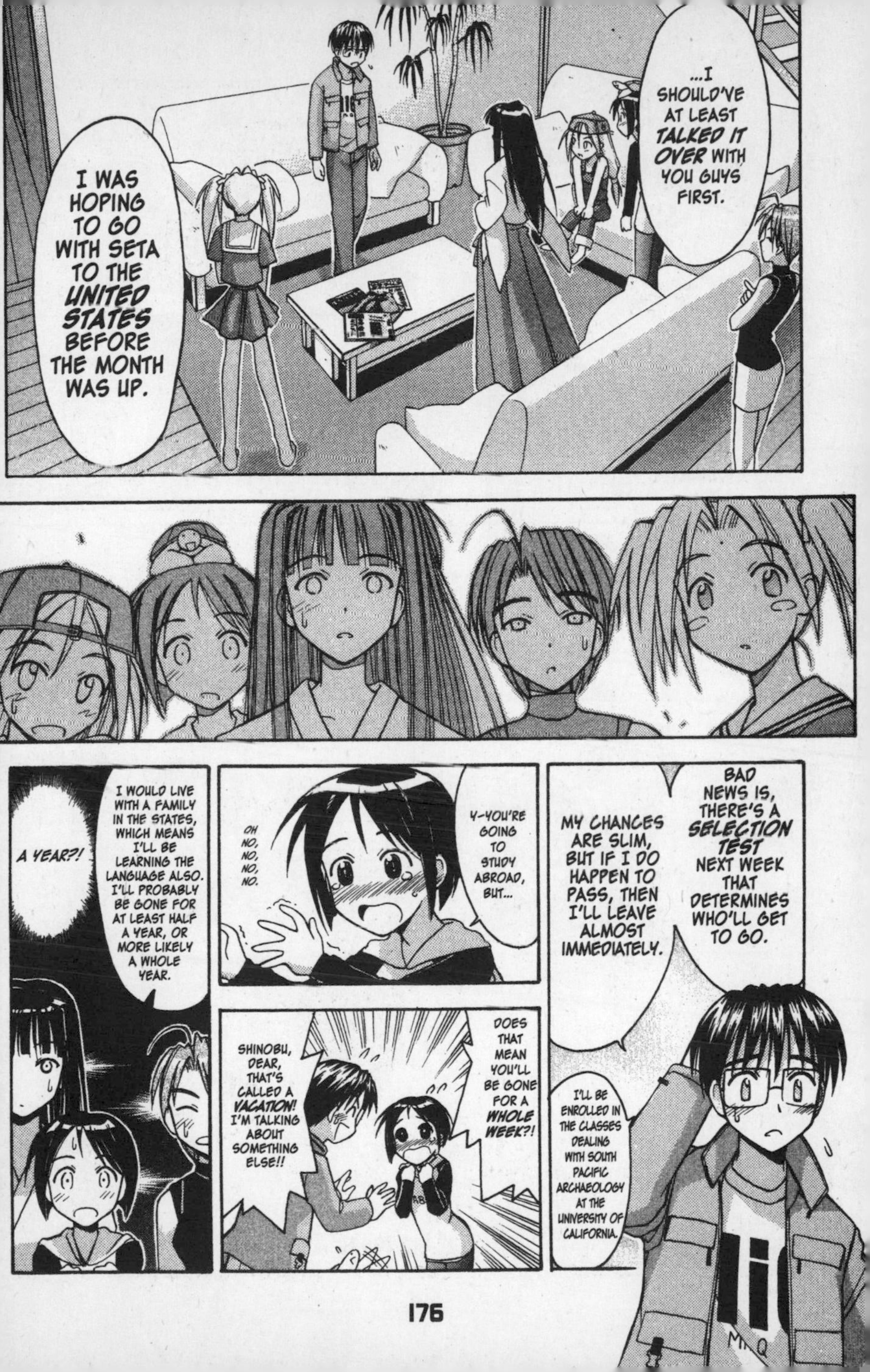
...I SHOULD'VE AT LEAST TALKED IT OVER WITH YOU GUYS FIRST.
I WAS HOPING TO GO WITH SETA TO THE UNITED STATES BEFORE THE MONTH WAS UP.
BAD NEWS IS, THERE'S A SELECTION TEST NEXT WEEK THAT DETERMINES WHO'LL GET TO GO.
MY CHANCES ARE SLIM, BUT IF I DO HAPPEN TO PASS, THEN I'LL LEAVE ALMOST IMMEDIATELY.
I'LL BE ENROLLED IN THE CLASSES DEALING WITH SOUTH PACIFIC ARCHAEOLOGY AT THE UNIVERSITY OF CALIFORNIA.
Y-YOU'RE GOING TO STUDY ABROAD, BUT...
OH NO, NO, NO, NO.
DOES THAT MEAN YOU'LL BE GONE FOR A WHOLE WEEK?!
SHINOBU, DEAR, THAT'S CALLED A VACATION! I'M TALKING ABOUT SOMETHING ELSE!!
I WOULD LIVE WITH A FAMILY IN THE STATES, WHICH MEANS I'LL BE LEARNING THE LANGUAGE ALSO. I'LL PROBABLY BE GONE FOR AT LEAST HALF A YEAR, OR MORE LIKELY A WHOLE YEAR.
A YEAR?!

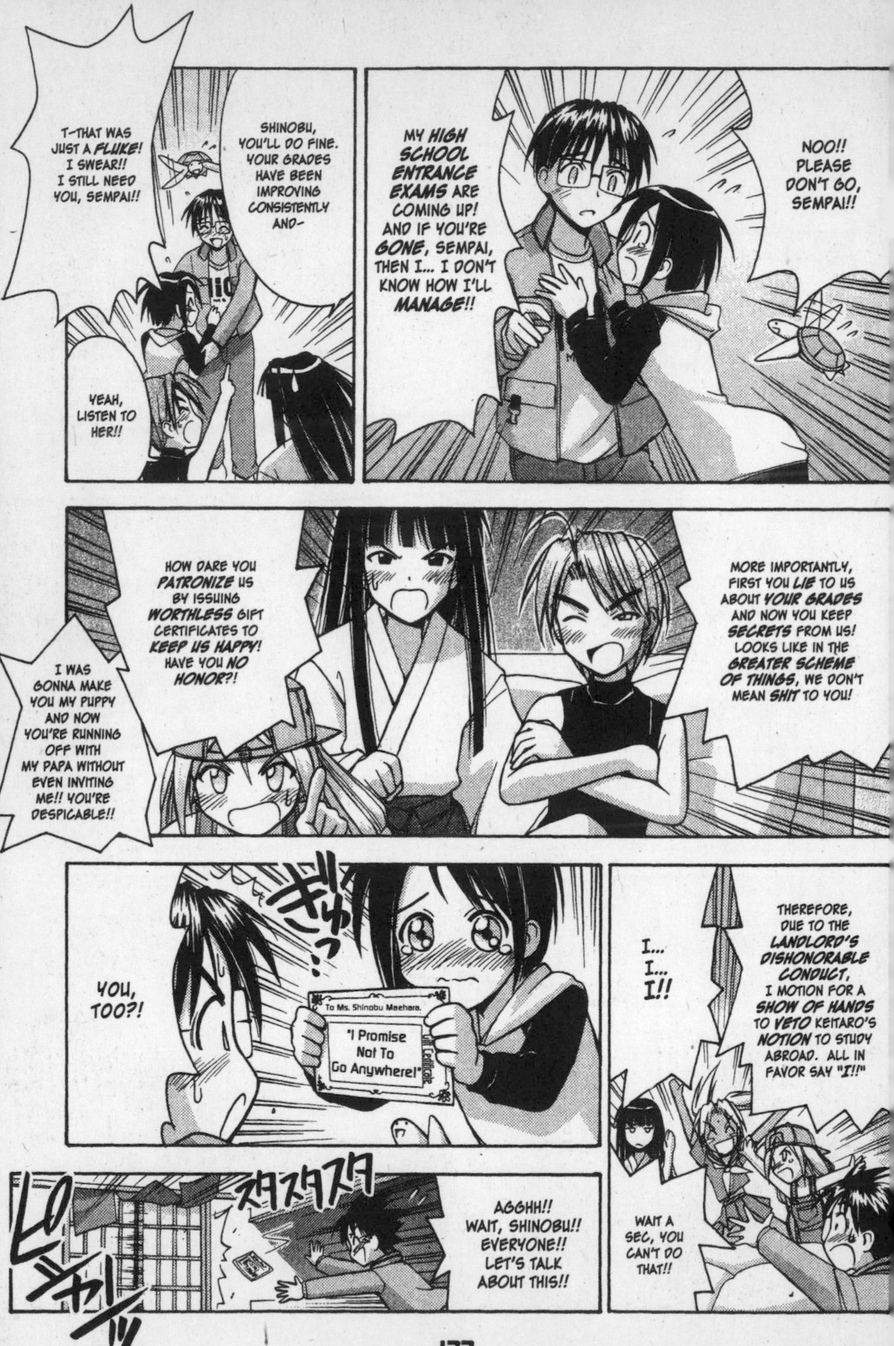
NOO!! PLEASE DON'T GO, SEMPAI!!
MY HIGH SCHOOL ENTRANCE EXAMS ARE COMING UP! AND IF YOU'RE GONE, SEMPAI, THEN I... I DON'T KNOW HOW I'LL MANAGE!!
SHINOBU, YOU'LL DO FINE. YOUR GRADES HAVE BEEN IMPROVING CONSISTENTLY AND-
T-THAT WAS JUST A FLUKE! I SWEAR!! I STILL NEED YOU, SEMPAI!!
YEAH, LISTEN TO HER!!
MORE IMPORTANTLY, FIRST YOU LIE TO US ABOUT YOUR GRADES AND NOW YOU KEEP SECRETS FROM US! LOOKS LIKE IN THE GREATER SCHEME OF THINGS, WE DON'T MEAN SHIT TO YOU!
HOW DARE YOU PATRONIZE US BY ISSUING WORTHLESS GIFT CERTIFICATES TO KEEP US HAPPY! HAVE YOU NO HONOR?!
I WAS GONNA MAKE YOU MY PUPPY AND NOW YOU'RE RUNNING OFF WITH MY PAPA WITHOUT EVEN INVITING ME!! YOU'RE DESPICABLE!!
THEREFORE, DUE TO THE LANDLORD'S DISHONORABLE CONDUCT, I MOTION FOR A SHOW OF HANDS TO VETO KEITARO'S NOTION TO STUDY ABROAD. ALL IN FAVOR SAY "I!!"
I... I... I!!
WAIT A SEC, YOU CAN'T DO THAT!!
ぎゅっ
YOU, TOO?!
To Ms. Shinobu Maehara.
"I Promise Not To Go Anywhere!"
Gift Certificate
スタスタスタ
AGGHH!! WAIT, SHINOBU!! EVERYONE!! LET'S TALK ABOUT THIS!!
ピシャッ

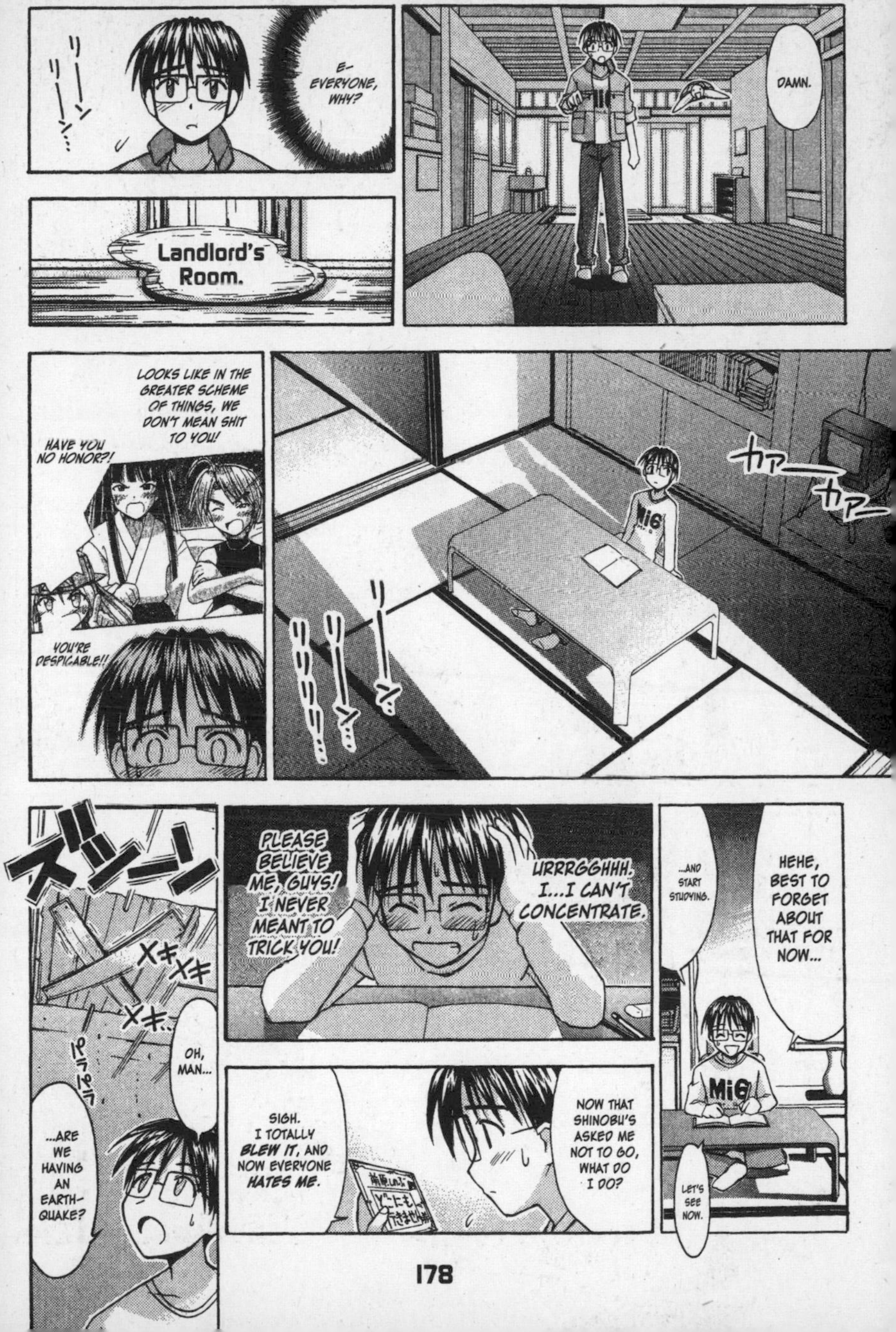
DAMN.
E-EVERYONE, WHY?
リーン リーン…
Landlord's Room.
カァー カァ
リーン リーン リリリリ…
LOOKS LIKE IN THE GREATER SCHEME OF THINGS, WE DON'T MEAN SHIT TO YOU!
HAVE YOU NO HONOR?!
YOU'RE DESPICABLE!!
HEHE, BEST TO FORGET ABOUT THAT FOR NOW...
...AND START STUDYING.
LET'S SEE NOW.
URRRGGHHH. I...I CAN'T CONCENTRATE.
PLEASE BELIEVE ME, GUYS! I NEVER MEANT TO TRICK YOU!
NOW THAT SHINOBU'S ASKED ME NOT TO GO, WHAT DO I DO?
SIGH. I TOTALLY BLEW IT, AND NOW EVERYONE HATES ME.
ズシーン
メキメキ
メキ
パラパラ
OH, MAN...
...ARE WE HAVING AN EARTH-QUAKE?

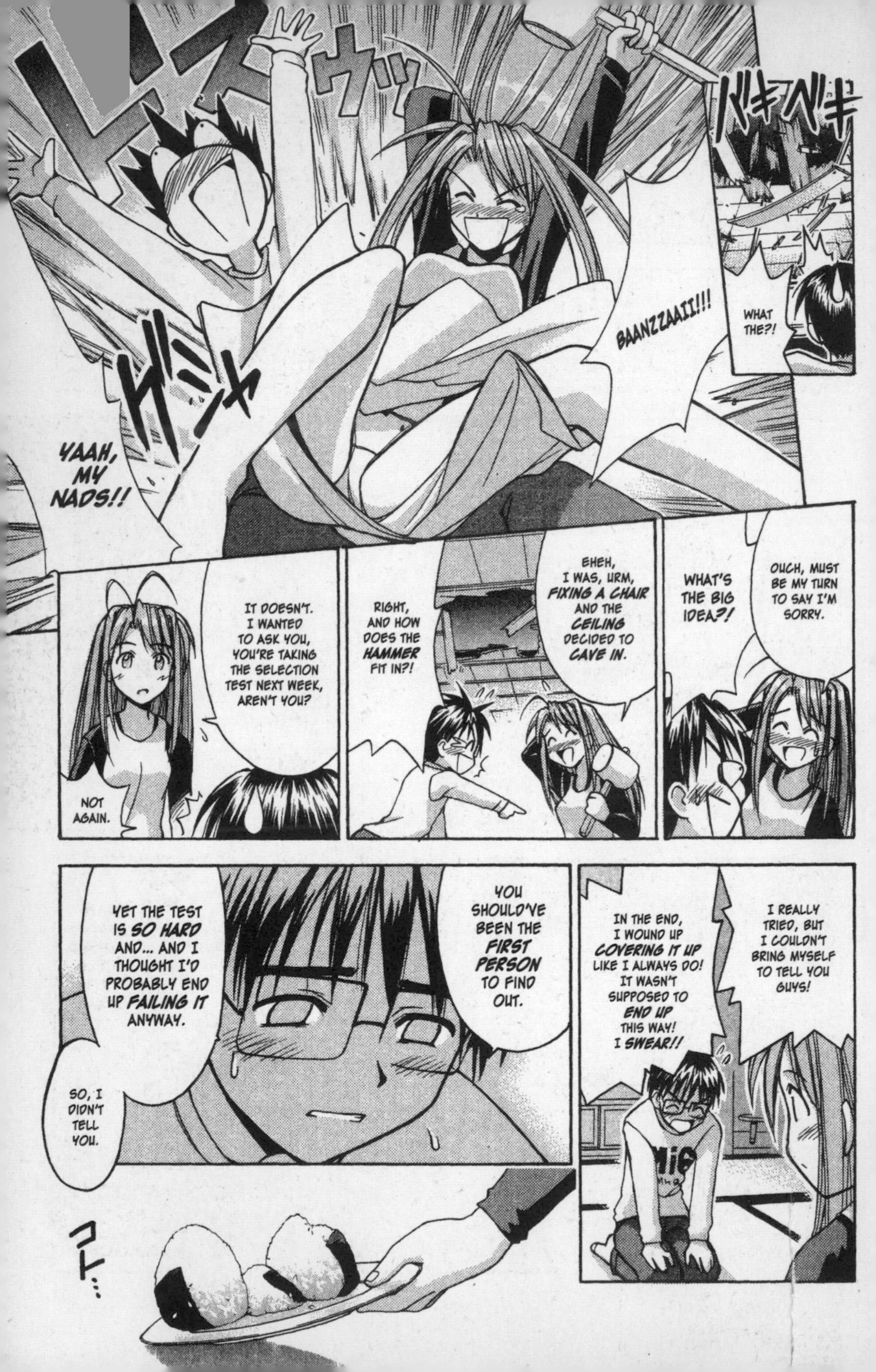
バキベキ
WHAT THE?!
BAANZZAAII!!!
YAAH, MY NADS!!
OUCH, MUST BE MY TURN TO SAY I'M SORRY.
WHAT'S THE BIG IDEA?!
EHEH, I WAS, URM, FIXING A CHAIR AND THE CEILING DECIDED TO CAVE IN.
RIGHT, AND HOW DOES THE HAMMER FIT IN?!
IT DOESN'T. I WANTED TO ASK YOU, YOU'RE TAKING THE SELECTION TEST NEXT WEEK, AREN'T YOU?
NOT AGAIN.
I REALLY TRIED, BUT I COULDN'T BRING MYSELF TO TELL YOU GUYS!
IN THE END, I WOUND UP COVERING IT UP LIKE I ALWAYS DO! IT WASN'T SUPPOSED TO END UP THIS WAY! I SWEAR!!
YOU SHOULD'VE BEEN THE FIRST PERSON TO FIND OUT.
YET THE TEST IS SO HARD AND... AND I THOUGHT I'D PROBABLY END UP FAILING IT ANYWAY.
SO, I DIDN'T TELL YOU.
コト…

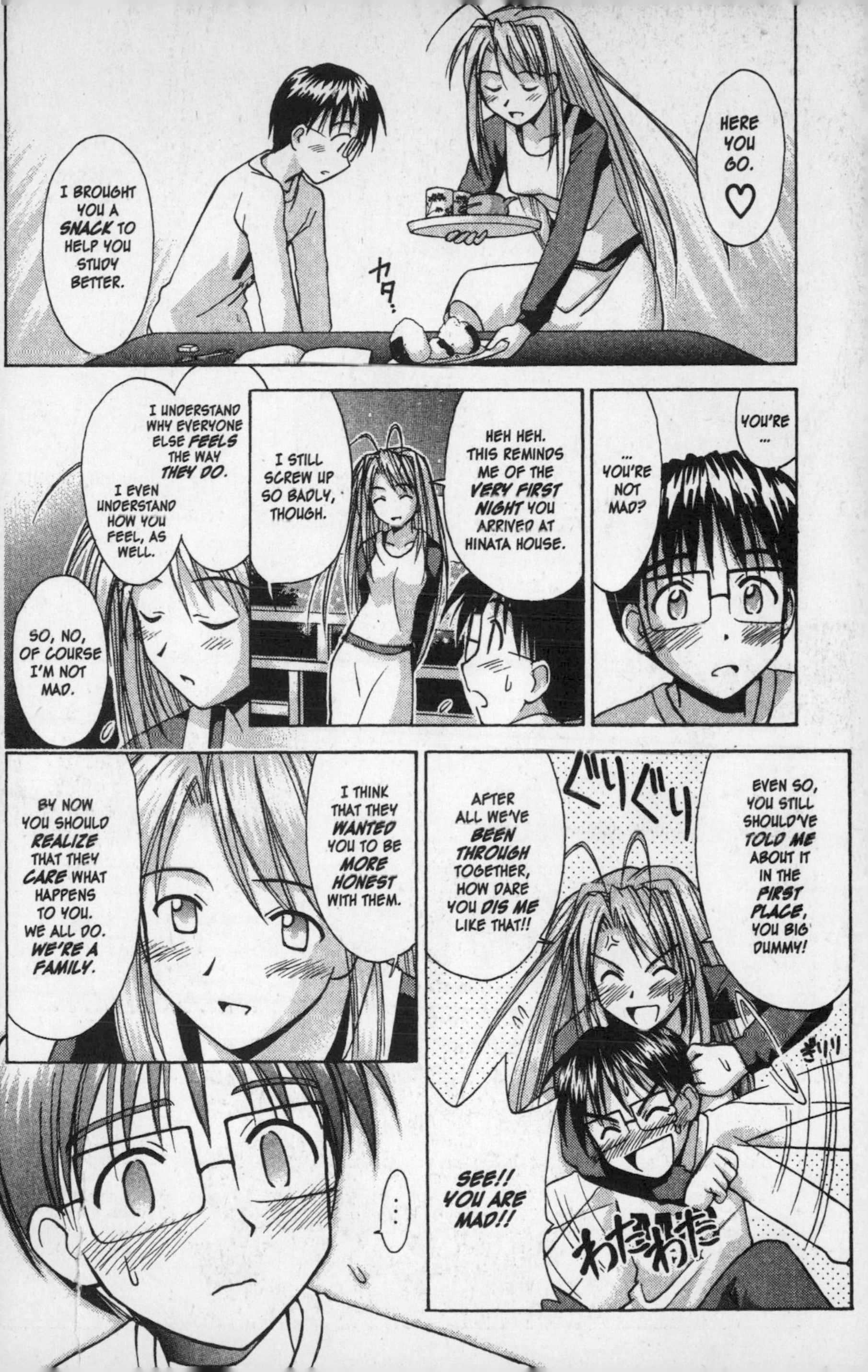
HERE YOU GO. ♡
I BROUGHT YOU A SNACK TO HELP YOU STUDY BETTER.
カタ
YOU'RE ...
... YOU'RE NOT MAD?
HEH HEH. THIS REMINDS ME OF THE VERY FIRST NIGHT YOU ARRIVED AT HINATA HOUSE.
I STILL SCREW UP SO BADLY, THOUGH.
I UNDERSTAND WHY EVERYONE ELSE FEELS THE WAY THEY DO.
I EVEN UNDERSTAND HOW YOU FEEL, AS WELL.
SO, NO, OF COURSE I'M NOT MAD.
ぐりぐり
EVEN SO, YOU STILL SHOULD'VE TOLD ME ABOUT IT IN THE FIRST PLACE, YOU BIG DUMMY!
AFTER ALL WE'VE BEEN THROUGH TOGETHER, HOW DARE YOU DIS ME LIKE THAT!!
ぎりり
SEE!! YOU ARE MAD!!
わたわた
I THINK THAT THEY WANTED YOU TO BE MORE HONEST WITH THEM.
BY NOW YOU SHOULD REALIZE THAT THEY CARE WHAT HAPPENS TO YOU. WE ALL DO. WE'RE A FAMILY.
...

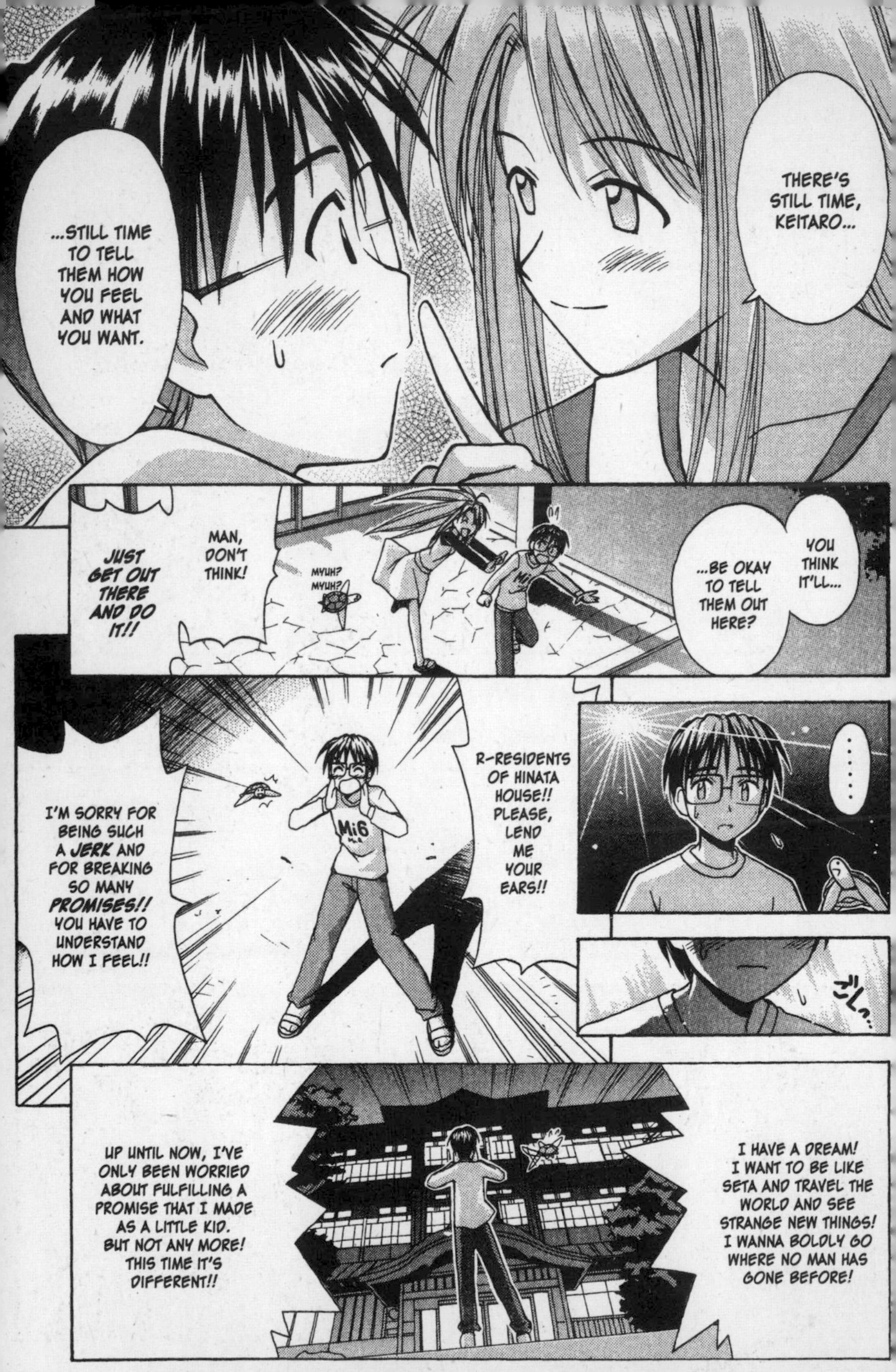
THERE'S STILL TIME, KEITARO...
...STILL TIME TO TELL THEM HOW YOU FEEL AND WHAT YOU WANT.
YOU THINK IT'LL...
...BE OKAY TO TELL THEM OUT HERE?
MYUH? MYUH?
MAN, DON'T THINK!
JUST GET OUT THERE AND DO IT!!
......
ごしっ..
R-RESIDENTS OF HINATA HOUSE!! PLEASE, LEND ME YOUR EARS!!
I'M SORRY FOR BEING SUCH A JERK AND FOR BREAKING SO MANY PROMISES!! YOU HAVE TO UNDERSTAND HOW I FEEL!!
I HAVE A DREAM! I WANT TO BE LIKE SETA AND TRAVEL THE WORLD AND SEE STRANGE NEW THINGS! I WANNA BOLDLY GO WHERE NO MAN HAS GONE BEFORE!
UP UNTIL NOW, I'VE ONLY BEEN WORRIED ABOUT FULFILLING A PROMISE THAT I MADE AS A LITTLE KID. BUT NOT ANY MORE! THIS TIME IT'S DIFFERENT!!

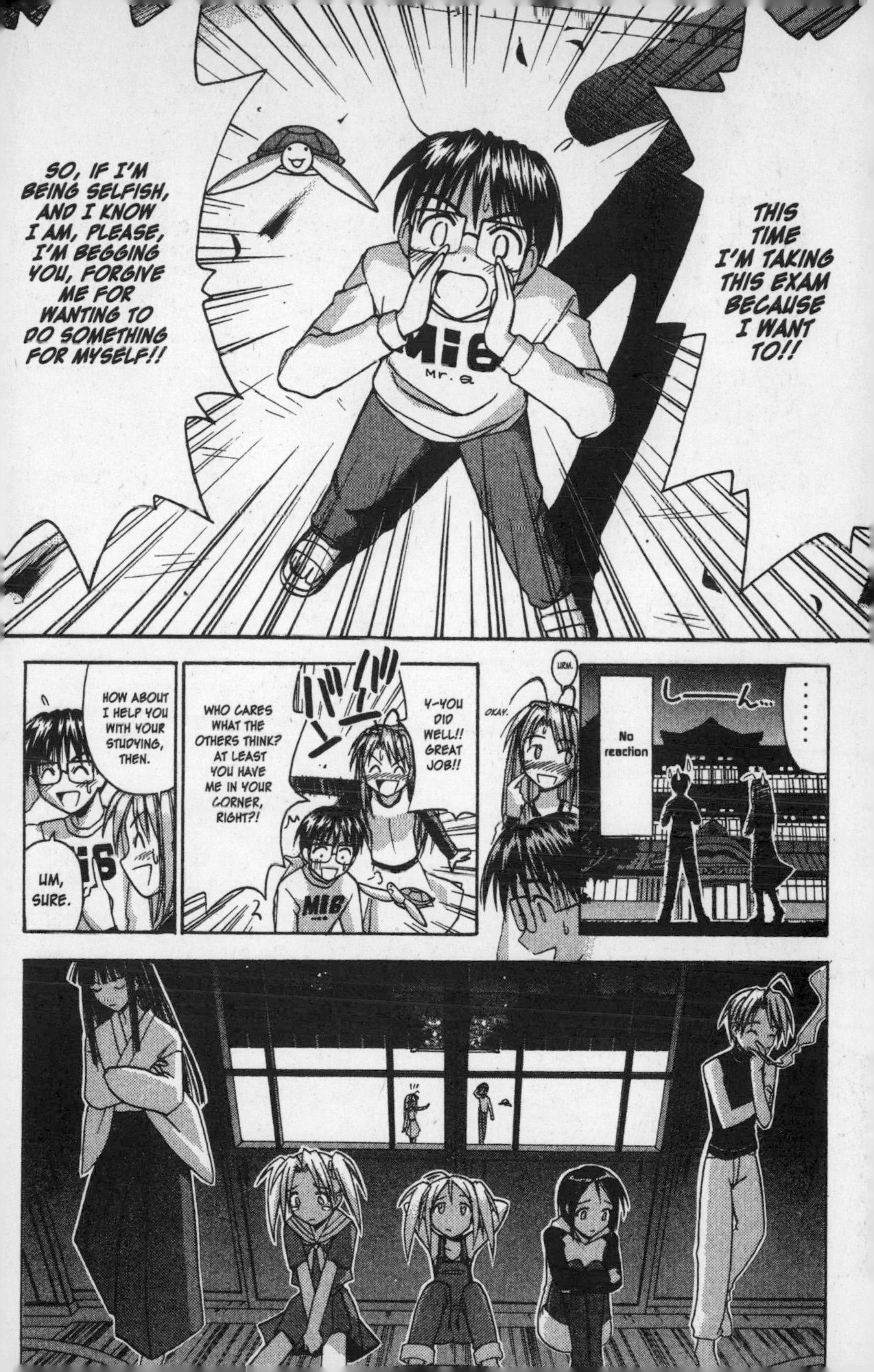
THIS TIME I'M TAKING THIS EXAM BECAUSE I WANT TO!!
SO, IF I'M BEING SELFISH, AND I KNOW I AM, PLEASE, I'M BEGGING YOU, FORGIVE ME FOR WANTING TO DO SOMETHING FOR MYSELF!!
......
しーん...
No reaction
URM.
OKAY.
Y-YOU DID WELL!! GREAT JOB!!
WHO CARES WHAT THE OTHERS THINK? AT LEAST YOU HAVE ME IN YOUR CORNER, RIGHT?!
HOW ABOUT I HELP YOU WITH YOUR STUDYING, THEN.
UM, SURE.

〈掲載／週刊少年マガジン2000年第39号～第49号、第40号第46号休載〉

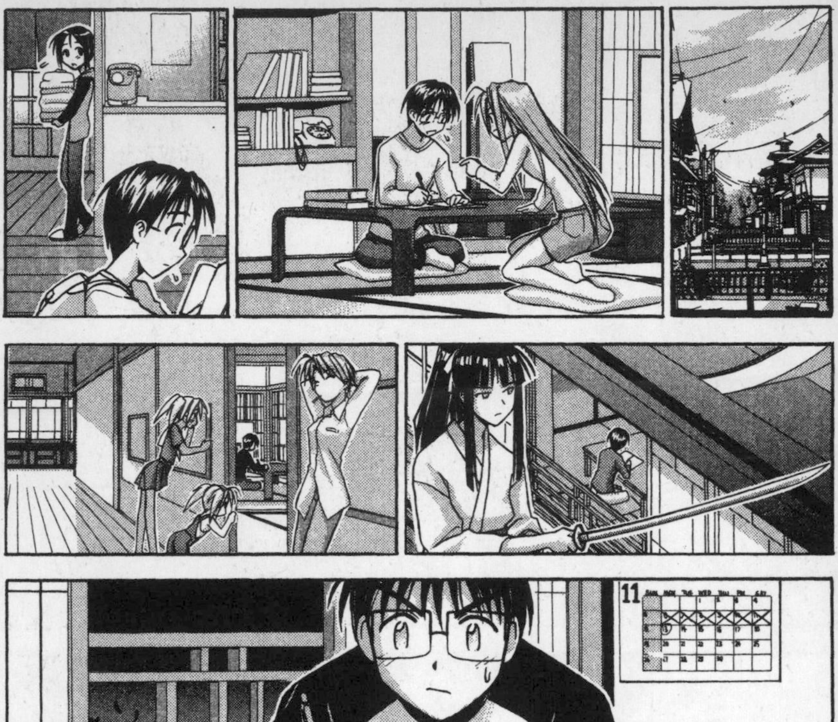

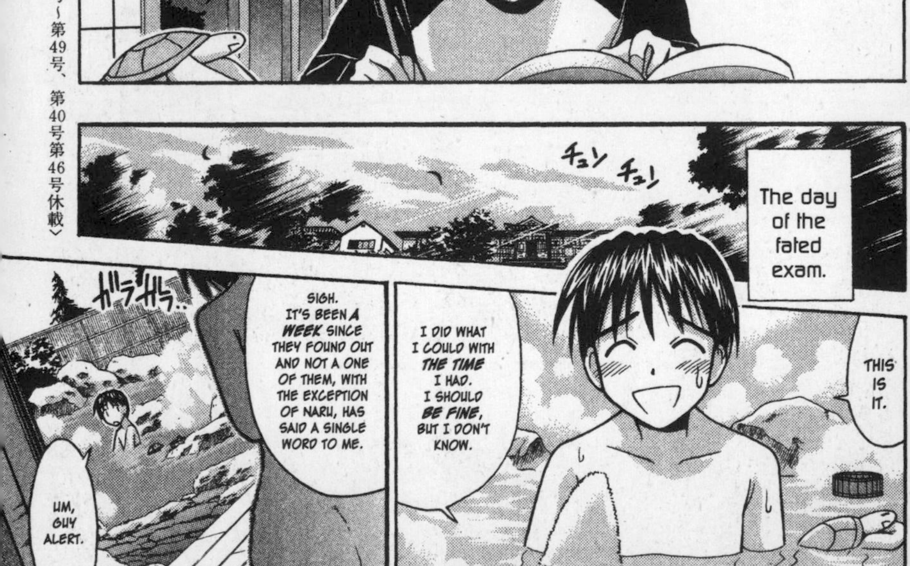
チュン
チュン
The day of the fated exam.
THIS IS IT.
I DID WHAT I COULD WITH *THE TIME* I HAD. I SHOULD *BE FINE*, BUT I DON'T KNOW.
SIGH. IT'S BEEN *A WEEK* SINCE THEY FOUND OUT AND NOT A ONE OF THEM, WITH THE EXCEPTION OF NARU, HAS SAID A SINGLE WORD TO ME.
ガラガラ
UM, GUY ALERT.

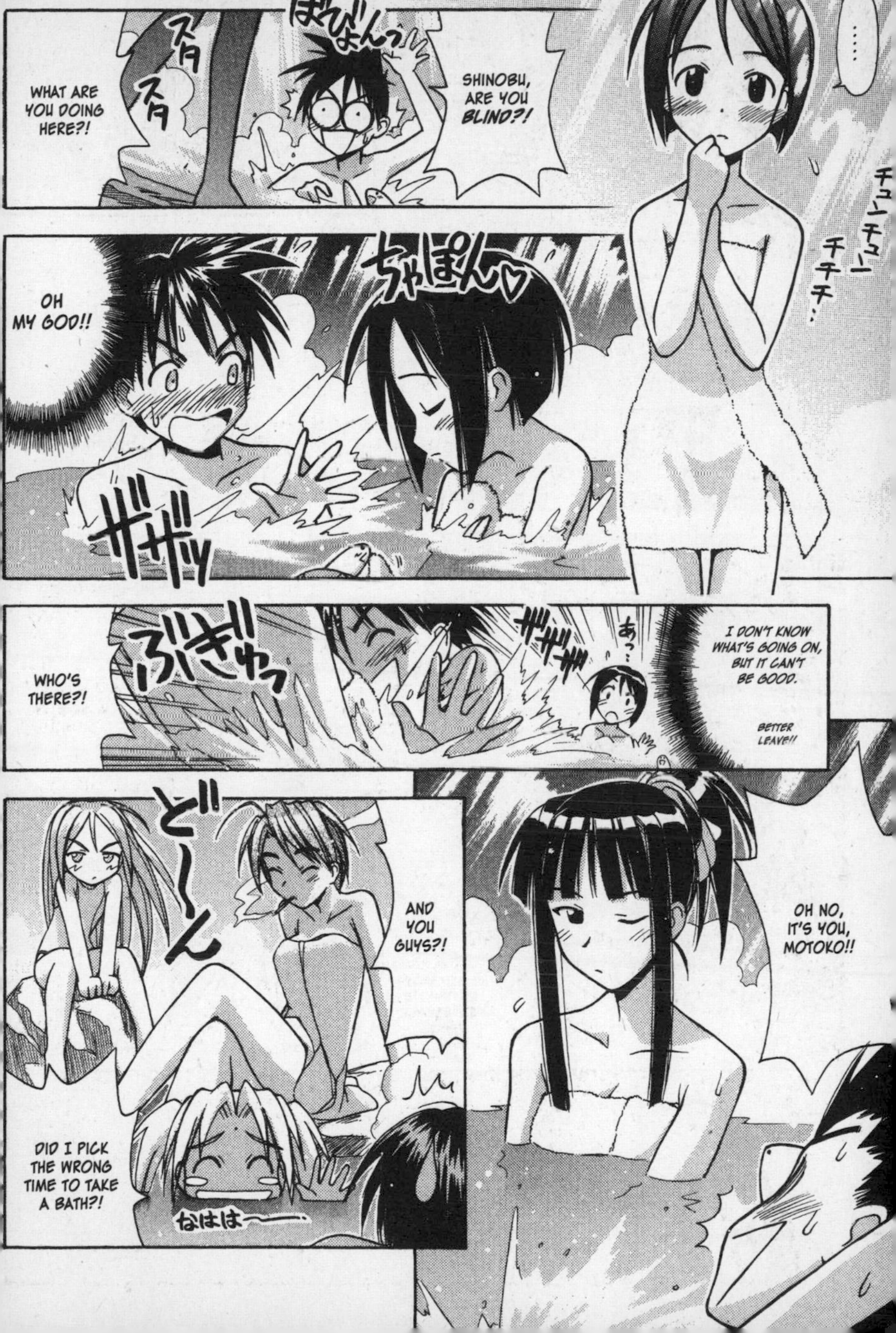
……
チュンチュン
チチチ‥
ばびょんっ
SHINOBU, ARE YOU BLIND?!
スタスタ
WHAT ARE YOU DOING HERE?!
ちゃぽん♡
OH MY GOD!!
ザザッ
I DON'T KNOW WHAT'S GOING ON, BUT IT CAN'T BE GOOD.
BETTER LEAVE!!
あっ…
ザザザ
ぶぎゃっ
WHO'S THERE?!
OH NO, IT'S YOU, MOTOKO!!
AND YOU GUYS?!
どーん
DID I PICK THE WRONG TIME TO TAKE A BATH?!
なははーー

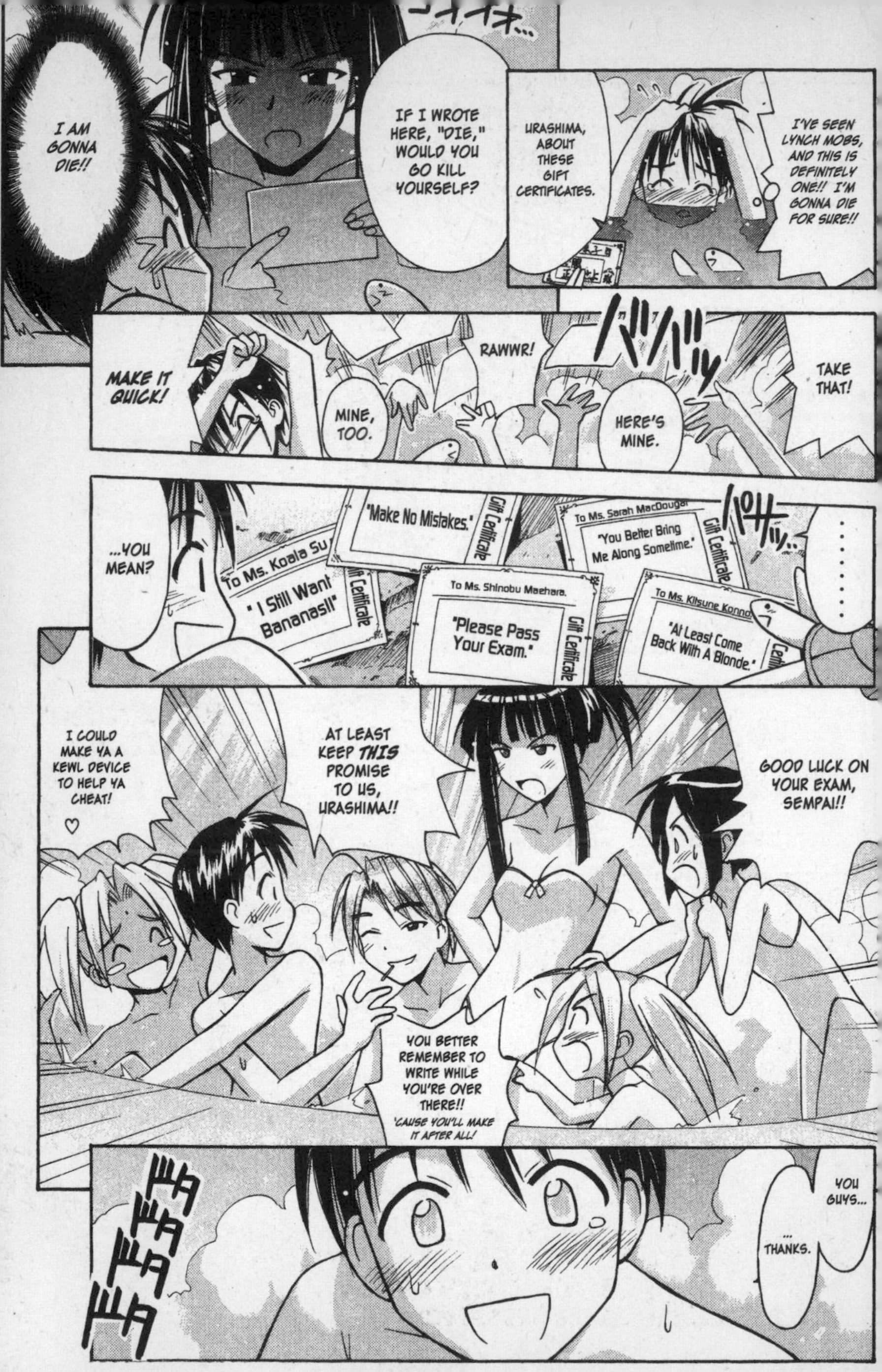

I'VE SEEN LYNCH MOBS, AND THIS IS DEFINITELY ONE!! I'M GONNA DIE FOR SURE!!
URASHIMA, ABOUT THESE GIFT CERTIFICATES.
IF I WROTE HERE, "DIE," WOULD YOU GO KILL YOURSELF?
I AM GONNA DIE!!
TAKE THAT!
HERE'S MINE.
RAWWR!
MINE, TOO.
MAKE IT QUICK!
......
To Ms. Kitsune Konno
"At Least Come Back With A Blonde."
To Ms. Sarah MacDougal
"You Better Bring Me Along Sometime."
Gift Certificate
To Ms. Shinobu Maehara.
"Please Pass Your Exam."
Gift Certificate
"Make No Mistakes."
Gift Certificate
To Ms. Koala Su
"I Still Want Bananas!!"
...YOU MEAN?
GOOD LUCK ON YOUR EXAM, SEMPAI!!
AT LEAST KEEP THIS PROMISE TO US, URASHIMA!!
YOU BETTER REMEMBER TO WRITE WHILE YOU'RE OVER THERE!!
'CAUSE YOU'LL MAKE IT AFTER ALL!
I COULD MAKE YA A KEWL DEVICE TO HELP YA CHEAT! ♡
YOU GUYS...
...THANKS.

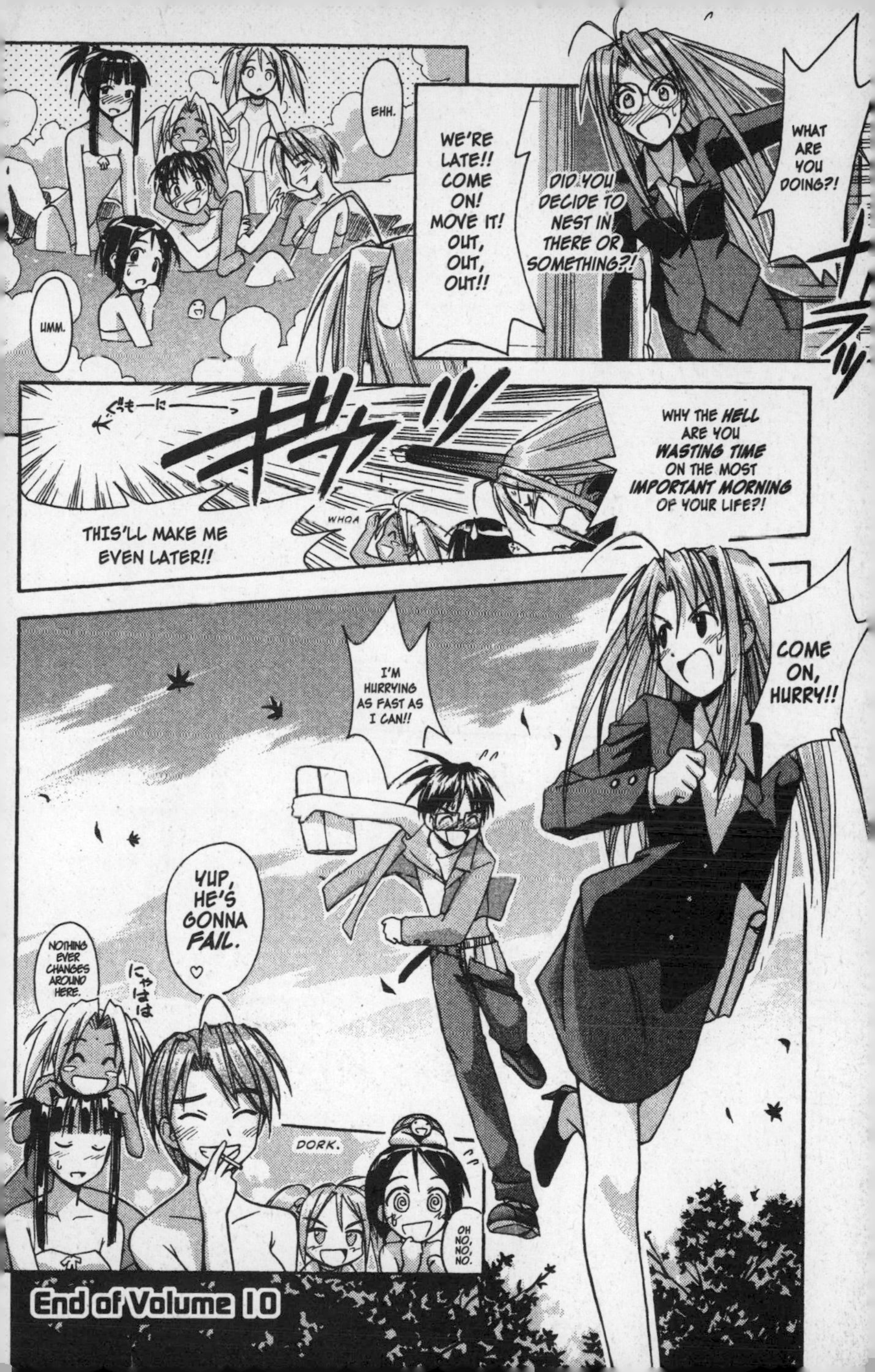
WHAT ARE YOU DOING?!
DID YOU DECIDE TO NEST IN THERE OR SOMETHING?!
WE'RE LATE!! COME ON! MOVE IT! OUT, OUT, OUT!!
EHH.
UMM.
WHY THE HELL ARE YOU WASTING TIME ON THE MOST IMPORTANT MORNING OF YOUR LIFE?!
WHOA
ギャッ
THIS'LL MAKE ME EVEN LATER!!
COME ON, HURRY!!
I'M HURRYING AS FAST AS I CAN!!
YUP, HE'S GONNA FAIL. ♡
にゃはは
NOTHING EVER CHANGES AROUND HERE.
DORK.
OH NO, NO, NO.
End of Volume 10

STAFF

Ken Akamatsu
Takashi Takemoto
Kenichi Nakamura
Takaaki Miyahara
Tomohiko Saito
Masaki Ohyama
Ran Ayanaga

EDITOR

Noboru Ohno
Masakazu Yoshimoto
Yasushi Yamanaka

KC Editor

Shinichiro Yoshihara

In the next volume of

Love Hina

Having miraculously landed a study-abroad position, Keitaro bids farewell to the girls of Hinata House, just as things between him and Naru are beginning to heat up. A chance flight delay offers Naru enough time to get all the bottled-up emotions she's never been able to properly express off her chest. This is definitely the moment fans have been waiting for.

Time passes and a new face proclaiming to be the new Hinata House landlord shows up on the girls' doorstep. This girl is none other than Keitaro's own little sister, Kanako Urashima. As resentments flair between the residents and Kanako, several feuds erupt that—if not tactfully resolved—could very well rip the close-knit family apart. And what's this about the girls' dormitory being turned back into an inn?

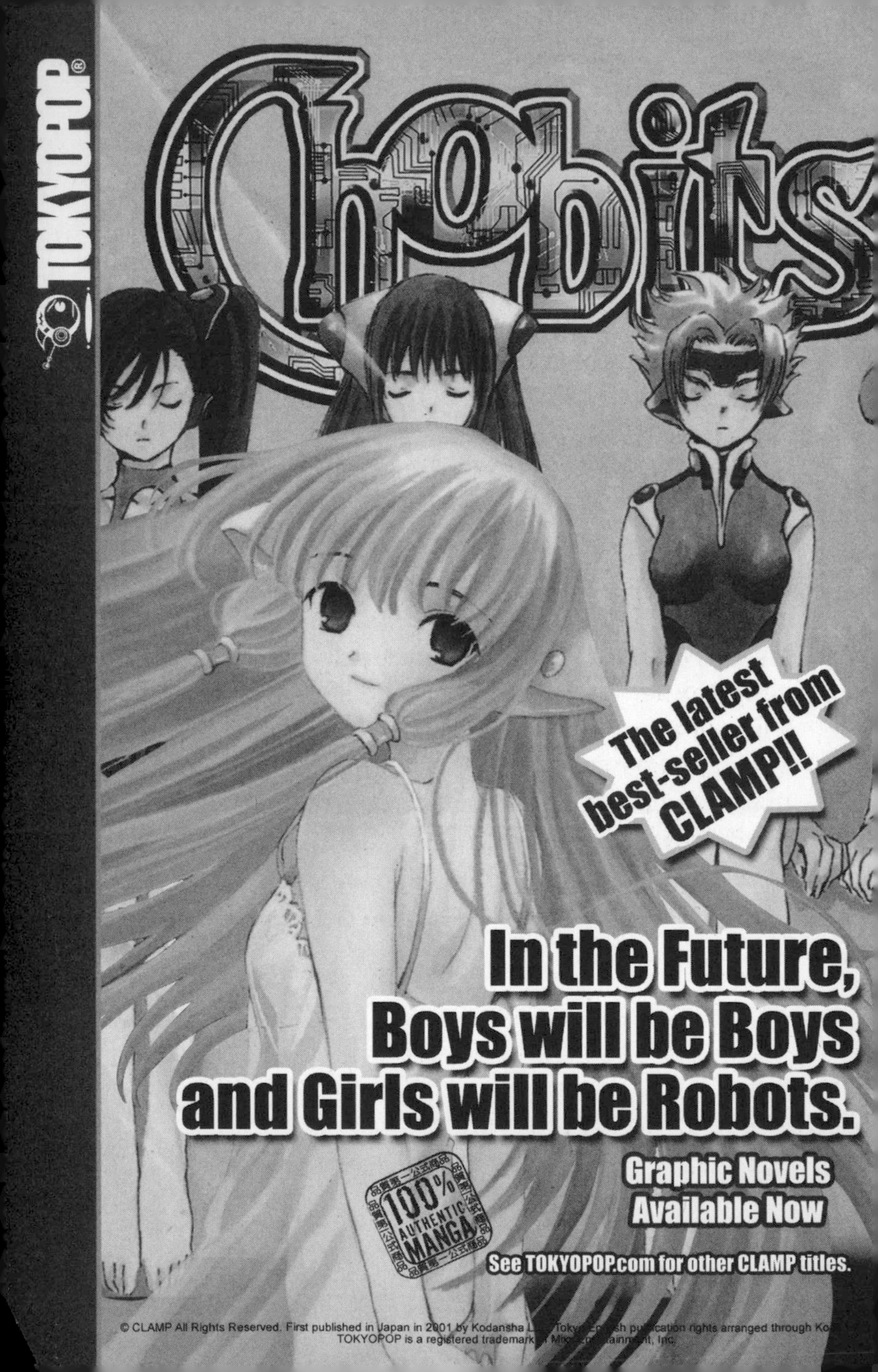
TOKYOPOP®
Chobits
The latest best-seller from CLAMP!!
In the Future, Boys will be Boys and Girls will be Robots.
100% AUTHENTIC MANGA
Graphic Novels Available Now
See TOKYOPOP.com for other CLAMP titles.
© CLAMP All Rights Reserved. First published in Japan in 2001 by Kodansha Ltd.
TOKYOPOP is a registered trademark

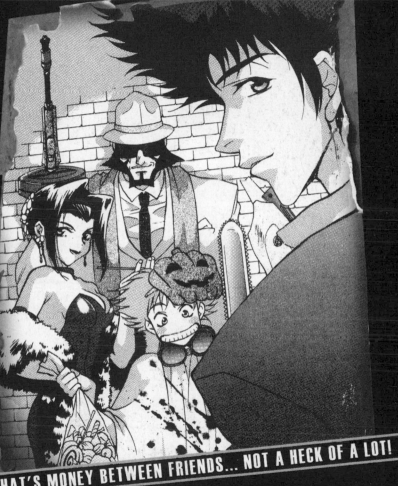

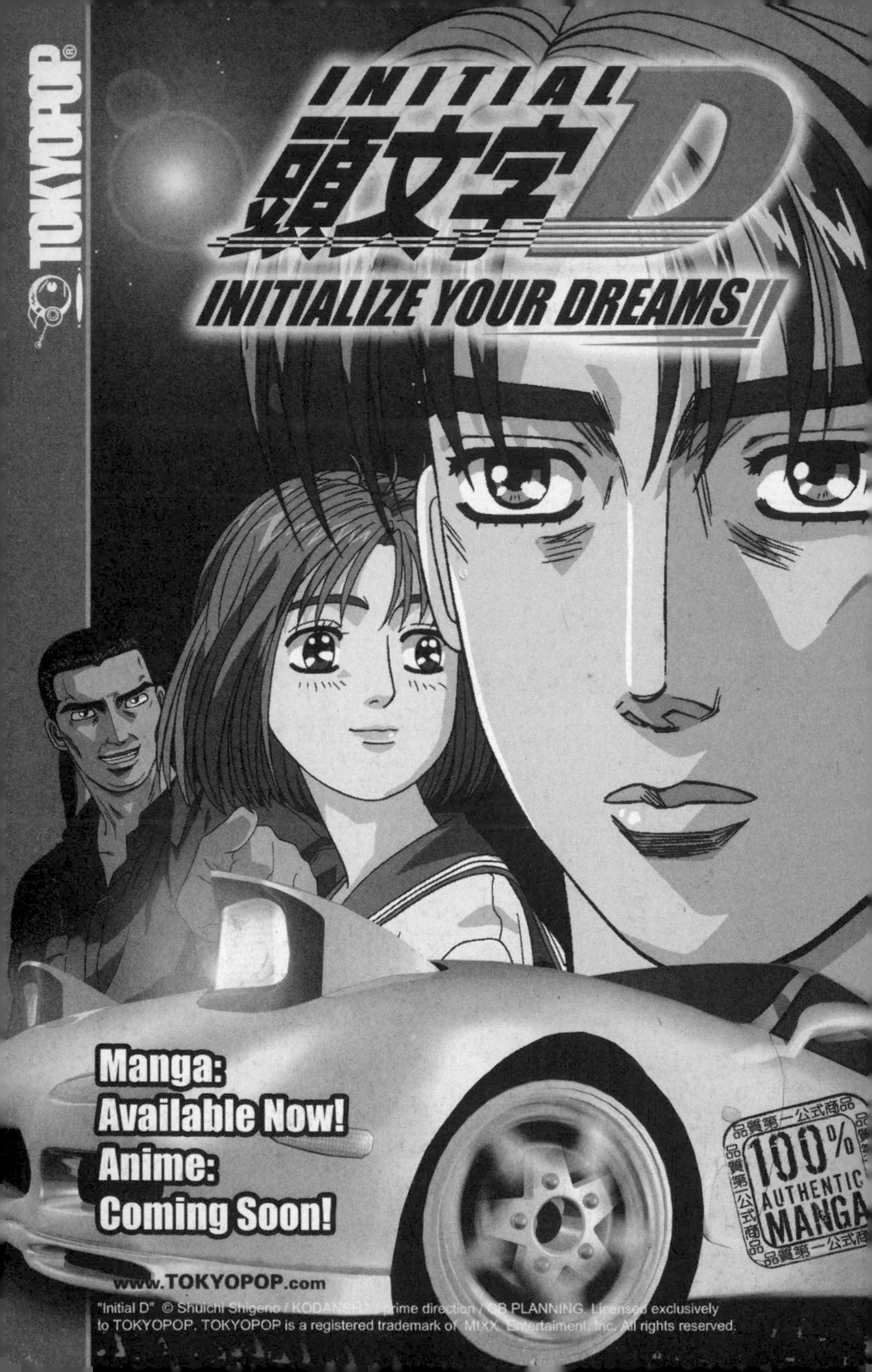
TOKYOPOP
INITIAL
頭文字D
INITIALIZE YOUR DREAMS!!
Manga:
Available Now!
Anime:
Coming Soon!
品質第一公式商品
100%
AUTHENTIC
MANGA
www.TOKYOPOP.com
"Initial D" © Shuichi Shigeno / KODANSHA / prime direction / OB PLANNING. Licensed exclusively to TOKYOPOP. TOKYOPOP is a registered trademark of MIXX Entertaiment, Inc. All rights reserved.

STOP!

This is the back of the book.
You wouldn't want to spoil a great ending!

This book is printed "manga-style," in the authentic Japanese right-to-left format. Since none of the artwork has been flipped or altered, readers get to experience the story just as the creator intended. You've been asking for it, so TOKYOPOP® delivered: authentic, hot-off-the-press, and far more fun!

DIRECTIONS

If this is your first time reading manga-style, here's a quick guide to help you understand how it works.

It's easy... just start in the top right panel and follow the numbers. Have fun, and look for more 100% authentic manga from TOKYOPOP®!

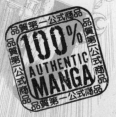

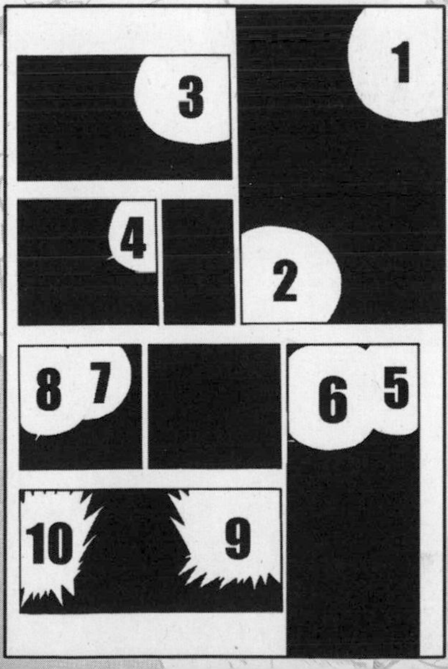